MANDATE '68

MANDATE '68

MARTIN SULLIVAN

Doubleday Canada Limited, Toronto, Ontario

Doubleday & Company, Inc., Garden City, New York

1968

Contents

Author's Note

IN TEN MONTHS, from September 9, 1967, to June 25, 1968, power in Canada passed to a new generation. This development was hardly surprising, since both of the former party leaders were in their 70's; the wonder was that they stayed so long.

But what was it like two years ago? Stalemate and irrelevance — there seemed no way that Dalton Camp was going to unseat the Chief, and even if he did, Pearson was the only winner the Liberals had. "New Politics" for Canada was little more than a dream shared by a few backbenchers and younger party workers. What no one could foresee was that the advent of Robert L. Stanfield and Pierre Elliott Trudeau would herald a new relevance and participation in Canadian politics, beyond that experienced in any contemporary democracy, least of all here.

This book tries to trace the maneuvers, the frustrations, and the lucky circumstances that allowed these men to accede to power. The emphasis in the beginning is on the role Quebec has played, for here was the crucible that created Trudeau, here the greatest threat to Confederation, and here its staunchest defenders. To understand Trudeau, one must first understand French-Canadian politics, and to understand *that* political animal is to understand Canada's own brand of democracy.

I claim no special expertise or inside information, nor do I presume to be a personal friend of Trudeau's, though I have known him since 1961 and have followed his career professionally. Certainly, it will be no secret to the reader that my respect and admiration for him runs deep. The day he entered politics, I remember being very touched, when he asked me if I thought he had made the right decision. "They need people like you in Ottawa, Pierre," was all I could muster.

Stanfield I know less well, perhaps because I have been based in Montreal, on and off, for the past twelve years. But I traveled with him during his leadership and national campaigns, and like Trudeau, he is a man of unfailing courtesy and consideration.

The genesis of this book may be of interest. The idea was born with Serrell Hillman, *Time's* bureau chief in Toronto, who mentioned it at lunch one day to David Manuel, Doubleday Canada's managing editor. Dave nursed it to the project stage, sought the author, and eventually wound up putting in nights and weekends on the manuscript, far beyond the call of duty. In a sense, the book also belongs to Blair Fraser, who had given much thought to the outline and would have written it himself, had he not died so tragically in May. (I now appreciate what he meant by the difficulty of attempting 'contemporary history.')

So then it came to me, and after much discussion (and no little trepidation), I agreed to take it on, providing I had *Time's* approval — which I received, along with their overwhelming support. Yet I would never have attempted this first book, had I not been asked to do so by my publisher, and encouraged so greatly by *Time* and by my friends and colleagues inside and outside politics.

Richard M. Clurman, chief of correspondents in New York, not only gave me leave of absence to do the book but allowed me to remain on staff during the writing. John M. Scott, editor of *Time's* Canadian edition, was most enthusiastic and gave me access to our "morgue" in Montreal.

I am also deeply grateful for the generosity of my fellow correspondents who let me use their notes and research: Marsh Clark, then Ottawa bureau chief and now in Saigon; Alan Grossman, Courtney Tower and Robert Lewis, all of Ottawa; Ed Ogle in Calgary; and of course, Serrell Hillman in Toronto — all of whom contributed to this book. If they recognize their handiwork, I hope they will regard it as further acknowledgement.

Luke Panet-Raymond and Joan Forsey were invaluable researchers; Anne Smith, Peggy McFetrick and Julie Findlay were typists any author would be thankful for; and my wife Anthea undertook the horrendous job of indexing it all, while simultaneously coping with two small children and a bearish husband.

November
1968

M.S.
Montreal

I

La Nuit de la St. Jean

The world is a strange theatre. There are moments in
it when the worst plays are those which succeed best.
— *Alexis de Tocqueville, Souvenirs*

EVERYONE SENSED something was going to happen.

Maybe it was the weather — muggy, humid, and overcast, with
the menace of a lurking thunderstorm. When the sun broke out, it
shone through the watery haze briefly, then disappeared again.

It was Monday, June 24, the red letter day of St. John the
Baptist, patron saint of French Canada, and the final day of campaigning for the 1968 general election. Both party leaders, Prime
Minister Pierre Elliott Trudeau and Opposition Leader Robert
Lorne Stanfield, had been in Ottawa overnight. Stanfield had left
early in the morning for London, Ontario, in Misajumax, a lumber-
ing, old, oil-streaked DC-7 that the Progressive Conservative Party
had hired for the campaign from Transair of Winnipeg. The plane
was named Misajumax after Stanfield's four children: Miriam,
Sarah, Judy and Max. But newsmen aboard nicknamed it the
Crashmaster, praying that it wouldn't and listening appreciatively
as the pilot went through his careful pre-flight procedures before
each take-off.

Trudeau spent most of the morning whirling through the ground
fog to Renfrew, Ontario, near Ottawa, where he told a small but
enthusiastic crowd that there had to be linguistic equality in Canada, that each Canadian must feel at home in all provinces.

Stanfield spent the morning in Jay Waldo Monteith's riding in
Stratford, Ontario, then headed East, dropping in on Lee Elgy
Grills in Belleville, George Hees in Cobourg, and Michael Starr in
Oshawa. Misajumax finally set a course for the Maritimes late

Monday evening, setting down briefly at Moncton for a last hurrah for Charles Thomas who was fighting a close campaign with Margaret Rideout. (The last stop was worth it, as it turned out; Thomas won.)

Both leaders were desperately tired. Stanfield in particular showed the paralyzing fatigue that comes from a 51-day campaign; his heavy-lidded eyes seemed sleepier than ever, and his gaunt, lean face more monumental. Deep-etched lines creased his neck and curved upward from his jaw to his hairline.

Trudeau, too, showed his weariness, in manner more than looks. His body, amazingly fit for a man of 48, never let him down, thanks to the stern regimen he has imposed on it through a lifetime of carefully measured diet and exercise. Right to the end, his movements were fluid, his balance precise, his step springy. But his eyes were tired, and his mouth tightened almost imperceptibly at irritations that would not have mattered six months ago. For Trudeau had been campaigning for half a year, from his cross-country tour as Minister of Justice, preparing provincial premiers for the Constitutional conference, right through the Liberal leadership convention and immediately, with hardly a pause, into the general election.

Stanfield travelled 25,000 miles in Misajumax, or once around the world, plus another 10,000 miles in smaller planes and helicopters, plus about 5,000 miles in cars and cavalcades. Trudeau spent 60 hours in his chartered Air Canada DC-9, which seemed to fly everywhere at about 600 miles an hour, or about 35,000 miles. His trips in smaller planes added up to at least as much as Stanfield's and so did his car rides.

Both were deeply tanned from open convertibles and shopping centers. But as John Turner put it on election night, "Outside, we all look great, but inside it's mush."

Trudeau was to wind up his campaign in Montreal, and attend the St. Jean Baptiste parade that night. Just about everyone disapproved of the plan. That included the Conservatives, who had a hunch that the Monday night parade could hurt them. Tory campaign manager, Edwin A. Goodman even went to Montreal to see if they could get Trudeau disinvited, but no way could be found to shore up the Tory's tactical position.

For the Liberals, on the other hand, there was the awful memory of Robert F. Kennedy's assassination only three weeks earlier. But there was nothing they could do, either. The St. Jean Baptiste Society had asked him to be a guest of honor, and there was no alternative. To back out would give the nationalists and separatists a tremendous moral victory. The French Canadian Prime Minister of Canada afraid to attend French Canada's "national day," and in his own home town, too. It was unthinkable. Yet more unthinkable was what might happen.

The DC-9 was filled with bustling activity as it stood gleaming, scarlet and white, impassively efficient, on the apron at Ottawa's Uplands Airport, waiting to take the Prime Minister on the 23-minute flight to Montreal.

Newsmen who travel with the Prime Minister are asked to be at the airport 30 minutes prior to take-off. Trudeau likes punctuality; those who keep him waiting are left behind — in theory, at any rate. Many of the newsmen at Uplands that Monday had followed Trudeau on every leg of the campaign, and the brief flight to Montreal would be the end of it. Most were there early, partly to lighten the take-off weight of the bar, but mostly for mixed feelings of apprehension and nostalgia. Nostalgia for a period of close cameraderie that was ending; for a long, salmon-pink tube that felt like home after six weeks, filled with its turquoise blue and orange seats; with its cheerful, sometimes beautiful stewardesses who were changed each week, in case anyone fell in love with them; and with its happy Captain, Ralph Leek, chief pilot of the DC-9 fleet, who enjoyed flying the irreverent press corps so much that he stayed on for the whole campaign, despite the passengers' tendency to call him "the driver" and their habit of cheering and clapping whenever he made a good landing, which was always.

The press corps was unusually free from deadlines that Monday. The mandatory 48-hour black-out on radio and television campaign reports had switched off the frenetic electronic journalists, while most of the columnists and reporters on board knew that their next big story would not come until the vote on Tuesday. Unless . . . but they tried not to think of that.

The plane took off soon after 12:30 p.m., and for most of the trip people tried to work out how far they had flown during the campaign. The mood was like the last day of vacation. Tomorrow, school would start again.

There was barely time for sandwiches before Captain Leek set the DC-9 down on Dorval's runway Six Right, braked hard and turned. Where the devil was he going?

The feeling of apprehension increased. Instead of heading for the terminal, Leek was taxiing to a parking space on the corner of the great Air Canada maintenance hangar, half a mile from the main building, shielded by jet-blast barriers of steel on two sides, the hangar on the third and a natural hillock on the fourth. Clearly, police were taking no chances, and all the combined municipal police forces on the Island of Montreal, the Montreal detachment of the Quebec Provincial Police and of the Royal Canadian Mounted Police were on duty that day.

Only police, political aides and half a dozen official vehicles were on hand, including the massive, closed-in black Cadillac the Prime Minister was to use. It was said to be armored, the glass bullet-proof. It certainly looked it. The gloom on the tarmac was relieved by the appearance of the Prime Minister — and his decision to choose the moment for one of his banister-slides — straight down the single rail of the DC-9's self-stowing stairway, side-saddle. He found the pitch steeper than expected. But it broke the tension.

The motorcade set off under lowering skies for Norgate shopping center, in the suburb of St. Laurent (Dollard riding), where one of Trudeau's closest political friends, Jean-Pierre Goyer, was running for re-election. He is one of the toughest and best young M.P.'s in Quebec, a federalist, one of the original Trudeau committee members, a *Cité Libre* contributor and Duplessis-battler since college days.

Goyer appeared to have no major problems in Dollard, but no one could be entirely sure of the extent of the threat posed by the NDP candidate, Charles Taylor, who had run well in Mount Royal in 1965 against Trudeau (and with Trudeau's help against Alan Macnaughton in 1963), coming second with 14,929 votes to Trudeau's 28,064. Trudeau was wearing one of the St. Jean Baptiste Society's blue and white plastic fleur-de-lis badges in his button hole, when he climbed onto the platform to hug Goyer and tell the partisan crown in the shopping center to vote for him. He went on to talk about unity, about the "incredibly rich and beautiful country" that Canada is, their Canada, and how important it was that it should be kept together. "The fundamental question of the campaign is our future as a united country" he was to say over and over again during that final day. He talked about "one Canada, one nation with two languages, no special privileges to any province, no *statut particulier* (special status)." He said he had confidence that the Canadian people had heard and understood and agreed with the Liberals, and he asked the crowd to agree too. "Will it be two nations as the NDP said in 1961?" he asked. The crowd growled negatively. "Will it be two nations as the Progressive Conservatives say this time?" he asked. The growl came again. "Or will it be one nation . . .?" He didn't have time to finish before a yell of "Yes!" bellowed back from the crowd and answered the question for him.

At 1:20 p.m. he was off to Duvernay, where Eric Kierans, the lonely outsider from the Liberal leadership convention was fighting as only an Irishman would in a riding that was 95% French-speaking and where before redistribution in 1965 the NDP got 27% of the vote. This time the NDP were out to win, with the Quebec leader Robert Cliche himself running, backed, it was said, by Daniel Johnson and the National Union. Trudeau's help was badly needed.

From Duvernay, which covers the eastern section of the new City of Laval, on Ile Jésus, Trudeau helicoptered across the St. Lawrence islands to the southshore textile town of St. Hyacinthe, a once-Liberal stronghold that has been Tory since 1957. This was where the Minister of Forestry, Maurice Sauvé, who lost his Magdalen Island constituency in redistribution, was trying to unseat a Diefenbaker loyalist, Théogène Ricard.

It was Sauvé's second choice as a riding. He had lost the nomination in Montreal-Gamelin to an underwear salesman with a knack for political organization. Sauvé was not popular with the Trudeau organizers who felt he had welshed on a promise to support Trudeau during the Liberal leadership convention by going to work for Paul Martin. It was hardly coincidental that Sauvé's riding was the last one Trudeau visited on the last day of the campaign. The visit would do Sauvé no good.

The thundery, murky weather seemed to thicken as 4 p.m.

approached. It was stifling in the Royal 22nd Regiment's armory
in St. Hyacinthe where Sauvé had held his wind-up meeting, and
the crowd's attention wavered between the platitudinous speeches
from the platform and the cordoned-off square on the parade
ground outside, where Trudeau's helicopter was scheduled to land.
Every heavy truck that passed within earshot made necks crane
skyward to catch a glimpse of an illusory helicopter.

When the helicopter arrived, it came quickly, and there was
barely time to spot it skimming over the trees from the north-west
before it hovered momentarily then fluttered down onto the
helipad. Tall men with crew-cuts seemed to close in around Trudeau as he walked into the armory, walled by well-wishers,
autograph-hunters, and clutching adolescent hands.

"I've touched him, I've touched him!" cried one pretty young
girl after Trudeau passed, running back to where her bearded boyfriend was standing. "I touched him" she said with glee, then,
catching the stern disapproval in his eye, she added, "Oh, I hate
him! Je le déteste!" The boyfriend smiled approvingly.

Trudeau told the good people of St. Hyacinthe that "*chez-nous*
is not just the Province of Quebec, *chez-nous* is the whole of Canada." He said it was a great and beautiful and rich country which
he had seen from coast-to-coast during the last few weeks, making
250 speeches "far too many, but making few promises — lots of
words which all add up to the same message, *vivons unis*, let us
live united." Trudeau spoke about the future of Canada and what
Canadians can hope for in a world where no future was certain
and where the greatest victories, such as Harold Wilson's in Britain
or Lyndon Johnson's in the United States, can quickly lose their
impetus if conditions change, conditions over which their rulers
have no control. "Look at France herself," he said, "plagued with
internal problems, trying to teach others how to run their countries,
when she can't do it herself!"

It was a good speech, almost entirely in French, and he told
them that in other parts of Canada he always said something in
French to the English-speaking audience and it was always warmly
received. Thus set up, the crowd could only cheer when he switched
effortlessly in mid-sentence into a few words in English.

Exhausted but exhilarated, Trudeau timed his plea perfectly. **By** now it was brilliantly polished, and it always ended with a mid-sentence switch back into French *". . . et c'est ça le Canada . . ."* he would say. The applause always interrupted him and he never did finish the sentence. He didn't have to. That's what bilingualism means, he seemed to be saying, not as a braggart or show-off but in the sense that "if I can do it, why not you?" Why not one country, one people, one nation but two languages, together, understood by all? "Our home is not just Quebec," he thundered, in conclusion pointing rhetorically off-stage to the one million French-speaking Canadians who lived outside Quebec. French Canadians all across the country who are proud to speak French and be at the same time New Brunswickers, or Manitobans or Albertans. "Our home, *chez-nous*, is not just the province of Quebec. It's the whole of Canada."

The nine Canadian maple-leaf flags in the armory seemed to billow momentarily with pride beside the two Quebec *fleurs-de-lis*. But the *fleur-de-lis* of the Bourbons would have its moment, too, that day, and it was only four hours away.

For Trudeau, it was back out through the crowd to the helicopter and, blades whirling faster and faster, up over the parade ground, over the armory and the trees towards Montreal and a quiet supper with his invalid mother at her modest brown-brick house in Outremont, a wealthy suburb on the backward slope of Mount Royal (*outre-mont* or "beyond the mountain").

La Nuit de la St. Jean.

The highlight of St. Jean Baptiste Day is the night-time parade along Sherbrooke Street. Sidewalk entrepreneurs set out chairs along the curb, and landladies lease their front rooms for the evening's entertainment, when floats with wondrous tableaux of flashing lights and twinkling girls, Go-Go dancers and bathing beauties, pay tribute to French Canada's progress to the tune of satin-suited bugle bands and the noisy pocketa-pocketa of hidden two-stroke generators and thudding diesel tractors. Street arabs hawk badges and blue and white Quebec paper flags and hundreds of dozens of bottles of Coca-Cola and Pepsi-Cola (beverages Quebeckers drink in such quantities that "Pepsi" is part of the language) that make *la fête de la St. Jean* truly a family affair, when children stay up late, and parents indulge them. It's all rather bucolic and wistful and good-humored, and all carried live on the French television network.

But this year it was different. Though the large families were there and the hundreds of six-packs of Pepsi, there was nothing bucolic or wistful or good-humored about it. The crowd was spoiling for a fight.

Newsmen and cameramen went ahead of the Prime Minister's group to take up positions on the observers' stand directly opposite the VIP platform, located as usual along the pseudo-Grecian facade of the Montreal Public Library, facing out into the dark woods of Lafontaine Park. Newsmen arrived at about 8:45 p.m., and the parade was due to start passing at 9:30. But by then the fight had started.

Soon after eight, the area behind the observers' stand was filled with perhaps a thousand noisy demonstrators dressed in the leather sports jackets and bell-bottomed trousers, the wispy beards and draggly hair that are almost the trademarks of the young, turned-on, and sometimes very attractive Montreal separatists. Most of the sidewalks were packed with spectators watching the separatists. Every few minutes a sheaf of leaflets would explode into the air above the demonstrators. "*Pouilleux!*" they read, "*débarrassez-vous de vos poux!*" (Referring to Trudeau's campaign remark about the "lousy French" spoken by French Canadians.) The translation is roughly "Lousy ones! Get rid of your lice. Don't vote! Lice to Ottawa! Quebec to the Quebeckers!"

The demonstrators also chanted, monotonously, "*Tru-deau au pot-eau*" (Trudeau to the gallows), occasionally varying it with the old separatist chant "*Le Qué-bec aux Qué-bec-ois*" (Quebec for the Quebeckers).

Police, uniformed and plainclothes, moved constantly through the crowd keeping it from bunching, breaking up groups by walking through them. Occasionally, a demonstrator would goad a policeman too far, there would be a surge of cops and the crowd would scatter like a shoal of fish, regrouping after the police had bundled away their captive to cool off in one of the half dozen blue and white police paddy-wagons.

Newsmen who wandered through the demonstrators got a good-humored reception at first. "Are you a Mountie?" one group asked. Then the press button with *Prime Minister's Party* on it caught their eye. They laughed good-naturedly. "Press, eh? Prime Minister's Party? It's going to be quite a party, we promise you." And they happily gathered some of the leaflets they had been tossing around to complete press documentation.

Another rush by the cops broke up the group. But the police were still in reasonably good humor. And the group was soon back again at the main taunting spot. "*Tru-deau au pot-eau!*" they shouted. "*Le Qué-bec aux Qué-bec-ois!*" Zap. The police swept in again.

By 9:15, the crowd was getting rougher. Among the trees four leather-jacketed toughs were talking in low voices. They were speaking English. One of them had a little black billie in his hand. "Let's stick together fellas, okay?" said the leader. They were Mounties. A gormless looking youth in a wind-breaker came through the crowd with a rusty old bit of pipe which he tossed onto the street. The plainclothesmen grabbed him. Rap, rap, rap went the little black billie on his head. He was led away to the paddy-wagon.

Then it started. It was 9:30, or a few minutes after. Something sailed through the air and smashed at the feet of the cops. It was a pop bottle. Then two more in close succession. They were coming from the crowd among the trees.

The police started getting mad. They do not appreciate a barrage of bottles at the best of times and particularly not when they had only regular cloth caps on. Their mood changed swiftly. Now there was blood on the prisoners they bundled into the paddy wagons. The crowd's mood changed, too. Things were getting rough. Sensible people left, but lots stayed to stare, even with young children.

The VIP stand filled up with assorted dignitaries. Trudeau, the late Quebec Premier Daniel Johnson, Archbishop Grégoire of Montreal, Mayor Jean Drapeau took their seats slowly, after staring aghast at the surging, bottle-hurling mobs on each side of the observers' stand fifty feet in front of them. Trudeau's appearance goaded the separatists to fresh efforts.

Soon after ten, a searchlight beam lit up the sky far to the East down Sherbrooke Street. The parade was coming. But most people were too fascinated by the medieval battle right in front of them to care. All pretense that it was just a disturbance had gone.

As paddy-wagons filled up and were driven away to dump their contents in neighboring police stations, replacements roared in. Panel trucks filled with a relief force of burly riot police in white riot helmets, armed with businesslike clubs, took the place of the battered traffic police who had been doing their best back of the stands. The area in front of the VIP platform and the Prime Minister became a relief zone where wounded were patched up before being loaded into ambulances or paddy-wagons. The situation was now a full-scale riot. Police ambulances, flashers twirling and sirens moaning, pitched and backed and roared away down the street with fresh loads of wounded policemen. Wounded bystanders also got solicitous treatment from police. A four-year-old boy, hit on the head by a piece of glass, was guided to first aid tenderly by a six-foot sergeant. Wounded demonstrators got a quick field dressing, if they were lucky, and were pushed roughly into the wagons. More often they were just allowed to bleed a little.

Pierre Bourgault, the president of the Rassemblement pour l'Indépendance Nationale, had a short-lived triumph when he came to urge on his forces. He was fingered immediately by a federal Liberal party organizer working with police, and was pleasantly surprised to find himself lifted up onto supporters' shoulders and carried to the heart of the battle. It was only when his men carried him into police lines and handed him over to six hefty riot police that he realized his "supporters" had been two plainclothes cops. Observers said Régis Chartrand, the boxer leader of the strong-armed Chevaliers de l'Indépendance, was treated less gently than Bourgault. Somehow the police forgot to open the door the first time they tried to put him into the paddy-wagon, and it took Régis awhile to recover.

Meanwhile, the Pepsi and Coke bottles continued to rain down like mortars, and a few were said to have contained acid, to liven things up. Several policemen were blinded with kerosene, then smashed in the belly or across the legs or face with a chunk of wood or crowbar. It had become very ugly.

Towards 10:30, just as Robert Stanfield was landing in Moncton, New Brunswick, for his final quiet pep talk to Tories in the airport parking lot, the mounted police arrived on 15 magnificent golden Palominos, the pride of Montreal's civic ceremonies. But there was nothing ceremonial about the riders, with riot helmets, goggles, and long batons with leather thongs at their ends. The mounted police charges were brutally effective, and minutes after their arrival the police had recaptured the area around the stands, driving the separatists — and hoodlums who had joined in by now — back onto the high-ground behind the trees.

And through it all, amid the shouts, the sirens, the clatter of horses' hooves and the crunch of broken glass, the big parade started to go by.

There were police cadets, the firemen's band, the band of the St. John the Baptist Society itself, with plumes and medieval tunics, and the fleur-de-lis flags of Quebec, celebrating the 20th anniversary of Quebec's own provincial flag. There was a float tactlessly recalling the Chemin du Roy, the northshore road from Quebec to Montreal, named for Louis XIV, in the 17th century, but only put to use by his 20th century successor, Charles de Gaulle, the summer before.

But the parade was a bore compared to the see-saw bloodletting going on behind the stands. A bottle scored a direct hit on the white helmet of a mounted policeman. He sagged forward onto his horse's neck, and the helmet fell off. A comrade retrieved it, and the policeman put it on again, apparently only momentarily stunned.

Again the horses wheeled and charged into the scattering separatists, choking off a renewed chorus of *Tru-deau au Pot-eau*. The motorcycle patrolmen joined in, gunning their engines furiously. The people broke and ran back into the safety of the dark wood behind. The director of the Montreal Police, Jean Paul Gilbert, had been a guest of honor in the VIP stand when the riot started. He left immediately to go down into the riot zone to take charge, and hatless and unprotected, as the bottles thudded down, he spent the rest of the evening walking through the area encouraging his men, keeping them calm.

The dirtiest guerrilla warfare took place in the dim areas to the left of the observers' stand, up on the hill, where gangs of young toughs took over with short crating crowbars, whacking cops, horses legs, car windows and each other, finally winding up with the primitive orgy of setting a wrecked patrol car on fire.

Just before eleven, as the parade continued to trundle past, and peace appeared to have been restored, a separatist flanking movement on the right hand side of the observers' stand broke through police lines and surged into the street just long enough for someone to toss a Coca-Cola bottle in a high arc at the Prime Minister. It sailed six feet over his head and smashed against the marble portico behind. There was an indecently hasty exit by VIPs, including the Archbishop and the Premier of Quebec, Daniel Johnson.

Trudeau, with RCMP plainclothesmen Bob Richardson providing a body shield and RCMP corporal Ron Corey getting a plastic raincoat to protect him from the glass, almost disappeared for a moment under his solicitous bodyguard. They were the only ones left in the stand. The other VIPs had vanished. Below, on the sidewalk, aides Bill Lee and Vic Chapman yelled up at him not to leave, while from the observers' stand opposite another aide, Jim Davey, bellowed one word: "Stay!"

But Trudeau did not need their advice. He had no intention of leaving. He stood up and brushed away the raincoat with a sweep of his left arm. "I won't leave, I am going to stay," he said angrily, or at least that is what aides and police think he said.

Montreal Mayor Jean Drapeau stayed too, having escorted his wife to the exit. A few minutes later they were rejoined by an ashen and shamefaced Premier Johnson.

But it was Trudeau's hour, Trudeau's triumph. And across the street in the observers' stand, there was an extraordinary sight. Virtually the entire press corps pocketed its notebooks, stood and cheered, breaking one of the most sacred traditions of the fourth estate. Yet there they were, from such top Ottawa columnists as Peter Newman, down to the rawest police desk rookies, clapping and shouting like teenage fans. Trudeau waved back and leaned forward onto the balustrade with his chin on his hands, as if to get a better look.

For the police, the break-through of the bottle-thrower was a severe loss of face, and when a second bottle was lobbed at the

VIP stand within seconds of the first, crashing harmlessly onto the sidewalk, the furious riot squads reacted with renewed vigor, hurling back demonstrators without ceremony, and the blood began to flow still more freely. Now the police were really angry. Few demonstrators under arrest reached the wagons without a kick in the backside or a crack on the head. Some police lost all control, viciously thumping rioters who were already pinioned by others.

No doubt several innocent bystanders were arrested, as the newspapers would report the next day, but how anyone could be classified as "innocent" who watched the riot for an hour and still stayed among the demonstrators, without a duty reason, is hard to see. Yet right up until the last float passed by, small boys were wandering through the crowd selling bottles of Coke and Pepsi — or ammunition, depending on your point of view. And parents strolled across the glass-strewn no man's land with tiny children And hard to believe, down beside the observers' stand, while police and rioters battled 30 feet away, there were even a couple of young lovers, necking. *L'amour toujours.*

By 11:45, it was all over, the VIP stand emptied, and a huge, menacing crowd started surging down towards the reviewing stands from Sherbrooke Street East. A phalanx of riot police, three men deep, with billies and riot helmets stood across the street, blocking their progress.

The crowd faltered. A couple of bottles mortared down among the police. Nobody was hit, no one moved. Everyone held their breath. There must have been 3,000 people to 300 uniformed police.

The police line held. The crowd stopped and slowly, reluctantly, it started to break up, an occasional defiant bottle plummeting down into the no man's land.

The riot was over. A police car burned quietly up the hill, belly up, like an enormous lamp. The separatist shouts, *Tru-deau au Pot-eau, le Québec aux Québecois*, grew fainter, more distant. And the empty stands stood like islands in a sea of broken glass, trampled separatist leaflets, burst plastic bags of white paint, smashed police crowd control barriers and the lesser litter of a normal crowd — paper bags and flags, newspapers and candy-wrappers. While all around shuffled groups of silent spectators kept moving like thoughtful cattle by the police. They had come to gawk at what was left, to reconstruct the savagery of 90 minutes that had become part of Canadian political history.

Slowly, they, too, began to disperse, and the police, good-humored to the end for the most part, began to relax too.

"Let's not kid ourselves," said one, "it was a war and we won it."

"All I want to do is go back to bed," yawned another.

"What I say," said a third, surveying the debris, "is that it's goddam lucky we don't have paving stones on Sherbrooke Street."

Goddam lucky. Lucky for Montreal, Trudeau and the Liberals.

Back at the Chateau Champlain, in Trudeau's suite on the 34th floor, the telephone rang until three in the morning. Bill Lee, who answered it, says one caller happened to be a Tory who had watched it all on television.

"I just want you to know I've been a Conservative all my life," he told Lee, "but Trudeau's got my vote tomorrow."

And in Halifax, Misajumax's big, balloon tires brushed the runway at 12:35 a.m., bringing Stanfield back home to a crowd of loyal Nova Scotians who had heard about Trudeau's triumph on the National News at midnight (Nova Scotia being an hour ahead of Quebec) and would never say die. It was a brave, defiant gesture. But in their hearts everyone knew it was hopeless. The Conservative strategists had known it right from the start. Goodman, for one, rated the Trudeau campaign as brilliant. "He never gave us a thing to get our teeth into. He realized that the only way he could lose it was to make a mistake. And he didn't make a single one. I feared all along that he was going to kill us at the last moment, but I couldn't do a goddam thing about it."

Stanfield was under no illusions either. "It was apparent from the outset that the contest of the election was not favorable to us," he said, and privately he would admit that "something between 75 and 90 seats" was the best he could hope for on election day.

Yet only eight months before, on November 3, 1967, the Gallup poll had shown the Conservatives under Stanfield likely to win the support of 43% of Canadian voters, compared to only 34% for the Liberals. It would have been a clear majority. Now the best they could hope for was 75 to 90 seats. How could it have happened? Victory had seemed so close that the party had started to take on the sober and sensible attitude of the next government. Some unkind observers even said it had fought the campaign as if it *were* the government, cautiously and defensively, leaving all élan and initiative to the Liberals.

Now, in the penultimate moment, the chance to become the 16th Prime Minister of Canada must have seemed a long way off to Stanfield; the years ahead as Opposition leader so interminable and so barren. Yet there was hope, there must always be hope. Trudeau was so suddenly a national figure, so recently a politician, so much a creation of the mass media, that there had to be hope that it might all come right in the end. The wheel always makes its circle. And if the wheel would be made to turn faster, the Conservative opportunity would come sooner. The Trudeau phenomenon would have to be analyzed, its history sifted for evidence, the gleanings evaluated and the antidote found. But first they would have to find out where it had started and how.

II

Where it all Started

"Of the past, I must say, it interests me only as far as it acts on future events, and in the sense that (André) Gide wrote: 'Le présent serait plein de tous les avenirs si le passé n'y projetait déjà une histoire'."
— *Pierre Elliott Trudeau,*
La Grève de l'Amiante

FROM HIS SUITE high up in the tower of the CPR's Chateau Frontenac hotel, in Quebec City, Maurice LeNoblet Duplessis, the bachelor premier of Quebec, was undoubtedly comforted by the thought that his own feudal Catholic fortress was hardly threatened by the Communist, socialist, atheistic insurrections which seemed so universal in 1948. On July 28, he had been returned to power for his second consecutive term (and third term as premier) with 82 out of 92 seats in the Legislature and nearly 60% of the popular vote. (A possible measure of Quebec's security — and devotion — perhaps, might be its entirely serious offer of sanctuary that year to the Vatican itself, should the Left-wing troubles in Italy threaten the Holy See.)

In fact, if there was any threat at all to his hegemony, it came in clerical dress from three old houses huddled together in that densely populated cliff-top part of Quebec City's Upper Town. The old houses that offended Duplessis contained Laval University's Faculty of Social Science, headed by a rubicund dean named the Most Reverend Georges-Henri Lévesque, whose fervent opposition to Duplessis was disguised by bubbling good humor and the white robe of a Dominican monk.

The medieval role of teacher-monk was less curious to the French Canadians of Quebec than it might have appeared to other

North Americans. In 1948, Quebec was still, politically, a feudal society, in spite of a growing urban and industrial base. Dean Lévesque, as a professor-priest, was merely filling the educational role that the Church had occupied since the conquest of 1759.

What surprised Quebec, on the contrary, was that he should want to change things at all. The man who found this least comprehensible was Duplessis who considered that he had contributed in no small way to the young monk's career, putting in a good word with the authorities and coming through with a $50,000 grant in 1944 which was 10% more than the School of Social Science had received from the Liberals. But despite the government money, the school continued to consider that its main function was mass education and not the perpetuation of a ruling elite, and, inevitably, Duplessis felt it was all rank ingratitude. He cajoled and pleaded and he even bribed Laval University to see things his way. In 1948 he gave the university half of a $4,000,000 grant towards a new campus in suburban St. Foy (pointedly promising: "you'll get the rest later") which he boasted would cost $100,000,000 and take 100 years to build. Duplessis had the mentality of a 19th century country notary, as Gérard Pelletier once put it, and there was no way he could ever understand the forces which were changing Quebec society.

For Father Lévesque understanding came easier. For a start, unlike Duplessis, he was not born into the Quebec establishment. His father was the sheriff of Roberval, a pretty little town on the western shore of Lac St. Jean in north-eastern Quebec, and even the top court officer's salary did not go far when there were 15 in the family. He got his *bachot* from the great seminary at Chicoutimi and went on to further studies at the Dominican Theological College in Ottawa, where he was ordained in 1928 and awarded his Ph.D. in 1930. The Dominicans sent him to northern France to take another doctorate at the University of Lille in 1932, then brought him back to Ottawa to teach social philosophy at the college. His reputation as an exceptional teacher spread quickly, and within a few years he was lecturing all over Quebec and giving regular evening courses as well at the University of Montreal and at Laval University in Quebec City. He soon attracted a following of bright young students, and in 1937 the Dominicans bowed to popular demand by letting laymen attend his classes in Ottawa as full-time students.

The laymen included Maurice Lamontagne, later to become a leading economist, politician and senator, and Maurice Tremblay, the distinguished Laval sociologist. Lamontagne, a poor boy from Mont Joli in Quebec's impoverished Gaspé region, had done brilliantly at the Seminary at Rimouski and had attracted the attention of the Bishop there, Msgr. Georges Courchesne. Lamontagne had met Lévesque in 1936 in Rimouski when the Dominican had lectured the seminarians on such niceties of Canon Law as diriment and impedient impediments to marriage. The lecture was so brilliant that Lamontagne remembers he decided on the spot to go to Ottawa to sit at the scholar's feet at the Dominican College on Empress Street. Msgr. Courchesne saw no impediment to the plan; it was duly arranged, and in the fall of 1937 Lamontagne began what was to be a life-long association with both Lévesque and Ottawa that would change the face of Quebec and ultimately of Canada itself.

Within a few months, in 1938, Lévesque was called away to Quebec City by Cardinal Villeneuve to become the head of a new school of social science that would be part of Laval's faculty of Philosophy. It was a full year before Lamontagne and Tremblay could get their transfers to Laval and continue their association.

Meanwhile, at Laval, Lévesque wasted no time. The "jolly monk", as he was called, breezed merrily through the musty corridors of the *Quartier Latin* much like the cool north-east wind which blows up out of the Gulf of St. Lawrence and buffets Cap Diamant winter and summer.

He knew from the start that Laval's new school of social science would amount to little until it broke away from the dreary curriculum of Jansenist crypto-sociology, philosophy and metaphysics which had hung around and smothered the study of social sciences in Quebec like seaweed since the shipwreck of 1759. But Lévesque also knew better than to take on the hierarchy from a position of weakness. First, he had to break away from the department of philosophy and establish the school as an independent faculty of social sciences. Second, he had to build up a teaching staff with the highest academic qualifications in order to disarm critics who tried to question the school's competence. Finally, he had to establish such a reputation for excellence in the community at large that opposition by the establishment itself would be neutralized.

By 1943, Lévesque had become Dean of the Faculty of Social Science at Laval and was free from control by the Faculty of Philosophy. The same year, Maurice Lamontagne and Maurice Tremblay returned from Harvard with master's degrees in economics and sociology respectively. By 1944, the late René Tremblay had graduated summa cum laude from Laval, got an M.A. in economics from McGill, then did postgraduate work at Louvain and Cambridge before returning to the Laval faculty. In the same period, Roger Marier, a contemporary of Lamontagne, went to study in Washington, and then returned to Laval to lecture in sociology. He is now a deputy minister in Quebec. Jean Charles Falardeau, another sociologist, went to Chicago before returning to Laval where he still teaches. Arthur Tremblay, now deputy minister of Education, was another. All told, it was an extraordinary feat of incubation. Within 10 years, Lévesque had created his own faculty of native, French Canadian social scientists. Yet there was no chauvinism in his achievement. The talent was local but the skill was international.

And with the returning graduates of Harvard, Paris, Columbia, Chicago, Washington, Louvain, Oxford, Cambridge and many other universities came new ideas — or rather, ideas that were new to Quebec. Keynes, Laski and Marx became names to be associated with interesting ideas rather than epithets tossed at non-conformists or exorcised with hasty genuflexion. These ideas spread through the student body at the faculty of social science and out into the dark regions of philosophy, medicine and law, policed by their drab legions of black-soutaned Jesuits and charcoal suited lawyers and notaries. And inevitably, the ideas reached the ears of the public, sometimes by osmosis but most often through the stream of graduates that Father Lévesque sent out into the world. Reactions were sometimes angry, but he always backed up his professors. For example, shortly after Lamontagne came back from Harvard reports started to reach Lévesque that his protegé had turned Communist. What had happened, it appeared, was that he had mentioned Karl Marx in an economics lecture on capitalism without pausing to disassociate himself from Marx's political theories. Lévesque finally called Lamontagne in for a chat. "Maurice," he said, "it's your business if you are a Communist, it doesn't concern me at all. But, because of the position you hold in the Faculty, if you aren't a Communist, say so, because it will simplify things enormously for everybody. Now if you are a Communist, in view of all the important work we have still to do together, please be discreet."

In 1948, Lévesque was only 45 and the average age of his faculty was under 35. The total budget for the school was only $150,000, yet Lévesque managed to keep 25 full-time professors on staff through personal devotion and perhaps the knowledge that he drew only $2,500 a year himself. Maurice Lamontagne spent eleven years at Laval, started at $2,500 a year and was only earning $7,500 as chairman of the department of economics in 1954 when he left to join the civil service in Ottawa. The devotion of the faculty to Lévesque was total and remained so long after he ceased to be Dean in 1956 (he continued as a professor until he went to Africa as rector of Rwanda National University in 1963, a position he still holds).

The roster of graduates from Laval's school of social science reads today like a Who's Who in French Canada. Graduates ranged from Marcel Pépin, now president of the *Confédération des Syndicats Nationaux*, to Louis Robichaud, the premier of New Brunswick. But the most distinguished was Jean Marchand, now Minister of Forestry and Rural Development in the Liberal government, who enrolled in 1939 because it was the only department at Laval which would let him work his way through school. He had a widowed mother to support and for most of his college days he worked nights as a stenographer for the highway patrol division of the Provincial Police, until he was fired "for political remarks" the cops did not like, then signed on as a clerk at Canada Steamship Lines for the rest of his university career. He graduated with a master's degree in 1942. The school had a long way to go in his day, he recalls, "I could have done that course in a year". But he stuck it out. "Only a few professors were worthy of the name," he says. "But Father Lévesque was a masterly animator. He had faith and tremendous enthusiasm. It really was not a faculty in the

real sense, but he believed in what he was doing. I don't think he
was so much a scholar as an intelligent man of action."

Lévesque had opposed Quebec's confessional co-operatives after
the war (an iconoclastic gesture that made him an immediate hero
with the avant-garde) by pointing out, quite logically, that they
would fail in cities and towns where there was more than one
denomination. And they did, too, which made Lévesque even more
unpopular.

Lévesque's interest in social action stimulated Marchand. From
Laval, Marchand worked briefly for the C.S.L. and for a fishermen's cooperative, and then, again at Father Lévesque's suggestion, he joined the pulp and paper workers' union as an organizer
in December 1942. In March, 1943, he led 2,000 workers from
Lake St. John Paper Co. and Price Bros. out on a strike which not
only forced a Royal commission of inquiry into the pulp and paper
industry in Quebec (Prevost report) but, in February 1945,
resulted in amendments to both the Quebec and the Canadian
Labour Relations Acts. But by that time Marchand was plunged
into other battles. In August 1944, at the age of 26, he became
the general provincial organizer for the *Confédération des Travailleurs Catholiques du Canada*, the catholic trades union of Quebec,
and a year later he set about reorganizing the asbestos miners in
the Eastern Townships.

It might be supposed that a nationalist such as Duplessis would
have been pleased to see such sturdy signs of life in Quebec's labor
unions which were, after all, both French Canadian and Catholic.
But this was not the case.

The Duplessis era was perhaps the apogee of what has been
called the "Holy Alliance" in Quebec, when the three great institutions, Church, Political and Economic still retained total control
over what had become a highly industrialized state. The rationale
for this extraordinary mid-20th century oligarchy was contained in
something called the "social doctrine of the Church", an amalgam
of nationalism, carefully selected Papal encyclicals and pure
hokum which was designed, basically, to keep the proletariat in its
place. This was highly satisfactory for the elite, of course, since
the growing industrialization of Quebec meant that huge profits
were to be made as a result. Quebec had to compete for industry

with other areas in North America and, as long as the labor force remained docile, its attraction to industrialists was overwhelming, and the profits they shared with their Quebec partners remained enormous. A restive labor force, on the other hand, not only threatened the economic institutions but directly, through finance, and indirectly, through influence, the political and clerical sectors as well.

So the influence of Laval's faculty of social science on the labor movement in Quebec, and the organizational success of Jean Marchand and others like him, became a direct threat to Duplessis' power base. It had to be stopped, in fact, and Duplessis employed every tactic in his repertoire as a master strategist to stop it.

The upshot was that the CTCC had started to organize the Quebec civil service in order to insure job security and prevent the wholesale dismissals that punctuated every change of government. Duplessis' response in 1948 was Bill 5, an odious piece of labor legislation which was so reactionary that he did not dare show it to his minister of Labor before tabling it. And even then the National Union's 89% majority in the Legislative Assembly was not prepared to put it through and the premier was forced to withdraw it. He blamed this humiliation on the CTCC and Father Lévesque and was determined to have his revenge. The asbestos strike in 1949 was the opportunity.

In retrospect, the strike had a cathartic effect on the province, it brought out the best and the worst in Quebec society, in every sector, involving everyone, and, before it ended, it had involved the rest of North America. As that most distinguished lawyer, professor and champion of civil liberty, Frank Scott, wrote in his introduction to *La Grève de l'Amiante* in 1956, "all were convinced that this even constituted a turning point in the social history of Quebec."

The strike took its name from a small town and a fibrous mineral both of which are found in the rolling, rocky hills of the Eastern Townships of Quebec, an area which is bounded to the east and south by Maine, New Hampshire and Vermont. It is a pretty countryside of woods and green valleys, an extension of the mountains of New England, with much the same industrial base, textiles, dairy farms, woods and little else.

All this changed in 1876, when construction gangs, building the Quebec Central Railway, blasted out a cutting near Thetford Mines and saw a vein of rock containing a strange grey-white fibrous material. This was asbestos, resistant to fire, heat and friction. Up until then, Italy had controlled the world market, but by 1928, Canada was producing 86% of the world's supply of asbestos, 180,000 tons, the entire production going to the construction and automobile industry in the United States. The town of Asbestos grew from 600 people in 1900, to 5,711 in the early 1950's.

Ironically, the boom in asbestos hardly brought prosperity. From the start, Canadian asbestos was short-fibred, hence less valuable than the long-fibred Italian variety. Then new discoveries in Southern Rhodesia flooded world markets with low-cost asbestos in the 1920's. And just when the automobile and construction industries seemed about to make Canadian short-fibred asbestos more valuable, the Depression came, and it was not until the Second World War that the Canadian industry started making a decent profit. But by that time it was barely Canadian. Of the seven producers remaining in the Eastern Townships, four were American companies, all linked to manufacturing divisions in the U.S. such as Johns-Manville (Asbestos) and Flintkote (Thetford), one was British (Bell, owned by Turner and Newall), and only two were Canadian, Asbestos Corporation and Johnson's Co. Ltd.

The ups and downs of the asbestos industry were matched by its labor history. The first attempt at forming a union took place at Thetford in 1909, but it was not until 1915 that the Western Union of Miners (American Federation of Labor) unionized the industry and struck for higher wages. Almost immediately they were undercut by a so-called Catholic union organized by a Thetford priest named Abbe Maxime Fortin. This then, was the inglorious beginning of La Confederation des travailleurs catholiques du Canada (now the Confederation of National Trades Unions) which was founded in 1921 in Hull, P.Q. The Thetford Catholic Union was a founder member.

As Trudeau put it in *la Grève de l'Amiante*, "the birth, by artificial insemination, of the catholic labor system, does not constitute the most glorious episode in Quebec's history." Quebec's Catholic labor unions were a by-product of chance; their motivation a nationalist reaction against outside ideas which had been neglected in Quebec; their philosophy xenophobic, authoritarian and unrealistic.

The strike at Asbestos changed not only the CTCC (it is now non-confessional as well as federalist), but the very society that created it.

What was that society?

Trudeau's background chapter in *La Grève de l'Amiante* was compelling. It was also passionate, and at times you feel he over-stated the case, which is easy to do when trying to persuade some well-loved person to your point of view. And this is a key facet of Trudeau which English Canadians ignore at their peril. He may love Canada patriotically, but he loves Quebec passionately. Quebec Nationalists, who admit his sincerity, accuse him of being too rigid in his attitude towards Quebec. They will point out that his viewpoint has not changed in 20 years. This is absolutely true, but the arguments he opposes have not changed in 20 years, either, nor in 120 years, for that matter; only the terminology is different — what used to be "*la race*" is now "*la nation*", as he says.

The society that would explode in 1949 at Asbestos was one in which the thinkers were out of touch with reality. In 1900, Quebec was 40% urbanized and by 1931 that percentage had risen to 53%, by 1951 it was 67% and by 1961, 74%, yet nationalist leaders such as Henri Bourassa would argue that Quebeckers were basically farmers, and a return to the land was the solution to their problems. This land myth had persisted since the foundation of the colony of New France in the 17th century despite early proof that French Canadians were unwilling and unexceptional farmers and Quebec itself unpromising farm country since only 5% of the land is rated arable.

But, as Trudeau points out, while Quebec's thinkers conjured their unworkable agrarian utopias, the ordinary worker faced reality daily, evolving his own way of resolving the dichotomy — sometimes by simply giving up, as Quebeckers did at a rate of 20,000 a year from the 1870s onward, emigrating to the United States and to the opportunities afforded by the American industrial revolution. Those who stayed behind took advantage of Canada's own industrial revolution 25 years later when, in Quebec alone, the value of agricultural products dropped from 65% of the gross provincial product in 1900 to 5.5% in the 1960s and the value of manufactured goods rose from 4% to 65%.

But the increasing industrial reality of Quebec in the first half of the 20th century made no impression on the nationalists. The introspection of nearly 150 years had been permitted to atrophy, and the 'system of security', as Trudeau puts it, that had allowed the French Canadian to get over the shock of "being beaten, occupied, leaderless, commercially barred and diminished in influence in a continent which they had, after all, discovered, explored and colonized", became permanent. "That's why, faced with an English atmosphere, Protestant, materialistic, commercial and later industrialized, our nationalists elaborated a system of defense in which all the prime forces were contrary: French language, Catholic, authoritarian, idealistic, rural.

"And out of the whole, our social theoreticians elaborated 'an astrology' which claimed to order the destinies of French Canada with the precision of a celestial system. Our 'providential mission' was thus accomplished. And while this fantastic scheme was being constructed by our thinkers, the people themselves were concerned with the real threats to their daily life . . . the result being constant selection between the demands of nationalism and common-sense survival. . . . A little pastoral dream of greatness was played out against an exodus to the United States."

Since it was unworkable and hence anchored in unreality, Quebec nationalism tended to become more and more rococo until, at times, it reached a state of high mumbo-jumbo, as in 1902, when Msgr. Paquet referred in a sermon to "a social priesthood, reserved for an elite people, to which we have the privilege to belong . . ." and went on to systematically reject all contemporary materialism "in favor of the honor of the doctrine and the palms of the apostolate".

Politically, authoritarianism fostered by the institutional "Holy Alliance" encouraged the belief that the state was somehow independent of the people and outside their control. This permitted political parties to control government without any pretence at democratic procedures, while those parties which might have taught elementary principles of democratic action, the CCF and later the NDP, were discouraged by the Papal condemnation of socialist atheism.

The world of the Social Doctrine of the Church, with its tenets of return to the land, small private enterprise, confessional cooperatives, catholic unions and corporatism was sometimes a wonderland that only Lewis Carroll would have invented, had it not invented itself, because nothing really worked. The land myth was just that. The small business ideal — that French Canadians should not attempt major industrial ventures — was destined to hamstring development of native industries and industrialists. Confessional cooperatives worked well among farmers and fishermen but collapsed when they were introduced into multi-lingual, multi-denominational urban communities. Catholic unions also worked, but they finally destroyed the system that created them and ultimately became non-denominational, destroying their raison d'être as well.

Corporatism, "evangelical corporatism", is by no means dead in the Province of Quebec as the survival of Quebec's Legislative Council, or Upper House, can testify. But the institutionalization of the elite in a legal superstructure representing all the vested interests in order to advise the elected government, would seem to require, as Trudeau notes, a degree of democratic evolution so far advanced that special interests would be subordinated. The Province of Quebec has shown no sign of such democratic sophistication and as a result one can only share Trudeau's suspicion that Quebec corporatism is just another means for the elite to discipline the masses. "Most of our thinkers see corporatism as a means of domesticating labor," he said. And as such, like all the other theories of the Social Doctrine of the Church, it will probably fail.

Clearly the Social Doctrine of the Church was only able to remain in force as long as it did, because the elite which supported it managed to perpetuate itself.

Trudeau explains this as a result of Quebec's educational system, controlled by the Church, remaining unchanged from 1837 to 1937, while the universities, also controlled by the Church, limited their degree courses to theology, medicine and law as late as 1920. Education was not compulsory in Quebec until 1942, and even after the act was proclaimed in May, 1943, making school compulsory from the age of six to 14, the National Union government never enforced it.

University education in Quebec's catholic colleges was described this way by André Siegfried in 1905. "The university, far from being, as it is in other countries, a milieu where new ideas are created and developed and prepared for tomorrow, has become an instrument for conservation. Left to itself, higher education in French Canada tends to stay what it is. Its directing principles do not direct it towards evolution. It will require exceptional leaders to push it towards organic and profound reform." According to Trudeau, it changed little until after the Second World War, and then it was the Asbestos strike which set fire to the campuses of Laval and the University of Montreal. Trudeau remembers that in his own law course at the University of Montreal, professors were mostly "harrassed lawyers who showed students how to find their way around the codes of the province" and little else. Public law courses were almost unknown, and the great streams of international law unrecognized. It was hardly surprising that, in such a blinkered, authoritarian legal group, only half a dozen lawyers were prepared to take briefs for the labor unions. And as late as 1949, Quebec had no family court, no legal aid bureau and no legal clinic.

Trudeau recalls that the business school at the U. of M. taught French, the History of Canada, physical geography and produced some good statistics but was abysmally weak in the burgeoning field of management. The school of social sciences taught home economy, hygiene for nurses, and evening courses.

Only the University of Laval could claim a school of social science worthy of the name and that was mostly due to a remarkable Dominican monk named Georges-Henri Lévesque.

And this is where it all began.

The asbestos strike started on February 14, 1949, but it did not burst upon the people of Quebec like some flood from a dam collapse. It was much more insidious, like a leak in a dike, which springs another and another until there is water everywhere and the dike has gone. Labor problems had plagued the industry from its inception. Working conditions were appalling; pay was poor. But appalling conditions and poor pay existed in many Quebec industries. And, while both conditions and pay were part of the CTCC union's demands (elimination of dust and a 15 cent an hour raise from 85 cents to $1.00), the key issue was recognition for the union. This came through clearly in such demands as a union supervised pension plan; union approval of promotions, transfers and dismissals; right to discuss production standards; and finally, application of the Rand formula, which recognizes the union's right in a collective contract to compulsory dues deduction for all workers covered by the contract whether members of the union or not. The formula owes nothing to Ayn but gets its name from the Hon. Ivan Rand, a retired judge of the Supreme Court of Canada, who developed the formula as arbitrator in the Ford Motor Company of Canada's labor dispute in 1945. Though almost universal today, the Rand formula was a contentious issue in 1949.

Negotiations for a new contract had started at Thetford Mines between the Asbestos Corporation and the Johnson's Company and *La Fédération de l'Industrie Minière* (affiliate of the CTCC) on December 10, 1948 and had continued through to January 7, 1949 with some progress. In Asbestos, the Canadian Johns-Manville Company started negotiations on December 24, 1948, and broke them off on January 14, 1949, after only five sessions. No meetings took place for a month and on Sunday, February 13, Jean Marchand, as secretary-general of the CTCC, called a meeting in the parish hall of St. Aimé d'Asbestos Church (the curé was the almoner of the union local) and asked for patience for another 48 hours, in order to make a final plea to the Minister of Labor, Antonio Barrette, who was still regarded at that point as a friend of labor (after all, he had not seen Duplessis' Bill 5 before it was tabled).

But the asbestos miners had waited long enough. They shouted him down and, as midnight approached, groups left the hall to call out the night shift and set up pickets at the factory, railroad terminus, mine shaft and mill complex. On Monday, strikes also closed the companies at Thetford Mines. Only Quebec Asbestos, at East Broughton, kept going throughout the strike; all the other ten mines were strikebound.

By Thursday, February 17, Flintkote Mines in Thetford offered to settle for whatever the others settled for, if their workers went back. It looked as if the union was winning. Flintkote's offer was rejected. But two days later Inspector General Norbert Labbé of the Quebec Provincial Police roared into Asbestos at the head of 100 troopers in 25 police cars and wagons. Duplessis' counter-attack had started. Police behavior in the streets of Asbestos was deliberately provocative; many were reported drunk on duty, and there were reports of indecent behavior.

On Monday, the Quebec labor relations board announced that it had arbitrarily de-certified the Mining Industry Federation. A delegation went to Quebec to protest to Labor Minister Barrette; they were told they would have to take their case to Duplessis — who refused to receive any delegation that included Jean Marchand. The delegation walked out. The break was total. No dialogue took place with government or management. And the pressure was increasing. QPP stopped all cars to check for the smallest infringe-ment. Miners who left licenses at home faced a unique sentence from Duplessis' magistrates — return immediately to work, or pay a $30 fine, or go to jail. Most preferred jail.

In the cities, meanwhile, Canadian Johns-Manville, which was the biggest employer (2,000 workers) and had the largest stake in the strike, published full page advertisements declaring the strike illegal (which technically it was) and demanding a return to work. The CTCC began collecting what was to become a strike fund of over $200,000. The same week striking bachelors started to receive $3 per week and married men got $4 plus $1 per child (along with free bread and milk for everyone).

The carnival atmosphere that had existed barely a week before changed to grey depression. Even the weather turned against the strikers. The thermometer plunged below zero, and cold winds blew the snow into deep drifts; just keeping warm became a major concern. For strikers with lungs weakened from years of breathing the fibre-laden air of the mines and mills, the weather was more than just a discomfort.

By mid-March the weather had improved but the strikers seemed more isolated than ever. Against the news that a social research group at the University of Montreal had started a collec-tion for the strikers, and that the international unions across Can-ada were sending in truckloads of food, came ominous signs that the establishment was closing ranks against them. Shopkeepers cut off credit, while police brutality increased. Strike-breakers started appearing in increasing numbers, brought in by company recruiters from the surrounding countryside. In March, Johns-Manville hired 122 strike-breakers, in April 252 went to work, protected from the anger of the strikers by Duplessis' police.

On March 14, somebody blew up the railroad line owned by Johns-Manville which was used to carry freight from Asbestos to the main CNR line at Danville (home town of the late Daniel Johnson, then serving his second term as a backbencher in Duplessis' National Union government). The Mounties investigated the dynamiting but found few clues, and no one was arrested. Two days later, strikers overturned a Johns-Manville truck driven by a strikebreaker.

Police were reinforced in Asbestos. And that Sunday, parishoners were treated to a new phenomenon, schism in the Church, with Curé Deslandes of St. Isaac-Jogues telling them that if the strikers had taken his advice (and not struck), all the trouble would have been avoided, while Curé Camirand of St. Aimé's Church read extracts from the Papal Encyclical, Divini Redemptoris, which said workers deserved a just salary, and told the strikers not to be discouraged but that they must rely on themselves alone to see the strike through.

Late that same night, Inspector General Labbé's men arrested two strike leaders in their beds and hauled them away for three days of old-fashioned interrogation at the Club Iroquois (owned by Johns-Manville, but serving as a boozy temporary police headquarters for the strike). From that time until the end of the strike, police tactics showed that, faced with organized opposition, the establishment would condone the use of any means to have its way. The use of violence was to occur frequently during the Duplessis regime and recur during the Lesage regime that followed in the brutal Samedi de la Matraque (Saturday of the Clubs) in Quebec City in 1964 during the Queen's visit.

The police arrested 173 people during the asbestos strike, held many incommunicado for days over the protests of the few lawyers who could be found to defend them, such as a young Montreal advocate named Jean Drapeau. But in the end, of the 173 arrested, only 31 were convicted (20 of them for "vagabondage"), and the rest were acquitted. Both sides broke the law, of course, but compared to the calculated travesty of justice perpetuated by Duplessis and his henchmen, the strikers' behavior was benign.

As March turned to April, the federal government: welcomed Newfoundland into Confederation with a golden handshake of some $200-million in federal aid, ratified the agreement setting up the North Atlantic Treaty Organization in a single day — and noted the strike at Asbestos only with homilies. On April 4, the Hon. Humphrey Mitchell, Minister of Labor, told the House of Commons, "constant vigilance is the price of liberty" but pointed out that the strike was a provincial matter. Badly hurt in the 1948 provincial election, and with a general election set for June 25, the Liberals were in no mood to take the advice of the Liberal member for Megantic, Joe Lafontaine, and pressure Duplessis into line.

It was to be the start of a long period of accommodation between Prime Minister Louis St. Laurent and Duplessis in which each minded his own business. It was to last, more or less unbroken, until 1958 when Diefenbaker, ferociously aided by Duplessis, would sweep the Liberals out of power for nearly five years. Those who abided by the accommodation, even briefly, were to become the "Old Guard" of the 1960s.

Imperceptibly at first, but then in a flood, came the change in public opinion which was to buoy up the strikers like an incoming tide until the settlement was reached two months later. On April 11, hundreds of students from the University of Montreal defied the disapproval of the authorities to drive 98 miles to Asbestos in a happy cavalcade of cars and trucks, shouting "Vive les grèvistes de l'amiante" ("Long live the asbestos strikers"), and demonstrating their support of the workers with gifts of food and money.

Five days later, the asbestos companies re-opened negotiations with the CTCC. They said they had no objection to re-certification of the union. A break-through seemed imminent. But hopes were dashed on April 18, when the provincial government rejected the suggestion. On April 20, Johns-Manville refused to accept rent from strikers who were tenants in company-owned houses. It was not charity that motivated the move: the company refused rent because it was serving eviction notices (up until then rents had been paid by the union out of strike funds to prevent evictions). But public reaction was so violent that the next day the embattled Labor Minister, Barrette, told Johns-Manville vice president, George K. Foster, to cut it out. Eviction notices were withdrawn.

It was at this point, on April 22, when relations between miners and the companies were at their bitterest, that Gérard Pelletier and a friend rattled into Asbestos in his battered, old right-hand-drive British Singer. Pelletier, the labor correspondent for Montreal's *Le Devoir*, had been in Asbestos and Thetford Mines since the strike started in February. His involvement as a newsman in the strike that cold winter was to turn him into an activist in the labor movement, but long before the strike started at Asbestos, he had been passionately interested in the problems of labor and its evolution in Quebec. Pelletier had been born and raised in Victoriaville, only a few miles east of Asbestos, where the textile mills had exploited cheap labor even more shamelessly than the asbestos industry. At the University of Montreal, he had taken a B.A. degree and had plunged into Catholic Action, then journalism at *Le Devoir*. His specific concern with asbestos occurred nearly 18 months before, when an American freelance writer named Burton LeDoux had submitted evidence to *Le Devoir* that asbestosis had reached epidemic proportions in the mining hamlet of East Broughton (ironically, the only mine to operate unchecked throughout the strike), due to lack of dust control. A year earlier, LeDoux's investigative reporting for another publication had led to the closure of a Quebec silica mine in which silicosis was endemic. LeDoux and Pelletier jointly authored a study of the East Broughton situation which caused a sensation. And when the asbestos strike broke out in February, *Le Devoir* became the first newspaper in the history of Quebec journalism to assign a reporter to cover a strike on location and for the duration. Pelletier was the reporter.

The man sitting beside him as he drove into Asbestos from Montreal that morning was an old college friend, just back from China and other trouble-spots on a round-the-world hitch-hike, and he was keen to find out where the action was in Quebec. They were the same age, but even at 29, the contrast was considerable.

Pelletier, thin, trim and as elegant as $35 a week from *Le Devoir* permitted, was already identifiably the slightly stooped, aristocratic figure that he is today. Pierre Elliott Trudeau was still the student — in fact, he had been at school almost continuously since their days together at the U. of M., first at Harvard and then Paris and most recently, until the previous spring, at the London School of Economics. He looked the part; his clothes, Marchand remembers, were usually jeans, sandals (weather permitting), old shirt, no tie, old jacket and tattered old raincoat. His face looked very much as it does today. There was more hair, of course, piled high and curly, and a scruffy, blond, chin-strap beard that would cause miners to call him "St. Joseph" in the days to come. But the huge almond-shaped eyes, leonine nose and high-cheekbones were the same; so was the sensuous mouth, the wide, tooth-filled smile, and skin that was weathering into pock-marked worldliness. Even then, it was a face and a style that had a devastating effect on women.

Pelletier was delighted to show Trudeau around but the sightseeing trip lasted only as far as the first policeman who ordered them to stop and, coming around to what he took to be the driver's side of the little English car, demanded to see Trudeau's driving licence. He had failed to note that Trudeau had no steering-wheel in front of him. When Trudeau couldn't produce a licence, the cop arrested them all and told them to follow him to the Iroquois Club. There, in a crimson session before Inspector Gagné, the cop discovered that the car had right-hand-drive and the driver, Pelletier, had all the legal documents required. Gagné told Pelletier and Trudeau that they had 30 minutes to get out of town, and stormed out of the office to further berate the patrolman who had caused him such a loss of face. Trudeau and Pelletier were left to pick up their belongings (the police had emptied the car, strewing the contents on the floor of the club) and, conforming to the legal niceties of being ordered out of town, drove out of Asbestos for an hour or two, until the police cooled down.

The effect of that brutal first day in Asbestos was apparent the same evening, when he met Jean Marchand for the first time and accepted his invitation to address a meeting of miners on the legal aspects of the strike. The speech Trudeau made in St. Aimé's church hall that night was so militant that Marchand still remembers that he was on the edge of his chair by the end. "Miners are not schoolchildren, you know," he recalls, "and while students might steal pencils, the miners steal dynamite. They use it all day at work, and they are very familiar with it. Now, I had managed to de-fuse two or three cute little plots by the boys which would have blown up the mine manager and most of his staff. So you can imagine that when Trudeau urged physical resistance by the strikers, I got a little bit worried." It took quite a while to get the men under control again.

Jean Marchand is a scrappy little terrier of a man with a brisk manner who, then as now, has a wisp of hair which stands straight up from his forehead, giving him an air of being constantly surprised — which he rarely is, as it happens. He is also one of the greatest stump speakers in Canadian politics. He can enter a hall in a tough district with a hostile audience and in minutes have it groaning, laughing, roaring, and happily eating out of his hand. He experienced few situations in his 23 years as a labor leader when things got out of control, or close to it, but that night with Trudeau in Asbestos was one of them. And while he did not ask Trudeau to address the miners again, he was impressed enough to invite him to join the CTCC as a legal adviser, once the strike was over. He also asked Pelletier to come on board as the public relations director and editor of the union paper. Trudeau turned down the job offer, because he did not want to be tied down to one area, but for the next 15 years he did serve on a casual basis as legal counsel in half a dozen cases involving the CTCC and its successor the CSN. Pelletier, on the other hand, joined the CTCC and remained with the labor movement until he returned to journalism as editor of *La Presse* in 1961.

Trudeau stayed in and around Asbestos for about three weeks in all, visiting the other strike areas and talking to the picketers. He was there when the strike moved into its most brutal and best known period.

On April 24, there was a rally in support of the strikers in the Palais Montcalm at which Father Lévesque made a famous speech in which he replied to the Jesuit argument that authority comes from God. "Ladies and Gentlemen," he opened, "Liberty *also* comes from God." Four days later, the rector of Laval, Monseignor Vandry, denied a report (in *Le Devoir* by Pelletier) that he had forbidden Laval Students to go to Asbestos to hand over a collection of money they had made for the miners. Maurice Lamontagne and two other faculty members had defied the rector to take the money to Asbestos for the students.

But the penultimate moment came on May 1, when the Archbishop of Montreal, Msgr. Joseph Charbonneau, a brave and outspoken man who was as big as he was courageous, towered over the congregation of establishmentarians in Notre Dame Church and declared that the Church must help the strikers in Asbestos. "There's a conspiracy to destroy the working class, and it's the Church's duty to intervene!" The effect of Archbishop Charbonneau's sermon was to split both Church and Establishment, and though it led to his own dismissal, it brought in a new era for Quebec.

The reaction of the strikers was euphoric. Victory was in sight. But the reaction of Duplessis was predictable. More squads of police heavily armed with tear gas grenades and sub-machineguns were sent in to Asbestos to protect the mine properties. Police tactics became rougher still and the strikers replied in kind, a car with four plainclothesmen was overturned and the cops roughed up by picketers.

On the night of May 5, without setting foot in Asbestos, the Director of the Provincial Police, Hilaire Beauregard, telephoned the mayor to tell him that the riot act would be read the following morning. (This illegal order was typical of police tactics). And when Judge H. O'Brady read the act the next morning, Beauregard's men swept through town arresting everyone in sight. In all, 145 people were arrested, 53 detained, and the Club Iroquois echoed to sounds of the Provincial Police questioning strikers. The riot act was in force for two days.

Feelings ran so high throughout Quebec that the late André Laurendeau, the distinguished editorialist at *Le Devoir,* wrote an open letter to the U.S. Ambassador asking him to take action against the American subsidiaries whose concept of democracy failed to travel well. "Will you permit men of money to undermine in Canada your reputation as a great civilized people?" he asked.

"Will you risk international assemblies where certain adversaries who seek your weaknesses can produce fearful dossiers about certain American employers? Would you have it said that for the United States neither democracy nor humanity nor justice are products for export — not even to a neighboring white race?"

The U.S. reply came on May 21, when visiting labor leaders, members of Johns-Manville's own company union in Manville, New Jersey, saw the conditions in Asbestos and declared that they would be intolerable in the U.S. and were 20 years behind the times.

But by then the tide of public opinion was overwhelmingly against Duplessis and the asbestos mining companies. The companies were ready to settle at almost any price. Only Duplessis was intransigent. He had been defied, and worse, publicly humiliated. The strike would last until he could recoup his prestige. At this point, the Archbishop of Quebec, Msgr. Maurice Roy, offered his services as mediator. A kindly man and consummate diplomat, Roy was the perfect mediator. He was accepted by both sides, and, on June 13, he went to work. By July 1, 1949, the strike was over, and the whole dispute was taken to an arbitration board.

As in all strikes, both sides lost financially, and when the arbitration board recommendation came down the following December, it did not give the union anything approaching a carte blanche. Wages were increased to 95 cents an hour and not the dollar the union asked; the Rand formula was rejected and even suppressed in those mines which had accepted it (Asbestos Corporation, Johnson's and Flintkote); and a union supervised pension fund was also rejected. In short, the new contract was little better than a saw-off. But that is all past history. Within three years, the Asbestos companies were paying the highest mining wages in Quebec, and in the 20 years that have passed since the strike, conditions in the industry have improved.

The "Holy Alliance" was broken. Recognition was at last obtained for labor, for unions and for the collective bargaining process in the province of Quebec which had never existed before. The "Holy Alliance" was broken. A new power structure had been erected. And an action group had formed around Marchand,

Pelletier and Trudeau which would transform Quebec and ultimately Canada itself.

While the asbestos strike was nearing its end, Canada went to
the polls in a general election. In it, the new premier of the newest
Canadian province, Newfoundland, Joseph Roberts Smallwood,
expressed his thanks for admission to confederation by campaigning actively for the federal Liberals and referring to Louis Stephen
St. Laurent as "the greatest man Canada has ever produced." In
Quebec, on the other hand, the National Union party fought hard
against St. Laurent and an editorialist described him culturally
as "more Stephen than Louis". St. Laurent's campaign was an
intensely personal one, and on June 25, 1949 he won a smashing
victory with a majority of 190 seats to the Conservatives 41 (CCF
got 13 and Social Credit, 10).

Nineteen years later, Joey Smallwood, still premier of Newfoundland, knew another good thing when he saw it and described
Pierre Elliott Trudeau as "the most brilliant man Canada has ever
produced". In Quebec, on the other hand, the National Union
fought hard against Trudeau and Premier Daniel Johnson referred
to him as "Lord Elliott," while the separatists said *"qui'importe les
trous d'eau"* and called him "Peter Elliott Waterhole". Trudeau's
campaign was an intensely personal one.

Plus ça change, plus c'est la même chose. For though Quebec
had been transformed socially in between time, its political attitudes had changed little, only the state itself had changed — from
passive nationalism to active separatism, from defensive autonomy
to aggressive autonomy. The task of making federalism relevant
to Quebeckers was still far from finished.

III

The Seedlings

THE ASBESTOS STRIKE had galvanized everyone involved in it. For Jean Marchand, the hero of the strike, there was no doubt about what he had to do: the CTCC had to be built up and this was no time to sit on its laurels.

Maurice Lamontagne, who had played a sideline role as adviser and fund-raiser during the strike, plunged into the central job of being the expert economic witness for the union during the arbitration board hearings. He had already made a name for himself doing economic research for the Ministry of Munitions and Supply under Clarence Decatur Howe (the ministry title changed to Reconstruction and Supply in January 1946), and his services were frequently requested in Ottawa. His sojourns at Laval became shorter and shorter, and, by 1954, he was deputy minister of Northern Affairs and National Resources under another Laval alumnus, Jean Lesage.

Father Lévesque had also become a favorite of the Ottawa Establishment. Since early in 1949, he had been on leave from Laval, serving on the Royal Commission of inquiry into National Development in the Arts, Letters and Sciences under the chairmanship of Vincent Massey, Canada's most distinguished scholar-diplomat. During 1950, the French government decided to honor Levésque for his outspoken support of the Free French forces during the Second World War (when most of the Quebec clergy were in favor of Vichy) and to make him a Chevalier de la Légion d'Honneur. This decoration led to a bristling exchange between a visiting French statesman and Premier Duplessis. "Some of your decorations are an insult to the Province of Quebec," snarled Duplessis at a reception at the French Consulate General in Quebec City. "When France decides to decorate a person, M'sieu, she does not have to ask for, or receive, the per-

mission of the government involved," replied the French diplomat
icily.

(When St. Laurent tried to appoint Father Lévesque to the
Senate, five years later, he probably wished he had the cool
assurance of a French diplomat. For while the Master-General of
the Dominican Order in Rome approved Lévesque's appointment,
the Canadian Bishops, led by Paul Emile Cardinal Léger, vetoed
the proposal. And it was left to Quebec's gentle Archbishop, now
Cardinal, Maurice Roy, to tell Lévesque, some say with regret,
that it could not be allowed.)

Trudeau and Pelletier came out of the asbestos strike badly
needing to get involved. Pelletier quickly found his role in the
CTCC as public relations man and editor of *Le Travail,* the
federation newspaper. For Trudeau the choice was much harder.

Today, when he looks back on that period, he is apt to imagine
that he really wanted to teach, but that Duplessis would not let
him work in a Quebec university. The reality appears to be somewhat different. One of the first people to try to hire him was
Marchand himself, who was in desperate need of a first-rate
lawyer to work full-time within the federation. Following close on
Marchand, was Maurice Lamontagne who wanted just Trudeau's
sort of talent in the economics department at Laval. As they
remember it, Trudeau turned down the job offers because he did
not want to live outside Montreal, or did not want to be trapped
into one thing.

"I tried to hire him as a conseiller technique," says Marchand,
"but he said 'it would tie me down too much. I need liberty' ".

Even Father Lévesque stepped in to put his weight behind
Lamontagne's offer. But he remembers, too, that neither Trudeau
nor Pelletier (whom he also tried to hire) wanted to live outside
Montreal.

"Sure he was under-employed in the Fifties," says Marchand.
"Pierre took a long time to get involved in things. He took a long
time to participate and collaborate. In any social or political
adventure he had a considerable reluctance to overcome. As soon
as he felt he was menaced with involvement, he left, for the south
of France, or Italy or Sweden."

"If he hadn't had money, he would have had to get involved," says Marchand, "if only to pay for the luxury of those trips to Europe. But whether being rich hurt or helped, I am not sure. I don't know. He might not have had the global experience he did, attaching himself to different milieux, being accepted everywhere. If he had been involved, it would have limited him in the experience he could have acquired. But as a man, in the Fifties, he was certainly under-employed."

For some reason, Trudeau finally made up his mind to accept a job as a junior clerk in the Privy Council office. With its great majority in parliament, the St. Laurent administration seemed to promise exciting, dynamic politics. The Massey Commission was only one sign. In January, 1950, the veteran diplomat and orientalist, Chester A. Ronning, Canadian charge d'affaires in Nanking, was sent to Peking by St. Laurent with orders to buy a house suitable for the Canadian Embassy. Great things were in the wind. A cultural inventory, radical changes in foreign policy — the Privy Council office promised to be action central. And Trudeau wanted to be where the action was.

But long before deeds could be drawn up on the house in Peking, the Minister of Defense, Brooke Claxton, was to rise in the House of Commons to report that on the previous day, June 25, the Republic of Korea had been invaded from the north. The Korean war had started.

There is evidence that Trudeau's disillusionment with Ottawa may have set in before Korea. For during the month war broke out, on newsstands and in bookstores acquainted with the avant-garde, a small, 6" by 8" magazine of political opinion made its appearance. It was called *Cité Libre* (Free City) because it believed in free expression of opinion. It was hence, by definition, opposed to just about everything the Premier of Quebec stood for.

Cité Libre first became an idea for an idea in Paris in 1946–1947, when Trudeau and his friends were students. The magazine was born during the winter of 1949–1950 at weekend meetings in Montreal, attended by Trudeau, Pelletier and eight others in their crowd. They were Charles Lussier, a lawyer and now deputy-minister of the Secretariat of State under Pelletier (the meetings were in his house 832 Rockland Street); Reginald Boisvert, a public relations man for a labor union; Jean-Paul Geoffroy and

Pierre Vadboncoeur; Guy Cormier, just back from studying in
Paris and about to become a newspaperman; Maurice Blain, a
notary and literary critic; Roger Rolland, a public affairs producer
for Radio Canada; and Pierre Laporte, a lawyer and reporter for
Le Devoir, now a prominent Quebec Liberal MLA.

As with the other group undertakings which mushroomed in the
1950's, *Cité Libre* got its impetus from the asbestos strike and
the evidence it produced that opposition to Duplessis was not only
conceivable but had a chance of success. One of *Cité Libre's* first
long-term projects, for instance, was to produce a document that
would examine the strike from a number of angles, political, financial, union, and relate it to the broader socio-economic field. This,
of course, was to become the book, *La Grève de l'Amiante,* published in 1956, and containing major contributions by four of the
founders — Trudeau, Pelletier, Lussier and Boisvert.

Cité Libre's short-term objective, however, was to produce a
more-or-less quarterly review of the best ideas and essays relevant
to Quebec — and Canada's — political development. The publishing schedule was irregular for many years and it was not until a
young journalist named Jacques Hébert became the production
manager, as well as a member of the editorial board, that *Cité
Libre* was able to become a significant intellectual force with a
small but effective distribution and subscription service. Hébert,
now the owner of Editions du Jour, the best-known paperback
house in Quebec, had roamed the world since he graduated from
the University of Montreal in 1945, financing his travels with
freelance articles, films and slide shows. But in 1954, he settled
down in Montreal and started *Vrai,* a crusading weekly newspaper,
sponsored by Mayor Jean Drapeau's Civic Action Party, which
folded in 1959, when he fell out with Drapeau and went into the
book publishing business. Hébert had become a close friend of
Trudeau's in the 1950's, and in 1960, he, Trudeau, Dr. Denis
Lazure and Micheline Légendre visited Communist China together.
The book, *Two Innocents in Red China,* co-authored by Hébert
and Trudeau, was the result. Hébert is a warm, vital, Zolaesque
personality, a defender of unpopular and often losing causes (he
has published dozens of books of social protest and written a few
himself), constantly in litigation, in short, what they call in Quebec
un original — a character.

Hébert's influence on *Cité Libre,* both as an administrator and as a board member, cannot be over-emphasized. But it was not felt until after 1954; during the early years, the driving force was Trudeau himself.

Theoretically, of course, *Cité Libre* was run by members of the editorial board, who were jointly responsible for the publication. Early on, they evolved a unique policy and system: each would-be contributor, whether board member or not, had to defend his essay ideas in debate with the others before being allowed to put pen to paper. This *viva voce,* they felt, would clarify ideas and avoid petty errors. But once the ordeal was over, the writer could be sure that his piece would run untouched by the editors. The editorial board also acted as a useful foil externally, since the founders felt that it created a collegiality that would at once avoid the personality cults that afflict "little" magazines and also prevent the authorities from persecuting any one individual.

Trudeau soon became so involved with the magazine that he decided to give up the Privy Council and return to Montreal full-time. Besides, his involvement with a magazine that was already incurring Duplessis' wrath made his fellow civil servants nervous.

"It was alright as long as I was writing about the theory of politics," he says. "But when I decided to write about the practice of politics, I felt I had to resign". In 1952, he left Ottawa to return to private practice as a lawyer in Montreal.

His two years with the Privy Council were uneventful. As did Mackenzie King before him, St. Laurent retained the Presidency of the council himself, so Trudeau was able to develop a close working relationship with the Prime Minister. And while he did become friends professionally with a number of civil servants, his weekends and spare time were spent in Montreal; as far as Ottawa was concerned, his private life remained in Quebec. He served as a very junior official on one or two Federal-Provincial conferences, earned the respect of his colleagues, but left little mark.

A measure of his disengagement at the time comes from the memory of Marc Lalonde, then a student, now his senior Privy Council advisor, who was trying to make up his mind at the time whether to go into law or social sciences and decided to get Trudeau's advice. Lalonde had read Trudeau's articles in *Cité*

Libre and had met him on shipboard coming back from Europe in 1951 (Trudeau visited Europe almost every year from 1949 onward). Lalonde wanted to go to the London School of Economics and asked Trudeau's advice as an old LSE graduate. Trudeau's reply was so unmemorable that Lalonde has no idea what he said. He presumes he must have taken it, however, because the upshot was that he decided to study law at the University of Montreal and then read economics at Oxford. The two men became close friends several years later, when Lalonde was a co-founder of the Institute of Public Law at the University of Montreal.

Another group formed in the early 1950's came to be known as the Jean-Marie Nadeau Society, although there is no evidence that it was ever more than a few people who supported the charismatic Montreal lawyer Jean-Marie Nadeau for the provincial Liberal leadership in 1950, and then continued a close association until Jean Lesage's election as provincial leader in 1958. A collection of extracts from Jean-Marie Nadeau's diaries was published in 1966 by Editions Parti Pris (publishers of the separatist magazine) and made fascinating reading. The foreword was by René Lévesque (an un-separated Liberal at the time), who knew him from the late 1940's, when they worked together at the International Service of the CBC — Lévesque as an announcer, and Nadeau as the Montreal lawyer and professor who came in each week to do his political commentary. "Though he was a lawyer, professor and even, I believe, 'intellectual', the man I remember always evoked the land for me," Lévesque wrote. "We other French Canadians were never far from the land, of course, one or two generations at the most. But Jean-Marie Nadeau was somehow closer. Though a graduate and member of the Bar, he remained identified with his native Saint Césaire (35 miles south-east of Montreal)."

Lévesque remembers that Nadeau could feel as indignant about a liquor permit in Sorel as he was about the crisis in China" . . . and yet still remain fiercely the villager from St. Césaire."

Nadeau became the chief Liberal organizer for Montreal and a close advisor of the man who beat him for the leadership, Georges-Emile Lapalme. He spoke out against the collaboration of Federal

Liberals and Quebec's National Union, and was a major force in restructuring the provincial wing of the party so that Old Guard influence was reduced. He felt very strongly that sources of party finance should be revealed and that honesty should be demanded as much of the elite as it was of the poor.

Trudeau was to write about "The New Treason of the Intellectuals" in *Cité Libre* in 1962. Jean-Marie Nadeau had already hit hard at what he called "The Treason of the Elite" in September, 1956, squarely blaming French Canada's moral and technological crisis on "our errors and faults", on the key people in politics, journalism, and teaching. "We must see the origin of these errors and how they came about," he wrote. "Corruption, laziness, desire to enrich oneself at no effort, egotism. Just define the profession of 'politician', from deputy to county laborer, via civil servant and all the other clients of politics. That's why 'being in politics' has taken on, in our milieu, the meaning of a particular alimentary function. In other times, in Rome, the magistrature was a position of public trust, but (with us) it is a source of money and enrichment. And exceptions are rare."

Nadeau had a part in every major political development in Quebec in the Fifties, and it was tragic that in 1960, a few days after he was appointed by the Liberals as special counsel to look into the National Union Administration, he should have been killed in an automobile accident. Quebec lost an exceptional man.

Nadeau's legacy was nothing less than the reform wing of the Liberal party in Quebec. His protégés were such men as Guy Favreau and Bob Giguère, both key figures in the machinery which was to produce and project Pierre Elliott Trudeau as a political figure. Favreau had been one of Nadeau's closest friends since he graduated from law school at the University of Montreal in 1940. He was active in the reform wing of the Liberal Party from the early 1940's, until he became an associate Deputy Minister of Justice in Ottawa in 1955. Giguère was Nadeau's campaign manager when he ran for the provincial party leadership and later turned his talents to organizing the French Canadian Institute of Public Affairs (ICAP), of which he became secretary-general. A labor mediator by profession, Giguère is today the federal Liberal campaign manager for Quebec.

And so, standing against Duplessis in the early 1950's, there was *Cité Libre,* the Jean-Marie Nadeau Society, the Catholic Labor unions — and little else. The provincial Liberals would recoup some strength (23 seats) under Lapalme in 1952, but they never caught fire and never seriously threatened the National Union while Duplessis was alive.

As for *Cité Libre,* from a unionist's point of view, it "had an effect on the intellectuals and on the men of action and hence on the public itself," says Marchand, "but it did not affect the public directly at the start."

Pelletier, one of the founders of *Cité Libre,* says its effect on Duplessis tends to be exaggerated. "We kept the flame alight," he says, and Trudeau would agree. "I don't recall any one big battle with Duplessis or any particular success," says Trudeau. "We did not actually defeat Duplessis. He died before we could."

In fact, as Herbert Steinhouse wrote for *l'Observateur* in Paris in December, 1950, it was by no means clear at the time that if Duplessis had been removed, a Liberal or even Democratic party would have succeeded him. "If Duplessis is kicked out, no one can say what would replace him. Catholic reformers have always, and increasingly, cherished the idea of a corporatist state (Mussolini always had a big following in Quebec). The danger is therefore that the 'good Quebeckers' will have to choose one day between the museum of the past and a new 'Wave of the Future,' comprising 'Peace Eternal' between management and labor and 'trains that run on time' ".

It was a depressing prospect. Yet there were signs of hope, if one knew where to look. One prophetic speech that sounds as if it had been made by Trudeau in June, 1968, and not by Father Lévesque 20 years earlier (while receiving an honorary degree at the University of British Columbia) had this to say: "Unity is impossible without what I would call democratic pluralism. The ideal of democracy demands respect for the will of all the people. Now the Canadian people are made up essentially of different ethnic groups who all, with reason, want to guard and develop their special cultures. That means to say that Canadian democracy will not achieve unity until it respects the diversity of its elements. This diversity is a resource that, unhappily, is not appreciated by either side: it constitutes a common asset which too few Canadians take the trouble to understand or draw upon. If only Canadians would get to know each other better, they would like each other better!"

In retrospect, the 1950's were strangely smug and complacent years. There was a war in Asia and almost ceaseless turmoil around the globe, but for Canada it was a period of unprecedented prosperity. Fortunes were made in dozens of fields, frequently in mining and oil, and these more often in the penny stock promotions that accompanied the boom than in the discoveries themselves.

Immigration soared as Europeans left austerity behind them at a rate unequalled since before the First World War, with an average of more than 155,000 newcomers settling in Canada each year throughout the decade. The population grew 30%, from 14,000,000 to 18,000,000, an increase only exceeded by the 34% leap in the first decade of the century. With the increased population came bigger markets, and as immigration soared, so did housing, automobile production and other secondary industries.

Politically, Canada developed internationally as a respected, impartial intermediary, yet domestically it stagnated. While the Liberal regime earned applause for its progressive Commonwealth and United Nations policies, it hunkered down at home into the seat of power, cushioned by backroom deals and cynical non-aggression pacts that stifled democratic principles.

Yet there, scattered in the debris and nearly suffocated, were the unmistakable seedlings of the new politics — frail but full of hope.

New Brunswick, September 22, 1952: the Progressive Conservatives under Hugh John Flemming upset the deeply-entrenched 12-year-old regime of John McNair and his Liberals, thanks to a brilliant, well-researched campaign by one Dalton Camp and his employers, Locke, Johnson & Company, a Toronto advertising agency.

The unexpected Tory victory was to start a legend about Dalton Kingsley Camp that would reach its climactic moment 15 years later in Toronto during the P.C. Leadership Convention, masterminded by Camp himself. A stocky, balding, monkish figure,

Camp personifies cool competence and yet, somehow, injects enough wry wit into everything he does to indicate that he does not take life, or himself, too seriously.

He is the son of a well-known Maritimer, Dr. Harold B. Camp, a Baptist preacher of renown, and he was born in Woodstock, N.B. on September 11, 1920. The family moved to California soon afterwards, and Camp spent most of his early life in Piedmont, returning in his late teens to Wolfville, Nova Scotia, to graduate from high school and go to Acadia University briefly before joining the army at the outbreak of World War II. He ended the war as a Lieutenant, finished his B.A. at the University of New Brunswick and took an M.Sc. at Columbia. He then won a Beaverbrook scholarship to spend a year at the London School of Economics, where he became an admirer of such disparate figures as Harold Laski, Winston Churchill and, in a funny way, of Lord Beaverbrook himself. (The latter used to get his pound of flesh from the scholars who accepted his largesse by summoning them to see him on Sundays at Cherkley to be terrorized.)

Beaverbrook happened to loathe Laski with all the vast energy that he could bring to that act. It seemed that he had asked Laski to talk sense into Aneurin Bevan during the war, when there was some coal-mining problems at the Ministry of Supply, and Laski had refused. So Beaverbrook never forgave him. Finding a Laski admirer among one of his own scholars was a shock, giving Camp in Beaverbrook's eyes the fascination that a mouse has for a cat, before it is eaten. "Laski's radicalism made me a Red Tory," says Camp, and he was summoned on several Sundays to sit on the terrace at Cherkley between Lord Beaverbrook and Brigadier Michael Wardell, his aide and confidant, both deep in Sunday newspapers, indulging in the affectionate rudeness that characterized their life-long friendship. The conversation Camp remembers went something like this:

Beaverbrook: "Captain". (Wardell was always "Captain," his demobilization rank from the 10th Hussars, although his reserve rank later rose to Brigadier). "Captain, what do you think about this trouble in the Middle East? What's it all about?"

Wardell: (Not looking up from his newspaper). "How the hell should I know Max."

Beaverbrook: "Well, what do you know about it Camp?"

And for several minutes thereafter, Camp offered whatever knowledge he had on the subject, horrified at the apparent insolence that Wardell displayed to the First Baron.

"Beaverbrook was the last man who ever frightened me," he says, and remembers stumbling through some improvised reply.

Wardell, who now lives in Fredericton, N.B., remembers the day clearly. "Camp was not frightened at all," he says dryly. "He was entirely in control of himself and very self-assured, and Beaverbrook found him rather astonishing. He was dumbfounded by his enthusiasm for Laski."

(Camp remained on friendly terms with Beaverbrook and Wardell for many years. However, when he marshalled the forces against Diefenbaker in 1966, Wardell remained loyal to Diefenbaker and vigorously defended him against Camp in his newspaper, *The Daily Gleaner,* and other publications. He characterizes himself to this day "as one of the last, lonely Diefenbaker loyalists," and his relations with Camp are strained, to put it mildly.)

On his return home, Camp became an active Liberal, and, in 1948, he was the national treasurer of the Young Liberal Association of Canada. But his first leadership convention was to be his last: he became so infuriated by the steamroller tactics of a 38-year-old Nova Scotian named Robert Henry Winters (who had refused to let a proposal for Maritime development go through the policy committee), that he resigned from the party and went over to the Progressive Conservatives.

Camp went on from the triumph with Flemming to win Nova Scotia for Robert Stanfield in 1956; Manitoba for Dufferin Roblin in 1958 (having played a secondary but important role in the 1957 and 1958 P.C. Federal victories); and Prince Edward Island for Walter Shaw in 1959. He kept his men in power, too: Flemming lasted eight years until 1960; Stanfield and Roblin both retired from provincial politics undefeated; and Walter Shaw lasted until 1966 — a record that works out 1952 to 1967 at 15 wins and five losses. Enough of a record to make him an ex-Liberal that the party could ill-afford to lose.

But in 1952, it was all just starting.

As the year turned, Pierre Elliott Trudeau reflected sadly on

French Canadian politics in *Cité Libre* (December) and the "profound immorality" he saw pervading the scene. "We corrupt the civil service, blackmail deputies, pressure courts, defraud the income tax, and wink at graft," he wrote. "And in elections, our immorality becomes positively scabrous. A peasant who would be ashamed to enter a brothel sells his conscience at each election for a bottle of 'whisky blanc'. A lawyer who would demand the maximum penalty for a thief who robbed a church, is delighted with himself for adding 2,000 fictitious names to an electoral list. Why? To say that 'Democracy doesn't take well with Latins' and that 'Nordic people have a better developed sense of civic responsibility' explains nothing."

As Trudeau saw it then, the whole thing was the psychological reaction of French Canadians to democracy. They had never had democracy before the conquest and had never had to fight for it, so, like other things imposed on them, "it was not to be used, but to be abused."

Trudeau also laid a case against the Roman Catholic Church. "Without prejudicing the future, it must be recognized that Catholics, collectively, have rarely been pillars of democracy — and I say it to our shame — for they often mix questions of temporal and spiritual morality."

In countries where the Catholic Church is strong, anarchy is avoided only by authoritarianism. Where the Church is weak, on the other hand, the separation of church and state "is accepted as a compromise," he said.

"That's another reason why, in Quebec, where everyone knows that authority comes from God, one attaches no importance to such affectations as elections: they are Protestant, Anglo-Saxon diversions whose significance is obscure and whose usefulness is immediately translated into a bottle of whisky to be received, a parish hall to be built, or a road building contract to be awarded."

Trudeau deplored the fact that though French Canadians "by nature adore political discussions" their colossal ignorance of the subject is due as much to prejudice as it is to laziness. Historically, he said, they have been "warned against the democratic system without ever having tried it, which explains why French Canadian (political) studies have always been in the direction of extremism

— Maurrasism (Charles Maurras, jailed for life for collaboration after the Second World War, preached an authoritarian theory in France in the 1930's), Fascism, authoritarianism — so that the activities in the 1930's led to a resurgence of nationalism rather than liberalism."

It is significant, Trudeau felt, that while the rest of the world in the 1930's was trying out new things; in the United States, the New Deal: in Britain, Keynesian economics: "French Canadians were wanting a reassertion of nationalism."

In 1953, Stalin died, the Korean War ended, and the first television network was established between Montreal and Toronto, just in time to broadcast the Coronation and the conquest of Everest. In August, taking vicarious advantage of all the goodies, St. Laurent went to the country for a new mandate and came back with a reduced majority of 173 seats to the Conservatives 51. When he got around to shuffling his cabinet in mid-September, he appointed Jean Lesage as Minister of Resources and Development, succeeding Robert Winters, who went to Public Works.

Lesage was a golden boy in politics. Clever, blondly handsome, and enormously ambitious, he was known as *un go-getter* in his native Quebec City, where he had graduated with honors from law school at Laval and almost immediately plunged into politics. It was no coincidence that Lesage's career as a star crown prosecutor in Quebec began and ended with the five-year regime of Liberal Premier J. Adelard Godbout, from 1939 to 1944, for that was the way in Quebec politics. Lesage adopted a strong anticonscription stand during the war but did not let it stop him from joining the Garrison Club as Premier in the 60's, for that was the way too. And when Godbout was beaten in 1944 by Duplessis, Lesage wasted no time hanging around to serve the opposition but jumped into the first federal election that came along, winning Montmagny-l'Islet on his first try, in 1945. St. Laurent had been one of the law professors at Laval, and in the way kindly old professors are wont, he kept his eye out for Lesage. After an apprenticeship as parliamentary secretary to the Secretary of State for External Affairs (Lester Bowles Pearson) and to the Minister of Finance (Douglas Abbott), Lesage got his reward. It was a textbook career of the old style.

Another ambitious fellow to emerge in 1953 was Maurice
Sauvé, a dark, burly man with permanently flushed cheeks, who
burst into Jean Marchand's office at the CTCC in Quebec City
one day in 1952 and insisted that he be taken on staff. "He really
laid siege to me," recalls Marchand. Sauvé had just arrived back
from studies in Europe and was literally off the boat. He was
exceptionally qualified, with a law degree, as well as an M.A. and
Ph.D. in economics. "He said he had to go to work for the unions,
but all he wanted was to be given a job in a small town, where he
would settle down for 10 years and do a study in depth." Marchand gave him a job with the CTCC in St. Hyacinthe, 30 miles
east of Montreal. "Within a year, he wanted out. He provoked the
same negative reactions in the union as he did in politics. He went
next to the metallurgists (*Fédération nationale de la métallurgie*),
but very few of them could stand him, and he wasn't there more
than a few months before he tried to organize an election to get
the president out. It was very badly organized, rather as it was in
Gamelin in 1968." Sauvé took a leave of absence from the metallurgists in 1955, to go to work for the Royal Commission into
Canadian economic prospects under Walter Gordon, one of the
sachems of the federal Liberal Party. It was a job with a future.
Working in Ottawa, Sauvé got to know Lamontagne, and through
him went to work for Jean Lesage as public relations director of
the Quebec Liberal Party, planning the provincial Liberal sweep
in 1960.

In 1962, Sauvé decided to run in the federal election for the
remote constituency of Iles-de-la-Madeleine, a group of islands
scattered in the Gulf of St. Lawrence. He won the riding, and
from the day he arrived in Ottawa, Sauvé made no secret of his
ambition to be the Quebec leader in Ottawa, and, if he achieved
that position, of kicking most of his "Old Guard" colleagues out
of the party. In 1953, however, he was just another *conseiller
technique* with the CTCC.

Early in 1954, St. Laurent set off on a world tour which took
him to eleven countries in six weeks and so exhausted him that it
was really the start of a long decline. He returned from it on
March 17, quite unable to deal with a series of little crises, ranging
from Duplessis' sudden demand for 15% of the personal income

tax paid by Quebeckers (six months later, St. Laurent finally settled for 10%), to a book written by Maurice Lamontagne, by then deputy minister in Lesage's department, which was hardly designed to endear Ottawa to Quebec. The book, *Canadian Federalism, Evolution and Problems* (University Press of Laval), is a lucid discussion of Canadian federalism from an economist's point of view.

Lamontagne traced Canadian confederation from its inception in 1867, to the actuality of 1954, and though some statements are obviously outdated, much of what he wrote about the latter period still holds true today. He saw Confederation essentially as a defensive system that was created as a result of unfavorable economic conditions in Canada that had been brought about by the first industrial revolution. There was a need for federal government intervention in industrial development — for example, the building of the trans-continental railway — and this need continued right up until the First World War. In the 1920's, the federal role diminished, because the arrival of such things as automobiles and the new development of natural resources created the urbanization and industrialization that allowed the provinces to play a dominant role in their turn. In the 1930's, however, it became obvious that the provinces were unable or unwilling to create a coherent social security system (i.e., Quebec and family support, old age pensions, etcetera) and the federal government had to step in again. Prophetically, in view of the Canada Pension Plan and now Medicare, Lamontagne wrote in 1954, that one may presume that the federal government will continue to bear the main burden in social welfare and take the initiative to satisfy demands.

But more important than social welfare, Lamontagne foresaw that "economic stability will be the main problem in the future." He said that provincial governments are limited in the role they may play, since economic stability is not local or regional, they do not have any trade or monetary controls, and their powers of taxation and borrowing are limited. "Thus economic stability requires a central direction," he wrote, "and an integrated economic policy. All factors indicate that the federal government must play a dominant role."

It is really a great pity that Lamontagne's book has not been published in English because his final chapter, "The dilemma of Quebec," was the cause of his *lutte à mort* with Duplessis. In it, Lamontagne relentlessly shreds every argument that Quebec had used (until then) to obstruct or attack the central government on constitutional matters.

Lamontagne dealt first with the economic objections to the constitutional situation, pointing out that Quebec's "hybrid and equivocal" position on the New Federalism meant that "it is inconvenienced by Confederation without benefitting from it, while the rest of Canada is prevented from seeking new goals." He suggested that the other provinces might wait awhile for Quebec, but not forever, and when they become convinced that Quebec will never move, they will leave it behind. "Could not separatism be more or less imposed one day?" he asks. He cites the absurdity of Quebec contributing to confederation through taxes but (in 1954) not taking advantage of what was offered in return in joint programs, university grants, forestry, highway, housing and agricultural programs. Quebec was losing millions a year in aid. And this was not just an economic loss but led directly into the political and cultural fields, through lower standards of living in broad terms and by lack of aid to artists, students and others who could have great cost-benefit potential. The result was frustration and apathy, he said, which had no outlet, because prejudice and ignorance prevented the truth being discovered and the vicious circle from being broken. "Post-war prosperity is the only reason why Quebec has been able to maintain its position so long, but prosperity won't last forever."

Put up or shut up, he told Quebec. "Either accept the New Federalism and integrate with it, or refuse and disassociate from it."

He found no possible justification for separatism, since, for a start, it would drastically lower standards of living. "The less educated a population is, the more it costs to administer per capita." Customs barriers between Quebec and the rest of Canada would discourage industrial location; the banking system would need to be reformed; and provincial borrowing power was extremely limited, in any case. "So there are certainly no economic grounds for separatism."

Culturally and psychologically he admitted Quebec had problems. But the solutions to these problems were nearly all in Quebec itself and had nothing to do with the rest of Canada. "But like all who feel culturally threatened, they won't seek answers in themselves, but try to blame it on others, the Americans, the English or the Jews." Lamontagne noted the contradictions of the French-Canadian character which can, at the same time as it attributes all its misfortunes on "foreigners," seek out, through its political leaders, American and English Canadian financiers to bring industry into Quebec. "The joyous hospitality towards American tycoons and capital that has been a Quebec tradition since Chapleau and Mercier," as Jean-Charles Falardeau put it in 1953.

Quebec, Lamontagne said, has total jurisdiction in education at all levels and is at full liberty to implement any cultural plans it wants to. But the province had never established a coherent cultural policy, nor was there any justification for supposing that greater autonomy, even separatism, would make any difference. "Separatism won't change a thing about the closeness of the United States for instance," he wrote. "French Canadians must stop looking nostalgically at the past and, in times of crisis, at separatism. Their future is tied to the rest of the country. Their great ambition should be to make Canada a truly bi-cultural country. And it is still the best way of serving their own cause."

Lamontagne's book caused a furor in Quebec nationalist circles, and Duplessis summoned Monseignor Alphonse-Marie Parent, the vice-rector of Laval, to see him in his office at the Legislature. The Monseignor is a diminutive man, barely five feet tall, but he is completely fearless. Five years later, in 1961, he was to become chairman of Lesage's Royal Commission on Education and the Parent Reports of 1964, 1965 and 1966 were to become the Magna Carta of Quebec education. He was an old friend of Dean Lévesque and of Lamontagne, and, like them, he believed in two essentials, Truth and Freedom. He knew what Duplessis wanted, and when the Premier asked him to disassociate the university publicly from Lamontagne's book, he quietly refused, firmly pointing out that it was a good book, solidly researched, and the fact that the Premier disagreed with Lamontagne's opinions was hardly relevant.

Duplessis was apoplectic. And when the Rector, Monseignor Ferdinand Vandry, returned a few weeks later, he repeated his demand. Laval must disassociate itself from Lamontagne or else. The threat was clear. Vandry, a weak, vacillating man, allowed himself to be bullied. That same day he issued a public disavowal of a distinguished work by a man who was at that time the most eminent economist in Quebec. It was a black day for the honor of Laval University.

Like a boxer who has knocked his opponent off balance, Duplessis pressed his attack on Laval. He wanted Father Lévesque removed as well, and Vandry bowed to this, too. The University established a rule that no dean could serve more than three four-year terms. Father Lévesque would have to resign in 1955. And on December 15, 1954, anticipating the event, the Order of Dominican Fathers and some rich Liberal supporters, bought Kent House, a run-down hotel that had once been the magnificent Haldimand House, residence of Sir Frederick Haldimand, Governor of Lower Canada in 1780. It stands on the cliffs on the north shore of the St. Lawrence River, across from the Ile d'Orléans, beside the 274-foot-high Montmorency Falls. One of the most famous and romantic places in Quebec, there Prince Augustus dallied one summer in the 1790's with Madamoiselle Julie de St. Laurent, and there a tall and lovely French girl is said to walk the cliffs on moonless nights looking for her soldier lover, killed in battle in 1759.

The Dominicans and their friends paid a quarter of a million dollars for the house and its 42 acre estate, and for the renovations necessary to turn it into what became known as *"la seule salle de liberté dans la province de Quebec"*, a place where people from all faiths and countries and walks of life could come to meet and talk and rest. "An open home for all who cherish freedom and seek happiness through truth, charity and justice, a listening post, a kind if catalyzer for the human needs of our times, a sort of spiritual laboratory . . ." was how it was described when the brochure was ready.

The Dominicans called it Maison Montmorency and asked Father Lévesque to become the superior, which he did, living and teaching both there and at Laval (the university refused to lose him as a professor), until he left for Africa in 1963, to become Rector of the National University of Rwanda, a position he still holds.

Lamontagne's book acted like a catalyst on the intellectual community. *L'Institut Canadien des Affaires Publiques*, was launched in 1954. So was Jean Drapeau's reform-minded Civic Action League and its crusading weekly newspaper, *Vrai*. The pace was quickening. The opposition to Duplessis began to consolidate.

With 1956, the political cauldron went from a quiet simmer to a rolling boil. It was a year of great activity at home and abroad. In Ottawa, the year started well, and federalism was strengthened considerably by the passage in January of the equalization payments legislation, guaranteeing each province federal subsidies to make up the difference between their actual tax yields and the average per capita yields in the two richest provinces. But the mood soon turned sour in May with the ill-omened pipeline debate, when the Liberal majority forced legislation through parliament to meet the pipeline builder's deadline, and paid scant heed to procedural rules.

It was also the year of the Suez crisis, when the canal was seized by the Egyptians on July 26, occupied in October by the Israelis, French and British and finally given back to the Egyptians in November, in part through Canada's efforts at the United Nations. Canadian members of the U.N. Emergency Force proposed by Lester Pearson had barely arrived in Egypt, before the world's attention was turned to Hungary and the brutal suppression of an unarmed, popular revolt by the tanks and machine-guns of the Soviet army. Canada opened her doors to the refugees, and a $1,000,000 fund was established for their transportation and settlement. Any doubts that Canada could afford the expense were soon settled by the announcement that the Canada Council would be formed with a $100 million-dollar endowment gleaned from the death duties of two multi-millionaires, Killam and Dunn; and a report from Walter Gordon's Royal Commission that Canada's economic prospects for the next 25 years looked bright indeed. Gordon's report, conservative as it turned out, was that the population would be 26.5 million by 1980, the GNP $70-million, and per capita income $3,000.

Of more lasting significance, however, was the formation in Montreal on September 8 of a strange new political action group named Le Rassemblement, not to be confused with today's separatist Rassemblement pour l'Indépendance Nationale (RIN). The purpose of the Rassemblement would have been much clearer, had they stuck to their original name, the League for Democratic Education and Action. For this is what the objectives were: first to show people what democracy was, and then to persuade them to use it. Its 600 members ranged across the political spectrum from conservative to separatist, and the only thing they had in common was a belief in the democratic process.

This diversity was both the Rassemblement's strength and its weakness. It acted as a powerful force to persuade people to use democratic means, but its orientation lacked the specific policy proposals which would have unified members into a single political group. Thus it both succeeded and failed. During the three years it existed, Trudeau served as a vice-president, director and finally president. Shortly before he took over the presidency from René Tremblay, he wrote an article for *Cité Libre* entitled "A democratic manifesto" (October, 1958) in which he wondered if the only way to instill democracy in Quebec was not to form a new party with very rigid basic principles which every would-be member must agree to before admittance. This would avoid the tendency for members of other parties to join without renouncing their previous affiliations, affiliations which often led to attempts to re-form a new group into an existing old party. At that point, Trudeau felt that joining an existing old party was hopeless, "since the fate and fortune of democracy in our province is confined to parties which believe so little in democracy that they have never applied it to their own structures." The article ended inconclusively with the thought that perhaps the idea of a new party, the Democratic Union, should be held in reserve for the time being.

But the Rassemblement did galvanize political action in Quebec. Its gatherings brought together such disparate people as Trudeau; Yves Ryan, a Conservative; Eugene A. Forsey, Research Director, Canadian Labor Congress; Madame Thérèse Casgrain, a socialist; Arthur Tremblay, a Laval professor, now deputy minister of Education for Quebec; Jean-Marc Léger, a writer for *Le Devoir*, nationalist and separatist; Jacques-Yvan Morin, a professor at the University of Montreal, now secretary general of the Estates General, who opted for special status; Gérard Filion, then editorial director, *Le Devoir*; and of course such people as Jean Marchand, René Tremblay and Gérard Pelletier.

Marchand remembers the Rassemblement kindly. "It was an instrument we tried to use to reunite, outside existing parties, the progressive influences in the province, a milieu where we could express our opinions without getting committed politically. I think the CCF tried to sabotage it. It might have achieved something without them. But the main thing was that without it, we could have met for 15 or 20 years without doing a thing and we would have achieved nothing. As a movement, the Rassemblement did not influence the masses. It influenced individuals who then acted inside their various parties. It was a timid attempt at political involvement, I suppose, because politics in Quebec were so sacred, so controlled, that nobody wanted to be alone against Duplessis. So the only way to oppose him was to enter the Liberal party, which did not seem like a very jolly idea. In that way, Le Rassemblement was useful, in the short term, as a trampoline."

Soon after the foundation of the Rassemblement, the great Conservative wave started to sweep across the country, provincially and federally. In October, Robert Stanfield became Premier of Nova Scotia for the first time, ending 23 years of Liberal rule and further burnishing the reputation of Dalton Camp.

Stanfield was invited to give the keynote address at the leadership convention in Ottawa in December as a reward for his giant killing efforts in Nova Scotia. He set the stage for John Diefenbaker's election as leader with a speech that declared Conservatives ready for "new leadership and a fresh force in the conduct of its public affairs."

Within six months the Canadian people voiced their agreement with Stanfield, and for reasons that, according to a national poll, were 38% pipeline, 26% old age pension and 5% Suez, they kicked out Uncle Louis and replaced him with Visionary John. Among the Liberals who went down to defeat in June, 1957, along with such great men as C. D. Howe and Walter Harris, was the Associate Minister of Defense of two months' standing, 33-year-old Paul Theodore Hellyer, who used the next six years to make himself a nest-egg in the home construction business and nurse his ambition to cap an extraordinary political career (first elected an MP at 26) by becoming Prime Minister.

With the arrival of the Diefenbaker years, the 'democratic union' of Liberals was nearly complete. Only three more people remained to be introduced and then the awesome thrust for power would start.

The first was Jean-Pierre Goyer, then a 26-year-old law student at the University of Montreal, who was to spend two months in Quebec City during the spring of 1958 sitting outside Premier Duplessis' door with Francine Laurendeau and Bruno Meloche, other executives of AGEUM, the student association dramatizing the plight of Quebec's money-starved universities. Goyer flunked his bar exams that year, which was hardly surprising (he passed in 1959), but found himself wired into such reform groups as Jean Drapeau's Ligue d'Action Civique and Trudeau's Rassemblement which led, in turn, to an active role with the Lesage Liberals in 1959 and 1960, and to a campaign slot in Maurice Sauvé's election team in 1962. Along the way, Goyer became friendly with the *Cité Libre* group.

The second was Timothy Porteous, 25, freshly graduated from McGill Law School, who was one of forty Canadians on a world University Service trip to West Africa and found himself in a group with Pierre Elliott Trudeau in Lagos, Nigeria. Both decided simultaneously that they had seen enough of English-speaking Africa and, with two attractive young ladies of like mind, jumped on a "Mammy-wagon" for neighboring Dahomey and a long, lost weekend at l'Hotel de la Plage in Cotonou. They have remained close friends ever since then.

The third was British-born James Davey, 27, four years out of Corpus Christi, Oxford, with a master's degree in physics. He had been with A. V. Roe's Orenda group in Toronto working in engine computing, when the cutback in defense spending sent him to Montreal and a job with the management consultant firm of Kates & Co. (now Kates Peat Marwick & Co.). He avoided being a casualty of Diefenbaker's "Arrow" cancellation by only a few months. In Montreal, Davey and his Winnipeg-born wife plunged into the bicultural life, learning French and taking a series of courses at the University of Montreal.

Davey met Maurice Sauvé in his professional capacity as a management consultant when he helped the University of Montreal's *Groupe de Recherche Sociale* in a survey they were doing of Quebec political opinion for the Quebec Liberal Federation in 1959. Sauvé was Public Relations Director of the QLF at that time and the two became close friends, Davey's professional interest in politics becoming a personal one to the point where he helped campaign for Sauvé in the Magdalen Islands in 1962.

With Diefenbaker running the country and unchallengeable for at least four years, Pearson and his Liberals set about rebuilding their party. There were two key men for this job: Walter Gordon and Maurice Lamontagne. Lamontagne's brilliance and devotion to federalism had been recognized swiftly in Ottawa and by 1955 he had been appointed economic advisor to the Privy Council. When the Liberals were defeated in 1957, he joined the University of Ottawa as chairman of the department of economics and worked part-time as a special assistant to both St. Laurent and later Pearson. Gordon had long been a friend of Pearson's and had served on half a dozen royal commissions during the Liberal years in office. Lamontagne and Gordon were the men who organized the Kingston Conference of 1960, when the Liberals sought out new ideas by inviting academics and activists to come and talk to them at Queen's University (Jean Marchand of the CTCC and Bill Mahoney of the Steelworkers were on one panel). They were also the men who went out to seek good candidates for the 1962 general election.

But unfortunately for Lamontagne, he was no politician. His best role, which he played superbly, was as advisor and thinker, but not as strategist or political infighter. He lost two elections before he finally made it into the house in Outremont-St Jean in 1963, with a senatorship promised to the man who made way for him, Romuald Bourque. His first two tries for Parliament were in the traditionally liberal Quebec City riding of Quebec East, which had returned Sir Wilfrid Laurier for ten consecutive general elections, Ernest Lapointe for six straight, and St. Laurent for four. St. Laurent had won in 1957 with a plurality of 17,000 votes. But

Lamontagne, ignoring the existing party organization in favor of a brain trust of Laval University colleagues, campaigned from a chauffeured car and let the Duplessis-backed Conservative take it by 636 votes. There was no doubt at all that Duplessis had thrown every available organizer and spare dollar into the fight to even the score with the author of *Le Fédéralisme Canadien* and with Laval University at the same time. But Duplessis should not have won. In 1962, Lamontagne tried again in Quebec East but lost it to a Social Credit candidate whose plurality soared to 8,699. In 1963, he had to make a deal with the Old Guard to get his seat and his credibility as a politician was lost.

In Quebec, Duplessis was nearing the end of his time, but as 1958 ended he made one final attempt to settle matters once and for all with Father Lévesque, who continued to irritate him with all the comings and goings and revolutionary talk at La Maison Montmorency. So Duplessis elaborated a strategy.

The little municipality of Courville, where La Maison Montmorency is located, had a private bill before the legislature to ratify a tax agreement it had completed with the Dominicans which stipulated (among other conditions) that taxes on the house would only amount to $1,400 a year for a 20-year period starting in 1955.

But Duplessis caught sight of the clause and "suspended" it, arguing that La Maison Montmorency was a hotel and should be taxed as such. He proposed instead a clause for five years at $2,000 a year.

The late André Laurendeau, then chief editorialist at *Le Devoir*, found the situation irresistable. And on December 19, 1958, he wrote a devastating editorial.

"This man is petty," he wrote. "Petty in his public behavior. Petty as Premier. Petty in his government's activities. This time again, see how he acts: we are in the private bills committee. Hundreds of bills are being passed. It's there that the great companies receive their scandalous tax concessions. But here comes a bill from the little municipality of Courville. A harmless bill? Wait. The Prime Minister has an eye like a lynx, when he's bent on revenge. Like someone refusing to eat his dessert before the meat course, he suspends a clause of the bill. What clause? It deals with La Maison Montmorency," and Laurendeau describes just how Duplessis is going to jack up the taxes and cut the term. Then he continues. "*That* will teach the people of Courville to deal with the Dominicans. That will teach the Dominicans to make Father Lévesque the director of the house. And that will teach Father Lévesque to think that he is the lay General of the Province. Mr. Duplessis is lucid in these matters. The little affairs of his great provincial village."

At the end of the editorial, *Le Devoir* announced it was starting a collection to pay the extra taxes Duplessis was imposing on Maison Montmorency. And to get the fund rolling, Filion and Laurendeau started subscriptions off with $10 apiece. Within hours of publication, Jean Drapeau was on the telephone with a pledge for $50. Within a week, the fund had reached $2,700. Duplessis was humiliated. Even his own party members refused to vote for the bill. It was withdrawn. And within nine months, Duplessis was dead.

The effect was like day following night. His successor, Paul Sauvé, tried to harness the new dynamism with a dynamic performance of his own. But after less than four months, Sauvé was dead too, and the mantel passed to a man familiar to the veterans of Asbestos, Antonio Barrette.

The National Union went out not with a bang but a whimper. Barrette waited as long as he could to call a general election, but by June 22 it was all over, Jean Lesage was Premier and the Quiet Revolution had started.

IV

The Activists

JEAN LESAGE's new regime seemed to offer everything that a reformer could possibly want. And for the first two years, it was hard to find fault with it. Lesage chose his cabinet carefully, to reflect the whole spectrum of Liberal opinion, from such Conservatives as Bona Arsenault to such left-wingers as René Lévesque. Moreover, Lesage ran the team with a loose rein, achieving just the right blend of audacity and responsibility that Quebec seemed to need.

The work of re-organizing the Quebec Liberals had been pretty well done by others, when Lesage arrived from Ottawa in 1958, and he spent the next two years fighting the Liberal propaganda battle outside the Legislature and adroitly resisting invitations from Duplessis to contest a by-election and risk defeat (the thankless job of Liberal house leader was retained by Georges-Emile Lapalme). He also persuaded some fine people to become Liberal candidates, notably René Lévesque, the Jean Marie Nadeau Society member who had become one of Quebec's best-known television commentators for his program, *"Point de Mire"* (aiming mark), and for his leadership during a strike of CBC French-language producers in 1958.

Another first-rate candidate, who had actually opposed Lesage for the leadership in 1958, was Paul Gérin-Lajoie, a Rhodes Scholar and constitutional expert.

Lévesque entered the cabinet immediately on election as Minister of Public Works and Hydraulic Resources, becoming Minister of Natural Resources a year later. Lajoie became Minister of Youth on election, a portfolio he retained throughout the administration although its name was changed to Minister of Education in 1964.

It is to Lesage's credit that he was prepared to surround himself

with excellent ministers — and potential rivals — for such mag-
nanimity was unheard of in the parish-pump politics that had
characterized Quebec until then. And, by those standards, there
was certainly no need for it. Lesage had delivered for the Liberals
beyond their dreams, turning 17 seats into a majority of 50, while
reducing the National Union from 71 to 44, and taking 51% of
the popular vote against the NU's 47%. The win took place,
despite National Union goon squads who terrorized certain polls
by vrooming around the block in battered convertibles, loaded
with baseball bats, trying to scare off potential voters. Where that
failed, the goons invaded the polls and stuffed the ballot boxes
with fake voting slips or simply made off with the ballot boxes
altogether. Even the Provincial Police, utterly corrupted under
Duplessis, got into the act on June 22, 1960, with phoney "raids"
for "weapons" on innocent Liberal committee rooms, which were
then left ransacked by the "search." Some QPP cops went too far
in Verdun, calling on Liberal George O'Reilly's wife to ask which
hospital she would like her husband sent to. Mrs. O'Reilly called
Verdun city police and the Provincials wound up in jail.

One of the first steps of the Liberal administration was to send
telegrams to every provincial construction job ordering contractors
to stop working until the government had reviewed the contract.
This politically-motivated step (most contractors were NU supporters) had excellent results administratively, since it marked the
start of competitive tendering in public works for the government,
saving the provincial treasury millions of dollars over the next few
years. Under the old system, as a Royal Commission pointed out
later, the government purchasing agent would give a contract to a
friendly manufacturer or contractor who was then expected to
add onto his bid a percentage that he would 'contribute' to the
party's campaign treasury.

Almost immediately, the Lesage administration started making
huge investments in all sectors of the provincial economy from
education to highways. Investment in education alone went from
$191 million a year in 1960–61, to $571 million in 1966–1967,
yet to illustrate to what extent total investment increased, education as a percentage of total expenditure went up only 2% (from
22% to 24%) in the same period.

The civil service was reorganized from top to bottom. French Canadian experts in the federal civil service were "invited home" and many accepted with alacrity, having given up hope that the Diefenbaker administration would ever recognize Canada's bicultural condition with anything more understanding than bilingual cheques. Departments were restructured, so that professionals and not patronage-seekers would be in charge of key sections. And the Liberals even made their new professionals secure from the mass dismissals that had characterized previous government changeovers by permitting unionization, collective bargaining, and, to be regretted later, the right to strike.

The province's public educational system, vitiated by division and subdivision along both linguistic and religious lines (English Roman Catholic, French Roman Catholic, English Protestant, French Protestant), was so dominated by the Church in the Roman Catholic sector, which made up 90% of the population, that no previous government had dared appoint a Minister of Education, let alone create a ministry that would control the schools.

The Liberals removed the Bishops as sole arbiters of the school system and placed the system under a ministry of education, advised by a council made up of teachers, parents, clergy and state-appointed experts. Arthur Tremblay was brought in from Laval to become the deputy minister of the department of Education (Laval was also tapped for two other senior civil servants — René Tremblay, who became Deputy Minister of Industry and Commerce, and Roger Marier, to fill the same function in the department of Family and Social Welfare), and to bear most of the odium for its administration from National Union reactionaries. However, Tremblay survived the Liberal defeat in 1966, and so did the Ministry of Education.

Though Quebec's school system is still confessional today, there is little doubt that growing demands for neutral schools would have been granted if the Liberals had remained in office after 1966.

The Quebec Liberals strove for excellence in so many fields that it was inevitable that they should fail in some. The resentment in certain rural areas over the lack of patronage festered on throughout their six-year administration. It was compounded too by the

Liberals' self-admitted failure in rural areas and in the city slums.

The country ridings were traditionally Conservative, while the Liberals were the party of the cities. The country was a low priority area, besides, since Duplessis had lavished his attention on it and its roads, its bridges, and its low taxes, for 16 years. And though the Liberals claimed to recognize the problems of the Quebec farmer, little was done to help him.

So when the Liberals, trying to raise the standards of education in rural areas, insisted that one-room schoolhouses be replaced by modern centralized regional schools, the farmers not only found their children unavailable for morning and evening chores, as they bussed to school early and returned late, but their farm taxes rose sharply to pay for the luxury. Only belatedly did the Liberals give farmers some tax relief. But for many, it was too late.

Ironically, the Liberals did well by the most severely depressed areas of the province, such as the Gaspé peninsula region of the lower St. Lawrence, where such Federal programs as ARDA and Provincial programs like BAEQ (*Bureau d'amenagement de l'Est du Quebec*) jointly brought much hope and at least the promise of comfort. These regions showed their gratitude both federally and provincially by remaining loyal to the Liberals. But in the ignored Lac St. Jean region and in the Rouyn-Noranda area of northern Quebec, in the Eastern Townships along the U.S. Frontier, and in the country around the big cities, the protest votes went to the have-not Creditistes federally, and to the National Union provincially.

Liberal disinterest in the city poor was less excusable. These were (and are) the dispossessed of the age of affluence and technology, unskilled, unemployed, under-nourished, unhealthy and hence finally, unwanted.

Except for free hospitalization, the Quebec Liberals failed to put through a single major social welfare program of importance. There were plenty of promises of course. But vast new buildings, highways, bridges, universities and, of course, Expo itself, were much more attractive to a government increasingly tempted by a crypto-Gaullist *politique de grandeur*. And the basic problems were left unsolved. It was the age of 'planification', but little actual planning; of the technocrat, when computers came before day nurseries; of highways before low-rental housing; magnificent subways before slum clearance. It was a challenging time for the skilled and professional worker; expertise of nearly every description was in demand to schedule, build, control and operate. Taxes rose steadily to pay for all the government expenditures, vital, important, not-a-moment-too-soon expenditures, to be sure, but in the slums the rising expectations of the poor were rewarded with higher taxes and an increased cost of living.

The activists of the 1950's naturally plunged into the action. Jean Marchand and his CTCC (in 1960 it was renamed CSN and, in English, Confederation of National Trades Unions) fought it out with the international unions to unionize a province that had suddenly become, if not exactly pro-labor, a sort of Tom Tiddler's ground. Gérard Pelletier became editor of *La Presse* following a palace revolution in which the editor, Jean-Louis Gagnon, stormed out with a redoubtable lady named Madame Anna DuTremblay, one of *La Presse's* major shareholders, and set up in lively competition with their *Nouveau Journal*, a paper which lasted about a year before Mme DuTremblay picked up her millions and went back to *La Presse's* board.

Pierre Elliott Trudeau also became involved, at the University of Montreal, as a co-founder of the *Institut de Recherche en Droit Public* and as a professor of public law.

The Institute of Public Law was a pet project of Paul Gérin-Lajoie's, before he became Minister of Youth in the Lesage administration. Under normal circumstances he would have had to shelve the project when he was named to the cabinet but luckily he did not have to. One of his most active campaign workers was a young man named Marc Lalonde who had just returned from Ottawa, where he had been an executive assistant in the Department of Justice. And Lalonde took on not only Gérin-Lajoie's interest in the Research Institute but also his old law practice with the distinguished St. James Street firm of Gélinas, Bourque. Since Lalonde was active in the Bar Association and with the group at *Cité Libre*, it was not surprising that he asked Trudeau to serve on the board of Directors of the Institute. Trudeau accepted, and it was the start of the close but highly professional association that continues to this day.

The two men are uncannily complementary. Physically, Trudeau's face has the cast of a Florentine nobleman, while Lalonde's has the long-nosed lugubriousness of a medieval Pope or Cardinal, and one can imagine them in 16th Century garb, dividing the clerical and temporal spheres of influence between them. Academically, they balance each other; both are lawyers and economists, and philosophically they tend to be eclectic in their attitude towards ideas. Even their backgrounds are similar, for Lalonde's father was a farmer on Ile Perrot, off the southern tip of Montreal Island, while Trudeau's grandfather farmed in St. Rémi de Napierville, 18 miles to the south-east. There the similarities end, for Lalonde, despite Oxford, is very much a man of the people, in dress and habits, whereas Trudeau is as casually but thoroughly aristocratic as a first-generation millionaire's son can be.

Lalonde is somewhat bemused if asked to define his friendship with Trudeau. "A personal friend? The question has not really arisen in my mind. He's not a man with whom I've ever spent weekends. Not a man I'd ever call to go to the movies with. We used to swim together sometimes at the Chateau Laurier. But I would say it was very much of an intellectual association. Something of a complementary association. He never talks to me about his problems in private life, and I would never talk to him about mine." Lalonde does admit that Trudeau has consulted him about personal matters on which his position as Prime Minister has a bearing, for instance what he should do with his investments and what events he should attend or not attend as P.M. But for strictly private things, he keeps his own counsel. "He is a man who has his own personal life. My best friends are those whose personal lives I have nothing to do with."

Disenchantment with the Lesage regime did not come all at once, nor was it ever a total thing. Someone once said, "*le Quebec, c'est un village*" (Quebec's a village), and the statement is both a fact and a warning. It's a fact that just about everyone in Quebec's French-Canadian community is related to everyone else, since they are nearly all descended from the 60,000 French colonists who had settled there before the conquest. This has meant that quarrels, for the most part, have tended to remain *en famille*, and political friendships and alliances which an outsider may note are often more apparent than real. Also, as in families, pettiness sometimes reaches bewildering proportions, so that the reason for what appears to be a fight on a question of principle, may, in reality, have its roots in a most trivial matter.

The quarrel between Lesage and Trudeau has been attributed to jealousy, for the most part. But Lesage had no reason to be jealous of Trudeau, when he rejected his name as a proposed member of the *Conseil d'Orientation Economique* in 1961. The real reason? Who knows?

The quarrel between Lesage and Marchand, on the other hand, comes from the simple fact that Lesage asked Marchand to run in the 1962 provincial election — and then reneged on the deal, after Marchand had accepted.

It seems that Alcide Courcy and René Lévesque suddenly got cold feet about having Marchand on the team. And the reason they gave Lesage, in persuading him to put Marchand off, was that Marchand was too widely thought of as anti-Creditiste. "It was an idiotic argument, really," says Marchand. "And so Lesage decided that it was not a good idea and called me up to tell me 'your name is to linked with the fight against the Creditistes'. 'O.K.' I said, 'so get off my back; I wasn't the one who was making the offer.' And that was the end of that."

Marchand stayed on the Quebec Economic Advisory Council, however, and his relations with Jean Lesage have since improved to the point where they could be described as cordial.

The dismissal of Gérard Pelletier from *La Presse* took place in March, 1965, nearly three years later, when Lesage's conservative phase was well established. And there were good grounds for dissatisfaction on both sides. *La Presse* had been struck for seven months and had lost millions of dollars in revenue, particularly through the Christmas period. The settlement with the union had been difficult, and Pelletier had played little part in achieving it. Actually, the board of directors of *La Presse* had been dissatisfied with Pelletier's editorship for some time. There was the matter of his serialization of "J'accuse les assassins de Coffin," by his *Cité Libre* friend, Jacques Hébert, which had plunged them into several libel suits and left the sour taste of poor judgement. Then there was his belief in journalistic freedom, which did not appeal to the authoritarians on the board.

Pelletier ran the paper on a very loose rein, encouraging journal-

istic enterprise and also permitting a fair amount of moonlighting,
which he could hardly object to, since he had remained on the
board of *Cité Libre* himself, frequently expressing opinions that
varied from *La Presse's* official pro-Liberal line. So it was that
Pierre Bourgault, the president of the separatist RIN, had a snug
niche on *La Presse's* magazine section. But the directors also felt
that *La Presse* was giving too much space to dissent, the separatists
and anti-establishmentarians, and not enough to the Lesage regime.
(As it happened, Liberal sachem, Claude Ducharme, was a director of *La Presse* and married to one of the company heiresses.)

The final straw was an "Open Letter" that Pelletier wrote, in
January 1965, just before the *La Presse* strike ended, to Quebec
Justice Minister, Claude Wagner (a Lesage favorite at the time)
which took him apart in scorching terms for his whitewash of
police tactics during the Queen's visit to Quebec City the previous
October, along with many other things. Unfortunately, the letter
was published first in *Cité Libre*, then picked up as front page
news by most of the daily newspapers in Quebec, notably *Le
Devoir.* "*La Presse* pays Pelletier $25,000 a year to write in
Cité Libre," chortled the University of Montreal's irreverent
weekly, *Quartier Latin*, whose separatist-inclined editors lost no
love on *Cité Libre* or its federalist editorial board. The directors of
La Presse made note of the letter and decided they could spend
$25,000 a year more profitably elsewhere. When the paper
resumed publication on January 5, there was no sign of Pelletier.
Three months passed before the news emerged that he had been
fired.

Pelletier's departure might have been expected to provoke some
sort of mass walk-out from *La Presse*. It didn't. Whether the
memory of seven months' unemployment was too fresh or some
other reason, those few staffers who did resign from positions of
authority made it clear they were staying on staff and not leaving
the paper. Others who mildly regretted Pelletier's departure even
allowed that perhaps it was not a bad thing, since he had been so
remote from the staff that they never saw him anyway. So much
for group loyalty.

Fortunately, Pelletier did not find himself completely friendless,
and within weeks he started writing a syndicated column for *Le*

Devoir, the Montreal *Star* and some newspapers outside Quebec under the title: "The Opinions of Gérard Pelletier."

So much has been written and said about the New Guard and Old Guard Liberals on the federal scene, as well as the conservative and left-wing Liberals on the Quebec scene, that one tends to forget that in 1960, they were all one amorphous group. This is borne out as late as 1962, with Lesage's offer of a provincial seat to Marchand and Trudeaus being considered for the economic advisory council. The relationship was even closer. As late as 1963, René Lévesque was regarded by the *Cité Libre* group as 'their' man in the Lesage cabinet, and he would meet regularly with Marchand, Trudeau, Pelletier and André Laurendeau once a month to try out ideas on what he (and they) used to refer to as the "brain trust." Sometimes visitors to this group included Lamontagne, who was looking for candidates to run in the next federal election, and Maurice Sauvé, who had an on-again, off-again relationship with *Cité Libre*. Paul Gérin-Lajoie and Marc Lalonde were other members of the group, ex-officio, as it were. There were also a number of others whose names are unfamiliar outside Quebec, such as Jean-Paul Lefebvre, Pierre Vadboncoeur, Jean-Charles Falardeau and other regular *Cité Libre* contributors like Guy Viau of the National Gallery.

In addition to government administration itself — federal, provincial and municipal (Jean Drapeau swept back into office as Mayor of Montreal in October, 1960) — the topics which interested the reform group in this period can be divided into three general categories: nuclear arms, constitutional amendment and splinter-party politics.

The nuclear arms question was on everybody's mind during the late 1950's and early 1960's, when the threat of a nuclear holocaust seemed to hang over the world, punctuated by nuclear test explosions and an ominous increase in fall-out.

The question of constitutional amendment was raised in October, 1960, at a federal-provincial attorney-generals conference in Ottawa. It sought a formula that would allow Canadians to amend their own 'constitution,' the British North America Act of 1867, without having to petition the British parliament at Westminster. Through no fault of the British, this colonial anomaly had bothered

Canadian politicians for years, since the provinces were simply unable or unwilling to agree on an amending formula. And until agreement was unanimous, the provinces naturally did not want to give up the right of appeal to the 'neutral court' at Westminster. After two more meetings, in November and January, the federal and provincial governments agreed in principle on an amending formula. This ultimately became known as the Fulton-Favreau formula (after the Conservative and Liberal Ministers of Justice who had produced it), which foundered on the reefs of Quebec objections in 1964–1965.

Splinter-party politics were also a subject of much interest to the *Cité Libre* group, many of whom were members of the socialist Commonwealth Cooperative Federation (CCF) which transformed itself into the New Democratic Party, and, on August 3, 1961, chose Thomas Clement Douglas as the new national leader. Unlike the CCF, the NDP had modified its socialism to the point where the big labor unions could promise their backing — and potentially enormous membership and financial strength. As it happened, it did not work out the way but, in 1961, the NDP looked like the wave of the future in federal politics.

The second splinter group which attracted attention was a constantly changing gaggle of separatist parties, ranging from the Communist-backed ASIQ (*Action Socialist pour l'Indépendance de Québec*), now defunct, to the nationalist, anti-semitic followers of Raymond Barbeau's Laurentian Republican Party. After several decades of hibernation, the separatist movement emerged in 1960, apparently inspired by the derring-do of Fidel Castro and Ché Guevara in Cuba. The Cubans, in turn, continue to take a close interest in Quebec separatism, as a matter of fact, but their influence has never regained the élan it had in 1961, when the Cuban consul in Montreal conducted regular lectures in guerrilla warfare and other niceties of *la revolucion* for a group of ASIQ members.

The silly season of Quebec separatism during which Dr. Marcel Chaput, formerly of the Defense Research Board, did most of his celebrated fasting, ended abruptly in the spring of 1963, when an organization calling itself the FLQ (*Front de Libération de Québec*) exploded a bomb in a trashcan, killing a night watchman. A month later, an army sergeant was permanently crippled by another

FLQ bomb in a Westmount mail-box, and within five months, the FLQ had been unmasked as a group of misguided students who were subsequently tried and sentenced to periods ranging from six months to 12 years. Police action has been equally swift and unerring on ensuing FLQ hold-ups and bombings. But while the FLQ stole most of the headlines, a far more serious movement was forming around the person of Pierre Bourgault and his RIN, who were dedicated (until the last St. Jean Baptiste Day, at any rate) to achieving independance for Quebec by non-violent, demo-cratic means. It was this group, with its appeal to the young, well-educated, professional classes, that concerned the pro-federal *Cité Libre* group.

The third splinter party was, of course, Social Credit (and its October, 1963, offshoot — *le Ralliement des Créditistes*) which was of concern to Marchand in particular, because most of its sup-port appeared to come from the same working class group that made up the membership of the Confederation des Syndicats Nationaux. The real strength of the Social Credit movement did not become apparent until the Federal election in June, 1962, when the party blossomed in Quebec with 26 seats which, added to four in British Columbia and Alberta, made it the holder of the balance of power in Parliament. Both Conservatives and Liberals naturally blamed the Social Credit vote for stealing their potential majorities in Parliament, and the Tories probably had justice on their side, since most Socreds in Quebec came from previously Conservative ridings. But in truth the persistence of the Socreds and Créditistes in 1963, 1965, and 1968, seems to indicate that the vote is one of protest against both the old parties. It has also been hard to identify the Socred/Créditiste vote beyond saying that it is from the "have-nots" and tends to be rural rather than urban, though not exclusively so.

Both Maurice Lamontagne (as a victim of the Socred wave in Quebec East) and Jean Marchand set out in the summer and fall of 1962 to do battle with the Socred/Créditiste phenomenon. Lamontagne provided the economic strategy to knock down the bizarre, inflationary theories that characterized the basic philo-sophy of Social Credit, while Marchand took the party apart on its anti-labor beliefs (against price controls, collective bargaining, closed-shop). The campaign by Marchand was waged on the level of the union locals and, as far as the CSN was concerned, it resulted in an official rejection of Socred/Créditiste philosophy and a personal triumph for Marchand himself. And although Marchand took no part in the 1963 election, his tactic of economic ridicule was taken up by Yvon Dupuis in his personal duel of the hustings throughout Quebec against the high priest of Créditisme, the mercurial and demagogic car dealer from Rouyn, Réal Caouette.

Marchand took no part in the 1963 federal election for a very good reason: nuclear weapons. As mentioned already, nuclear arms had become an emotional issue in Canada. The Liberal Federation had adopted an anti-nuclear weapons stand at its convention in Ottawa on January 12, 1961, and the party platform had contained it during the 1962 campaign.

In December, 1961, *Cité Libre* carried a bad-tempered article by Trudeau (title: "War! War!"), decrying French Canada's fascination with separatism, when the world itself was facing nuclear annihilation. "Today's youth speaks of separatism and Laurentia," he wrote, "turning their faces resolutely to the past and energetically attacking problems that were solved a century ago!"

Trudeau evoked a delightful Quebec tableau of anxious huddles among "40-year-old businessmen in their clubs, women in their literary and sewing circles, clergy in their presbyteries, politicians seeking voters, professors at dinner, press and radio executives . . . all speaking about what? Giving sententious consideration to what? Separatism, Independence, Laurentia!

"Nero" he concluded, "was judged harshly by history for having played a violin (or something else) during the destruction of Rome. But today's damned brood could well escape such condemnation — for mankind may have no future."

If Trudeau's piece was a *cri du coeur* for realism, it was also a declaration of war on Quebec's separatists. His scorn for that "damned brood" well reflected his opinion of separatism then and now — though today he takes the threat, if not the philosophy, more seriously. For their part, the separatists were quick to respond, and *Cité Libre* gladly joined battle — the entire April, 1962, issue was devoted to Separatism.

Trudeau and Pelletier converted to Liberalism late in 1962, through a logical system of elimination. The New Democratic Party had failed to live up to its hopes in the June general election. It won only 19 seats to the 25 the CCF gained in 1958, the last comparable period before the Diefenbaker sweep. Moreover, the NDP had fallen for "special status" as a solution to Quebec's constitutional problems, alienating Trudeau and Pelletier who considered the proposal woolly and illogical. They were forced to look elsewhere. Conservatism was evidently unthinkable. The provincial Liberals did not want them and, in any case, were showing signs of nationalism. So the federal Liberal Party started to look like the least of all evils. But did the federal Liberals want them?

The answer to this, back in 1962, was probably negative. But the federal Liberals wanted Jean Marchand very much indeed; in fact, Lamontagne had been trying to persuade him for years. Marchand had turned down an offer to run in the June federal election. But before he did, he had discussed it with the *Cité Libre* brains trust, allowing that, if he ever did decide to go, he would not want to go alone, and would any of them come with him? Trudeau and Pelletier said they would run with him whenever he was ready. Which was the way they left it, until December, 1962, when Marchand called them together. "I'm ready to cross the threshold; how about it?" he said. They agreed, and a month later, Marchand, Pelletier and Trudeau were poised, ready to become Liberal candidates as soon as the next general election was announced.

Several things had made Marchand change his mind. One was the Créditiste challenge. Another was the humiliating treatment he had received from Lesage and René Lévesque — who had gone on to a stunning victory in the November 15 provincial election on the issue of nationalization of private power companies in Quebec, an idea created and polished for them by the *Cité Libre* group.

There was one other new reason for Marchand wanting to go to the House of Commons in 1963: Maurice Sauvé. Sauvé had been the only member of the reform group to win a seat in 1962, and as matters stood in January, 1963, the Member for the Iles-de-la-Madeleine could rightfully claim to represent, and lead, any

New Guard that might emerge in a Liberal win. As Marchand put it, "Sauvé and I were never cordial."

And so it came to pass. Speaking to the Liberal Association in the Toronto riding of York-Scarborough on January 12, 1963, the Liberal Opposition leader, Lester Pearson, arbitrarily reversed the party stand on nuclear weapons, flatly telling the Diefenbaker government to honor its obligations and accept the nuclear weapons it had agreed to take.

It was an extraordinary about-face in view of Pearson's solid record of opposition to nuclear weapons, repeated again and again. In Ottawa, in January, 1961, he told the Liberal convention that the country did not need to "be tied to an American dollar, to an American BOMARC . . . (and) specifically, we should not require or use nuclear weapons under any kind of national or joint control." He was so forceful about it that the convention agreed to a resolution that a Liberal government "should not acquire, manufacture or use such weapons either under separate Canadian control or joint U.S.-Canadian control." This resolution was repeated at the federation meeting a year later, and a statement that "Canada will contribute fully to collective security but without nuclear force" was issued for the election in June that year. As late as October, Pearson was saying "it's important that countries which don't have nuclear arms yet should do what they can to prevent their distribution on a wider circle."

The first result of Pearson's self-contradiction was that Marchand, Pelletier and Trudeau told the Liberal party brass that there could be no question of their running at that time or in the foreseeable future. It was a sad blow to Lamontagne who had worked long and hard to line up an exceptional Quebec contingent. Apparently, it also hit other regional organizers at the wrong time, because a little while later Pearson modified his statement to say he was still against nuclear weapons and would enter no further agreements to possess them after the current Tory commitment had been honored. This soothed most objections, but it did not mollify Trudeau. In April, 1963, the very month of the federal election, *Cité Libre* appeared with a devastating attack on both Pearson and the Liberal party, which not only tossed back at Pearson everything he had ever said against nuclear arms, but added in the note that, as for the author, Pierre Elliott Trudeau would work and vote for the New Democratic Party in April 1963.

"Pearson — of Spiritual Abdication" is a piece of journalism that Trudeau probably regrets. It is conspicuous by its absence from the judiciously edited collection of Trudeau's writing, *Federalism and the French Canadians* (Macmillan), which made a well-timed appearance before the Liberal leadership campaign in early 1968.

At one point in it, Trudeau noted that Pearson argued that failure to use nuclear weapons on the CF-104 or Bomarc would mean $750,000,000 down the drain. "One is tempted to ask our Nobel Peace Prizewinner what would happen to peace if the U.S.A. and the Soviet Union shared this concern for money, and also refused to renounce the use of certain arms on the grounds that they had cost them a lot of cash . . .?" Trudeau also wondered why Pearson should suddenly be so solicitous of agreement with the U.S., when the Americans had themselves felt no compunction to deliver weapons previously agreed upon (Skybolts to the British and launching pads to the Turks), and had, besides that, treated Canada pretty casually in recent months. He cited no consultation over Cuba, nastiness about wheat to China, pressure over what the O'Leary Commission said must be done to American publications, and so on.

What lay beneath it, according to Trudeau, was that the Americans wanted to get rid of Diefenbaker, particularly since his three-day delay in snapping to attention when President Kennedy called the Cuban alert on October 22. "Mr. Kennedy's 'hipsters' could not tolerate this," wrote Trudeau. "It could be a bad example to others. Diefenbaker must go!"

"Do you think I dramatize it?" he asked his readers. "How do you think politics work? Do you think General (Lauris) Norstad, former supreme commander Allied Forces in Europe, came to Ottawa on January 3 as a tourist to tell the Canadian government publicly to respect its agreements? Do you think it's by chance that Mr. Pearson was able to rely on the authority of General Norstad in his speech on January 12? Do you think the State Department inadvertently gave newspapers the press release on January 30 which reinforced Mr. Pearson's position and called

Mr. Diefenbaker a liar? Do you think it's by accident that this communiqué gave the Opposition leader the arguments with which he larded his speech to Parliament on January 31? You think it is coincidental that this led to events which ended in the fall of the government on February 5?"

Trudeau said he doubted that the U.S. would treat Canada "any differently than Guatemala when reasons of state demand it and circumstances permit it — but reasons must demand and circumstances permit."

Since the Pentagon could provide "the final push," he said, all that "was asked of Mr. Pearson was that he should betray the program of his party as well as the idealism with which he has always been identified. Fund raisers promised to be munificent. And Gallup showed that a pro-nuclear arms policy would not wipe out a majority of voters. Power offered itself to Mr. Pearson: he had nothing to lose except his honor. He lost it. And his entire party lost it with him."

Trudeau said that even if he had been in favor of nuclear weapons he would still denounce the Liberal structure. Power was the goad, he said, and he had never seen "a more degrading spectacle than all those Liberals who changed colors with their leader."

Trudeau also expressed considerable contempt for those who would not speak out, because . . . "It's always after the ultimate defeat that there is someone brave enough to attack the chief," he said. "Before the battle, as after victory, one risks compromising one's chances of being named a minister, parliamentary secretary, judge, senator, pubkeeper, elevator operator, table or bowl."

He did not mourn Diefenbaker's defeat, of course, only the way it was done. "I regret that a Canadian government has been defeated in the House on a question, and according to a strategy, cooked up by the Americans. It's sad to think how these Johnny-come-latelys to power are scandalized and tremble with indignation because the National Union bought votes with refrigerators. I well remember the federal Liberals of 1957. They were cynics who believed that power belonged to them only — and they came within an inch of putting parliament in tutelage. One might have hoped that six years of opposition would have purged them. Alas. The events of the last two months have proved not."

The Liberal party appalled him that spring of 1963:

"I detect among the old guard the same brutal cynicism: I see in the youth associations the same selfish docility; and between them, men of my generation, who tremble with anticipation because they have seen the rouged face of Power," he said.

He bid it farewell, and he urged others to do likewise: "I think it is the duty of all who believe it is urgent to divert the course of Canadian political thought away from absolute degradation."

Many Liberals, when they finished reading the article, put *Cité Libre* down with a vow that never, while there was a breath in their bodies, would Pierre Elliott Trudeau ever be considered as a Liberal candidate again. One such was Guy Favreau. (Trudeau's second conversion to the Liberal party, three years later, is as much a comment on him as it is on them.)

The Liberals went into the April, 1963, election fully confident that they would emerge with a majority. They had set up Diefenbaker's defeat — with a little help from their friends — and from the mood of the country, there was every reason to suppose that the Conservatives would be soundly beaten. But two factors seemed to have been forgotten in their strategy. First, the country was not pleased with the behavior of Parliament since the June 1962 election, when obstructionism had become the rule rather than the exception, so that a second election within ten months was not appreciated. Second, a lot of people refused to believe that Diefenbaker was as ineffectual as his record indicated.

The Conservatives, on the other hand, torn and tattered though they were by the defections of Douglas Harkness, George Hees and Pierre Sévigny and by the less emotional departures of Donald Fleming and Davie Fulton, knew that if they could get Diefenbaker to work his visionary charisma on the small towns, they could retrench until more favorable times returned. Furthermore, they had recently elected as national organizer just the man for the job: Dalton Camp.

"If he ever sweats, it's from work, never from worry," someone said of him that spring. And with his cool, sophisticated approach, Camp moved into the office of the ex-director, Allister Grosart, winced at the "Keep Smiling" sign on the wall, but left it there "because to take it down would give unwarranted significance."

Camp's advice to Diefenbaker was blunt. The election was a

holding operation; therefore, he should run a folksy, whistle-stop campaign by train, capitalizing on his touch with the "ordinary" people, as President Truman had done in 1948. Secondly, he should deal from strength, starting his campaign out West, where his support was. Thirdly, he should play up Liberal obstructionism and work on the nuclear arms issue as unwarranted American interference.

Camp personified quiet confidence. "Sometimes I think I've been a kind of lucky charm watch-fob for the Conservatives," he said. "I've been a pallbearer at the funerals of more Liberal governments than anybody in the party."

He was also meticulously loyal to Diefenbaker, despite personal reservations which he will admit to today ("I'm afraid he is paranoic"), but which were never revealed during his leadership. It was an extraordinary performance, for few men have been so provoked or publicly vilified as Camp was by Diefenbaker, and yet he managed to avoid recrimination, never criticized Diefenbaker on a personal level.

The result of the election was far better than the Conservatives had any right to expect, for although they were defeated, the Liberals were denied a majority. The success of Camp's strategy of playing on Western sensibilities was underlined by the fact that in Saskatchewan the Conservatives actually improved their position, taking all 17 seats and wiping the Liberals out. The splinter parties were also hurt. Social Credit were cut back by six seats in Quebec, while the NDP, despite Trudeau's support (he campaigned for fellow U. of M. professor, Charles Taylor, in Mount Royal) had a net loss of two seats, to 17 and again failed to win a single seat in Quebec.

The Liberals were disappointed by the lack of a majority, but they returned to power with the 26th Parliament in a dynamic mood and determined to govern. The first session started exactly six weeks after the election and with the ink hardly dry on the writs.

The party had closed its ranks after the nuclear controversy and with the excitement of power there was no open break between the New and Old Guards in the Quebec caucus for the first few weeks. There were twelve new members from the province, and

Prime Minister Pearson wasted little time in putting them to work. The cabinet had been sworn in on April 22, and the faithful Maurice Lamontagne, elected at last in the safe Old Guard riding of Outremont-St Jean, was rewarded with the Presidency of the Privy Council. Guy Favreau, who had been in private law practice in Montreal since leaving the Department of Justice in 1960, became Minister of Citizenship and Immigration. René Tremblay, who had been persuaded by Lamontagne to leave the Quebec civil service to run for Parliament, became a Minister without Portfolio.

The old guard was also there in commanding force, led by Lionel Chevrier, the Minister of Justice and Quebec caucus leader.

Only one major figure was left out in the cold. That was Maurice Sauvé, and his feelings about being passed over for the second time (he had been elected in 1962) can be imagined. Very quickly, the Quebec members polarized around Chevrier and Sauvé, whose personality, despite absence of cabinet rank, far out-drew the less dominant Lamontagne, Favreau and Tremblay.

Lamontagne, still regarded as the embryonic Quebec leader by Pearson, if by no one else, did his best to grow into the part. But MP columnist Douglas Fisher of the NDP soon gave him a *zéro de conduite* in his regular run-down of Cabinet competence. Nevertheless, the Liberal image-makers were busy, and Lamontagne's newly-furnished house at 18 Lakeview Terrace, beside Ottawa's Dow's Lake, appeared in the *Journal's* Home Section on May 25. In June, Lamontagne launched a vigorous, summer-long campaign against separatism in Quebec by calling the National Union leader, Daniel Johnson, a separatist fellow-traveller. By November, the RIN felt he had done such a good job that they petitioned the Queen to dub him "Sir Maurice."

Yet for all the fun and calumny leveled at him, Lamontagne was responsible for many of the truly important programs implemented by the Pearson administration. As President of the Privy Council, he was the man who planned and pushed through the Economic Council of Canada, the Centennial Commission and the Royal Commission on Bilingualism and Biculturalism. He also brought in several changes recommended by the Glassco Royal Commission on government organization. His work on the policy committee of the Liberal party, along with Tom Kent and Walter

Gordon, brought about such things as the science council and the Consumer Affairs department. Their recommendations for labor-management and prices and wages review boards have still to be implemented. Even as Secretary of State in 1964, an appointment that ended any leadership ambitions he might have had, Lamontagne initiated some major legislation — the revised Broadcasting Act and the grants to encourage Canadian film-makers. But he was never a practical politician, and fate was still to test him cruelly.

Tremblay was another brilliant and devoted man who was ill-used by Parliament. Like Lamontagne, his best role was that of party mandarin. He had done well as president of the Rassemblement and later as secretary of the Quebec Liberal Federation and chairman of the political program committee for Lesage's Liberals in 1960, but his performance as minister without portfolio (and subsequently as Minister of Citizenship and Immigration, succeeding Favreau) was not impressive.

Pearson had to look elsewhere for his Quebec leader.

Under the Liberal Party principle of alternating French and English-speaking leaders, the next leader of the federal party should be French. Quite clearly, the man who led the Quebec caucus would stand a better chance than most to become Pearson's successor in the not too distant future (he was 66, and the next election would probably be his last). So when Lionel Chevrier decided to retire in the fall of 1963, and accept the job of Canadian High Commissioner in London, far more than the Quebec leadership was at stake, and the jockeying for position became deadly serious.

One man who considered himself suited to the job was Maurice Sauvé, the *de-facto* leader of the reform wing. Another was Maurice Lamontagne, who had Sauvé's support if his own candidacy was rejected. But there were still a number of Old Guardsmen who felt their claims were prior. Yvon Dupuis and Guy Rouleau were the main power brokers in this group and their candidate was Guy Favreau. Although Favreau did not have an enemy in the world, he was not strong, and Sauvé felt that the *vieux gang*, led by Dupuis and Rouleau, would control him. He and Lamontagne urged Pearson to consider a triumvirate — the candidates suggested were Favreau, Lamontagne and one other, either Tremblay or Sauvé. But the *vieux gang* won out, and in February, 1964, Pearson ended the matter by naming Favreau Minister of Justice and House leader (an incredible appointment for a man with exactly nine months parliamentary experience). In addition, Pearson disarmed a revolt by naming Sauvé to the Forestry portfolio and Dupuis as a Minister without Portfolio.

If Favreau did well in Justice and as House leader, it was clear the Quebec leadership would be his. Pearson had found the perfect compromise.

Joseph Albert Guy Favreau was probably the most likeable man to enter politics in this decade. He threw himself into the smallest human problems with the same energy he would use for the most extreme government crisis. And this was both his strength and his weakness. A rumpled bear of a man, six feet tall and weighing over 200 pounds, he became as familiar a sight around Ottawa as he had been in the Montreal law courts, with a thatch of curly black hair and an absurd little mustache which failed to hide his humorous, self-deprecating grin or detract from his striking blue eyes. He worked incredibly hard, from 9 a.m. to past midnight, year-in, year-out, eating on the run, sleeping too little, and sometimes playing hard too, chasing down double martinis with a Bass Ale or slipping away to New York like an undergraduate for an innocent night on the town with an old classmate when both their wives were in the country for the summer. His personal kindness and generosity were legendary. A typical example was when as Minister of Citizenship, he sacrificed his own weekend, driving from Montreal to Ottawa one Sunday morning in 1963, to prepare a passport for 28-year-old Herbert Hemberger, whose father had died in Germany the day before and the emergency found him without travel documents. Favreau made sure Hemberger was on the plane to Mannheim that night.

His work in the thankless junior portfolio of Citizenship and Immigration had earned widespread praise. Said columnist Fisher in the *Telegram*: "He is rejuvenating a much scrambled department and has won friends everywhere."

He seemed so capable and willing and impressed Pearson so much with what appeared to be an inexhaustible capacity for work that by New Year, 1964, the temptation was to pile it on. Urged on by Rouleau and Dupuis, Pearson did just that.

Four months later, Favreau became Quebec leader. The job brought with it the obligation to speak regularly and widely inside and outside the province, a task Favreau accepted with his usual gusto, hitting out at separatism in speeches to the Canadian Manufacturers Association, the National Liberal Council, and many others.

But it took its toll. On October 22, after a harrowing time with such government items as the flag debate, the Fulton-Favreau formula to amend the BNA Act, and of course the first squalls of the soon-to-be-revealed Rivard case, Favreau was told by his doctor that he must cut back drastically on his work load. Faced with a doctor's ultimatum, Pearson at last gave the house leadership to George McIlraith, the president of the Privy Council, and a member of parliament for 25 years.

The story of that sad winter of 1964–1965 has been told many times. In retrospect, the achievement of a national flag, redistribution, the Columbia River Treaty, tri-service integration and student loans have far outweighed the scandals that seemed to break in parliament every other week. But in January, 1965, it seemed that the Liberal dossier was dominated by the Rivard affair, the Dupuis affair, the Furniture affair, and the Asselin affair.

By far the most serious was the Rivard case in which a convicted Montreal gangster, Lucien Rivard, was awaiting deportation to Texas to be tried for drug-trafficking, when the lawyer representing the U.S. government received what he took to be a bribe offer from a ministerial assistant. The department of justice investigated the matter, and accepted the resignation of the man involved, but Favreau decided not to press charges.

To the Conservatives' Erik Nielsen, MP for the Yukon, who learned about the case by means that have never been revealed, the solution sounded like political whitewash. And on November 23, in a dramatic speech to the House, Nielsen revealed what he knew about it. The result was an uproar in Parliament, widespread controversy and the Dorion inquiry which continued to titillate newspaper readers through the winter and well into spring.

The commission headed by Mr. Justice Frederic Dorion sat

for 42 days, and on June 29, the judge handed in his 150-page report. It criticized Favreau's judgement in making a personal decision rather than obtaining advice from his senior civil servants — though Judge Dorion agreed with Favreau that there was not enough evidence to prosecute on the basis of the RCMP report at that time.

Favreau immediately resigned the Justice portfolio and later accepted the position of President of the Privy Council.

The Rivard case and the ensuing Dorion inquiry ruined Favreau's career, unjustly perhaps, but a measure of how his fellow Liberals assessed the matter was that as early as January, Jean Marchand was being urged to enter Parliament and become the Quebec leader. Marchand refused (temporarily, as it turned out), because he did not want to join the party until certain Quebec members had resigned, and the party structure had been changed to include democratic control of the treasury and public disclosure of the source of financial contributions. But the search was on for credible new Quebec leaders. The reason was not hard to find.

Soon after the Rivard case was revealed to the Commons, another *histoire* broke which touched two other cabinet ministers — Maurice Lamontagne and René Tremblay. This turned out to be the furniture affair, and it was essentially a matter of poor judgement. Lamontagne and Tremblay had bought large amounts of furniture from Futurama Galleries, a Montreal store owned by the Sefkind brothers, Max and Adolf, and had taken advantage of a pay-as-you-can purchase plan that was so generous it seemed to explain why the brothers had gone bankrupt. On further investigation, Tremblay's involvement appeared blameless; he had paid his bills and the only account outstanding was for furniture he had not received. Lamontagne, on the other hand, had bought some furniture in 1961, some more in 1963, but had only started settling his $6,056 account at $1,000 down and $200 a month after the Bank of Montreal, as creditors, had reminded him of his unpaid balance, in January 1964.

John Diefenbaker could not resist wondering aloud who would get the title of "Lord Chesterfield" if Canada were ever to restore the nobility. And so, the furniture case started an open-season on past *histoires,* which Liberal reformers and Tory crusaders had been longing to unearth. One such was the Asselin affair, which involved Montreal MP Edmund Asselin and the $62,605 profit he made in a real estate deal with the Protestant School Board of Greater Montreal, but *before* entering Parliament. This came closer to witch-hunting than many Liberals care to admit, and Asselin was forced to stand down at the next election as part of the pound of flesh demanded by the Liberal reform wing. Asselin later had the satisfaction of winning, with costs, a lawsuit brought against him by the school board, thereby disproving a Quebec royal commission claim that the profit he made was either "unlawful" or "unconscionable." The profit, it seemed, was just shrewd investment.

But the three *histoires* had one feature in common, which escaped no one, and that was that all the people involved were French Canadians.

More would follow. On January 22, another story made the rounds. This involved Yvon Dupuis, the Minister without Portfolio, who was accused of accepting a $10,000 bribe to obtain a race-track for a group in his home riding of St. Jean-Iberville-Napierville. Dupuis never denied that he had received the money but always claimed that he handed it over, as requested, to an unidentified member of Quebec's Revenue department, whom he offered to pick out if he was allowed to go through the department.

This suggestion earned the scorn of Quebec's Revenue Minister at the time, the redoutable Eric Kierans, who challenged Dupuis to name the man. The case ultimately came to trial and Dupuis was convicted of influence peddling. He was acquitted on appeal but his career as a politician was over.

The cumulative effect of all the *histoires* was to strain relations still further between Canada's English and French-speaking communities. To the *anglophones* it looked as if Pearson, the first Prime Minister to pay more than lip service to biculturalism, was being stabbed by his own Quebec members.

To French Canadians, on the other hand, in view of the flimsy evidence being produced against them, it looked as if Favreau, Lamontagne and Tremblay were three good men being victimized by an anti-French conspiracy. As the Toronto *Star's* Bob McKenzie wrote in January, 1965, the feeling in Quebec City was that "the shadow on (their) careers . . . is out of all proportion to the seriousness of the mistakes they may have made."

The situation was tragic and destined to grow worse. Within three years, Favreau and Tremblay were dead, and Lamontagne had been relegated to the Senate. It was an appalling price to pay for such trifling mistakes.

One of the stranger facts of that strange month of January, 1965, was that the Liberals were convinced that the country was ready to give them a majority. The chief organizer, Keith Davey, told newsmen that campaign readiness had gone "from red to yellow", and party polls were giving the Liberals a majority of between 140 and 180 seats in the 265-seat house.

How the Liberals could have believed their polls is one of the continuing mysteries of politics. What might have been affecting their judgement perhaps was the knowledge that though the Liberal Party was in poor shape in Quebec, the Conservative condition across the nation was even worse.

The Conservatives had not done well since the 1963 election. Diefenbaker had been unwilling to permit a reassessment of party policy or to allow a more communal approach to party direction. And while there were a few who openly rebelled, such as a prominent Ontario Conservative, "Eddie" Goodman, most of the party members occupied the middle-ground typified by Dalton Camp, who remained loyal to Diefenbaker but demanded a reorientation of the party.

As a result, at the annual convention in February, 1964, every forward step appeared to be countered by one, sometimes two, sideways moves. While the party elected Dalton Camp as the national president, and endorsed his party-wide call for a national conference on Canadian goals in Fredericton the following September, it got into an unnecessary hassle over whether the vote of loyalty to the leader should be secret or open. After a one-and-a-half-hour wrangle, the motion for a secret ballot was defeated by 3 to 1, and the show-of-hands vote of loyalty carried. Ironically, a secret ballot then would have actually been more effective in restoring party unity, because Diefenbaker would have won it, and it would have shown the world that he still had the support of Conservatives without fear or favor. Another unnecessary blunder was Diefenbaker's emotional acclamation of Leon Balcer, the Tory MP from Three Rivers, as "another Cartier," and his subsequent incomprehensible refusal to admit that Balcer was the Conservatives' Quebec leader, which was certainly the implication of the Cartier label.

Quebec Conservatives were further irritated by Diefenbaker's attitude to the question of a new national flag, and they helped end the filibuster which lasted for 37 sitting days, when cloture (recommended by a Quebec Tory) was invoked, finally passing the measure on December 12.

The high point of the Conservative year, such as it was, turned out to be Dalton Camp's conference on Canadian goals in the Chemistry Building at the University of New Brunswick, in Fredericton, September 9 to 12, where among others — and other things — Marshall McLuhan said that "political parties must now begin to think seriously about their responsibility to teenagers," which prompted Eugene Forsey to ask if he was suggesting Diefenbaker should wear a Beatle wig? Camp had called the conference because of his belief that "there are business and professional men, and the rising generations of younger people, who do not find political organization in its traditional form either appealing or challenging." And at Fredericton, welcoming the participants, he had said he hoped the party would develop "from fresh springs of awareness new channels of thought, inquiry and purpose. What we cannot do again is merely ingest the realities of a new society into an inert doctrinaire conservatism."

The best sparks at the conference came from a major speech by Professor William L. Morton, of the University of Manitoba, who flatly rejected a special status for Quebec, which had been increasingly discussed during the year, and said he felt Quebec was a province like any other. Professor Morton's viewpoint was predictably attacked by two other conference speakers, *Le Devoir's* Claude Ryan and the president of the *Trust Général du Canada*, Marcel Faribault. But it received support from an unexpected source, Marc Lalonde, whom Camp remembers as "very bright, very tough and unconsciously belligerent" and who allowed that in his opinion "a strong platform in favor of federalism would sweep in Quebec the proponents of the Associate State or the special status for Quebec." Within four years, Lalonde had practiced at what he preached, as Trudeau's top strategist.

The Fredericton conference pointed the way, even though the party was not going to adopt its guidelines for another two years. It had been a bright moment in an otherwise gloomy year. And for the Tories the year was getting gloomier. In November, the Conservatives lost a seat to the NDP in an Ontario by-election. And by year's end, having broken party ranks over the flag debate (seven of the ten Quebec Tory MP's voted with the government), it looked as if the French Canadian wing of the party was about to collapse altogether.

By December of 1964, the Cartier-like non-leader from Three Rivers, Leon Balcer, threatened to sit as an independent, unless there was a national leadership convention. Soon after New Year, Balcer and nine other Quebec Conservatives were huddled in a hotel in Montreal, preparing an ultimatum for the party. Only intervention by Dalton Camp and Egan Chambers, a Montrealer and ex-president of the association, persuaded them to modify their positions. Even so, three weeks later, after a four-and-a-half-hour meeting in the scarlet Royal Suite of Montreal's Windsor Hotel, Balcer and his group drove to Ottawa to call a press conference and demand that a date for a leadership convention be set before Parliament returned on February 16.

The second challenge to Diefenbaker's leadership in as many years had occurred. On January 25, Camp polled the 133-members of the national executive as to whether they should meet to consider the leadership question; and if so, should they meet before February 16, or at the next regular executive committee meeting?

Before the answers were received, Diefenbaker had returned to Ottawa and ordered a two-day caucus of Tory MP's for February 11 and 12.

Five days later, Camp had finished counting the national executive poll, and ordered a meeting for the following Friday and Saturday, February 5 and 6, a week before Diefenbaker's party caucus. It was a gamble that did not work.

Enraged at the attempted finesse, Diefenbaker rescheduled his party caucus for February 5, when he received an emotional open vote of support and defused the threat of the national executive meeting which was to follow suit the next day.

Diefenbaker had won round two. Only Rémi Paul, the Tory

lawyer from Louiseville, was prepared to stand on his rebel principles; he became an independent on February 18.

Balcer waited until February 15 to make up his mind to remain after all (though he finally quit in April) and two days later, Diefenbaker went on "The Nation's Business" to talk to his fellow Canadians. "I have been maligned," he said. "I have been condemned. No one since the days of Macdonald has gone through the like . . ." And so it went in vein, appealing to the people to support him against "them." He concluded: "I will follow the will of the people. Will it be the will of the people or those that are all powerful?"

The revolt died slowly, as spring turned to summer and it became clear that the Liberals were being afflicted by election fever. By September 7, with the tocsin for an election, the Progressive Conservative party closed its ranks again: back came George Hees, who had declared unconvincingly that Parliament held no temptation for the president of a stock exchange; back, too, came Davie Fulton, disabused of his provincial ambitions in British Columbia. It looked like 1958 all over again and, predictably, that is just what Diefenbaker said.

As John Saywell wrote in the *Canadian Annual Review* that year "it was less a rallying of the clan behind the chief, however, than a feeling that the clan must be kept alive to fight under new leadership another day."

V

Into the Arena

"Many important historical facts can only be explained
by accidental circumstances; and many others remain
totally inexplicable, although I believe that chance does
nothing that has not been prepared beforehand. Ante-
cedent facts, the nature of institutions, the cast of minds
and the state of morals are the materials of which
are composed those impromptus which astonish and
alarm us."

— *Alexis de Tocqueville, Souvenirs*

IT WAS Friday, September 10, 1965, and at 3:55 p.m. there was
not a seat to be had in the coyly-muraled Alpine Room of
Montreal's Mount Royal Hotel. Newsmen were crowded shoulder-
to-shoulder down both sides of the long, green, felt covered
conference table, leaving a narrow microphone-clustered space at
one end, in front of the long orange draperies. Television cameras,
tape-recorders, and portable power units filled all the space behind
the seated newsmen on both sides of the table.

The news conference had been called by the Liberal Federation
of Canada (Quebec section) for what had been described confi-
dentially by Liberal public relations man John de B. Payne as
important news. Payne was in constant touch with the chief Liberal
organizer for Quebec, Louis de Gonzague Giguère, who was in the
vice-regal suite of the Windsor Hotel, two blocks away on Domin-
ion Square. There, Favreau, Lamontagne and Sauvé, on the one
side, and Marchand, Pelletier and Trudeau, on the other, had been
closeted for most of the past 24 hours.

For months, Giguére, Lamontagne and Favreau had been trying
to persuade Jean Marchand to run as a Liberal candidate in the

next general election. Marchand was holding out for a triumvirate that would include Pelletier and Trudeau. The Liberals were not at all happy, but they needed Marchand desperately.

In Ottawa, Keith Davey and Walter Gordon had planned a June election but first the Dorion Report and then the federal-provincial conference had forced a postponement. The first snow usually falls on Eastern Canada in mid-November, ending the election season for six months, and since 60 days are needed between dissolution and voting, Davey and Gordon had set Labor Day, September 1, as the deadline for a 1965 election decision. When Labor Day passed without a decision by Marchand, they persuaded Pearson to wait no longer. On September 7, Pearson announced that Parliament had been dissolved and an election scheduled for November 8.

By the next evening, the negotiations with Marchand, Pelletier and Trudeau had reached a crisis point. Lamontagne had become exasperated, and Giguère had taken over as discussion leader. He's a tough, broken-nosed little man of enormous charm and a will of steel. Naturally, he comes from the Lac St. Jean region of Quebec, like Father Georges-Henri Lévesque, who used to take out his sister when they were teenagers.

Giguère's first problem, the following morning, was to get everybody together again, since Wednesday's meeting had broken up with strained feelings on all sides. "It's a musical comedy," said Payne. "Everybody's sitting by their telephone at home, waiting for somebody to call. Next time we'll set it to music; you bring the piano, and I'll give you the lyrics."

Compounding the problem were the newsmen who were besieging everyone involved. Giguère called one meeting, then announced that it had been cancelled. Pelletier had flown to Winnipeg, which complicated matters, and he would not be back until late that night. Giguère decided to go with those that were available. He took the vice-regal suite at the Windsor and invited Marchand, Trudeau, Favreau, Lamontagne and Sauvé to meet him at 7:30 for a leisurely evening of drinks and supper — which Pelletier would join when his plane got in shortly after 10 p.m. Sauvé also arrived late, about 8:30. A trolley with three servings of spaghetti and meat sauce, coffee, rolls and a bottle of Valpolicella was wheeled into the suite a good three hours later, after which Maurice Sauvé, in shirtsleeves, checked to see that the orange "Do Not Disturb" sign was still on the door. Shortly after eleven, Gérard Pelletier arrived, shielding his face with a newspaper. Trudeau, a non-smoker, appeared briefly at the door to get some fresh air. "It's pretty thick in there." An hour later, the room service waiter returned with fresh ice, glasses, six bottles of Vichy water, four beers and a bottle of Courvoisier brandy. Another hour passed, and Trudeau again came out for a breather. "It seems that they don't need us badly enough," he said. Just before three, Pelletier and Trudeau came out and left the hotel, walking quickly. Ten minutes later, Marchand left. No one would say anything. They would meet again in the suite at 12 noon.

Friday morning passed, while newsmen vainly tried every ploy in their repertoire to penetrate the veil of secrecy, and at noon, they were back in the suite. The meeting broke up at three, and there were smiles. All would be told at the news conference an hour later.

Just before four, Favreau, leading Sauvé and Lamontagne, eased his bear-like bulk sideways past the tripods, and they stood in line like a corporal's guard, leaning against the wall at the head of the table. There were no seats to spare. Marchand, in a shiny brown suit, looking unusually well-tanned and rested in spite of only five hours' sleep the night before, wandered into the room, puffing on his pipe. Pelletier appeared next and took a seat on Marchand's right. His blue suit jacket and pants did not match. There was no sign of Trudeau.

"If you will bear with us for a few minutes more," said Marchand, "we have another visitor to come." At five minutes past four, immaculate in dark blue summer cords, white shirt, and blue knitted tie, Trudeau arrived. The conference started. It was all in French. They spoke in turn, first Marchand, then Pelletier, and finally Trudeau.

Marchand's statement was simple and straightforward. He said he had decided to run for the Federal parliament, because "I consider that there are certain problems facing Canada which are not only important but which demand quick, immediate solutions. And I believe that everyone who is able must do everything he

can to support the government and provide a new presence in
Ottawa. It's not a question of replacing a team but of reinforcing
a team which is in action. We believe that one of the most important problems is to reinforce the team which is representing the
province of Quebec."

It was a diplomatic speech. Everyone knew this was a new team
and no amount of reinforcing would help the old one. But it
sounded good.

Pelletier echoed Marchand. "I believe that certain problems
remain to be resolved if Canada is to reach her political ideal."
He spoke of Canada facing a deadline and that the Liberal party
"seems to be the best one to meet that deadline and have the will
and means to solve Canada's problems."

Trudeau was cool and cerebral, carefully analyzing his reasons
and treating his audience to a delightful little lecture, delivered,
alternately, in impeccable English and Paris-accented French.

"There are really two questions here," he started. "First, why
did I enter politics? And second, why the Liberals?

"To answer the first question: I think it's only normal, after
spending 15 years in the role of a critic, after telling others what
to do, to try and get out and do it myself. I should try to do
something. I should turn from examination to direct action.

"Now, why the Liberals? I believe that is a question I must
explain in terms of priorities. When one has a plan, one has to
follow an axis of priorities. Our people, the French Canadians,
have neither the time, nor the energy, nor the inclination to finance
too many revolutions. We must try to choose.

"My discussions with the Liberals didn't start yesterday, or 24
hours ago," he said. "But I came to believe that the party was
ready to accept the concepts of people with ideas and attitudes
like my own, not because Canada has been around for 100 years,
or has the second highest standard of living, nor because of my
ability to see the French Canadian role, nor because I think it
would be a tragedy to turn inwards — but because it is a party
where a French Canadian can belong without humiliation, and
because I opt for the Canadian hypothesis."

It was done. Guy Favreau said a few words to welcome them
officially to the party. "Marchand, Pelletier and Trudeau are not

people whose arms you twist. They decided they would join us after long and deep reflection. There was no deal, promise, or condition, and that is perhaps what makes this such an encouraging event for both the Liberals and the entire country — *province et pays*. We all, in this room, know how important the presence of these three new political men will be, for the party and the country. We know, equally, of the great awareness of their political engagement. The Liberal Party welcomes them and their common desire to work together with us for Quebec and the rest of Canada. Their decision to involve themselves constitutes a moment of joy and great pride for the Liberal Party."

(The full story of the previous evening did not emerge until years later. For the first four hours, Favreau, Lamontagne and Giguère explained why they did not want Trudeau and Pelletier. Finally, Maurice Sauvé said the discussion was obviously going nowhere, and he, Marchand, Trudeau and Pelletier withdrew to the bedroom to talk tactics. Sauvé told Marchand to say to Favreau: "Okay, we've made up our mind, we want to come in, and I've called a press conference for tomorrow at 4 p.m. to announce it." Sauvé then told him to call *La Presse* and *Le Devoir* from the bedroom so that the news of the press conference would be in the Friday papers. They then went back and presented Favreau with a *fait accompli*. We want in — and we've called a press conference. What are you going to do about it? For good measure, Sauvé added that if Favreau, Lamontagne and Giguère did not accept Marchand, Trudeau and Pelletier, then he himself would not run again and would resign from the party. Favreau knew he had been beaten. The Friday noon meeting was just to save face. At first, Favreau decided he did not want to go to the press conference. "You have to," said Sauvé. "You're the Quebec leader. Who will welcome us into the party if you're not there?")

Few novilleros have ever been so warmly welcomed into the political arena, and when one considers Trudeau's published opinion of the Liberal Party only two years previously, Favreau's attitude was generous indeed.

Yet the metamorphosis was not really surprising. The Liberals were in trouble, and they needed Marchand badly enough to welcome the Devil himself, if that were a condition. And while

Trudeau's angry denunciation of Pearson in April, 1963, annoyed several Liberals, it did not receive wide circulation and, for many people, only said out loud what they were thinking. What hurt the party more, in all probability, was Trudeau's active campaigning in the Montreal riding of Mount Royal for Charles Taylor, his old friend and U. of M. colleague. For the sad fact was that the number of people who subscribed to *Cité Libre,* let alone read it, was infinitely smaller than the number interested in federal politics — and that was small enough.

One of the myths that has grown up since Trudeau became a national figure is that *Cité Libre* was somehow a lonely Chevalier Bayard of a magazine, *sans peur et sans reproche,* hacking away at the National Union hordes. In fact, *Cité Libre's* circulation was always tiny (it is only 2500 copies today, less than half of those subscriptions) and its influence tangential at best because its readers were nearly all academics or professional men, rarely active in politics. "If a dozen politicians actually read it before 1965, I would be very surprised," says Maurice Sauvé.

Thus the fall-out from "Pearson — or spiritual abdication" remained low. Trudeau not only continued his teaching and research at the U. of M. (civil liberties was his special interest) but took on a side-line as a research consultant for the Royal Commission on Bilingualism later that year.

Another recruit to the Bi-Bi commission was Jean Marchand, named one of the ten Royal Commissioners in July, 1963. Marchand's role as a commissioner, and the frequent trips it required to Ottawa and other parts of the country, became a source of increasing irritation to the executive of the CSN, who naturally felt that the president should devote himself full-time to union activities — or else take leave of absence and let someone else get on with it. For a year and a half Marchand did neither. This internal conflict with the CSN continued until the spring of 1965, when Marchand finally promised to resign on May 8, on the assumption that a June general election would take place as planned by Davey, Gordon and Lamontagne.

The big news of the year was separatism, which had at last emerged from its conspiratorial back rooms to put bombs in garbage cans and mailboxes. Quebec's schoolboy terrorists proved a mercifully docile lot, in spite of their proclaimed Cuban and Algerian models; far more serious to political observers, was the re-emergence of nationalism, the shrill demands for constitutional change, not, as might be hoped, to make confederation work any better, but to permit Quebeckers to be *maitre chez-eux*. Many observers detected behind the accusations tossed at the *maudits anglais* (damned English), an increasing undercurrent of anti-clericalism, particularly in such journals as *Parti Pris*, the Marxist-Leninist separatist magazine. Yet the Church was in the throes of liberalization, thanks largely to Pope John XXIII, and even Quebec's Jesuits and Dominicans were at last getting along together. But increasingly, instead of grasping the opportunities confederation offered, Quebec's young intellectuals devoted themselves to the old outworn themes that they were exploited and colonized and it was the fault of the English, the Americans and the Jews. (Anti-semitism, never far from the surface in French Canada, was to emerge with depressing frequency.) To Quebec intellectuals who had fought nationalism in its authoritarian era under Duplessis, the reappearance of nationalism in the guise of socialism was one giant step backwards.

At first, it was dismissed contemptuously — "another wasted generation of French Canadians," was how Trudeau put it on several occasions. But the mood of Quebec refused to change; separatism and its camp followers would not go away because some intellectuals said they were a waste of time. No, it had to be taken seriously, as one more enemy to be beaten, and early in 1963, the strategy was laid for that battle.

The man who took the first step was not Pierre Trudeau, but Marc Lalonde. Lalonde had worked with Paul Gérin-Lajoie during the provincial election in November, 1962. He had close links with most of the young political activists in Quebec through Lajoie's team, and through his own continuing contacts as a practising lawyer, frequently consulted by the governments in both Ottawa and Quebec. During the 1962 campaign, Lalonde started to detect a persistent undercurrent of nationalism which disturbed him. He decided to pay close attention to the theme, seeking out arguments, mapping out the extent of the feeling and its depth. What he discovered worried him increasingly, because he was, and is, a dedicated federalist — convinced that Quebec is better protected and better able to evolve within the Canadian confederation than it could outside. One day, early in 1963, he met Albert Breton, a close friend and fellow contributor to *Cité Libre* and a professor of economics at the University of Montreal. "Breton and I discussed the rise of ardent nationalism in Quebec and we found that we agreed that the wind was blowing in that direction," recalls Lalonde. So they decided to get some other friends together and talk some more. Breton brought his brother, Raymond, a professor of sociology at McGill, Lalonde brought in Trudeau, and so the group collected — Claude Bruneau, a Montreal lawyer and friend of Lalonde; Dr. Yvon Gauthier, a psychiatrist; Maurice Pinard, a professor of sociology at McGill. The group met every Friday evening in the board room of the Social Research Group, on Laurier Avenue West. "We did not intend to publish anything at first, but it soon seemed to be easier to get our ideas down on paper, and that's how the manifesto came about," says Lalonde.

The "Canadian Manifesto", sub-titled "an appeal for realism in Canadian politics", was published simultaneously in the *Canadian Forum* and in *Cité Libre* in May, 1964. The full text was also published in the Montreal *Star*. It is probably one of the most important political documents of the 1960's, and a blueprint, in many ways, for the Trudeau administration.

An interesting comparison for Trudeau buffs can be made between the *Cité Libre* version of the manifesto, entitled "Pour Une Politique Fonctionelle", of May, 1964, and the first article Trudeau ever wrote for the magazine, in June, 1950, also titled "Politique Fonctionelle". Aside from the title, there are other, similarities close enough to suggest that Trudeau played the major role in drafting the manifesto.

The Manifesto started with a declaration of concern for Quebec and Canada. "Canada today is a country in search of a purpose," it declared. The Manifesto went on to express concern that the reform movement in Quebec was losing its direction and in danger of being compromised. It reaffirmed its "faith in man, and it is on the basis of human criteria that we demand policies better adapted to our world and our times. This is the only 'appeal to pride and dignity' we find worthwhile.

Declaring that human resources were limited and work abounded to be done, the Manifesto listed eight main problems as critical: first, unemployment, which would be corrected only by expansionist economic policies calculated to absorb manpower and reduce unemployment. Thus did nationalism work against full employment. "Among other things, it is inconceivable that politicians should continue to dread budgetary deficits and that, even when resorting to them, they should continue to pay homage to the sacred cow of a balanced budget," it said, in part.

Second, the Manifesto was concerned about regional disparity, the fisherman in the Gaspé and the farmer in the maritimes; the need for government policy to permit mobility of labor, described as a key to maximum yield.

Third was the administration of justice: Canada's Criminal Code sought vengeance rather than rehabilitation. The whole process of arrest, detention, and interrogation in Canada infringed basic individual rights. The Manifesto was particularly scornful of the Quebec Civil Code "vaunted as the cornerstone of our society" for more than a 100 years. "If this claim is true, then it must be said that our society rests at least in part on rather weird foundations." It went on to criticize the courts as "antiquated and inadequate" (they still are) noting that in May, 1964, the Superior Court in Montreal had a backlog of 17,000 cases, most of them three to five years old.

The fourth problem was the low investment in Human Capital; fifth was adaptation — not only the need to re-train workers affected by automation, but a precise policy to re-adapt both men and their families to an age of rapid change; sixth was health, and it pointed towards medicare; and the seventh was federalism. The Manifesto criticized the lack of policy in federal-provincial relations. "One thing is certain. The kind of haphazard political expediency which has inspired so many sharing schemes and federal subsidies for so long has got to stop."

Finally, there was a need for political leadership in Canada. "We deplore the absence of leadership in political affairs. Public figures, federal and provincial, do not provide the people with a clear idea of the direction in which they want the country to go. They appear to be the toys of the communications media and of their ghost writers." It deplored the vagueness and the incoherence of Canada's leaders and their use of "propaganda loaded with emotional slogans", for example, the statement: " 'we owe it to ourselves to have a steel industry.' As though it were simply a matter of pride and without any need to publish the studies on the subject."

The Manifesto listed many other things as major problems with perhaps lower priorities, and concluded with a simple creed in Canada. "Most valid trends today are towards more enlightened humanism, towards various forms of political, social and economic universalism. Canada is a reproduction on a smaller and simpler scale of this universal phenomenon. The challenge is for a number of ethnic groups to learn to live together. It is a modern challenge, meaningful and indicative of what can be expected from men in the days ahead. If Canadians cannot make a success of a country such as theirs, how can they contribute in any way to the elaboration of humanism, to the formulation of the international political structures of tomorrow? If this country is to work, federalism must be preserved and refined at all costs."

The effect of the Manifesto in political science circles was sensational. At last, the federalist option had been defined with clarity and precision, and what's more, two of the people responsible for the definition were prepared to commit themselves to political action — Trudeau and Lalonde.

Meanwhile, between the Manifesto's conception early in 1963, and its publication in 1964, the rise of nationalism in Quebec had increased. Early in 1963, Lesage had started to put the brakes on his Quiet Revolution, and René Lévesque, nationally famous from the power nationalization fight, started to take his battles outside the cabinet room and directly to the public. In September, 1963, he found an ally and soon close friend in Eric Kierans, who had left the Montreal and Canadian stock exchanges late in the summer to join the Lesage cabinet as Minister of Revenue, winning election in the traditionally senior Anglo-Saxon provincial riding of Notre Dame de Grace.

Kierans' political ambitions were not new. He had been defeated in 1957 for the federal nomination in NDG and few doubted that his entry into provincial politics would ultimately lead him to Ottawa. In fact, Quebec offered a perfect springboard, for as early as 1963, Jean Lesage was starting to prepare himself to return to Ottawa as Pearson's successor. In 1964 a very definite pattern emerged as he closed ranks with Pearson in resisting demands that the Royal visit scheduled for the fall should be canceled. His speaking engagements, to the Ontario Legislature and to the University of Moncton, N.B., took on a tone and manner calculated to make English Canadians see in Jean Lesage the hope for confederation.

But while Lesage hobnobbed with Pearson and tried to turn himself into a national figure, happenings back home indicated that he was woefully out of touch with the real mood of Quebec. Early in 1965, separatists robbed a Montreal armory of 100 rifles, 10,000 rounds of ammunition, and Dr. Chaput warned that the Queen would be in grave danger if she came to Quebec City in October.

In April, the first meeting of the Estates General, sponsored by the nationalist St. John the Baptist Society and 17 other groups, took place and endorsed associate statehood for Quebec. Early in May, René Lévesque also came out for associate statehood "without rifles or dynamite as much as possible. However, if it comes to guns, dynamite and other devices, so be it. I think that it is morally justifiable when there is no alternative." Soon afterwards, 85 people were arrested for demonstrating against Victoria Day in Montreal, and on June 26, 10,000 Quebec farmers marched on the Legislature to protest against the failure of Lesage's Liberals to do anything for the agricultural sector. On July 5, René Lévesque and the president of the Quebec Liberal Federation, François Aquin, succeeded in persuading the provincial wing of the Liberal Party to break completely with the federal party. Only five of the 1,400 delegates at the convention opposed the motion.

Lesage's counter-attack took place at the annual convention of the Quebec party in mid-September, when he managed to install Dr. Irénée Lapierre, a right-wing Liberal, as president of the provincial party, replacing Aquin. He also threw his full support behind the increasingly reactionary activities of his new Minister of Justice, Claude Wagner, who was elected to the Legislature for the Montreal suburb of Verdun at a by-election on October 5, the day the Queen set foot in Canada.

Five days later, the Royal yacht *Britannia*, constantly patrolled by naval and police frogmen, tied up at Wolfe's Cove and the Queen entered Quebec City for the most disastrous Royal Visit in Canadian history. For weeks beforehand, newspapers on both sides of the Atlantic had given full coverage to separatist threats. In London, before her departure, the *Daily Mirror* bannered an assassination threat by a "Canadian Killer Gang", while the stately *Times* urged that the tour be canceled, since "an innocent life is at stake, as well as the dignity of a great, if dual, nation." It was perhaps unsurprising that Quebeckers stayed home in their thousands to watch the visit on television from the safety of their living rooms, and the only crowds to greet the Royal Progress were knots of curious late fall tourists and long lines of troops and police, separated by yellow barricades. The Quebec tour ended on Saturday, October 10, with the Quebec City Police, in riot helmets and flare orange coats, armed with three-foot long baseball bats, smashing their way into small knots of separatists and students who had the temerity to jeer the Royal Couple as they arrived and left the Chateau Frontenac Hotel before and after a state banquet. It was a hideous example of authoritarian over-reaction, of officially sanctioned police brutality, and it went down in the annals of Quebec as the infamous *Samedi de la Matraque* (Saturday of the Clubs). It was a humiliating experience for both Lesage and Pearson, the planners of the Royal Visit, but for Lesage it was also a severe set-back to his timetable for returning in glory to Ottawa. On the one hand, it seemed clear that he had to put his Quebec house in order before thinking of moving to larger quarters. While on the other, the scandals involving French-Canadian cabinet ministers in Ottawa made it appear most unlikely that the Liberal Party would be ready to pick another French Canadian as the national leader in the near future.

And this was the rub. Lesage was anxious to go to Ottawa but he would not consider leaving Quebec City unless his position as Pearson's successor was cut and dried. And he told Pearson as much on January 2, 1965, replying to an offer of a senior cabinet position if he would join the federal government.

Obviously Pearson himself could hardly commit the party to a successor, even if he had wanted to, and there are grounds for suspecting that Pearson did not entirely approve of Lesage, his style or ambition. His reaction to Lesage's demand that his position as successor be assured without recourse to democratic procedures can only be imagined.

The result of the January confrontation was that Lesage spurned the cabinet post proffered by Pearson and retired to the frustrating role of observer. In fact, Lesage must have been fairly seething with ambition on the sidelines during the spring of 1965, as the federal Liberals went fishing for federalists in Quebec. Unable to offer either himself or his advice, thanks to the separation of provincial and federal parties brought about by his own nationalists, Lesage just had to sit and wait and watch while first Marchand, then Trudeau and Pelletier were sought out for the federal team. Lesage had always approved of Marchand. He was a known quantity, a Quebec City man, an acquaintance. Lesage calls Marchand "a professional," a man who knows what it is all about. "You build people the way I was built. You start at eighteen, and you participate in every election." He was contemptuous of Pierre Trudeau and Gérard Pelletier. "You don't take people like that and put them in politics. You need professionals. Not dilettantes. Not 'deep thinkers'."

Lesage urged Pearson to persuade Marchand to get some 'real' professionals with him. He suggested Guy Gagnon, Lesage's executive secretary and chief provincial organizer (brother of Jean-Louis Gagnon of the Bi-Bi Commission and formerly *Le Nouveau Journal*). Gagnon had Quebec politics in his veins since childhood. He was a professional. He knew Quebec and every key organizer in every riding. He also suggested Claude Morin, the deputy minister of Federal-Provincial affairs.

It would have been such a perfect set-up for Lesage's own accession to power, that it must have been all he could do to keep in the background from January 2 until the election in November. As it was, he was often on the telephone to "Mike" (Pearson), "Gordon" (Robertson, secretary of the Cabinet) and "Tom" (Kent, of the PM's office), as he liked to put it, trying to persuade them against Pelletier and Trudeau, those intolerable deep thinkers — knowing full well that what chance he had left for the succession would rise or fall in inverse proportion to their success or failure in Ottawa.

For Jean Lesage liked Ottawa. He had thoroughly enjoyed the pomp and ceremony of the capital in the St. Laurent era, and had done his best to give Quebec City's old gingerbread Legislature some of the same dignity. Legislature openings had a panache under Lesage that they have rarely displayed before or since. Motionless Provincial Policemen would sweat at attention under television lights in heavy blue colonial serge uniforms, white belts, gloves and spiked pith helmets — relics of an Empire long since relegated to Hollywood back-lots and late, late shows.

Some said he rather overdid it for bourgeois Quebec City. The entire parliamentary complex was redecorated in the six years he was premier, and some of the offices and facilities that emerged from the remodelling were very impressive indeed. Most imposing of all, of course, was the suite occupied by Lesage himself, a symphony of dark-green leather furniture with complementary curtains and rugs, and heavy oak paneling, all of which took up an entire wing of an annex. So many secretaries and flunkies guarded his privacy, so many doors stood between him and the public, that some of his own ministers actually swore that from 1964 onward, they were unable to see him outside of Cabinet for six months at a stretch.

Some of his ministers, it should be noted, adopted his style of political grandeur, so that, by 1965, it was said in Ottawa that if you wanted to talk to a Quebec minister, you sent a telegram. They simply did not receive telephone calls.

Outside the legislature, the presence of the Quebec politician was equally impressive. Every cabinet minister was supplied with a chauffeur and a limousine. On occasion, there were veritable traffic jams of long, black Buicks and Cadillacs outside the Cap Rouge Golf Club or the Quebec Winter Club, as ministers took their ease.

In Ottawa, where ministers sometimes traveled by bus during the Pearson administration, it used to be one of the attractions of federal-provincial conferences to watch a Quebec delegation arrive on Parliament Hill. Invariably, a seemingly endless line of somber limousines, with blue and white *fleurs-de-lis* fluttering at the fenders, would sweep up to the main portico, and everybody would try to guess how many secretaries, under-secretaries, *conseillers techniques* and stenographers the delegation would bring with it.

But for all its pseudo-Gaullist pretension, the domicile at 1175 Bougainville Avenue was not the Elysée Palace, and short of the Elysée itself, Lesage still hankered for 24 Sussex Drive, Ottawa, and some scarlet-uniformed Mounties he could call his own.

Lesage would make two major attempts to recapture the initiative. In mid-September, 1965, he toured Western Canada for three weeks in Quebec's private DeHavilland executive jet, telling the people "what Quebec really wants". It was a disaster. In Calgary, he denounced the unilingualism of the Mounties; in Victoria, he told Empire loyalists that French Canada would put up with English Canada if it got reciprocity; and in Vancouver, he allowed that there were only two things that would keep Quebec in confederation — a special status and national recognition of Canada's bicultural duality, which sounded like having your cake and eating it too. Quite apart from what he said, the Westerners did not like the way he said it, and his pompous, rather florid style did not go down well at all. In Toronto, on his way home, he appeared to change his mind about what Quebec really wanted after all, declaring that perhaps a new constitution was not really necessary.

Back in Quebec, watching the campaign leading to the federal election running its course, Lesage thought it all over again. Only one thing, he decided, could yet give him the stature he needed to push his candidacy as Pearson's successor ahead of the French Canadians likely to be in the cabinet (Marchand, his prime rival, was guaranteed a seat when he ran, and was slated for Minister of Citizenship and Immigration after election). It would be necessary for Lesage to have an overwhelming personal triumph as Premier of Quebec. And since overwhelming personal triumphs did not come tailor-made, Lesage decided to order the one thing he could, a provincial election. All he needed for that was the excuse.

Meanwhile, the federal election took precedence.

Persuading Marchand had been a long, hard process involving Maurice Lamontagne, Guy Favreau and Maurice Sauvé. Lamontagne brought in Bob Giguère who took Marchand golfing. Maurice Sauvé brought himself in, to the irritation of just about everybody, to press his conviction that Marchand should go with a team or not at all. Sauvé says he was only warning Marchand that if he came along he would be swamped by the old guard, which he identified as those behind Favreau and Lamontagne. Marchand remembers it otherwise.

"Maurice Sauvé pretends he played a role in bringing me into the party, but he didn't do anything. He detested Favreau and Lamontagne and everything they did he tried to undo. His purpose in coming to see me at Cap Rouge was to persuade me not to go into politics because it would diminish his influence. Evidently, Favreau and Lamontagne had used the possibility of my entry as a threat. You know, 'you watch out, *maudit* Sauvé, or Marchand will come in, and you have to go back in your hole'. And Sauvé came to tell me 'it makes no sense, their using you against me.' "

Marchand could hardly believe his ears. But he knew Sauvé well enough from his union days not to be surprised. Marchand remembers that Sauvé tried to get a leave of absence from the national federation of metallurgists when he left them in 1955 to join the Gordon Commission on Canada's economic prospects, but the union had refused, insisting that he resign. Sauvé went from the commission into the Quebec Liberal Federation in 1958 (on Maurice Lamontagne's recommendation) as public relations director, and never returned to the union. "He had annoyed the negotiating committee, then the executive committee, and then the general assembly," Marchand remembers. "They all wanted to kick him out. He's a sort of machine, humorless, incapable of generosity, quite impossible for a team. Lamontagne and Favreau made mistakes, but they were not bandits. Sauvé is so preoccupied with his own ambition that he was the one who destroyed the first federal experience. And I was determined he wasn't going to play the same pig's ass with me. I had a bit more experience, and I was not going to let him do to us what he did to Lamontagne.

The sad thing about Sauvé, says Marchand, "is that he was the best French Canadian minister in the federal government. He knew his job, and he was very competent. But completely unmanageable. I kept telling him, don't stab everybody in the back. But he wasn't interested at all."

As soon as Marchand became leader of the Quebec caucus, Sauvé started campaigning to get the job abolished. (Sauvé's *pièce de résistance* would come three years later, during the Liberal leadership convention of 1968. "He double-crossed us royally. One day he said we are all on the same team, and we have a job to do, and the next day, he's working for Paul Martin.")

Meanwhile, the Federal election and its prologue took precedence.

It was a hard year to be a federal politician. For the younger MP's, there was the frustrating knowledge that there was a majority waiting in the country for the first party that managed to re-establish contact with the Canadian people; but as long as old men led, relevance would remain remote and the public disinterested.

For the older members, the death of Churchill, at the end of January, reminded them that the generation gap was not just a catchy label dreamed up by some over-zealous whippersnapper. And as Pearson, Diefenbaker, and Newfoundland's Joey Smallwood joined other representatives of the free world at St. Paul's Cathedral, to pay homage to the grand old man, looking around, they must have realized with a shock that they were old men, too.

While Pearson was in London, in fact, a reform group of six backbenchers in his Quebec caucus, led by August Choquette and Jean Chrétien, petitioned him for a complete reorganization of the Liberal structure in Quebec, proposed a full-scale meeting of the 47-member caucus in Quebec City to kick out the Old Guard. Gérard Pelletier, writing in *Cité Libre*, called for "clean sweep, brutal in fact" — and Guy Rouleau, implicated in the Rivard affair, obliged everyone by resigning as chairman of the Quebec caucus on February 14, the day before the new flag was officially proclaimed on Parliament Hill before a crowd of 10,000.

Yet symbols were not enough, as the preliminary report of the Royal Commission on Bilingualism and Biculturalism would indicate early in March, warning that there was "serious danger to the continued existence of Canada" and that the country was passing through the "most critical period of its history since Confederation."

But if the Bi-Bi report was depressing, Liberal hopes rose again towards the end of March, when the Gallup poll told them that 45% of Canadians preferred Pearson as Prime Minister and only 29% liked Diefenbaker. The news did not worry the Chief; at a party celebrating his 25th year in Parliament a week later, he noted that Gladstone returned to power at the age of 82.

About the only person really concerned with youth that month seemed to be the leader of Quebec's National Union party, Daniel Johnson, who called upon it "to seize the party" at the policy convention March 19–21 in the Queen Elizabeth hotel. Johnson was an enigma in Canadian politics, a protégé of Duplessis, and Minister of Hydraulic Resources in his government, he had fought hard to win the leadership of the party in October, 1961, and had worked hard to reorganize and improve its image since then. A charming and courteous man, Johnson's even temper and unself-conscious manner contrasted strongly with Lesage's increasingly autocratic style. Yet behind the charm and courtesy, was concealed an ambition and a political skill the equal and in some ways greater than Lesage's. For instance, while Lesage became daily more Olympian, Johnson never forgot the basic lesson of parliamentary democracy: power comes from the people. He never lost contact with his electors personally or spiritually. No birth, marriage, or death took place in Bagot county, without Johnson knowing about it, and offering his congratulations or sympathy. So he was able to detect the rural unhappiness with Liberalism long before anyone else. And when 10,000 farmers marched on Quebec City to demand government action, the fine hand of the National Union was seen behind such catchy banners as "La Belle Province, Oh How Charming, Come and See the Peasants Starving," which drew national attention to farm incomes that ranged from $700 to $2,300.

Riding by riding, Johnson reorganized the National Union and, building on the resolutions passed at the 1961 leadership convention, he produced an acceptable election program in 1962. In March, 1965, he was responsible for the first full-scale policy convention in the party's history, ringing in such neutral panelists as Jean Marchand of the CSN and Louis Laberge of the Quebec Federation of Labor, Claude Ryan of *Le Devoir*, Economist François-Albert Angers, Jean-Noël Tremblay of Laval, Marcel Faribault, and Professor Jacques-Yvan Morin, to talk about constitutional issues facing Quebec. More than 3,000 delegates attended the Montreal convention and neutral consensus was that

Johnson's efforts at democratization seemed to be paying off with a good program, younger members in the party and the promise of good candidates in the next election.

Meanwhile, in Ottawa, the 2nd session of the 26th parliament was slowly coming to an end. On April 3, Parliament was prorogued, amid speculation that the Liberals would go to the country without calling a third session. The session had certainly been long enough (248 days) and wordy enough (14-million) for an MP to feel that an election might be pleasantly relaxing. And in terms of legislation, the 26th had been productive — the pension plan was through, so was the flag, redistribution, a new labor code, and the Columbia River treaty.

But the party leaders clearly felt otherwise. And on April 5, after a two-day break, Parliament was back in session for the third time. The throne speech contained enough new material to keep the house in session for two full years: the Company of Young Canadians, the War on Poverty, the Fulton-Favreau formula to amend the BNA Act, parliamentary procedural reforms, the Canada Development Corporation, medicare, an ombudsman, and a science council were but a few of the proposals. All of which led observers to suspect that an election could not be far away.

When Walter Gordon brought down his budget on April 26, election hawks were delighted. It showed government spending down $536 million, while the GNP had grown 9%, with hardly any inflation, while government revenue was up 14%. Gordon's 10% cut in personal income tax was not only justified but was clearly the stuff elections were made from. "It will," he said, "encourage and stimulate our working force . . . upon whose efforts our prosperity and progress depend." To say nothing about votes.

The upturn for the Federal Liberals coincided, as it often does, with provincial depression. In a prophetic piece, the Toronto *Star's* Richard Daignault and Dominique Clift wrote on Friday, April 9, "the Quiet Revolution is sick, sick, sick." Lesage was getting more conservative by the month and discouragement and weariness had set in throughout his Cabinet. "René Lévesque now acts as if he's fighting for his political life," they noted, while "Eric Kierans keeps mumbling that he's sick of the whole business. And Paul Gerin-Lajoie is keeping a stiff upper lip that doesn't quite hide his anger and his anxiety." They said the basic atmosphere of the Quiet Revolution had gone sour, and the signs were all around — Gérard Pelletier fired from *La Presse* the Friday before, a hold-back on reform legislation, and the ascension of conservative elements in the Liberal Party.

In *Le Devoir*, Claude Ryan detected the same thing and offered his own lucid interpretation: "It is the reflection of a group which, in a society undergoing rapid change, is hanging onto the levers of power, but which no longer has the nerve necessary to maintain the position that money and birth have conferred upon it." When once-docile public opinion slips away, "the bourgeoisie gets into a panic," said Ryan.

Everyone agreed that Lesage's ear now belonged to his Justice Minister, Claude Wagner — "a rigidly conservative mind," as Ryan put it.

Pelletier's re-appearance in print on April 14, as a twice-weekly columnist for *Le Devoir*, the Montreal *Star* and the Ottawa *Citizen*, was some comfort to Quebec's reformers. But on April 23, signs of real problems in the heart of the Quebec Liberal organization showed up with the angry resignation of Maurice Leroux, Lesage's senior public relations man (and architect of the November 11, 1962 television debate with Daniel Johnson, which was credited with providing the final push for the Liberal sweep four days later) declaring "I am leaving the Quebec Liberal Federation because I do not want to be an accomplice to the retreat now being carried out by the government." Leroux later became a separatist.

In May, it looked as if the campaign against the old guard politicians of the Quebec wing of the Federal Liberal party was likely to end in one of the bloodiest floor fights in party history. For months, Maurice Sauvé, the Minister of Forestry, had been marshalling his forces. A show-down would have destroyed all the bonhomie and up-beat feeling that had developed in the party since the end of the second session early in April. And this all on the eve of the symbolic "founding" of the Quebec wing of the Federal party, a $50-a-plate fund-raising dinner at the Queen Elizabeth to honor Pearson, Favreau and St. Laurent and set a confident mood for a soon-to-be-announced election.

There were long interpretive articles in *Le Devoir* on "what

Maurice Sauvé really wants" by Jean Pierre Fournier, and by the time the reader got to the fourth or fifth installment he had developed a deep sympathy for both the Liberal leadership and Sauvé himself, known by wags on Parliament Hill as "the James Bond of Confederation," who had threatened to resign three times in only three years as an MP. "The real reason (people don't like Sauvé) is that he is feared," Fournier concluded. "He represents a new type of Quebec politician whose strengths and intentions are still unknown but of whom one knows he is troublesome."

As it turned out, Sauvé's reform threat was de-fused by the skillful diplomacy of Lamontagne, Favreau and Bob Giguère, notably the last. And they did it, essentially, by giving Sauvé everything he wanted, except personal power.

Time and scandal had thinned the ranks of the Quebec campaign committee. Lionel Chevrier had gone to London as High Commissioner in 1964. Yvon Dupuis and Guy Rouleau, the chairman, had resigned voluntarily. Only Senators J. Eugène Lefrancois and Azellus Denis remained to be persuaded to step down, and the job was done, leaving Giguère as the only remaining member. "I am the only Old Guardsman left," he chuckled, and welcomed on board a new slate of officers that included such Young Turks as Michel Robert, the president of the Young Liberals, and Eugène Lapointe, his predecessor. "It's not a question of cleaning-up," said Giguère, "it's rejuvenation."

As to the election, Giguère allowed "I'm ready to go now." He predicted confidently that the Liberals would win 63 out of the 75 federal seats in Quebec. His enthusiasm was infectious, and the May 7 banquet in the garish ballroom of the Queen Elizabeth was fund-raising with a vengeance.

A fresh Liberal red carnation lay at each place setting at the banquet tables and, beside it, a maroon cardboard tube containing a miniature nylon maple-leaf flag, a flagpole, and a copy of its red-black-and-gold proclamation. And if that was not enough to set a mood of partisan sentimentality, they even shunted out old "Uncle Louis" St. Laurent for the occasion. Pink cheeked and very frail, his charcoal-grey, double-breasted suit hanging two sizes too large, forlornly recalling a statesmanly embonpoint, St. Laurent shuffled happily along behind Pearson to the table of honor, a fixed look of childlike delight on his face and a distant gleam in his eye, like an old thoroughbred who hears the hunt go past and dimly remembers the excitement of the chase.

There was a mood of expectancy, but it did not last long. By the end of May, with no election in sight and Guy Rouleau, Yvon Dupuis and Edmund Asselin still members of the party, Gérard Pelletier declared flatly in his column that the Quebec wing of the Liberals "will undergo no change of any importance between now and the next election." And he asked: "Is this a defeat for Maurice Sauvé alone or for the whole party?" Then Sauvé re-entered the controversy by telling members of the Montreal Labor Council that "the machine age in Quebec politics must be brought to an end."

Things were moving fast. On June 13, Rouleau and Dupuis were read out of the party and soon afterwards Edmund Asselin announced that he would not contest the next election. On June 28, the Dorion report was given to the government and, on the following day, Guy Favreau resigned as Minister of Justice. A week later, Pearson shuffled his cabinet. Favreau was made president of the Privy Council and retained his job as Quebec leader. His old portfolio was given to the Associate Minister of Defense, Lucien Cardin, a quietly competent neutral in the Quebec caucus's Old Guard versus New Guard battle. Maurice Sauvé stayed where he was in Forestry. The only new face in the cabinet was Jean-Luc Pepin (who had been a parliamentary secretary to the Minister of Trade and Commerce, Mitchell Sharp), who became a Minister without Portfolio. One observer called it a "listless game of musical chairs."

But what seemed listless in Ottawa, took on an entirely different sort of animation in the tortuous political byways of Quebec, where the new cabinet looked like a distinct triumph for Jean Marchand. In retrospect, the Quebec interpretation was right, and this is how it went: Marchand had decided long ago that he would not enter federal politics alone. Over the years, his short list of acceptable running mates had been whittled down to four people — Gérard Pelletier, Pierre Elliott Trudeau, Marc Lalonde and Jean-Paul Lefebvre. The two he wanted most were Pelletier and Trudeau, but Favreau had been trying to persuade him against them ever since the party made its offer at the end of January.

Favreau wanted Marchand to come alone, and he had made it clear that he considered both Pelletier and Trudeau unacceptable as Liberals, because of their past record of criticism and attacks on the party. Favreau also felt they would be political liabilities, but most of all, he could not forgive their personal attacks on the Prime Minister.

But the combination of the Dorion Report and the cabinet shuffle had unexpectedly placed Marchand in a position of unprecedented strength. The Dorion report had neutralized Favreau as a power-broker in the party, and his continued position as Quebec leader was window-dressing. Simultaneously, the cabinet shuffle, bringing in Jean-Luc Pepin, one of Maurice Sauvé's friends in the New Guard, had skillfully disarmed any criticism from Sauvé that the Old Guard was still in command. Finally, Pearson's refusal to promote Sauvé out of Forestry and into a more powerful portfolio had virtually left the field open to Marchand. His whim was now the party's command.

It was hardly surprising, therefore, that by early August control of the party finances had passed to a three-man committee chaired by Bob Giguère, and that talks between Giguère, Marchand, Favreau, and Lamontagne had been renewed with vigor. Marchand confidently told reporters on August 6 that he would be "making a decision before the end of August." He did not miss the deadline by much.

By the end of August, all of Marchand's demands had been agreed to except his choice of running mates. He still insisted on Pelletier, Trudeau and Lefebvre. The Liberals still did not want them. After one inconsequential session, a negotiator exploded, "Marchand's demands make Maurice Sauvé look like a piker." Giguère was slowly coming around to the idea, yet, still he balked at Trudeau. "One day he does his hair one way, another day it's different. The farmers wouldn't go for it. Then there's his leather jackets and jeans. It would be too hard."

But finally, early in September, the party agreed and at last, on September 10, the whole agonizing process ended. For better or worse, they were in.

Claude Ryan had forecast their entry in a typically perceptive editorial in *Le Devoir* the week before. "In the choice these men will make is the outline of the option of a generation . . . the phenomenon can be summed up as follows: we are perhaps on the verge of witnessing the meeting of the post-war neo-democrats with the ingenious assimilator that the Liberal Party has always been in Canada."

Marchand, Pelletier and Trudeau were quickly nicknamed "The Three Wise Men," in English Canada, while in nationalist Quebec they were dubbed "*Les Trois Colombes*," — the three pigeons, a rather less romantic image.

Marchand and Pelletier were both well known to the public, and it took no time to find them ridings. Marchand had counties in both Montreal and Quebec City vying for the honor. He finally settled on the tough Créditiste riding of Quebec West to test his mettle. Pelletier went to Montreal Hochelaga, where the Liberal incumbent wanted to retire after 25 years of unbroken service, and the association had asked for someone with a labor-union, working-class background to suit the area. "They were tickled pink when we suggested Pelletier," said Giguère.

But Trudeau was a different matter. Trudeau possessed every draw-back a Quebec politician could have. He was unknown, unconventional and unmarried. Moreover, he was an intellectual and was believed to have radical left-wing tendencies. As Giguère and Favreau had realized long before, it was now clear to the party that he would be unacceptable in a French-Canadian riding, and awfully hard to sell in an English one.

Giguère and Favreau rapidly concluded that they would have to parachute Trudeau — and teach him how to jump at the same time. They selected the Montreal riding of Mount Royal, because it was going to be vacant, because it was polyglot and sophisticated enough to accept a 'special' candidate of Trudeau's style, and because it was Liberal and likely to elect another Liberal.

Mount Royal was the riding of the Speaker of the House, Alan Macnaughton, who wanted to retire from the House to return to private business. But he also hankered after the Senate, and that hankering gave Favreau and Giguère the lever they needed to persuade Macnaughton to leave the choice of his successor open. They knew they could not ask Macnaughton to endorse Trudeau, because he had already told one of his campaign workers, Dr. Stuart Smith, that he could have the succession.

Macnaughton was understandably miffed at not being let in on the negotiations with Trudeau ("he just wanted to perform the laying-on of hands" said one organizer) and at being put in an embarrassing position with Smith. So, on September 13, he decided to announce his retirement without tipping anyone off in advance. This threw the party organization into chaos — a bit of willfulness, that Macnaughton was made to pay for; he had to sweat it out for nine long months before being summoned to the Senate.

Within hours of Macnaughton's statement, party headquarters were besieged by would-be candidates for the Mount Royal riding. Leading the pack was Milton Klein, the incumbent in Cartier, who regarded himself as representative in Ottawa of Montreal's Jewish population. His argument was that the Jewish population was falling in Cartier but rising in Mount Royal, therefore he should go to Mount Royal and Trudeau to Cartier. But when party headquarters checked it out with Mount Royal Liberals, the answer they got was that they would prefer Trudeau to Klein. Yet there was no way they could convince Klein of this, until a number of prominent Jewish people entered the Mount Royal nomination race, including Dr. Victor Goldbloom who is today a member of the Quebec Provincial Legislature.

Another problem in getting Trudeau nominated was a fight between party headquarters and the riding association on who was eligible to be a voting delegate.

But at last, on October 7, in the town hall of the Town of Mount Royal, 400 voting delegates approved Trudeau as their candidate by a wide majority, and the third wise man was home.

The rest was anti-climactic. The most vigorous opposition during the election campaign for the next four and a half weeks came from Trudeau's old friend Charles Taylor — the same NDP candidate in the same riding that he had worked so hard for, just two years earlier. Trudeau applied himself to campaigning with the thoroughness with which he approached everything else. He did what his organizers asked him to do, went to coffee parties, charmed the women, and impressed the men with his clear logic and articulate style. He wore sober, three-piece suits and ties and never once had to be sent home to change, as Giguère had to tell him to do before his nomination, when he showed up in filthy jeans and a ragged pullover to meet some dignitaries on a Sunday after-noon. In short, he was the model candidate. And he took friendly advice about not spending his own money so literally that his total campaign contribution was $150, and the county carried a $4,000 deficit until early in 1968, when party headquarters finally paid up.

Thanks to hard work of his own and careful management by Giguère and others, he won the riding easily, with a plurality of 13,135 (against Macnaughton's all-time record of 28,793 in 1963), doing far better than either Pelletier (7,029) or Marchand (849).

If only the Liberal Party as a whole had done as well. The November 8 election was a near disaster to the Liberals who returned with only 129 seats, a gain of exactly two over 1963, while the Conservatives were up seven with 99 and the NDP gained three for 21. As *Time* put it, "if the TV networks had merely replayed films of election night 1963, it would have saved everyone a lot of money and trouble."

Walter Gordon, the Minister of Finance, paid the required political penalty for the failure of his election strategy, resigning from the cabinet on November 11. Keith Davey, the national Liberal organizer, soon followed suit and was made a Senator at the aged of 39, confirming suspicions that Pearson's plans to reform the Senate had been postponed indefinitely.

And so, when Jean Marchand became Minister of Citizenship and Immigration on December 18, 1965, (succeeding Tremblay) all effective opposition had vanished.

The Conservatives also returned to Parliament with their prob-lems partly solved. It was now clear beyond any doubt that they would not regain power with Diefenbaker — clear, that was, to everybody except Diefenbaker. Since January, columnists had been suggesting candidates for the succession. As Anthony Westell wrote in the *Globe & Mail Magazine* back in January, "Stanfield, Fulton, Roblin, Hees, Hamilton, Robarts — round and round goes the same list of names, as Conservatives endlessly discuss possible successors to the Old Chief. If there is an election this spring, and Diefenbaker can win it, he will, of course, be unassailable as Tory leader. But barring that improbable event, his days in politics are numbered."

But Diefenbaker beat back the challenge in early February and Robert Stanfield, the man most often mentioned as his successor, reduced speculation further by rejecting the idea of leaving Nova Scotia for Ottawa. To a question of whether he had considered federal politics, he replied memorably, "Yes, in much the way I have considered ski-jumping." With that, the Tory revolt went back to a state of suspended animation, flaring briefly now and then, as when Leon Balcer finally quit in April, and Davie Fulton announced that he would return to federal politics at the next election.

By May, with an election almost certain, Dalton Camp and the other party leaders were actively involved in cosmetic repairs to the party image. "I'd rather see our party reconstructed from the ashes of its defeat in the 1963 election, than attempt to rebuild a party on the quagmire of Federal Liberalism in Quebec," he said bravely during the height of the Sauvé revolt. And a month later, he could say without hesitation that Diefenbaker "had been more sinned against than sinning," while at that very moment Conservatives in Diefenbaker's own province of Saskatchewan were tapping each MP for a $500 contribution to keep their office in Saskatoon open due to lack of public support.

Peter Newman noted that the Chief was "trapped between his eroding authority and his desperate dreams. John Diefenbaker has become a politician without a party." On June 8, the Conservative caucus refused to go along with Diefenbaker's plan to obstruct Liberal proposals for parliamentary reform.

For a brief moment in September, it looked as if Diefenbaker might be making a come-back. The Conservative party had closed ranks completely, and while touring Quebec's solidly Tory Eastern Townships, Diefenbaker observed that "It's like 1957 and 1958, I can feel the under-current. Things are starting to roll." But the sensation was illusory.

Dalton Camp himself entered the election in Toronto, challenging Trade Minister Mitchell Sharp in Eglinton and lost; Frank McGee, a bright young hope of 1957, reappeared in York-Scarborough, and lost also; while George Hees tossed up the Montreal and Canadian stock exchanges at a moment's notice to plunge back into politics in Northumberland, Ontario, beating Professor Pauline Jewett, the able Liberal incumbent, by 563 votes, to the regret of all Liberals and many Conservatives. About the only Conservative who stuck to his principles was Leon Balcer, who resisted all blandishments to return to the fold, declaring "there is no place for a French Canadian in the party of Mr. Diefenbaker."

For any normal politician, the results of the November 8 election would have been a clear vote of no confidence. And this was what the Tory strategists were hoping. By making a genuine and massive gesture of support, they were determined that Diefenbaker would not be able to say later that the party had let him down. Right across the country, throughout September and October, Conservatives campaigned with the Chief in shoulder-to-shoulder displays of federal-provincial solidarity. On October 8, in Toronto, 7,000 party members were witness as the panjandrums of Conservatism, Ontario's John Robarts, Manitoba's Duff Roblin and Nova Scotia's Robert Stanfield all joined Diefenbaker on the platform for a mass rally at the University of Toronto's Varsity Stadium off Bloor Street. No greater display of support could have been asked.

But it made no difference. When the votes were counted on November 8, the Progressive Conservatives wound up with a net gain of seven seats. It was no longer a question of whether Diefenbaker had to go; the only question was when and how. For a time, the party hoped that Diefenbaker would make the decision himself.

From November until May, the Conservative chieftains waited to hear his resignation, like officers in a Prussian regimental mess anticipating the shot that would tell them their disgraced colonel had taken the gentlemanly way out. It never came. And slowly, reluctantly, the dread machinery of court-martial was set into motion.

VI

A Boundless and Bottomless Sea

I conclude, therefore, that unless it commands its own
arms no principality is secure; rather, it is dependent on
fortune, since there is no valor and no loyalty to defend
it when adversity comes.

— *Machiavelli*

WHILE THE Conservatives waited for Diefenbaker, and the rest of
the Liberals got over the shock of not getting a majority, Marchand,
Pelletier and Trudeau quickly consolidated their position inside
the party. By the time the Quebec caucus met in early January,
their position had been strengthened still further by another
Favreau gaffe: the appointment of dental technician, Jean Pierre
Côté, to the Postmaster General's portfolio. Since Côté's only
apparent qualification for the post was his close friendship with
Favreau, caucus reaction was summed up well by the Member for
Bonaventure, Albert Béchard, who wondered, "if they are looking
for someone insignificant to stuff in the cabinet, why not me?"

The progressive elements in caucus who polarized around the
"three wise men", included the Minister of Mines, Jean-Luc Pepin,
the Minister of Industry, Charles Mills Drury, and of course
Maurice Lamontagne. Strong support also came from the younger
members, most notably from a regular contributor to *Cité Libre*,
Jean-Pierre Goyer, who had won Guy Rouleau's old seat in
Montreal Dollard.

Goyer realized, perhaps more fully than his peers, that Pearson
was on the verge of retiring and that a French Canadian had to
be found soon for the leadership. He was convinced, moreover,
that the only man, French or English, who could solve Canada's
constitutional problems was Pierre Trudeau, and it was only
Trudeau's entry that made him run, too.

"Giguère called me about two months before the election was

announced, saying that the party needed young people. I was very hesitant. It did not seem to me that much could be done to reform the party. But then Marchand, Pelletier and Trudeau agreed to go. And that decided me."

To prepare himself as the self-appointed Trudeau propagandist in caucus, Goyer re-read all his back copies of *Cité Libre*, plus anything else of Trudeau's he could find. "I know Trudeau best by what he's written — and it's the best way to know him. He doesn't deviate from his writings. Just about everything he thinks is there."

Like most other new members, Goyer was horrified by the attitude of the Quebec caucus, which seemed to spend most of its time squabbling over patronage, and the rest of it pussy-footing around trying to avoid offending anyone. At one of his first meetings, for instance, he heard the supposedly reform-minded Minister of Forestry, Maurice Sauvé, make the astonishing statement that Quebec Liberal MPs should not publicly disagree with Quebec Liberal MLAs. (And this at a time when a Quebec provincial MLA, Eric Kierans, had caused consternation in Ottawa by writing directly to American officials, without telling Ottawa, to tell them that the Johnson administration's voluntary "guidelines" for restricting foreign investment infringed upon Canadian jurisdiction, since they affected Canadian companies which were U.S. subsidiaries.) Sauvé was rebuked in front of caucus by Drury who indicated that such a suggestion would lead to "dangerous" passivity. But Sauvé, it seemed, was more anxious to keep on the good side of his friend, Jean Lesage, than he was to make the federal presence effective in Quebec. (Sauvé's attitude to Lesage would change drastically after June 5, but by then his semi-detachment from the reform wing would be well established.)

Another person frozen out by the reformers was the Quebec leader, Guy Favreau, whose role they quietly took over without actually attacking the man himself. Though they did not conceal their scorn for the idea of a Quebec leader. "The concept of a Quebec lieutenant is really the black Negro king theory translated into the federal field," said Trudeau, who drew the analogy between the Colonial Governor and a tribal chief. "It would really be more sensible for the Prime Minister from now on to ask for a consensus from his Quebec colleagues," he suggested.

The reformers also organized a weekly lecture series to acquaint members with the problems facing the country and with their duties as members of Parliament. Professors of law, economics and sociology from Ottawa and Montreal would lecture the caucus twice a week, with permission from the party whips. "And the boys accepted it," says Goyer. "They found out that there were problems in politics apart from patronage." While old guardsmen pointedly stayed away, younger members who came to sneer, stayed to learn.

Not surprisingly, one of the most frequent caucus lecturers was Pierre Elliott Trudeau, and as his influence spread so did his followers. Within months he was the unrivaled intellectual leader of the caucus. And it was no accident that when Pearson decided, early in 1966, that the Privy Council should have a full-time Quebec constitutional expert on its staff, the man they called was Trudeau's alter-ego, Marc Lalonde.

As it turned out, Lalonde was too busy in his private law practice to spare the time the Privy Council job required, so he took another, on a task-force that was looking into securities regulations and corporate disclosures.

When that job was over, in November, 1966, Lalonde stayed on Pearson's staff for yet another six months, as an adviser in federal-provincial affairs, still commuting to Ottawa three days a week. Finally, in March, 1967, he joined the Privy Council office as a special advisor on constitutional matters, specifying that his leave of absence from his law firm would be for more than six months but less than a year. It was not until August, 1968, that Lalonde resigned himself to the fact that his tour as a civil servant was not going to be temporary and finally gave up his Montreal law practice.

Thus, within months of Trudeau's election as a Member of Parliament, Lalonde became a constant element in his life as a politician. His role as adviser, friend and confidant continued unbroken, and the architects of the Canadian Manifesto of 1964 were to become the plotters of the Canadian Phenomenon of 1968. By maintaining close contacts with Montreal through his law practice, Lalonde was able to keep Trudeau constantly informed of every twist in Quebec political thought. Trudeau, in turn, through his position as a parliamentary secretary to the Prime Minister, was able to maintain his ascendancy in the Quebec caucus and at the same time, with all the extraordinary political skill that he was starting to display, he was becoming invaluable to Pearson, complementing the role played by Lalonde.

By mid-February, the reform group had elected their own nominee as chairman of the Quebec caucus, soundly defeating the candidate put up by Favreau as Quebec leader. And with control of the caucus now total, it was no trouble to make sure that the French-language co-chairman for the Federal party's policy convention was one of their men, too. Claude Frenette, then just 27, was designated for the job at the convention in October, 1966. He was a Montreal lawyer and former executive assistant to Maurice Sauvé. An old-young man, with the bland face of a buddha and a mind with the precision of a computer, Frenette was to play an important part in the plans of the reform group, providing he handled himself well in October, which he did.

Thus, with everything cut, dried and packed, it was not surprising that the founding convention of the Quebec Section of the Liberal Federation of Canada, at Quebec City's turreted Chateau Frontenac on March 24, 25, and 26, was dominated by Marchand, Trudeau, and the reform group around them. For it was they who planned it, invited most of the speakers, wrote most of the speeches and then graciously accepted all the credit for what was indeed a triumphant reassertion of the federal presence in Quebec.

As several observers ironically noted, the success of the convention in Quebec City was made possible by René Lévesque and the other Quebec autonomists who had forced the Liberal party to break into federal and provincial units, thus permitting the federal half to pass resolutions that would have been roundly rejected had the provincial half been there.

Thus the most important achievement of the Quebec City convention was a near-unanimous decision to keep both Quebec in Confederation and the existing constitution, the British North America Act.

Trudeau summed up the convention: "The main thing is that we rejected any kind of special status for Quebec. In essence the meeting was an affirmation that federalism can't work, unless all the provinces are in basically the same relation toward the central government, and that the federal system as it was conceived by the Fathers of Confederation is still sound." He pointed out that the provinces already have jurisdiction over everything that closely involves the individual, such as health, education, and social welfare, while the central government controls only those things which govern the overall welfare of the nation, such as the general economic situation and its controls, and monetary and fiscal policy.

Prime Minister Pearson, who was beginning to feel his successors panting on his neck, made a strong speech at the convention which put them back in line. "I am resolved to carry on as long as I have strength and vigor, and the party wants me," he declared. "Let there be no doubt about that."

That was fine by Trudeau's timetable.

"When you think of the next big hurdles, bilingualism and constitutional rights, Pearson is the best man to achieve results. If these battles are won, Pearson will probably emerge very strong," he told Peter Newman in the Toronto *Star*. "If they are lost, better to lose them and then change Liberal leaders, than to change leaders and then lose them."

The *Star's* Quebec correspondent, Dominique Clift, noted the effect Trudeau's speeches had on Federal Liberal delegates in Quebec. "Trudeau's ideas supply them with a kind of respectability and help them overcome the open contempt with which they are held by provincial Liberals."

The question of leadership had never been far from the surface in the Liberal Party, since Pearson, for the third time, failed to win a decisive victory in April, 1963. The debacle of November, 1965, merely confirmed the narrowly held but growing conviction that Pearson would have to step down — soon. This point of view was not discouraged by Pearson, despite his statement in Quebec, March 26, that he would carry on as long as he had "strength and vigor and the party wants me," clear enough indication that he would not outstay his welcome.

Running hardest in the non-race during the spring of 1966 was Paul Theodore Hellyer, 43, the Minister of Defence, whose program to unify Canada's army, navy and air force into one unit was progressing and had successfully infuriated the Opposition.

The final task was to pass an act saying that Canada's armed forces would in fact be unified, and as Parliament headed to this juncture, late in 1966, Hellyer was the victim and beneficiary of widespread publicity, ranging from a controversy over the purchase of 125 Northrop F-5 tactical jet fighter interceptors to the actual benefits that had accrued from unification.

A growing number of people saw Hellyer as the next Prime Minister, certainly he did himself and so did his rivals, with the result that by March, Paul Martin, Mitchell Sharp, Robert Winters, John Turner and Allan MacEachen were all seeking platforms to keep their names fresh in the public mind. But Hellyer seemed to be leading the pack, and until Pearson cried halt at the Quebec convention, he was all set to take the Chateau Frontenac by storm, with a tape recorder full of French lessons in his attaché case.

All that was lacking to make the still-undeclared race a major one was a French-Canadian entry. But there, all eyes were on Lesage.

Jean Lesage wanted to be Prime Minister of Canada, there was no doubt about it, and the ambition was a reasonable one for a man who had achieved so much for Quebec in such a short time. It became an open secret that there would be an election in 1966, and party propagandists hastened to disarm criticism by pointing out that although their mandate ran until late in 1967, it would be inappropriate to hold an election during Centennial Year, when Expo would be taking place and the Premier of Quebec playing an important role.

Lesage himself steadily burnished his statesmanlike image, alternately squelching and supporting Kierans (as soon as he saw which way the wind was blowing on the guidelines, for instance) and Lévesque, and making vague speeches.

The director of *Le Devoir*, Claude Ryan, took him to task, on February 11, for his rather misty views, quoting two extracts from a speech Lesage had made earlier in the month on Quebec's constitutional desires, to prove his point.

Lesage had said: "The emergence of a special status for Quebec comes much less from a juridical position on our part, than from the evolution of our political regime, in which most of the provinces do not reject the idea of centralization of powers in Ottawa, while we, on the contrary, hold out for the existing decentralization."

Lesage added: "Quebec never asked for a special status, just recognition of her constitutional rights."

Ryan felt this position was alright as far as it went, but it did not go far enough: Quebec wanted to play a greater role than that conferred upon her by the constitution, he said, and that desire had led to unprecedented international initiatives. (The Quebec desire for a cultural treaty with France had caused a ruckus between External Affairs Minister Paul Martin and Quebec Education Minister Paul Gérin-Lajoie in April, 1965, but had led to the *accord cadre*, or cultural umbrella treaty, that Canada had signed with France seven months later, which gave Quebec the right to go ahead with any agreements it wanted to under that protocol.)

However, Ryan said, there was still a widespread feeling that a new constitution was needed. He also chided Lesage for his pride in his government's constitutional "pragmatism" and warned that pragmatism pushed too far could be termed opportunism and could force a statesman or a government "to renounce today a word given yesterday." He cited the Fulton-Favreau amending formula that Lesage applauded in 1964 but abandoned later as impractical.

The legislature recessed over Easter, which was early that year (April 11), and Lesage decided it would do his ministers good to lose their winter pallor in the sun on Miami Beach. All cabinet ministers, except Kierans, who was looking after things in Quebec and who had taken a cruise in the Caribbean in March, were summoned to Florida — at government expense. Lévesque, on holiday in Bermuda with his family, was ordered to fly in too. The cabinet was divided between the Surf Club and the Seaway Apartments on Collins Street and augmented by certain prominent Liberal advisors and financiers such as Claude Ducharme, the director of *La Presse* and close friend of Lesage and Maurice Sauvé; Guy Gagnon, the chief organizer; and Arthur Dupres, the campaign manager.

Their decision: a team election that would use all their big guns and draw maximum support. The date would be Sunday, June 5, exactly eight weeks away.

The cabinet filtered back to Quebec City during the week following Easter weekend. And on Monday, April 18, well-tanned from daily rounds of golf at La Gorce Club, on Indian Creek, Jean Lesage summoned newsmen to the pale-oak panelled cabinet room shortly before noon to give them the word. "Gentlemen, the house has been dissolved."

His ministers smirked confidently as Lesage allowed that the reason for the election was that he needed "a mandate" for the upcoming federal-provincial conferences. He had, of course, asked Pearson to put the one in Victoria back a week or two, he said, so that he could get the election out of the way before attending it. He predicted "an immense" Liberal majority and the Organizer-in-Chief, Alcide Courcy, chimed in with the estimate of 90 seats in the enlarged 108-seat house.

The Liberal strategy, as planned in Miami, was to promote Lesage and his team, as the slogan said: *"Les 108 candidats de l'équipe Lesage; pour un Québec plus humain — les droits et le bien-être du citoyen."* The message was clear, Lesage and his team of 108 candidates were for a more humane Quebec, the rights and welfare of the citizen.

But as the campaign progressed, disturbing rumors started floating back that even though the team was the main attraction, only the coach was doing any traveling. Such key speakers as Claude Wagner, René Lévesque, Eric Kierans, Paul Gérin-Lajoie and Pierre Laporte were told to stay in their counties unless the speakers' bureau called for them. All ridings had to place their requests through campaign headquarters.

Meanwhile, Lesage swept around the province like President de Gaulle, hogged all the television time and kept his hand firmly on the half-million-dollar war chest that had been made available for the election. He spoke sonorously about the $463-million Quebec had spent on super-highways, when the audience wanted to hear about jobs and taxes — specifically, more of the former and less of the latter.

Finally, it was Sunday, June 5, election day, and 3,190,904 Quebeckers went to the polls.

That evening, the turreted Winter Club was ready for a triumph of a size and baroque display deemed fit for Lesage's *politique de grandeur*. No location in Quebec City would have filled the role better, with its pseudo-Chateau exterior and its dark and massive oak beams, glassed-in spectators' bar, and huge indoor tennis courts, overlooking the plains of Abraham.

Lesage was there early, soon after 8 p.m., the tan he acquired at Easter in Miami deepened by a round of golf that afternoon at his favorite Cap Rouge Club, exercise he eased by using an electric golf cart. As a result, he was rather rotund, and even his new pale grey silk summer suit could not hide his portliness. His wife Corinne, on the other hand, had been on a diet, and she was the picture of an elegant first lady, dressed for the triumph in a new partisan red-and-white silk dress. Jules, their eldest son, as porky as his papa, was at his jovial best. Only little Raymond, a pre-teener, seemed subdued.

The family was escorted upstairs to the spectactors' gallery and Jean and Corinne were royally esconced in two matching yellow high-backed upholstered chairs, facing a 24-inch television set. Applauding, Liberal party supporters and strategists, wives and friends, clustered around them, grabbing vacant chairs and sofas, occasionally glancing from the screen to one of the huge return boards, which had been erected around the walls, manned by young Liberals wearing head-sets.

Miles away, in St. Pie de Bagot (population, 4,000), the leader of the Opposition had no such elaborate party or potted palms. Daniel Johnson, then 51, leader of the National Union, was spending that night as he always did, at his country home in the quiet Southern Quebec farming country that he had represented for 20 years.

Both men were attended by squads of assistants and newsmen, plugged into the world by the snaking black coaxial cables and power lines which feed on the agonies of leadership. But there was no doubt that Lesage was awaiting apotheosis while Johnson merely wanted votes.

They did not have to wait long. By 9:30, results were sagging badly, and a few minutes later, stern ward-heeler guards expelled newsmen from Lesage's presence. By the time another hour had crept past, disaster had struck with such finality that the guards abandoned their posts for the bar, and Lesage was again accessible.

He sat hunched forward in his chair, elbows on his knees, chain-smoking his way through his victory cigars and then onto any brand of smoke he could bum from his neighbors. His face was vacant, mouth slacked open, only his rheumy eyes remained animated. He stared at the set myopically from about four feet away, as if he were trying to will it to report good news.

Corinne was so upset she could no longer remain seated and she wandered through the crowd of standees, biting her nails and eyeing the television nervously as each return came in.

Son Jules was convinced it was all a journalistic plot. "They are all a bunch of whores waiting to be paid off," he repeated loudly. His mother soon caught the refrain. "I hope the *Union Nationale* take away your freedom to write what you please," she said.

Only Lesage managed to keep his temper. "Voyons, Maman," he said to his wife in gentle reproof. "It's not their fault."

By 11:15, the victory crowd had thinned to a point of embarrassment; Lesage and his cronies were left to face disaster alone. Even the newsmen, sensing a family tragedy, went quietly downstairs.

Five minutes later, the first of four Lesage ministers had been defeated and the NU went into a 54 to 52 lead.

By midnight, it was all over. Jean Lesage ceased to be a factor. Moreover, due to the separation of the federal and provincial Liberal parties he could not even be a king-maker. Suddenly, there was a whole new equation. For the Liberals, a French-Canadian candidate had to be found within the federal ranks. For the Conservatives, there was the tantalizing hint of power if they could get along with the new Quebec leader.

Yet there was also something chilling about the National Union victory. About Daniel Johnson's victory statement, when he rejected Lesage's claims of "moral victory" because of the Liberals' 6% plurality: "If you leave out the Montreal English vote, and the Montreal Jewish vote," the National Union got a good majority. It was an ominous foretaste of the old nationalist xenophobia reasserting itself — a revealing sign that, however much the NU appeared to have reformed, it was still the same old authoritarian, clerico-bourgeois group at heart. What of all those bright young candidates? Bright young people live in cities, and most of the NU's most promising candidates were in city ridings, soundly trounced by the Liberals. So Johnson came to power with his rural members, many of them holdovers from the Duplessis era whose concept of parliamentary democracy was to keep quiet and do whatever you were told.

A man who watched the National Union victory in Quebec with close attention was Dalton Camp. Only two weeks before, he had been the main speaker at a super-secret private dinner in Toronto's Albany Club, a Tory Mecca at 91 King Street East identifiable only by the foot-high brass numbers by the door.

The dinner was black-tie and attended by a group of Senators and multi-millionaires who make up Canada's top Tories. They were the members of the Albany, and they had asked Camp, as national president of the Progressive Conservative Association, to talk to them about the most pressing subject in the party — its leadership.

Several disturbing things had precipitated the dinner. In mid-April, Tory problems had worsened, with the dismissal of Flora MacDonald from party headquarters in Ottawa. She had served the party well for 10 years, but her inspiration was not John Diefenbaker. Thus she was dispensable.

The man who wielded the hatchet was James Johnston, the acting National Director of the party, described by Peter Newman as "probably the only Ph.D. in economics, in or out of captivity, who has unbounded faith in John Diefenbaker." Only the intervention of Diefenbaker loyalist "Yukon Erik" Nielsen had stopped caucus from passing a unanimous vote of confidence in Flora, and that was only by pointing out that it would mean unanimous no-confidence in Doctor Johnston, as he called himself.

Obviously, the party had to reassert itself. Then, the day before the Albany Club meeting, the Young Progressive Conservatives of Canada had satirized the monarchy in a sketch and had expressed doubts about its validity in Canada. Fraser Kelly reported to the *Telegram* from the convention that "the young men and women at these conferences are fed up with present politics and politicians." These were happenings that scandalized top Tories. But what was to be done? So they called on Camp.

"This is perhaps the story of my life," he said at the start. "I am becoming the last resort of the Tory party — and when all else fails, including plots, plans and palace revolutions, they turn to me for a speech to sum it all up. Roblin once told me I was becoming 'the lay Pope' of the Conservative faithful."

The opening may have been inauspicious, but what followed would become a landmark in the history of the Conservative Party in Canada. For this was the speech which contained the essence of his widely-publicized address to the Toronto Junior Board of Trade, on September 20, and of the speeches that followed. But the Albany speech was the first, and the best. It pulled no punches. It was blunt to the point of being terse and in terms of the party itself, it had an effect out of all proportion to the size of the audience. It gave the party the rationale it was seeking to demand a leadership conference without being disloyal. It was a tour de force — fifteen pages, triple-spaced, and in a lean, serifless type-face in keeping with its message: Diefenbaker must go.

Camp knew he was putting his political neck on the block, and that on past form his chances were not good. It was a brave thing to do; as the *Globe & Mail* said in an editorial on September 22, "it is a service to his party and indeed his country."

He moved into his topic swiftly, all the same, admitting to "some inward trepidation. It seems to me there are limits to the power of political leadership, and these should, from time to time, be examined and appraised," he said. "Baldwin once told his party that it had but two choices in its relations with its leader: 'Either back him or sack him'. Like much of what Baldwin would say, it was not without some measure of truth and hypocrisy.

"Leaders are fond of reminding followers of their responsi-bilities and duties to leadership. And followers sometimes need reminding. What is seldom heard, however, is a statement on the responsibilities of the leader to those he leads. Leaders are fond of saying how arduous their labor, how complex the circumstances, and how unfair the press criticism, as though they had been called to their high office by some supreme power rather than by those they are addressing."

Camp said some leaders really do consider their promotion ordained by divinity. Certain politicians on the other hand, he noted, think that the only job of a leader is to win elections. "If this were true, then the party system is a deadly waste of time and enterprise and we would do better to recruit leaders through the classified pages or by public opinion polls."

He went on to note that leaders are chosen "through the admittedly imperfect" convention system, based on mutual support. "It is not, as every politician knows, a lifetime contract. And this is the point. A leader inherits both a party's history and the title deeds to its future. In fact, he is likely, unless he is a Kennedy, to be the embodiment of his party's recent history, since it is assumed he will have the virtue of a considerable past political experience."

Thus, he leads the party "along its natural course," and by accepting responsibility for its future seeks "fresh insight in new circumstances, and the assistance of contemporary lieutenants, from among whom will come inevitably his successors. This latter is part of the British genius for parliamentary democracy. Again, the leader should give at least as much loyalty to his followers, as he demands from them. This is not personal loyalty, but rather loyalty to the party, to its continuing strength, best interests and well-being. . . . In the relationship between the leader and the led, there is a mutuality of interest and, as well, a continuing common experience of discovery, learning and revelation. Where the leader does not know the limits of his power, he must be taught, and when he is indifferent to the interest of his party, he must be reminded."

Camp dismissed as absurd the philosophy which says a leader does not need support when he is right, but requires it when he is wrong, since it would "convert supporters into hacks, and leaders into tyrants. The party is not the embodiment of the leader, but rather the other way round; the leader is transient, the party permanent. The argument is made that to question at any time, or in any matter, the acts of leaders will invoke a grave question of non-confidence. This is an argument for sheep, not for men."

He described the Conservative Party as being in "an unusual hiatus. The spokesmen for our party stand on public platforms and, badgered by the leadership question, they retreat behind vague sophistries." He said the situation could not continue "where the party appears to have leadership it follows but will not support" . . . "because the response of silence makes all of us conspirators. This is not a role anyone wants. No one could want it less than I do. So you can either resign your office, or resign yourself to events, or make some effort to resolve the question."

He spoke of the responsibilities of party officials, and he proposed three steps. "First, what almost everyone suspects and hopes should be confirmed — and that is that in the next general election, whether in 1968 or 1969, the party be under fresh leadership and equipped with new policy. There is not any value any longer in avoiding that consideration. There is great benefit to the party if the principals to such a decision would simply indicate the inevitability of that fact. To have such an understanding would, more than anything, close the gulf between caucus and party at large, between the various factions, and between the regional blocs within the party.

"Second, that potential candidates and aspirants for the leadership be encouraged to make their views known as to their position, if any, on various matters of public policy and that the National Association provide suitable occasions for such discussions by providing party forums where this may be done."

Here Camp clearly forecast the Montmorency policy conference of the following August, in many ways the most important party meeting of the decade.

"The next leader of this party should not take the party by surprise," he added, and the audience laughed.

Finally, Camp recommended that "we should agree that a convention be called no later than the spring of 1968. If there is to be a change of guard within the party, and new men are to come forward, I would hope they would arrive before, and not after, the convention, so that the policies passed by that body will bear some reasonable resemblance to the new force and new attitudes of the new guard." He paused. "It was rather the other way around in 1956." Laughter again.

Then he became serious. "If only we could, as a party, forget the past and have some secure knowledge of future decisions, we could then unite as we have not been united in many years. All it requires is a confrontation with reality. I would like to see the party give to its present leader the respect, loyalty and affection his contribution and his courage merit. I would like to see the parliamentary party and ourselves, outside it, united in common purpose and harmonious understanding."

Many of Canada's leading young Conservatives were at the

dinner, as well as the most prominent senior Tories in the land, and Camp cautioned all of them with firmness and resolution. "We cannot reconstitute this party without Quebec. We cannot do it without youth. We cannot do so without the cities. . . . The future of this party is not in any man's hands, but the responsibility of all of us, each to his own as he sees them."

Camp finished with a quotation by Michael Oakshott, "the Chancellor of my sometime old school, the London School of Economics". The quotation was a good one: "In politics, men sail a boundless and bottomless sea; there is neither harbor nor shelter, nor floor for anchorage, neither starting place nor appointed destination. The enterprise is to keep afloat on an even keel; the sea is both friend and enemy, and the seamanship consists in using the resources of a traditional manner of behavior in order to make a friend of every hostile occasion." The Tory revolt had turned onto its final tack.

Camp's concern with Quebec increased with Daniel Johnson's unexpected victory. He was no stranger to Quebec or Johnson, who had helped him plan the French Canadian guest list for the 1964 Fredericton conference, which Marcel Fairbault attended. Camp spoke Berlitz-improved French and had become deeply involved in the problems of the Quebec caucus since the Balcer-Paul revolt of 1964. He was under no illusions about the help the federal party could expect from the National Union. Nevertheless, the Johnson victory, while hardly a cause for unbridled rejoicing by Tory sophisticates, did prove that conservatism was not extinct in Quebec, whatever the mutation of the NU variety.

This added immediacy to the question of party leadership, since a new leader who was acceptable to Quebec could clearly make for greater headway than one who was not. Another factor making leadership an issue was the continuing decline in the popularity of the Liberal leader, Lester Pearson, whose resignation was now favored by 40% of those polled (33% wanted him to stay). This meant that a Liberal leadership convention might soon intervene, and Camp was certain that the party which changed leaders first stood the best chance of winning the next election. The Conservatives had to be first.

A provincial election in Manitoba kept Camp busy most of June electioneering on Premier Duff Roblin's behalf. His efforts were rewarded on June 23, with a fourth straight win for Manitoba's Conservatives, though a slightly reduced majority.

But enough people were wearing "I Luff Duff" buttons to convince Camp that Roblin was still a primary contender for the leadership.

By the inverse ratio rule of political fortunes in the two party system, Conservative prospects brightened perceptibly in June and July as the Liberals got rapped for a grossly inflationary, 30% pay raise to the Seaway workers in mid-June, and Paul Hellyer was forced to contend with some admirals who were willing to sacrifice their lifelong careers in protest to his unification program.

In August, the government over-reacted the other way and the country had to put up with a futile two-week rail strike.

In four months, Camp's sounding of the party was complete and he was ready to put his now public demand for "a reassessment of policy, a reform of party organization, and the reconfirmation — or otherwise — of the leadership" on the line for the annual convention in Ottawa, November 14 to 16. "If I am wrong," he told the Junior Board of Trade, "then the usual penalties of politics will apply. But is is important that we no longer perpetuate instability, indecision, and expediency."

Three days later, on September 23, the government obligingly released Mr. Justice Wishart Flett Spence's report on his commission of inquiry "into matters relating to one Gerda Munsinger."

The Spence report exonerated George Hees, whose association with Gerda, it said, "would appear to have been a casual one, not at all improper in character", but it roasted both Diefenbaker and his Associate Minister of Defense, Pierre Sévigny.

Predictably, the official Conservative reaction was that the commission had been partisan in its conclusions, but privately the anti-Diefenbaker forces were delighted. If there were any lingering doubts the Spence report on the Munsinger case ended them. More than ever, Diefenbaker had to go. It took some doing.

"Some of the mice have turned into rats," said Diefenbaker loyalist, Tommy Van Dusen. While acting campaign director, Dr. Johnston, declared, "I don't think anyone is going to tar and feather John Diefenbaker." Gordon Churchill called for Camp's resignation and described the speech as a "public attack on our leader."

But Davie Fulton countered by observing, "I think Mr. Camp's views reflect the thinking of a large segment of the Canadian people." And such other Camp supporters as Gordon Fairweather, Heath MacQuarrie, Gordon Aiken and Tom Bell fell in behind him.

And while Diefenbaker loyalists recalled bitterly that Camp "had spent $43,000 to lose in Eglinton" against Mitchell Sharp, his supporters retorted with a prophetic Camp remark "that I don't want to be known as the Jim Farley of Canada; I would rather be the Karl Marx of Eglinton".

Diefenbaker kept silent. His opinions were well-known. At his 71st birthday party on September 18, in Ottawa, he had reminded well-wishers that Sir John A. Macdonald, Canada's first Prime Minister and a personal (Conservative) idol, had fought his last election at the age of 76.

But on October 1, he finally laid it on the line: "No one has the right of leadership unless the grass roots support him". Then later, in the West, he promised that as long as he had health and support, the leadership will not be turned over to any small group." Yet always he came back to the need for merely a vote of confidence and nothing more — no secret ballots, no reappraisals, reform or new policy.

Throughout October, while the Liberals had a battle of their own in the Ottawa policy convention (preventing Westerners from passing resolutions that would invade provincial jurisdictions, and defeating the economic nationalism proposed by Walter Gordon), the Conservatives were dividing sharply into pro and anti-Diefenbaker factions, with Camp's proposals gradually getting increasingly impressive endorsement across the country. Camp himself traveled constantly to drum up delegate support, making speech after speech.

"In Canada there has been no Jacksonian age," he said at one point, "no Kennedy era. The business of politics is nearly bankrupt, run-down by obsolescence and over-run by change. No one can remember when the passions of politics were so far removed from the consensus of their constituents. We have never had a political renaissance in this country, but it is vital that we have one now, and that it be launched in the spirit and resolution of a true revolution."

It was heady stuff. And there was the ever-present threat.

"If my party is not the first to reform," he warned, "it will become an artifact of history."

By the end of October, the desperation of Diefenbaker's supporters began to show through. Since they could find no compromise candidate to run against Camp for the presidency at their annual convention in three weeks, they had to turn to a loyalist, Toronto lawyer Arthur Maloney, a former executive assistant to the Minister of Labor in the Tory government.

Their second gamble was to put out an unauthorized agenda for the convention in November, scheduling election of officers on the final day in the hope of getting a vote of confidence in Diefenbaker the day before and, with luck, defeating Camp on the strength of it. When that failed, and Camp ordered the national executive of the party to meet November 13, they tried to force an armistice on the grounds that open conflict might wreck the party. On November 3, Senator Allister Grosart, Camp's predecessor as national director of the party, tried to arrange a saw-off that would save face for both sides. "Blood-letting is a very old-fashioned cure," he said. "I've seen a few of them, and I don't think any were very successful."

Nevertheless, Diefenbaker's fulminations ("I don't call them the Bay Street crowd, but I know them, I can pick them out . . . they threw out R. B. Bennett in 1935, then R. J. Manion, then Arthur Meighen and then John Bracken . . .") and Camp's silence assured anyone who doubted that a blood-letting it would be.

It was worse than anyone feared. The national executive met in the Salon Renaissance, at the Chateau Laurier, on that grey Sunday in November and by a vote of 80 to 41 changed the agenda to place the election of the president and officers at 2:30 p.m. Tuesday, November 15, before the resolutions were debated.

Camp puffed his long, thin cigar and permitted himself a ghost of a smile. "It was a triumph for democracy," he said quietly, as he left the national executive meeting to return to his first floor suite, 176-178.

To Diefenbaker, four floors above in 578, it was disaster.

On Monday, the meeting, which was merely to hear the president's report and a welcome to delegates by Diefenbaker, was due to start at 7 p.m. in the Chateau's baroque ballroom. But by 5 p.m., the room was packed with Camp and Diefenbaker supporters, the former occupying the first 20 rows of seats in a solid phalanx. Late-comers had to watch the meeting on closed-circuit television in other rooms. When Camp arrived he was booed by Diefenbaker-Maloney supporters and cheered energetically by his own followers. When Diefenbaker arrived at least half of the people in the ballroom refused to stand or applaud, and the silence was deafening. The hoped-for standing ovation flopped miserably.

The first major speaker was Camp, and despite the mood of partisan bitterness, he pleaded for party unity. "My friends," he said, "this is surely not going to be an exercise in democracy by applause meter. This is not going to be a clash of claques . . . are all united by a common bond as Conservatives." But the opposition was not listening. He read the report of his stewardship as president to a constant buzz of conversation in the hall. "I have done my best," he shouted above the noise, "but we are all made of human clay", and he wound up by promising to do his duties "with tolerance toward all and malice to none."

Angry young Conservatives followed, speaking of "a complete loss of confidence in the leadership of the house of Parliament" and the need for "responsibility and leadership to be transferred to younger people".

Diefenbaker was the last speaker and TV personality, Joel Aldred, introduced him with the mellifluous, sun-lamped polish of the professional, rolling out platitudes about "old-fashioned" things like loyalty, and how they seemed to be disappearing; hailing Diefenbaker for "a strength and courage unrivalled by any leader since Macdonald."

It was definitely not the time for nostalgia, but Diefenbaker paid no heed. Half the audience failed to stand or even clap when he was introduced, and from the moment he started speaking, until he finished, three-quarters of an hour later, the heckling was merciless. "I come to deal with issues, not personalities," he said, and a heckler yelled: "Get on with it, then". But no issues were forthcoming. He took his glasses off, then put them on again, fumbling with his speech and his too-low lectern (Diefenbaker likes one exactly 4 feet 6 inches high, according to Peter Newman). And he rambled. "All my life, human values have been uppermost with me . . . disunity and self-criticism are a sweet sympathy to the Liberal party", he said. "I have had a long life from the days of my youth when I dreamed of the opportunities to serve this country." His voice quavered. The heckling continued. "Is this a Conservative party?" he asked finally, in exasperation. "Yes, yes," came the reply. He accused the hecklers of wanting "to go back to the dinosaur days." A heckler shouted, "we're in them now."

He spoke about policy only briefly, and finally, he lashed out blindly, words tumbling out in a welter of non-sequiturs. The conversation in the ballroom was so loud he could hardly be heard above the noise. But he ploughed on. "They say that criticism is healthy. If it is, then I'm exhibit A . . . it is easy to stand when those around you are worshipping false gods . . . no leader can stand when he has to turn around to see who's trying to trip him from behind. Ladies and gentlemen, you know in your hearts that that is true. No one can go forward unless there are men and women behind him who will stand . . . ladies and gentlemen, would you just please go home and think about this. You're not hurting anybody but yourselves. You will destroy the party from within. Ladies and gentlemen, I'm asking you to unite. Ladies and gentlemen, let us go forward a people's party . . ."

Mercifully, it was over. "I wanted to cry," said Eddie Goodman, the Resolutions chairman. And many women were weeping already.

At midnight that night, 40 Camp strategists gathered in the Chateau suite of Quebec Tory Claude Harari to discuss Tuesday's tactics. But already the consensus of reports was that Diefenbaker had been beaten.

The rest was anti-climactic. On Tuesday afternoon, in their speeches, there was an ocean of difference between Dalton Camp's cool, reasoned appeal and the angry, partisan approach of Arthur Maloney. The delegates, 1,100 of them, voted for two hours by province and in separate rooms, and then the ballots were taken to the Burgundy Room to be counted. At 7:55, the result was announced: Camp 564, Maloney 502. The leadership convention would be inevitable.

The Diefenbaker years were over, and outside, it was starting to snow.

VII

The Great Leadership Race

"Ffight on my men," says Sir Andrew Bartton,
"I am hurt, but I am not slaine;
"I'le lay mee downe and bleed a-while,
"and then I'le rise and ffight againe."

— *Old English Ballad*

BLUE EYES BLAZING, white hair bobbing, surrounded by 300 elderly supporters, John George Diefenbaker stood in the brown marble lobby of the Chateau Laurier, huffing defiant verse and looking like an angry old eagle. He had refused to return to the convention floor itself, in the Chateau's ballroom, but he had trudged through the snow from his office in the center block to rally his supporters, many of whom were weeping openly, both men and women, amid tearful shouts of "Lead on, John!"

In the ballroom, meanwhile, a resolution to hold a leadership convention before January 1, 1968, was passed effortlessly by 563 votes to 186, in a secret ballot. There was also a unanimous resolution giving the convention's "wholehearted appreciation of John G. Diefenbaker's universally recognized services."

The likelihood that Diefenbaker would now retire gracefully into the West with the setting sun was never more than a forlorn hope. Almost as soon as he reached Stornoway, the official residence of the Leader of the Opposition, Diefenbaker let out the news that telegrams and letters supporting him were "coming in from everywhere". While in the House of Commons, 71 of the 95 Tory members signed a Diefenbaker loyalty pledge, effectively poisoning relations between the caucus and the party-at-large still further. Later, the Diefenbaker loyalists carried their cause to the point of absurdity by pushing through a vote of confidence not only in Diefenbaker but in his wife, Olive, as well.

Under the circumstances, with the season of good-will approaching, Dalton Camp's decision to maintain "a low profile" until January was a wise one.

Meanwhile the Liberals had been growing accustomed to the new Premier of Quebec, Daniel Johnson, and to his tendency of saying one thing in English Canada (or the United States) and quite another back home in Quebec. What had emerged, obviously, was that the National Union was committed to a nationalistic approach to constitutional problems. As early as June 28, Johnson had said that everything would work out, providing English Canada recognized the existence of two nations and was prepared to draft a new constitution. In September, Johnson arrived at the Tax Structure committee meetings with a demand for 100% of the personal, corporate and succession taxes collected in Quebec; he was also angry at the Federal Government's attitude at the conference which, in effect, was to tell the provinces that they had better start raising some extra revenues of their own. As Finance Minister Mitchell Sharp put it: ". . . both Parliament and the provinces must accept their financial responsibilities . . . each should look to its own electors for direction as to what money should be raised and how it should be spent."

"If Ottawa does not cede, it's independence," retorted Johnson. In fairness to Johnson, while he was the only one to threaten secession, he was not the only premier upset by the Federal government's tough, six-point program for taxes. After all, the program reversed the Federal government's previous policy, if policy it was, of permitting ad hoc tax arrangements with different provinces. Sharp's principles were as follows:

1. A recognition that both Federal and Provincial governments needed enough tax revenue to do their jobs.

2. A recognition that each level of government was responsible to its electors for the money it spent and the taxes it raised.

3. A recognition that the Federal government would continue to make equalization payments to poorer provinces so that their citizens could enjoy the same standard of living as those in richer

provinces without having to pay taxes that were higher than those in richer provinces.

4. A recognition that the Federal government needed sufficient fiscal powers to pay its bills and make those delicate tax and monetary adjustments that keep the national economy running smoothly.

5. That all provinces would have the same fiscal arrangements with the Federal government.

6. That the fiscal arrangements would harmonize policies and priorities of both levels of government.

Sharp also proposed phasing out shared-cost programs over a number of years, in return for a 17% abatement on personal income tax.

The Tax Structure committee meetings in September and October marked the public inauguration of the "new federalism" that had entered the Liberal party with Marchand and Trudeau. The Federal government flatly refused to be brow-beaten by the provinces, and the formula approved on October 28 was the formula Sharp had proposed on September 14. By that time, however, all the provincial premiers from the Western have-provinces (Alberta, B.C. and Saskatchewan), as well as those of Ontario and Quebec, were so angry that Ontario's Premier John Robarts seemed to sum up the feelings of his colleagues when he said what was needed seemed to be a conference on confederation.

For the Federalists, on the other hand, confederation had not seemed in such good shape for years and, with solid backing from Quebec's 500,000-strong trades unions (their September 28 brief rejected separatism and special status in favor of federalism) and a boisterously successful $50-a-plate Federal Liberal party dinner in Montreal a month later, it was no surprise that Jean Marchand and his team moved quickly to consolidate their position. "We are acting with the mandate given us by the people of Quebec, and we represent Quebec as much as any others," Marchand told a cheering audience. "We (Quebec MP's in Ottawa) will not be treated as strangers," he said. The federal Liberals had won respect for Quebec's constitutional rights, he said, and their conception of Canada was decentralist, not centralist.

Within days, the Quebec federalists took the offensive in their counties across the province. In Mount Royal, the "Three Wise Men", Marchand, Pelletier and Trudeau, told a large meeting that "our adventure has not been in vain".

But how confident Marchand and company would have been if Jean Lesage were still in office is a fascinating but hypothetical question. There is no doubt that Lesage would have been just as tough as Johnson at the tax table — and quite possibly less easy to dismiss. There is also no doubt that a federal-provincial showdown was coming no matter who held office in Quebec. Thus one must conclude that Lesage's defeat made it all very much easier.

As for Lesage, he declared that "as a Quebecker I feel Quebec was humiliated at the last federal-provincial conference", which sounded like the sort of thing an Opposition leader is expected to say and was taken as such. Lesage had other things to think about. The Quebec Liberal Federation was about to hold its annual convention in Montreal, and a section of the party was in open revolt at Lesage's administration. The reformers, led by René Lévesque and Eric Kierans, stopped just short of demanding Lesage's resignation, but they did want a complete change in the organizational structure, including the creation of a committee to handle party finances.

The final solution was a compromise. Eric Kierans was elected president, defeating Dr. Irenée Lapierre by 768 votes to 542, but the other members of his reform-slate, Marc Brière and Philippe Casgrain, were beaten. By the time some semblance of unity had been restored, Lesage found himself faced with the problem of Quebec's bond markets, which had declined disastrously to the point where institutions literally refused to buy Quebec government or Hydro bonds. Since one reason for the decline was excessive borrowing during the Lesage administration, the Opposition leader had to take part constructively in the debate. And since another reason for Quebec's diminishing credit was Johnson's separatist-tinged nationalism, the situation offered more potential than verbal attacks in Ottawa. For a while there was peace.

Even Parliament seemed a mite less fractious as January 1967 approached. A $105-a-month guaranteed income for all Canadians over 65 was passed with minimal bother, capping an impressive three and a half year record of social welfare legislation for the

Liberal government. As the University of Manitoba's R. C. Bellan put it, "there now isn't much that a fully fledged welfare state has that Canada does not have." Though welfare spending by all levels of government had risen to $4.5 billion, there was a lot to show for it: a universal pension plan; family allowances to schoolchildren to 18; the Canada Assistance Plan; a War on Poverty; and a $500-million medical training plan. Medicare too, had been passed but was not to come into force for 18 months, until July 1, 1968, due to the economic situation.

Then, at last, it was Centennial Year. Prime Minister Pearson, fur-capped against the frigid January night, brought it in three hours after sunset on New Year's Eve, for the benefit of a national color television network, lighting the Centennial Flame of natural gas that wells up through water from a shallow bronze fountain on Parliament Hill, a perpetual memorial to Canada's first 100 years.

It was a moving ceremony amid the snows of winter, and the warm, golden flame that Pearson lit somehow matched the euphoria the country felt. Later that night, as 1967 really arrived in each of the seven time zones across Canada, the bells of 22,000 churches were rung for five minutes, bonfires were lit, and 100-gun salutes boomed out. The amazing thing about the euphoria of centennial year was not that it lasted at all, but, on the contrary, that it lasted so long. The year 1967 was to be one of peace and unity, a year for the world to come to Canada's birthday party and wish her well. It was to be a year of stimulation and excitement, crowned by the opening in April of the greatest exhibition the world had ever seen, Montreal's Expo 67, on its islands in the St. Lawrence, a setting so perfect that at night it looked like a cluster of glittering jewels on an exquisite necklace.

In Parliament, the spirit of unity was understandably absent among Conservatives, but the Liberals were filled with warm cameraderie. On January 5, Walter Gordon, who so nearly quit after the policy conference in October, was invited back into the Cabinet as a Minister without Portfolio. Three weeks later, the mystery about his function was cleared up when Pearson appointed him head of a task force to study foreign investment in Canada. "The study will include the significance, both political and economic, of foreign investment in the development of our country," Pearson said. It would also, he went on, find "ways to encourage greater Canadian ownership of our industry and resources, while retaining a climate favorable to the inflow of foreign investment, as required, for Canada's optimum development."

The resignation of ailing Guy Favreau as leader of the Quebec wing of the party cleared the way for Jean Marchand to take over the position. Marchand was naturally hesitant. He and Trudeau and others had made it clear that they disapproved in principle of the idea of a Quebec leader. But on January 18, with reluctance, Marchand accepted the job.

The control of the caucus by the new guard was now complete. It had taken barely 13 months. The placing of Claude Frenette as co-chairman of the October policy conference had been completely effective also. The party's policy was now their policy, or vice versa as some might say.

It had been a master-stroke, and the strategy had worked. With Marchand, Sauvé and Pepin in the Cabinet; Trudeau and Marc Lalonde working in the Prime Minister's office, the influence brought to bear on Pearson, however subtly or indirectly, must have been irresistible. He was soon persuaded that their method of dealing with French Canada was the best. Trudeau's role was particularly effective as parliamentary secretary, where he got to know Pearson well and was actively involved in drafting speeches for him, as well as being a close advisor.

In caucus, the weekly lectures had worked to perfection. Quebec Members were by now well prepared to face hostile questioning about the theory and practice of federalism — preparation they needed in the difficult political climate in Quebec where the National Union had declared war on the Federal Liberals after their humiliation at the Tax Structure Committee. Quebec MP's were now able to go back to their ridings and take on separatists, nationalists and all others with the devastating logic of convinced federalists. This they did with increasing effectiveness, zeroing in on two members of the National Union in particular, Marcel Masse, an ex-school teacher and Minister without Portfolio, whose babyish moon-face disguised a rabid nationalism; and Jean-Noël Tremblay, the Minister of Culture, an emaciated little man with a viperous tongue and an epicene manner, whose hysterical flights of fancy had earned him the nickname "Noëlla" in the Legislature.

The Quebec MP's were in good shape, but there was still the party organization at large to be dealt with. In order to reform the party at large, the reformers had to control the president, and here again they decided that young Claude Frenette was their man. Plans were made to groom him to be the reform candidate at the party's next convention which was scheduled for the fall of 1967. (It actually took place at the end of January, 1968, purposely postponed, in order to provide Trudeau with the right launching pad for his leadership bid).

The accession of Marchand to the post of Quebec leader created some new problems, however, because it meant that he, and not one of the other Quebec MP's, would be first to stand in line as a French Canadian candidate when Pearson stepped down. This of course suited most of the reformers well enough but it was upsetting to Marc Lalonde, Jean Pierre Goyer and Gérard Pelletier who had been convinced since 1965 that the French Canadian best suited to be Canada's next prime minister was Pierre Elliott Trudeau.

Furthermore, it was becoming obvious that Marchand would not do as a leadership candidate from Quebec. Marchand is not a man people feel neutral about. You like him or you loathe him, and, in his brief 13 months in Parliament, he had collected a small but dedicated group of enemies in the Quebec caucus (and in the party at large where his frequent Gallic threats to resign were not appreciated). He had been used to having things his own way in the trade union movement — or fighting for them — and he brought much the same ruthless union boss technique to the Quebec caucus. So, however devoted the reformers were to Marchand, they had to admit that he would probably not work out as Prime Minister. The other question was whether he could win the job if he ran for it? This too seemed doubtful. His health was not good; nor was his English. So there was considerable risk that if he did decide to be a candidate he would not do too well — a loss of face that the reformed Quebec caucus felt it could not afford.

Their concern about the need for a strong French Canadian candidate was heightened by Pearson's announcement on February 9 that he wanted the party to choose his successor at an open convention. This statement, reported by the *Globe & Mail*, increased speculation that Pearson would step down sooner than expected, in the fall of 1967, rather than 1968, and its effect on would-be successors was immediate. By general consensus the line-up as Centennial Year started was Paul Hellyer, whose scraps with the admirals and unification program continued to place him center stage; followed by Paul Martin, the Minister of External Affairs, whose claim was mostly based on seniority (35 years in parliament); Mitchell Sharp, whose handling of the Finance Portfolio had been impressive; Robert Winters, the Minister of Trade and Commerce, who *looked* like a Prime Minister and whose cabinet record was first rate; Allan MacEachen, the Minister of National Health and Welfare, who was one of the best debaters in the house, and Jean Marchand, the Minister of Manpower (Citizenship and Immigration had been changed to Manpower in October, 1966), because he seemed to be the leading French Canadian candidate.

The Minister of Agriculture, John J. Greene, and the Minister without Portfolio, John Turner, soon to become Registrar General, were also tacked onto most lists. Greene, because he had made a hit with Westerners; Turner, because he had made the right moves without making any enemies (he was to reverse his position on the death penalty in November, voting with the majority for total abolition).

The euphoria of the Centennial, combined with the obvious disunity of the opposition, both federally and provincially, renewed Liberal confidence that Spring. A measure of how they felt was the abolition on January 25 of an inter-departmental committee to study the economic effects of Quebec's secession. In February and March, Jean Marchand continued to denounce separatism in Quebec as "ignorant, unrealistic and childish" and to point to the increasing recognition being given to Canada's bilingual status. And indeed events were proving him right. In March, the Canadian armed forces introduced a new policy on bilingualism; in April, the province of Manitoba reversed a 1916 statute and permitted

French instruction in schools for 50% of the curriculum; while in August, Ontario announced that French language high schools would be added to the educational system, complementing the French primary schools and universities already in existence. Long before the Confederation of Tomorrow Conference in November and the first report of the Royal Commission on Bilingualism and Biculturalism in December, it looked as if the nation had taken already anticipated the B & B recommendations. (The essential recommendations were that French and English be recognized officially in Parliament and Federal institutions and in all provinces where French-speaking people represented more than 10% of the population; that French and English be recognized at all levels of government throughout Canada; that parents be given the right to have their children educated in either language.)

The New Federalism was obviously working well, and no one was surprised on April 4, when Prime Minister Pearson decided to reward its architects, promoting Jean Chrétien and Pierre Elliott Trudeau to the Cabinet, and Gérard Pelletier to the "junior cabinet" as a parliamentary secretary to the Minister of External Affairs.

What was significant, however, was Pearson's decision to give Chrétien a job as Minister without Portfolio, while he appointed Trudeau to the senior and most prestigious post of Minister of Justice — in the full knowledge that he would have to propose major amendments to the Criminal Code within a few months (they had been kicking around since the Diefenbaker administration), and that his total Parliamentary experience was exactly 16 months. (Chrétien, by way of contrast, had been in parliament for four years.)

In their own leadership race, the Conservatives had forged ahead.

On the evening of January 18, John Diefenbaker had suddenly appeared on CBC's "The Nation's Business" to tell the Canadian people that "I believe there should be a national leadership convention at an early date, the earliest possible date." And while he refused to say whether he would be a candidate or not, he added ominously, "I assure you, this is no swan-song."

Dalton Camp heard the news in his suite at the Ritz Carlton

Hotel in Montreal fifteen minutes before he was due to go to Westmount High School to help inaugurate the new Montreal-Westmount Progressive Conservative Association brought about by redistribution.

He had already sent out notice to the 25-member national executive committee of the party to stand by for a meeting in February, at which they would be asked to set a date for the convention whether the national leader had made up his mind or not. And the substance of his speech at the high school was to prepare the party to accept whatever decision the executive would make.

After a round of telephone calls to party executives, Camp braved the sub-zero temperature and icy streets to reach the school auditorium and, after apologizing for his lateness, got a round of applause when he asked the fur-bundled stockbrokers and their ladies "how would you feel if you had worked up a speech only to find that it is now substantially irrelevant?"

But he wasted no time. The national executive was summoned to Toronto for the following week, meeting in the Metropolitan Room of the Royal York on Saturday, January 28. Twenty-four members showed up, and that weekend, they decided by a 65% majority to elect delegates to the leadership convention on the basis of redistributed ridings, five delegates per riding of which one must be a woman and one a Young Progressive Conservative (under 30). It was decided that all delegates must be elected and not appointed.

Eddie Goodman, a well-known supporter of George Hees' candidacy, was made one of the convention co-chairmen while Roger Régimbal, one of Diefenbaker's last, lonely supporters in Quebec, was made the other.

The Diefenbaker forces fought bitterly against basing delegate representation on redistributed ridings. But the argument that the next election would be fought on the basis of redistribution won out. Camp chuckled. "Redistribution gives us 100 ridings versus 89 before; there will be 500 delegates from urban ridings, and at least 75% of the delegates-at-large will come from urban areas. The youth delegation has been sizably beefed up. Now whom do you think all that helps?"

Redistribution was, in truth, vitally important to Camp's plans and, in view of the final closeness of the vote, a key factor in his triumph.

So while Diefenbaker went off to Marathon, Florida, for a winter fishing holiday along the Keys, swearing that "I shall fight to the limit against any group or interest attempting to make the party something other than what it has become, a people's party", Dalton Camp and the national executive observed his wishes to the letter. The convention would be the most democratic in Conservative Party history — and why would Diefenbaker complain about that?

There would be five delegates from each of the 265 ridings in Canada; all Tory Senators and MP's, ex-candidates and members of Provincial legislatures (including the Quebec National Union); plus the 140 members of the national executive if they were not eligible under one of the other categories; 150 members of student groups; and 356 delegates at large, named by provincial associations on the following basis: Ontario and Quebec, 90 each; B.C. 30; Alberta, Saskatchewan and Manitoba, 25 each; Nova Scotia and New Brunswick 20 each; Prince Edward Island, 10; Newfoundland 15; Yukon and the North West Territories, three each. In all, a whopping 2,500 delegates eligible to vote. They telephoned the decision to Diefenbaker in Florida.

Three weeks later, the executive committee met again to decide on a time, place and someone to run the convention.

The location had been discussed at the first meeting, and Dalton Camp had decided to oppose Toronto — not because he did not like it, but because he did not want to appear to get his way on everything. But in fact, as everyone knew, including Camp, Toronto was the only possible location. Half the delegates would come from Ontario and Quebec and since Montreal was out of the question because of Expo 67, the obvious answer was Toronto, the only other Eastern city capable of accommodating 7,000 visitors (delegates plus wives and communications media). The only question was, when could Toronto do it? A check with hotels showed that immediately after Labor Day seemed best, and on February 12 it was decided that the convention would be held the week of September 4, with Wednesday, September 6, the official opening day, and balloting on Saturday.

Serious consideration was given to a Western city, notably

Calgary, which was anxious to have the convention. But quick cost analysis showed that accommodation would be a problem, and that travel costs would increase horrendously, from $100,000 in Montreal or Toronto, to $400,000 in Calgary. Since the party equalized travel expenses of delegates, Calgary was clearly out of the question.

The man selected to run the convention was big, ebullient Gene Rhéaume, former Tory MP for the Northwest Territories, a political pro who was finding life as an official of the Department of Indian Affairs somewhat restricting. So while the rest of the party concentrated on the leadership race, Rhéaume and Goodman set about making sure that the convention itself would be as foolproof as was humanly possible.

By April, Rhéaume and Goodman had set up an office in Toronto and had completed arrangements to hold the main convention activities in Maple Leaf Gardens, a huge and ugly yellow-brick hockey arena (home of Toronto's NHL Maple Leafs) on Carlton and Church Streets. They had booked 6,700 hotel rooms in Toronto for the week and had returned from a fact-finding mission to Washington loaded down with photostats of key organization documents they had borrowed from the convention planning departments of the Democratic and Republican parties, notably from the GOP's Ray Bliss and Josephine Good.

The convention was to be the first American-style event of its sort in Canada, quite apart from being the largest political convention of any kind ever held in the country, and Rhéaume and Goodman wanted to be sure that they knew all the problems in advance. They were concerned particularly about security — in credentials, floor management and voting, to eliminate any possibility of fraud; and, of course, against assaults on any of the candidates since the emotional content of the convention was likely to be high.

It was decided that three things would maximize security: first, the use of American voting machines, which are impossible to rig, unless the voter has bribed two poll clerks, two machine attendants (as well as the scrutineers) on all 20 voting machines, since teams were rotated after each ballot. The machines also eliminated recounts because there could be no such thing as a spoiled ballot.

Second, an elaborate IBM-devised credentials system which was based on matching signatures on pre-registration documents (countersigned by the credentials co-chairman) with signatures at registration; plus a color photograph of the delegate taken during the actual registration; plus a delegate number; plus a color code; all annealed in plastic so as to be worn on the lapel as both badge and credential, instantly verifiable at a glance at all times. The credentials system alone cost $15,000 extra — $2 per delegate more than at any previous convention. Thirdly, elaborate arrangements were made to prevent violence through regular security guards stationed in the arena; through the Toronto Metropolitan Police department, which had an eight-man squad of armed and uniformed police on duty in a strategically located room under the stands; and finally, in case medical aid was needed, by the planned presence of doctors as actual voting delegates in the arena. In addition, one of Toronto's leading heart surgeons was also in the arena standing by to give first aid if an assassination attempt took place. Naturally, none of the medical or police security details were revealed at the time. "You could imagine the headlines," says Rhéaume, "Tories Plan for Attempted Assassination".

But while Rhéaume and his staff planned for all eventualities, the Conservative Party had its eye on the candidates. The first entry for the leadership contest was John MacLean, a Hertz car rental agency operator from Brockville, Ontario, who had run unsuccessfully as a Conservative in the previous election.

The next was Edmund Davie Fulton, the former Conservative Minister of Justice and MP for Kamloops, B.C., who jumped in the day after Diefenbaker's television speech, billing himself as "a hard-hitting intellectual."

On January 24, non-candidate Robert Stanfield, made it clear that he was still not a candidate. "I have no desire to get into federal politics," he said. "And I have no intention of doing so. I wouldn't consider getting into federal politics unless I thought it awfully important."

The third candidate, on February 16, was the former Minister of Trade and Commerce, George Hees, who told newsmen at his Ottawa press conference that day that "I've never got into any contest I thought I couldn't win." Taxed about a statement the previous fall, in which he had recommended a cut in foreign aid, Hees gamely admitted that "once in a while a person in public life makes a damn-fool statement — and I did in that case."

But, as someone said, George Hees suffered from the unlikelihood of anyone calling him another Adlai Stevenson, and there were reports of increased pressure on Stanfield to run to head off Hees who was unquestionably the front runner. The two other provincial premiers most often mentioned as candidates seemed to have definitely rejected the possibility. Ontario's John Robarts, the possibility with the greatest potential of all, was in poor health, while Manitoba's Dufferin Roblin was plainly unwilling.

By April, Stanfield was sounding a lot less reluctant as he said things out West which sounded awfully close to the sort of policy speech a potential candidate might make. "What do we Conservatives — Progressive Conservatives — stand for?" he asked a rally of Manitoba Conservatives in Winnipeg on April 5. "What is our role in Canada?" he asked again, and then went on to list what he felt were the four basic party roles, stability; a sound opposition to the government; an orderly change of government "when the electorate wishes"; but also "it must represent a national consensus, to use a word now popular south of the border; not a mere temporary happenstantial consensus but rather one related to the continuing needs of the nation."

Some said Stanfield and Roblin had met to work out "a deal" for one of them to run as a candidate. Both men strongly denied the suggestion. Yet it was becoming apparent, as Peter Newman had said on March 18, that it was "not just a leadership contest but a struggle for control of the Conservative party."

By mid-April, it didn't seem that either Fulton or Hees could provide the sort of leadership needed to re-unite and re-orientate the party as it had to be if the Conservatives were to capture the young, educated urban population. Camp was convinced that the first party to attract this so far apolitical group would sweep the next election. If necessary, he was prepared to run himself, knowing that his candidacy would rip the party in two but at least permit something to grow around the half that followed him. The alternative was continued stagnation and irrelevance. It was last-resort strategy, of course, and he wanted to avoid it if either Roblin or

Stanfield could be persuaded to enter instead. But if a vacuum were allowed to persist, it was as clear as night follows day, that the candidate who would step in would be the man from Prince Albert, John G. Diefenbaker.

Camp flew several kites in April on his return from a brief holiday in France, and the reaction was not encouraging. "The Conservative party owes Dalton Camp a great debt, but it does not owe him the leadership," said Tory MP Gordon Fairweather, a solid Camp supporter at all other times. "If Camp runs, it will inject a whole new element into it," said a Diefenbaker man, ominously.

At the end of April, Parliament recessed to permit MP's to attend the opening of Expo 67 in Montreal and also watch further progress of the Tory race. On April 20, Robert Stanfield had dissolved the Nova Scotia parliament and had called a general election for May 30. Quite clearly, his maneuver would be timed perfectly, results permitting, for him to go on in triumph as Nova Scotia's favorite son to the Conservative convention in September.

May also marked the entry to the race of yet another candidate. (The fourth candidate had been Michael Starr, the former Tory Minister of Labor, who entered late in February, had no staff, ran no campaign, published no campaign literature, and was known to be a diehard Diefenbaker loyalist. The conclusion? His candidacy was not serious except as a stalking-horse for Diefenbaker.)

The fifth candidate was a refreshingly reactionary figure named Senator Malcolm Wallace McCutcheon, a financier and industrialist, who called himself the alternative to the "new socialism" and was memorably described by one observer as "an elderly Canadian multi-millionaire whose candidacy is aimed at keeping Canada safe for elderly multi-millionaires." With his ever-present cigarillos and pithy comments on most subjects, Senator McCutcheon became an early favorite of newsmen. "In a day of egg-walking and mincing words, he deported himself admirably," said *Time's* Marsh Clark.

Instead of struggling with school-boy French like all the others at a Montreal press conference, McCutcheon made his position quite clear. "I do not speak or understand French," he said, "so please address your questions to me in English."

He was asked if he thought a party leader should speak French?
"Not at all," he said.
Would he learn it if he became leader?
"Nope," he said, "I'm too old."

His right-wing philosophy gave him some curious bed-mates,
at times, such as his contention that universal family allowances
should be abolished in order to give families that really need
allowances more money. This position put him into total agreement with such left-wingers as Quebec's René Lévesque.

The sixth candidate was the former Minister of Agriculture,
Alvin Hamilton, a Diefenbaker loyalist with reservations. A former
RCAF navigator and leader of the Conservative party in Saskatchewan, Hamilton had been the best man in the Agriculture portfolio
in decades and had earned himself a place in Western folklore
with an imaginative policy that produced massive wheat sales to
Communist China and the Soviet Union. He was a candidate to
be reckoned with in terms of the Western vote.

On May 30, Robert Stanfield won another landslide in Nova
Scotia, returning to power with 40 seats in the legislature to the
Liberals six seats. But within days he squelched rumors that he
would run in the leadership race by stating firmly "that I have no
intention of standing as a candidate for the leadership of the
National Conservative party."

Perhaps reassured by this statement, the seventh candidate
promptly declared himself and Canada heard once more from
Donald Methuen Fleming, who had bowed out of politics as
Minister of Justice in 1963 for family reasons. Fleming, like Paul
Martin in the Liberal leadership race, was destined to be a tragic
figure. Like Martin, it would be the third time he had tried to
become leader of his party, confident of widespread support that
existed only in his mind. Like Martin, Fleming had a brilliant
academic background, a record of long service to the party, and
qualifications that would have suited him for the leadership on
each of the previous occasions, if better men had not passed him
by. But like Martin, Fleming would come to the convention representing an old-style in politics which had lost touch with reality.
Finally, both Martin and Fleming presumed too much on their
fluent bilingualism and French Canadian backgrounds (Fleming's

name had been Flamand and his family came from Lotbiniere, 20 miles south-west of Quebec) as the guarantee of support in Quebec. For though Quebec likes people who speak French, it likes people who win even better.

By mid-June there was an element of desperation in the situation. "There was going to have to be someone new in the race," recalls Camp. "But if I became a candidate, it was guaranteed that Diefenbaker would be a candidate." Several friends in the caucus and in the party were urging him to run. But Camp was shrewd enough to realize that there had to be more of a consensus than that. He went to Ottawa on June 13 to consult a key group of MP's. They decided by a narrow margin to advise him against running for the unity of the party. It became even more imperative that either Roblin or Stanfield should run. Camp did not mind whom, "I was really in the position of dealing with two people I liked," he remembers, "but there was no question that Stanfield would have stayed home had Roblin entered first."

During the latter part of June he had lunch at Expo (where his daughter was a guide) with Marcel Faribault, a friend since 1964 and an astute observer of the national scene. The main purpose of the luncheon was to discuss the outlook for the policy conference the party was planning to hold at the Dominican Maison Montmorency, August 7–10. The meeting was being organized by Eddie Goodman, Richard Bell, Bill Davis and Faribault and was designed to prepare policy resolutions for the policy committee which was to meet on the Monday and Tuesday before the convention started in Toronto on Sept. 6. It was felt that no useful policy discussions could take place that week and it was better to do most of the thinking and talking beforehand. The Montmorency Conference was to be a major mile-stone (and some would say mill-stone) in Conservative Party history. But at Expo in mid-June, everything seemed to be going well. Marcel Faribault, in fact, was much more concerned about developments in the embryo Liberal leadership race. He told Camp that he was concerned particularly about the possible candidacy of Pierre Elliott Trudeau.

Much of lunch that day in the Atlantic Provinces pavilion was given over to Faribault's assessment of the problems Trudeau would create as prime minister.

The discussion made Camp's subsequent missions to Halifax and to Winnipeg even more urgent. In Halifax, once more, Stanfield resisted all pleas. In Winnipeg, on June 20, on the other hand, Roblin seemed warmer. Manitoba Tories had been pressing him hard since Camp's last trip and had asked Camp to return because it looked as if a break-through was close.

But Roblin was listening more closely to rumblings from Prince Albert, where Diefenbaker was holed up like the Old Man of the Prairies, muttering that Camp was "flitting from flower to flower". Roblin felt he needed Diefenbaker's support — or at least neutrality — before committing himself and was keen to disassociate himself from Camp in order to achieve it. So he, too, turned Camp down, and the national president returned to his summer cottage at Robertson's Point, beside Grand Lake in New Brunswick to plot some more strategy.

First, he told both Roblin and Stanfield that if either of them entered the race, he would resign as party president, if they so desired, and would also work for them as he had done in their provincial campaigns. He gave Roblin July 10 as a deadline for entry. He also told him that he was wasting his time if he expected Diefenbaker to help. "It was a total misunderstanding that anybody was going to get Diefenbaker's support," he says. "Diefenbaker never helped anybody but himself — and he had a marvelous spy network, a sort of private army, to watch every move. Diefenbaker's a counter-puncher, and I was determined to wait him out."

It was a tense period, thankfully ignored by most of the Canadian press and public as a result of Quebec Premier Daniel Johnson's visit to Paris and his regal reception by President Charles de Gaulle, and the unconnected but ensuing Arab-Israeli War which dominated the front pages of the newspapers for most of June.

But by July, national interest had focused again on domestic affairs. July 10 had passed without word from Roblin. There were now slightly more than seven weeks to the national party convention in Toronto, barely enough time to plan and mount a new campaign.

Camp emerged from Robertson's Point for one final assault on Stanfield's reluctance. He enlisted the aid of all the top Tories he could persuade. Stanfield's telephone started ringing. Camp also flew to Ottawa to appeal to Senator Grattan O'Leary, the editor emeritus of the Ottawa *Journal* and High Lama of the Conservative Party, for his personal help in persuading Stanfield. O'Leary flew immediately to Halifax.

It was an agonizing two weeks, as slowly, in Ottawa and in Halifax, Stanfield was persuaded that Roblin was not going to run. The July 10 deadline was past. He was faced with the fact that a new, credible candidate was needed. By the end of the week Stanfield had agreed to run, providing his close friend and colleague, the Minister of Economics and Finance, George Isaac Smith, would take over from him and fulfill the election promises they had made together in May. Smith reluctantly agreed. But just before the weekend of July 15–16, Ike Smith had second thoughts. A new financial report from the provincial treasury indicated that the Nova Scotia sales tax would have to be raised. Smith rushed to see Stanfield and argued that he could not leave the government to handle this without him. Stanfield immediately agreed that he could not, and the Tories were informed that his candidacy was off again. It was Friday afternoon, July 14. There was consternation in the national party.

When Camp and his colleagues found out what had turned Stanfield off again so quickly, they descended on Smith in a black rage on Friday night and told him as bluntly as possible to let Stanfield go. Smith thought it over during the weekend and then told Stanfield on Monday, July 17, that he had been wrong to insist on him staying, and he should reconsider. He did, he decided to run once more, and that same day it became an open secret in Halifax that Stanfield would run.

On Wednesday, July 19, at exactly 8 p.m., Stanfield entered the Red Chamber of Halifax's lovely old Georgian legislature, Province House, and sitting in the great red chair beneath the portraits of portly King George III and sensual Queen Caroline, he announced his decision. "After much earnest discussion during the past fortnight," he said in an even voice, reading from the two-page statement on the massive mahogany table in front of him, "with my colleagues in the Nova Scotia government and with provincial and federal members of the Progressive Conservative party, I have come to the decision to declare myself as a candidate for the leadership of the Progressive Conservative Party of Canada. I never thought I should reach this decision, but in my heart I feel it is what I should do. Nova Scotians will understand that this has been a difficult decision for me. It is especially difficult, following, as it does, a general election in this province as a result of which the government was given a very satisfactory vote of confidence."

The Red Chamber was packed with newsmen and every important Conservative in the East. But conspicuous by their absence were Dalton Camp and his close associate in Halifax, tall, white-haired Finlay MacDonald, executive vice-president of the PC national association, and the television commentator-owner of Halifax's CJCH-TV, the largest private television station in Nova Scotia.

Stanfield had asked both Camp and MacDonald to help run his campaign as a candidate, but he had asked them to keep a low profile, working by telephone and mail and in private meetings in order to minimize the amount of ammunition available for a Diefenbaker counter-attack. His first request was to ask them not to attend his Wednesday declaration. The second was to make sure that neither of them resigned their official positions in the party — where they would be much more useful as "neutrals" than as open partisans. Camp was surprised and touched that Stanfield did not take up his offer to resign as soon as his candidacy was announced. "After all, I was an albatross to Stanfield," he says.

The contest took on an entirely new momentum with Stanfield into the race. Excitement increased. Stories about the lean, Lincolnesque Premier of Nova Scotia appeared overnight in dozens of newspapers across the country and the nation chuckled at his dry, self-deprecating wit.

Would he now take-up ski-jumping?

"No. I think one bit of foolishness is enough for one time," he replied in his slow, thoughtful way, maintaining a poker-face.

Was there any truth in the charge that underneath his slow, dry manner, he was just plain dull?

Stanfield never denied it. "I don't want to sound presumptuous," he replied, "but Mackenzie King was a little dull, too."

It was all rather shy and good-natured, in keeping with Canada's mid-Summer mood. Expo was a tremendous success, well on its way to breaking all records for a world exhibition, but it was no longer front-page news across the country. Canadians were delighted by the gaunt, dour Nova Scotian with the light sense of humor who had decided to entertain them. And to students of politics, it seemed entirely appropriate that a Maritimer should run for the leadership of a party which had brought about Canadian Confederation 100 years ago — a confederation which owed its existence in large part to proposals made by Maritimers and to conferences held in the Atlantic provinces.

But the mid-summer mood of euphoria and innocent entertainment had only one more weekend to go before four words by a visiting statesman would plunge the country into a major political crisis. Even as Stanfield announced his decision in Halifax, the great French battle-cruiser *Colbert* was about to raise its anchor off the French island of St. Pierre, 350 miles to the north-east, and steam up the Gulf of St. Lawrence to Quebec City, carrying President Charles de Gaulle on his self-appointed mission with destiny and the French Canadians.

De Gaulle's reception in St. Pierre had been close to hysteria. Almost alone among France's overseas territories, the tiny islands (population 5,000) off the south coast of Newfoundland had rejected Vichy during the Second World War and voted unanimously to join the French forces under the Cross of Lorraine. De Gaulle had never forgotten their loyalty, and it was said, with some seriousness, that of the five thousand people who lived on the bleak, rocky island of St. Pierre and its sandy neighbor, Miquelon, 4,999 were civil servants.

Who knows what dreams of Empire and tableaux of history must have passed through President de Gaulle's mind as the *Colbert* knifed her way through the grey-blue sea of the gulf on the route that Champlain and Cartier had sailed for the King of France, three and four centuries ago? The distant shoreline no doubt reminding him of the kingdom they had carved for monarchs who never deigned to visit.

President de Gaulle had been to Canada before, and most recently as a head of state, so it was hardly a case of the greatest living Frenchman making up for the preference of King Louis for

Versailles, over what Voltaire had described so cuttingly as "a few acres of snow".

The July state visit was different. Canada was 100 years old as far as *les anglo-saxons* were concerned, and theoretically it was to celebrate that event he was invited. But more important to France was the fact that the 30.4% of the Canadian population who were of French origin (1961 census) were starting to assert themselves, notably in the province of Quebec. The French-speaking world was growing stronger, or so it seemed, and France as the mother-land of French culture was bound to be interested. The Quiet Revolution had been much discussed in France in its twilight years, and in 1964, the daunting minister of culture, André Malraux, had gone to see for himself — evidently reporting back to the Elysée Palace that French Canadians, despite their regrettable accents and manners, were becoming *évolués* or close to it. Moreover, as Malraux must have noted, Quebeckers had overcome their complex about Frenchmen and were actually grateful for France's interest, eager to speak better French, establish closer cultural ties and generally go more than half-way to bridge the gap of two centuries. The Quebec government had even bought an enormously expensive mansion in Paris's 16th arrondissement to serve as a home for the Quebec government in Paris. And when the French government was nice enough to offer quasi-diplomatic status to Quebec's representatives, the French Canadians promptly bought a second, even more expensive house just off the Avenue Foch. By 1966, Quebec government investment in Paris real estate was well over $1,000,000.

Ever since de Gaulle's decision to visit Canada became known, early in 1966, the government of Quebec had been determined that the federal government would have as little as possible to do with arrangements. With the change of provincial governments in June, 1966, relations became even more strained, as the embassy in Paris and the department of External Affairs tried vainly to get in on the planning stage, only to be told, none too politely, that the President of France was the guest of Quebec, and they were to mind their own business. Ottawa was finally let in on the actual details barely a week beforehand, long after the Mayor of Montreal, Jean Drapeau, and Premier Daniel Johnson had jointly planned the triumphal procession along the *Chemin du Roy*. (Drapeau had the political foresight to mix Maple Leaf flags with the Fleur de lis when the parade route entered Montreal city limits, however.)

What happened is now history. At the end of his drive from Quebec City to Montreal, along the road named for Louis XIV, President de Gaulle acknowledged a huge crowd outside Montreal's City Hall by appearing on a previously unused balcony that overlooks Place Jacques Cartier beside Mayor Drapeau and Premier Johnson. Crowd estimates ranged from 5,000 to 20,000, and whatever it really was did not matter, the square was jammed with people, excitement was high and President de Gaulle made an impromptu speech, "I want to tell you a secret," he said in a voice trembling with emotion, "this evening I find myself in an atmosphere like that at the Liberation . . . Long Live Montreal, long live Quebec, long live a free Quebec!" Few who understand French will forget how General de Gaulle pronounced the last four words, "*vive le Québec libre*", rolling the last syllable with the inimitable, back-of-the-throat precision of the French aristocrat.

In Paris, the anti-Gaullist newsmagazine, *l'Express,* described de Gaulle's behavior as "the biggest diplomatic scandal since the war". In New York, on the other hand, the New York *Times* concluded, somewhat circuitously, that de Gaulle was really sticking a needle into the United States. In London, the *Times* decided it was all aimed at Britain and her attempt to enter the Common Market. While *Le Monde* of Paris, though pained at the way he had done it, was generally sympathetic to de Gaulle and felt it would remind "Ottawa and London" that they would have to give French Canadians and English Canadians equality; a rap on the knuckles for colonialism, as it were.

Time soon proved, with what became known as the First and the Second Declarations of Paris, on July 31 and November 26, that the President of France was indulging in no feat of diplomatic ventriloquism, but that his shafts were aimed at Canada itself.

De Gaulle did not go to Ottawa, of course, but cancelled the rest of his trip the following day. Soon after 3 p.m. on July 26, he climbed aboard a French Air Force DC-8 Freighter and flew back to Paris to a full-scale post-midnight reception from his cabinet at

Orly airport and to repeat again, on July 31, what he had said in Canada — with knobs on. Over the Atlantic, on his way home in the jet, de Gaulle radioed his thanks to Premier Johnson and Mayor Drapeau for their hospitality, thereby ensuring that it would be noted that no such message reached the Federal government in Ottawa.

Since July, 1967, Canadian relations with France have worsened progressively, and those of Quebec with France have improved in inverse proportion.

(In fact, the welcome planned for Premier Johnson's second visit to Paris, in October, 1968, would have rivaled that given the late Chancellor Adenauer, of West Germany, in the balmiest era of Franco-German post-war relations. Johnson was to have stayed at the Trianon palace and to have been the host at a state banquet for de Gaulle at Quebec's *Délégation Générale*. The visit was cancelled by Premier Johnson's sudden and fatal heart attack on September 26, only days after returning from Bermuda where he had spent three months convalescing from an initial attack in July.)

The effect of de Gaulle's statements on Canadian political life was immediate and severe. The rapprochement that seemed to have taken place between French and English Canadians during the Centennial was abruptly shattered as partisans on both sides issued angry statements for and against the General. Separatism received an enormous boost, intended or not, from de Gaulle's use of the long-time separatist slogan *Québec Libre*.

There is no doubt that politically the option of separatism became "respectable" for the first time soon afterwards. Constitutional reform suddenly became much more urgent than it had seemed earlier in the year.

As Claude Ryan wrote in *Le Devoir,* General de Gaulle's words were "excessive," but English Canada had fallen asleep, "intoxicated by the atmosphere of the centennial celebrations," and the effect of the speech was "like an electric shock." By August 15, a letter from Pearson was on its way to all provincial premiers inviting them to a constitutional conference in February, 1968, and suggesting that linguistic guarantees through a bill of rights should be a first priority in the discussions.

Meanwhile, the political furor had even reached the municipal level.

The man who emerged momentarily, as *Time* put it, "a sort of Superhomme", was the prim, toothbrush-mustached Mayor of Montreal, Jean Drapeau, who had taken advantage of a city-sponsored luncheon on July 26, the day of de Gaulle's departure, to make an impromptu speech which tried to clarify the complex feelings that French Canadians had about France and about de Gaulle's person. The speech was not a deft put-down on Drapeau's part, as was widely reported in the English press, but instead an emotional declaration of one French Canadian's rather nationalistic view of Quebec's desire for self-assertion, which, with France's help, as partner more than parent, could be achieved. Drapeau told de Gaulle that the feeling of French Canadians towards France was neither nostalgia nor gratitude, "since the existence of French Canada, and the role it could play in North America, was never, until you arrived, Mr. President, an object of much interest (to France)," he said. Rather, the emotion was a personal one directed to him and to the France he represented. Drapeau drew a curious analogy between the way de Gaulle had saved the French nation, twice, and "how our ancestors, our grandparents, our parents saved French Canada, and now, like France under your direction, French Canada resolutely turns to face the future."

It was all reminiscent of Abbé Lionel Groulx and the "honor of the doctrine and the palms of the Apostolate," but English Canada hardly noticed. It sounded like a put-down to them, because that's what they wanted to hear, and Drapeau found himself between the Devil and the deep blue sea.

So, wisely, Drapeau thanked everybody who called him, made no further comments, and confessed to his nationalist friends that he could not understand how English Canada could have misunderstood him so completely.

Suddenly, on August 3, perhaps prodded by all the activity, Dufferin Roblin called a news conference in Winnipeg, to announce, in English and French, that he too intended to run for the leadership of the Progressive Conservative party. "I think there is something useful I can do," he said, and climbed into a twin-jet Aero-Commander with his pretty wife Mary, at max. power, to catch up with all the others. "We have an embarrassment of riches," said Dalton Camp when he heard the news at Expo, where he was trying out the Gyrotron at La Ronde on his eight-year-old son Michael's recommendation. ("I didn't find it very exciting, but I think you'll like it, Dad.")

Roblin's rationale was quite simple. "Ever since Stanfield came in he has raised the status of the contest," said his close confidant, Louis Ralph Sherman, Tory MP for Winnipeg South. Roblin felt Stanfield "has given it prestige and stature. Prior to that it was a fight largely confined to the old wolf pack fighting for the mantle," he added in a welter of metaphors.

Another reason for the delay, advanced by Ralph Hedlin, was that Roblin did not like long campaigns. Provincially, 30 days was all he needed and he saw no reason why the federal party campaign should be any longer.

Another factor was that Roblin felt he was assured of the support of Quebec Premier Daniel Johnson and the National Union organizational machine.

A final factor, mentioned by some Roblin strategists, was that Stanfield was now identified as Camp's man in the contest, removing the odium from Roblin.

It all sounded pretty opportunistic, and that's the way most of the Conservative reformers took it. Roblin had waited for others to test the water before coming in himself.

Camp was not disturbed by Roblin's entry as a threat to Stanfield; he was confident Stanfield could win it now, and whatever he thought of Roblin's tactics, he never revealed it to anyone. Stanfield, on the other hand, was quietly furious and there was new steel in his campaign style as August went by. Publicly, however, he welcomed the competition, and even admitted that if he found himself losing in the final voting, he would throw his support to Roblin so one of them would win. (Significantly, Roblin never replied with similar generosity.)

Stanfield even admitted he was not worried by the low-key image of his campaign style compared to the foo-feraw of the others. "I couldn't possibly be trying to be interesting," he told one questioner, "so I must be telling the truth, mustn't I?" And he disarmed delegates at a reception in the Windsor Hotel in Montreal by saying that with all the other attractions, like Expo, "I wonder why anyone comes to see me at all."

Yet the temptation to explode must have been almost irresistable when, two days after Roblin's entry, the president of the Quebec PC Association, Paul O. Trepanier, publicly announced his support for Roblin and claimed that he had 300 delegates with him. On that basis, Stanfield's team estimated that Roblin would get 600 votes (or nearly half the 1250 he needed) on the first ballot and must be the man to beat henceforth; they altered their campaign accordingly.

The *mano a mano* between Roblin and Stanfield had an immediate effect on the public. Early in August the Gallup poll reported that Conservative popularity had soared from a low of 25% in February to 39%, while the Liberals had held steadily at 41% and the NDP had sunk from 28% to 18%. The Tory policy conference at Maison Montmorency could only improve the picture.

VIII

Conference at Montmorency

That Canada is and should be a federal state.
That Canada is composed of two founding peoples (*deux nations*), with historic rights who have been joined by people from many lands.
That the constitution should be such as to permit and encourage their full and harmonious growth and development in equality throughout Canada.

— *Montmorency Conference*

ONLY HISTORY will decide whether the Tory policy conference at Maison Montmorency, on the cliffs above the famous falls, was a monumental mistake or a monument to progressive conservatism. On the one hand, it almost certainly led to the election of Robert Stanfield as leader of the party and was responsible for the adoption of the philosophy of humanism which Stanfield represents. On the other hand, Montmorency produced one of the worst misunderstandings in Conservative Party history, a misunderstanding which was deliberately aggravated by the Liberal Party, which was only fair, and by John Diefenbaker, which was not. The misunderstanding involved just two French words, *deux nations*, which, taken out of context, seemed to imply that the Conservative Party advocated the establishment of "two nations" in Canada. In fact, any participant who took the trouble to read the key paragraph of the policy recommendation (quoted above) finds that the Conservatives approved no such establishment and those who implied that they did were either ignorant or mischievous and probably both.

This misunderstanding was not helped by the combined statements, temperate and otherwise, of the notary-president of the

General Trust of Canada, Marcel Faribault, a brilliant and complex man who personifies, at its best, the Quebec establishmentarian nationalist. He tends to be didactic, hard to follow, and undiplomatic in public statements, though in private, when professional dignity is unimportant, Faribault is a charming and courteous man. Unfortunately, the Montmorency Conference was a public affair and Faribault behaved accordingly. For $2, payable to the Progressive Conservative Party of Canada, any member of the public can buy the 145-page summary of the Montmorency Conference, which offers a good sample of the Faribault style from pages 92 to 101.

It also offers a clue as to why some people at the conference itself became somewhat confused about the interpretation that should be placed upon those two little words, *deux nations* (Faribault devoted two single spaced pages to the subject). Reading further, one comes upon "Mr. Faribault's informal statement to the Plenary Session", which was widely quoted and contained some very blunt statements, which Faribault was perfectly justified in making, considering the provocation he received. Some of the 130 people taking part had rudely referred to his Constitutional remarks as "poppycock", and had taken his mild suggestion about the monarchy ("if allegiance to a monarch has the effect of giving one power predominance over another, it would be better to replace this allegiance to the Crown with allegiance to the constitution") as a demand for abolition. One member of the audience, the Rev. George Ross, a lawyer turned United Church Minister, said flatly "the question of the monarch is not negotiable." The Rev. Ross also interrupted Michel Doyon, president of the Young Progressive Conservatives, who had talked about a "free Quebec in a Free Canada", with the comment, "that's baloney."

"I seem to have stirred up a hornet's nest," said Faribault, "but I want to make my position quite clear. I start from the same premise . . . that all the provinces are equal, but I reject absolutely the statement that so many things are not negotiable that no discussion can be had. I think we can discuss anything. There may be consensus: at the end there will be. But I refuse absolutely to be told that this is not negotiable, or that the paramountcy of the federal government is not negotiable. If you don't discuss, then you will lose the country."

Faribault said "the situation today is no worse than it was in 1864, and people sat down and discussed and obtained consensus." He pointed out that in his book three years before (*Confederation Wager*, with Robert M. Fowler) he had rejected a particular status for any of the provinces or constituent states. "I have not changed my mind, however, the people have changed their minds . . . the question of two nations is no longer debatable in the province of Quebec. Admit that you will put, you must put, at the preamble of a new Constitution, something which will be the recognition that there are in this country two founding peoples. You put that down," he said, his voice choking with emotion, "we might translate it in French 'two nations'. You will translate it 'two founding races or people' if you want. We cannot say 'people' because 'people' in our case doesn't mean nation, the same way as nation in English does not mean *nation*."

The nub of the constitutional issue, as Faribault saw it, was the need for the federal government to respect provincial jurisdiction, particularly in property, civil rights and social questions. "We don't want any more votes of money for education when the constitution says, in black and white, 'this is the exclusive field of the provinces' . . . 'exclusive' means 'exclusive' and there is no distinction whether in French or in English." He also questioned the intrusion of the supreme court of Canada in constitutional affairs. "There is no hope for this country unless you admit that the federal government cannot, by itself, decide that the Supreme Court will be, through its own selection, composed of judges who don't understand a damn thing about civil law as we have it in the Province of Quebec . . ." he was interrupted by applause . . . "and who render judgements that are unacceptable to the people of this country."

That night, and all the next day, on radio, television and in the newspapers the only thing people seemed to hear was not the indignation of a man who had been slighted, but the defiant statement of a Quebec nationalist in his out-of-context quotation, "the question of two nations is no longer debatable in the province of Quebec."

In terms of policy, the conference explored no new territory, but it did clarify Conservative thinking in a few murky areas, while the rest remained murky. Paul Stevens (who participated in the Constitutional section) and John Saywell used an apt quote from the *Globe & Mail* in their account of Montmorency in the Canadian Annual Review: "The thinkers were not so much thinking as borrowing — borrowing Liberal thoughts and New Democratic thoughts and not even bothering to apply much of a Conservative polish." As Saywell and Stevens said, "many Conservatives must have wondered whether they were in the right meeting."

Constitutionally, Montmorency was in favor of a Canadian-domiciled amending formula; for a constitutional tribunal to insure impartiality in disputes (replacing the Supreme Court); for the affirmation of the right of French Canadians to use their language in the courts and legislatures throughout Canada; and finally, for entrenchment of the Bill of Rights in the constitution.

The Montmorency meeting provided leadership race watchers with a fine opportunity to compare the candidates, superficially at any rate, since none of them took part except as observers. It also set off a claim-staking race. Paul Trepanier, the president of the Quebec PC's, told newsmen that Roblin would get 300 of Quebec's 535 delegate votes. "Roblin is the fair-haired boy as far as Quebec is concerned," said Trepanier. He was immediately contradicted by Fulton's campaign manager, Lowell Murray, who said that he knew that three out of five delegates in Trepanier's own riding were for Fulton — and he named them.

On August 10, Donald Fleming announced that he was 100% for the monarchy, and demanded that all the other candidates declare their positions. He got no answers. He also lost further French Canadian support by refusing to commit himself on special status for Quebec beyond saying that he recognized Quebec's role as the guardian of French culture in Canada.

With tongue in cheek, the *Globe & Mail* reported that everybody seemed to claim overwhelming support in Quebec, and decided to total it all up. It noted that Fleming claimed 400 votes, or 75%; Roblin was given 300 votes by Trepanier, or 56%; Fulton and Hees each claimed 178 votes, or 33%; whereas the Stanfield and McCutcheon forces expected 75 votes, or 14%. That worked out to 1,206 votes or 225%. Said the Globe: "Perhaps the only solution is for the convention organizers to increase

Quebec's allotment to, say 1,500. That way, there'd still be a few votes left over for Mr. Diefenbaker if he decided to become a candidate." One candidate, Senator Wallace McCutcheon, promptly denied having any support in Quebec at all. Noting Fleming's claim of some 70% of Quebec delegates and Roblin's of nearly 60%, McCutcheon declared "that leaves me 30% under water right now."

But by mid-August, the field had opened up enough for a preliminary guess at the finishing order. The leader was still easily George Harris Hees ("Our Man With Elan"), who was being so energetic that it was exhausting just to watch him. A millionaire and a health-buff, Hees, at 57, was fitter than most men half his age, as well as a good deal richer. "It's the fellow who meets the delegates who'll win," he said. "It's as simple as that." And to prove his point, he hurtled across the country by jet, spent three weeks with a private helicopter just visiting Quebec delegates, and whenever time hung heavily on his hands, he would plunge into the nearest swimming pool for a brisk twelve lengths. Wealthy by inheritance from the Hees family hardware company, he was a charter member of Toronto's establishment. He had been to all the right private schools and colleges, including Cambridge, and he epitomized the Toronto WASP, from the tab-collars of his Welch Margetson shirts, to his waisted, custom-made English suits and lustrous imported shoes.

He was frequently dismissed as a likeable, amusing, light-weight — a verdict that perhaps he brought on himself, to a certain extent, but which was hardly fair. Hees had been an outstanding minister of Trade and Commerce and a good parliamentarian. He was hard-working and, in reality, rather humorless, approaching his job as a minister and later as president of the Montreal and Canadian Stock Exchanges with the same serious thoroughness that he applied in all other endeavors from football and swimming — to campaigning for the leadership of the Progressive Conservative Party. But somewhere the nickname of "Heesie" stuck, and in spite of powerful backers in Ontario, delegates refused to take him seriously.

Number two into the stretch was Davie Fulton, 51, a West Coast establishmentarian who had won a Rhodes Scholarship to

St. John's College, Oxford, and had become the favorite of
Canada's campus Conservatives during the Diefenbaker administration. Fulton was heir to a family political tradition in British
Columbia, and when he fell out with Diefenbaker in 1962, after
serving as Minister of Justice, he had returned to his native
Kamloops to run for the leadership of the provincial Conservatives
and establish a new Tory beach-head on the coast. He won the
leadership but was crushed in the election — the Conservatives
failing to win a single seat and Fulton himself being humiliated
by "Flying Phil" Gagliardi, the Social Credit Minister of Roads
in B.C. — and he had returned to federal politics much subdued in
1965. His decision to run for the national leadership surprised
many Conservatives but, by campaigning harder than ever since
February, and by gathering a strong team of young strategists
around him, Fulton had shown that he had retained his appeal
in academic circles and among the younger Conservatives.

Number three, after less than three weeks of campaigning,
was Duff Roblin, whose Manitoba "mafia" had shown skill and
imagination in the jet-image campaign they created for him. Roblin
was well launched and climbing fast.

Number four was Robert Stanfield, and his impact seemed to be
diminishing. "I've seen low-key political campaigns in my time,
but never one so deep as that being conducted by Nova Scotia's
premier Robert Stanfield . . ." wrote Southam News Service chief,
Charles Lynch, in the Ottawa *Citizen* on August 15. "Mr. Stanfield has to be classed as a basso profundo among campaigners.
He's no more excited about national challenges that he has been
up to now about the challenges of Ecum Secum, Antigonish or
Tatmagouche. He radiates quiet confidence. The riddle is whether
he radiates it strongly enough to carry the convention." Lynch
wisely refrained from trying to answer the riddle. Stanfield, polls
showed, had a solid power base in the Maritimes, with 400
delegates out of 452. He also had some support building in
British Columbia and Saskatchewan. But if he were to get the
1,250 votes needed to win, Ontario and Quebec would be crucial.

His first major swing into Quebec, on August 18, was a dreary
failure. The weather was dull grey except for a momentary patch
of sun in Mont Joli, and it rained solidly in Chicoutimi and Que-

bec. And right from the start, everything went wrong. The plane he took from Halifax to Mont Joli did not have the right equipment for an IFR landing, so a Nordair DC-3 was diverted to Fredericton, N.B., to pick him up, delaying the whole day's schedule one and a half hours. Dr. René Lepage, the National Union national committee member and chief Progressive Conservative organizer in Mont Joli, had managed to keep half a dozen delegates waiting to see Stanfield at the Hotel Commercial. But the others had gone back to work. It was harvest time in the Gaspé, the best in years, and since most rural Tory-National Union supporters are farmers, they were not going to waste time away from their fields. Newsmen outnumbered everyone else. At the hotel, Stanfield and delegates sat at a long head table facing an empty banquet hall. Those who remained seemed to be solidly for Roblin. Stanfield headed back to the DC-3 with relief. The next stop, Baie Comeau was abandoned altogether, as the weather was uncertain on the other side of the gulf, and that would make up some of the lost time. The plane flew straight to Chicoutimi.

At Bagotville airport, the closest to Chicoutimi, half a dozen organizers were waiting, slightly bewildered because the plane was now ahead of schedule. It was raining hard. Downtown, the reception room in the Hotel Chicoutimi was deserted, chairs around the walls and three plates of malevolent canapes, archetypes of Peter de Vries' "pimples on toast", waited on a serving table. There were no people. No barman. Eventually, the room started to fill with familiar National Union rural figures, red-necked men in their 50's, with shiny suits and peg-bottom pants, their wives stout country-women with florid hats and complexions. There were no young people.

Stanfield read his speech, all in French, with the mystified expression of the unilingual Anglo-Saxon. It could have been Zulu for all the difference it made to the crowd, stony-faced or noses hidden in high-ball glasses to hide the smiles. It was a dreadful performance, sheer disaster.

Then someone had the bright idea of asking Gerry Doucet, 30, Canada's youngest cabinet minister (Stanfield made him Nova Scotia's provincial secretary in 1964 at the age of 27), to say a few words as an Acadian from Nova Scotia. Doucet saved the evening. He charmed the Chicoutimi audience with his fluent French — just sufficienty *joual* to be familiar — and he was unstinting in his praise for the boss. "I am the first Acadian in Nova Scotia ever to become a provincial cabinet minister," he said. "This doesn't give much credit to me, but it gives a lot to my premier, M'sieu Stanfield." He told them that Stanfield "is sympathetic to the aims of French Canada . . . and I think it is more important to understand the aims of French Canada than it is to speak the language." His little speech got a tremendous reception — and one NU organizer could not help wishing wistfully that the candidate were Gerry Doucet. Maybe Stanfield wished, too.

And on the way back to Montreal that night Stanfield vowed that learning adequate French would be a first priority. "I certainly wouldn't want to be Leader of the Opposition for any length of time without a significant facility in the language."

On August 17, less than four weeks before the convention, there were the first faint stirrings in the Diefenbaker camp, as word got out that a young Montreal advertising man, Graham Watt, had put together a record of Diefenbaker reciting and reminiscing. "I am a Canadian" appeared in music stores under the RCA Victor label on August 25, at $5 and sold 8,800 copies.

One of the Chief's best anecdotes was about Liberal Prime Minister William Lyon Mackenzie King and the Conservative Opposition leader, R. B. Bennett. Someone in the House of Commons had asked King what he would do if he were faced with a half a dozen Doukhobor ladies "devoid of all raiment?" King replied: "I would immediately call in the Leader of the Opposition." To which Bennett swiftly retorted: "The right honorable gentleman exaggerates — dispensing patronage outside of his own party has never been characteristic of him."

While the record made no major inroads on the hit-parade, the widespread publicity did underline the fact that John George Diefenbaker was, as one columnist put it, "the great X factor." And if the record were not enough, the convention committee received a request from Diefenbaker's staffers two days later for space in the Royal York Hotel, with extra telephone lines to be installed.

On August 19 a ghosted article in French under Stanfield's by-line appeared in *Le Devoir*. It contained a key phrase, edited into bold-face type, which said, "the Quebec situation presents certain distinctive aspects. Quebeckers feel that, in order to achieve their aims and ambitions, they must be given more authority over economic and social affairs in their province. I don't think any solutions that we will find for the problems of our federation will be able to ignore this feeling in Quebec."

There were few occasions in the weeks that followed when *Le Devoir* failed to note Stanfield's open-minded constitutional position, generally by contrasting it to the overly vague or rigid point of view of a competitor. As the convention drew closer, candidates began cranking out policy statements like life-boats from sinking ships, and opportunities to mock or applaud became more frequent. In the last week of August, it seemed to be possible to place the field with some accuracy.

Roblin, it was clear, was ahead. Hees was second and holding his position. Fulton was in third place but was receiving an increasing challenge in Quebec from Stanfield's editorial if not delegate support. Fleming was far behind in fifth place, followed by Hamilton, McCutcheon, Starr and MacLean.

There were several memorable vignettes during the final days before everyone went to Toronto. On August 21, Duff Roblin played to a French-Canadian audience in Chicoutimi when he told them in his fluent French that "it is necessary for all of us to understand the particular status of Quebec." But he failed to elaborate.

There was George Hees at a reception in Montreal's Windsor Hotel the next day, maneuvering himself so that photographers would be unable to snap his meeting with Pierre Sévigny ("Pierre Sévigny" he called, as if there were no one he would rather see, his 6 ft. 3 inch, 215 pound frame carefully offering only a back-view to cameramen, "how the hell are you?"). Sévigny's reply was lost to posterity.

There was Senator Wallace McCutcheon, in the appropriate luxury of the dark walnut paneled Albany Club, telling his peers in his familiar gravelly voice that "I stand before you as an unrepentent and unrevised Tory. I'm tired of watching Liberals trying to outflank the NDP," McCutcheon went on, "and then the

Tories trying to outflank the Liberals. I want a polarization of views. If Canada is going to maintain its strong political institutions. The Liberal government is a socialist government, aided and abetted by its NDP allies." The next day the Senator gave his assessment of the two nations theory, but it was no comfort to Quebec. While maintaining that Canada was a sovereign state, he admitted that it had two nations in it, "or maybe more, just as in Great Britain there are Welsh, Irish, English and Scots."

On August 25, there were also signs that the "X Factor" was about to apply itself. Diefenbaker loyalist Erik Nielsen had arrived in Toronto, ostensibly to help Michael Starr with the campaign that he wasn't running, while Diefenbaker himself chose the day to visit an old family house in the village of Neustadt, Ontario, which he had left when he was two years old. Nevertheless, the Chief pointed confidently to a second-story window, telling newsmen "I was born in that room up there." Later that day, in Hanover, Ontario, Diefenbaker fulminated about the *deux nations* issue. "We've got an answer to those who say Canada is two nations," he glowered, adding that there would be no "second class citizens" in Canada again. This met with the approval of an audience whose ethnic origin was largely German (Diefenbaker's father was a United Empire Loyalist of German extraction), and who could still remember when anti-German feeling during two world wars had led to the renaming of such places as Berlin, Ontario (now Kitchener).

There was Stanfield, also in southern Ontario, declaring that "the authority of the Federal government must be preserved." Adding, with a Churchillian flourish, that he was "not prepared to participate in the dismantling of the federal authority . . . I see no point in having a country that is not able to pursue an effective policy of economic development and growth." (A comment which ought to have put him in total agreement with Justice Minister Trudeau.)

And there was Davie Fulton, who had covered 75,000 miles during his six-month, six-day-a-week campaign, wearily climbing onto the stage at Your Father's Mustache, a Montreal night club, edging past a bored, straw-hatted combo, in order to deliver one final pre-convention pep talk to his youthful followers. To dispel the aloof, upper-class, intellectual image, which haunted him, Fulton had done everything he and his publicists could think of to be a regular guy, from barbecuing hamburgers and using four-letter words to riding a sorrel quarter-horse for two hours in the Calgary Stampede parade, in spite of incipient influenza. Yet, in his familiar brown suit, on the stage of the Clossé Street club, Fulton still looked very much the 51-year-old square, the "Adlai Stevenson of Canada" — stodgy, moralistic, academic. It made no impression on the 200 youngsters in the club. They were loyalists to a man, and they listened patiently and cheered loudly when he said that "with the new Conservative Party in Quebec, I am sure we can win the next election."

On the following day, August 26, Fulton issued his policy statement — as always, a lucid and thoughtful document. Of confederation, he said, "it was never conceived to be a quiet, or quieting, arrangement. It united two proud and powerful races in express anticipation that their separate strengths would stay and their common strength increase . . . the quest of Quebec today, is to restore that original partner's role. I am convinced that their goal is not the rejection but rather the reassertion of the spirit of confederation. That can be the common goal of all our people."

Not all was noble eloquence and *beau geste*; the gloves were starting to come off between certain candidates. In one speech, Roblin suggested a cut-back in welfare spending by the federal government. He found himself reproved by Stanfield, who said "I can't imagine the Conservative party abandoning existing welfare schemes to cut taxation. We need a good floor of security."

And while Roblin had been glad to have Stanfield tagged with Camp's support, he was becoming increasingly edgy about reports out of Quebec that the National Union and its premier, Daniel Johnson, were behind himself. Though Johnson's NU had little of Duplessis' party left in it, openly at any rate, it still was not quite respectable in Conservative circles and Roblin used an Ottawa press conference on August 25 to unhitch the NU wagon. He said he doubted the NU would take a stand on the Conservative party leadership but added that "I'm very happy if any Premier of any province is for me privately."

Roblin also refused to be squeezed about Diefenbaker ("a

towering political personality of our time") and his own candidacy ("I am a candidate because I want to have a share in my party's tremendous renewal"). Nevertheless, newsmen continued to squeeze all the same. For some season, Roblin never quite managed to win the confidence of the national press, and he always came across in reports as a rather prissy, preachy sort of individual, "like the little man on the wedding cake," as one Ottawa reporter put it.

(Fulton emerged as the favorite of the press gallery, while Stanfield, as Lynch indicated, was so different to most politicians that he received a sort of protective respect from the fourth estate. Hees was dismissed as a frivolous candidate, while McCutcheon, Starr and Hamilton got a neutral press and very little of that.)

In Vancouver, on August 28, as in Ottawa the weekend before, Roblin was asked about his relationship with Quebec's Daniel Johnson, in view of the news that a reception was planned for him in Montreal the following day at the Renaissance Club, home of the National Union party. "I have made no arrangements to meet him whatsoever," Roblin replied quite sharply. But he clearly had one eye on news reports in Quebec, when he told 400 people at a "Rally Round Roblin" meeting that night that "I never did believe in homogenized Canadians . . . English speaking and French speaking Canadians are in separate corners of the room. They must get together in the center and start a dialogue."

And at the Renaissance Club in Montreal next day, he got a rapturous reception when he said "once and for all, the two nations concept is indispensable for Canadian unity," and he urged the rest of the country to accept the French Canadian "as a partner in all sectors of the Canadian political, economic and social life."

It was practically the end of the campaign. Hees issued his policy statement on August 29, calling for new agricultural policies, a reorganization of the department of external affairs and co-ordinated foreign, defense and economic policies. Mike Starr told newsmen that he was "in this all the way," despite the total absence of any campaign. While Dr. Jim Johnston anticipated Diefenbaker's press conference of September 1 by announcing that as far as he could see the list of people who attended the Montmorency policy conference was "full of names that I've never heard of, and I'm meant to know Conservatives."

Roblin pacified those who thought he had turned into a Quebec separatist by saying that he did not want "to throw the old constitution away, the present British North America Act has been very durable, and it is amazing what we have been able to do with it," and assured an audience in Halifax that "the sooner Canadians realize that this is one nation politically but two nations culturally and on the sociological level, the quicker they will be able to stop the drifting process."

Donald Fleming, on the other hand, refused to rise to the "special status" bait during a last swing through Quebec and would say only that provinces and municipalities "must be assured of the resources necessary to enable them to assume their responsibilities." It was noted that Jean-Paul Cardinal, the National Union's Montreal organizer, was Fleming's Quebec campaign manager.

One of the most telling wind-up speeches during the week before the convention was Stanfield's policy statement in Montreal on August 31, at a rally at the Queen Elizabeth. In it, he defended the right of French-speaking Canadians "to enjoy their cultural and linguistic distinctiveness," as it was understood by the fathers of Confederation. A first step, he felt, was to guarantee French Canadians the same rights in the rest of Canada that English Canadians enjoyed in Quebec. But Stanfield emphasized his conviction that French Canadians did not want to impose their language on others. "What French-speaking Canadians outside Quebec seem to want," he said, "is to possess the mechanisms necessary to safeguard their identity, and, when it is practicable, to be able to use their own language in their dealings with public bodies. These are surely not unreasonable requests. In endorsing them, however, let it be clear that I am not suggesting that the federal government ought to become involved in matters of provincial jurisdiction. What I wish to do is to establish my belief that we should try to define these matters clearly and precisely in the constitution."

Stanfield defined his understanding of "special status", not as special rights and privileges (he thought the term unfortunate for this reason), but as a formula to allow Quebec a "measure of authority in respect to social and economic affairs which will enable them to fulfill themselves as French-Canadians". He said he did not think this requirement constituted a threat to the federal government's authority, until it was known precisely which controls Quebec wanted. Thus, Stanfield skillfully endorsed both *deux nations* and special status, while carefully re-defining the terms for himself.

The campaign was over — almost. But while candidates and their finance committees used the lull in battle between campaign and convention to add up some of their expenses ($100,000 was a minimum figure), John Diefenbaker continued his house and garden tour.

This time the tour went West, to the Saskatchewan prairie, where the Diefenbaker family moved in 1906, when John G. was eleven, building their own farmhouse near the hamlet of Borden, 40 miles north of Saskatoon. The Saskatchewan government had restored the old Diefenbaker pine-wood homestead at a cost of $15,000 and moved it to a place of honor in Regina's Wascana Park, not far from the legislature where Diefenbaker's political career almost started in 1926 (he suffered a series of defeats, both provincially and federally, for 14 years, until he was elected to the House of Commons in 1940).

After admiring the old homestead and the pioneer furniture inside the three-room house, Diefenbaker thanked the Liberal Premier, Ross Thatcher, ("from the bottom of my heart") for his non-partisan gesture and headed back to Ottawa, where his supporters had been busy with more contemporary projects.

The most active, as usual, was the National Director, James Johnston, who had rapped off a sharp telex message to convention headquarters in Toronto that week, accusing co-chairman Eddie Goodman and Roger Régimbal, and secretary Gene Rhéaume, of packing the convention, most notably the Ontario delegation. Johnston had also been busy calling the Ottawa bureau chiefs of all important newsmedia, warning them to stand by for important news on Friday, September 1. This was interpreted, correctly, as a Diefenbaker press conference, at which it was surmised, incorrectly, that the old chief would finally announce whether he would run.

On Friday, Diefenbaker was in chuckling good form at the news conference at the National Press building, and spotting his old *bête noire*, Charles Lynch, he saluted him, "Ha! Ha! My, my, there's Mr. Lynch, my favorite statesman," and sundry other comments about newsmen with whose opinions he did not concur. He also talked about a new transcontinental railroad — as if the country was not hard-pressed enough to utilize the two transcontinental railroads it possessed already. He spoke of an "undiminished" NATO contribution, and, warming to the subject really on his mind, launched into a diatribe against the Montmorency proposals, announcing that *deux nations* meant the same thing in French and English, despite the fact that most authorities disagreed with him, including the French dictionary of synonyms which gives *peuple* as a synonym for *"nation"* (i.e. *"Les USA sont un* peuple *formé d'un mélange de differentes* nations"). Finally, he said that Montmorency simply was not a Tory meeting. "Montmorency was not representative of Conservative thinking is this country. Insofar as the problem of national unity is concerned, the acceptance of the concept of two nations is contrary to every principle that this party has stood for for 100 years and more." And "special status", he added, "was detrimental to the unity of our country."

He spoke about the "six or seven million" Canadians whose origin was neither French nor English and who would have no part of the argument. "There's only one Canada," he rumbled, shaking his head and wagging his forefinger. "Only one nation, one national idea and one national dream." But would he run? Would he not run? Diefenbaker refused to answer.

As the weekend approached, Pierre O'Neil predicted in *Le Devoir* that 65% of the delegates would change their minds at least once during the convention. And Dalton Camp, emerging from Robertson's Point, for the first time since Stanfield's entry in July, agreed with him. "I don't give a damn what you've heard and read, half those delegates haven't made up their minds, and a lot of them haven't seen any candidates at all." While Roblin might be in front in a straw-poll, Diefenbaker's entry could cut away support in his own Manitoba delegation, where "Charlie", as Camp called Dief, still had a lot of impact.

"The man who makes the best impression in Toronto will win," said Camp. "After a couple of ballots, that delegate in the voting booth isn't going to remember the candidate who called on him or poured him a cup of coffee a couple of months before."

On Sunday, September 3, the 25-member convention committee

met at the Royal York to finalize arrangements for the convention and to hear Dr. Johnston's complaints against 88 delegates — which had boiled down to 15 by the time the committee met. Johnston could only substantiate six charges, and an infuriated committeeman moved that Johnston be thrown off the committee for questioning the integrity of the convention chairmen.

Though Johnston deserved to be tossed out, the convention co-chairman, Eddie Goodman, persuaded the committee member to withdraw his resolution, if Johnston would make another motion, declaring the motives of the convention offices "above suspicion". Johnston did just that, and it was seconded by Dalton Camp. To have tossed Johnston out at that point would have done more harm than good, since it would have confirmed Diefenbaker's suspicions that the committee was stacked against him. But Johnston was badly rattled.

"Look fellows, I don't want to be the black bastard in all this," he protested at one point, in complete retreat.

"Hey, baby, watch how you talk," said Hamilton lawyer and chief elections officer, Lincoln Alexander, a Negro, as the luckless Johnston put his foot in it again.

And Then There Were Ten

CONVENTION (kon-ven-shun) n. 1. Act of convening.
2. A body of delegates, representatives, members, or the
like, periodically convened for a common purpose . . .
— *Webster's New Collegiate Dictionary*

TORONTO HAS HAD larger conventions and quite possibly noisier
conventions, but no convention in civic memory came close to the
sustained excitement and increasing drama of the Progressive Conservative Centennial Convention, September 6 to 9, 1967.

The Conservatives went into it with a Gallup poll reporting
that 41% of the voters favored the Liberal Party, 30% the Tories.
By mid-October, when Gallup had time to ask the same question
again, the results were Conservatives 43%, Liberals 34%, a
complete reversal.

The job of organizing the convention had started in February
with appointment of the co-chairmen and the convention secretary.
By April, a permanent office had been set up in Toronto, accommodation blocked off at 27 hotels and motels, and a planning staff
of 40 put into action. The site of the main events, the Maple Leaf
Gardens, had of course been chosen, not for beauty or convenience,
but simply because it can hold up to 18,000 people, 15,656 of
them in seats. Organizers were expecting about 8,000 people, and
they wound up with at least that many, plus an unknown number
of Torontonians who were determined to join in the fun, whether
or not they were Progressive Conservatives.

The concept of the convention, or rather the televised part of
it which took place in Maple Leaf Gardens, was one of national
participation, says Rhéaume. "After all, it was live for only a few
people, so in convention planning we decided that we were really
holding it in four million living rooms."

The result was special care in the "production". No less than 2,000 prime red section seats were set aside for television, radio and other newsmen. CBC alone had 400 accredited staffers in Toronto, working for various divisions of the corporation. News-media also got prime accommodation at the Royal York and the Westbury. The age of color television had arrived in Canada "and we decorated the Maple Leaf Gardens on the 'living room' principle," recalls Rhéaume, "colors had to be just right for television, so did the other decor." By careful planning, and working closely with CBC and CTV television networks, the convention committee made sure that the TV cameramen would have all the latitude they wanted without spoiling the convention for the delegates. As a result, it cost the party $40,000 for the carpentry, scaffolding and fixtures needed to turn the Gardens into a convention TV studio.

The scheduling of activities was also important for full TV coverage. Outside the Gardens, candidates were told not to overlap their events if they wanted coverage; inside the Gardens, all events were timed critically.

The organizers were not going to risk the sort of thing that happened to the American Democratic Party convention in 1936, when applause for Franklin Roosevelt went on for 75 minutes. At the PC convention, nominations were limited to only 10 minutes; seconders, five minutes, and each candidate, 20 minutes, including demonstrations.

One minor rule that indicated the finesse that went into the planning was that all hospitality suites had to be closed during plenary sessions of the convention. This meant that when something was going on in the Gardens which was likely to be televised, there was no danger of a happy drunk lurching in from a pub-crawl of candidates' suites to find himself swaying with a glass in his hand in four million living-rooms. Since the only bars in the Gardens were in the Hot Stove Lounge and in the Directors' suite, both closed to delegates and public, the only beverages on sale were coffee and soft drinks. "We took a lot of flack from our annual meeting, where TV cameras tended to zoom in on those people with glasses in their hands," said Rhéaume.

Transportation would have been a horrendous problem for

convention delegates (and it was pretty bad as it was) since Expo and other centennial activities had jammed airline and rail services. Fortunately, Rhéaume, Goodman and Régimbal remembered in April to block off 3,000 seats on airlines into Toronto for key dates before and after the convention, and most delegates who registered in time, got transportation. While in Toronto itself, a shuttle bus service took delegates from their hotels to the Gardens and to events around town.

The planning staff, prior to convention week itself, consisted of the co-chairmen and Rhéaume, plus 40 university students. During convention week, the staff increased to 150 employees, not counting 200 security guards and 500 volunteers.

Summer decided to stay on during convention week, ignoring its traditional Labor Day deadline, and this created one problem the highly-efficient convention committee could do nothing about. If only there had been some way to use the ice surface, but that was boarded over and used as a floor for delegates chairs Thursday and Friday, and for the voting booths on Saturday. So while television arc lamps beat down on them, and the Gardens' extractor fans did their best to suck out the hot air, most of the delegates peeled off their jackets, flapped their red-white-and-blue "Roblin for Canada" fans, and steamed quietly as the temperature rose into the 90's.

The convention proper did not start until Thursday, but the important policy committee of the party held a meeting on Tuesday evening in the Royal York, to hear the candidates' policy speeches. And on Wednesday its 400 members held a plenary session in the hotel to decide, on the basis of the Montmorency conference recommendations, and what they had heard from the candidates the night before, what policy recommendations they would submit to the convention as a whole.

Therefore, by Tuesday afternoon, the hotels in Toronto were starting to fill up with delegates arriving to attend the policy committee meetings and with candidates and their supporters, newsmen and the general public. And by evening, all the key people were there.

The candidates were an impressive group. As the Montreal *Star* noted, on September 5, "if they were ever to come together in a government, they would provide a cabinet rivaling that of Laurier's administration in 1896."

The noise in the lobby of the Royal York, a tomblike place in normal times, seemed to reach a crescendo, that sustained itself for the next four days, echoing off the marble walls. The noise decreased only late at night and early in the morning. The Canadian Pediatric Association found it so noisy that it had to move its convention to a quieter place.

Tuesday was the day you noticed slogans. "Go Hamilton!, Go Canada!" "Fleming is Ready Now!" Stanfield, "The Man With the Winning Way". Hees' "Canada's Next Prime Minister," and, if in doubt, "Hees Can Win". Then there was "Fulton Now!" and "It's Fulton All Across Canada". There was "Roblin For Canada". McCutcheon's "Man of Decision". Starr's hand-drawn children's signs, "Our Next Bright PC Starr", and "Starr Light, Starr Bright", all daubed with gold sparkler dust. There were even, finally, the new "Keep the Chief" signs newsmen had failed to find in an Ottawa Valley printshop the week before.

There were also hundreds of pretty girls in their ubiquitous miniskirts, red, white, blue, for Roblin; blue and white for McCutcheon; blue and orange for Hees; orange and black for Fulton, and so it went. Some supporters were clearly there for a lark. Said a man with a "Keep The Chief" button to a girl with a Hees straw boater: "My button, for your boater?" "Done," said the girl, and they swapped.

Most of the candidates were in the Toronto vicinity well before Tuesday. Stanfield spent the weekend 50 miles north on the Barrie farm of his main Ontario organizer, lawyer Don Guthrie, 38. McCutcheon was on his own farm at Gormley, Ont. Mike Starr was at home in Oshawa and John Maclean in Brockville, all within easy driving distance. Fulton arrived from Ottawa on Monday. George Hees spent the weekend on his farm at Cobourg, 70 miles east of Toronto, but decided to get maximum publicity out of his arrival by flying in to Toronto's International Airport where his dixieland band, the "Metro-Stompers" met him with a scarlet, double-decker London bus.

Tuesday afternoon, Roblin arrived legitimately at the airport from Winnipeg, lost his way in the airport terminal, and soon afterwards lost his demonstrators when he arrived downtown at the Royal York. Roblin and his wife Mary finally gave up trying to find their supporters in the lobby of the hotel and headed for an elevator, in which Roblin was heard to say to Mary, "It's the ones with delegate badges who count, dear."

The Roblin strategy in Toronto was to create the Wendell Wilkie image — no establishment support but the grass-roots are for us — but the $750-per-day white and brown Jet Commander, the high-powered Manitoba cabinet level organization, and Roblin's own smoothly-tailored little 5 foot, 8 inch, figure were hardly the attributes of a man of the people. Far from being the boondocks candidate, Roblin came through as the city slicker just as strongly as those whom the Ontario establishment was backing.

One of the first things his Manitoba "mafia" did was call a news conference in their third floor suite. It was far too small. A zealous public relations man suggested newsmen at the front should kneel to give those at the back a better view. "What, already?" someone asked. It was not a success. Somehow, they got through the 23-minute conference and adjourned. Roblin and his wife went to their 7th floor suite to change, have a light supper, and work on the 10-minute speech he was due to give that night at the policy session.

The reality of hard competition was a shock to Roblin and his staffers. They had no idea that, in Stanfield and Fulton, they were up against two highly sophisticated election teams. Fulton's, as mentioned already, came from his strong position amoung young PC's. They seemed to be everywhere, skillfully exploiting every situation, such as Roblin's confused arrival in the lobby of the Royal York, where they successfully detached the candidate from his supporters and turned chants of "Go, Roblin, Go" into "Home, Roblin, Home."

The Stanfield demonstrations were quieter but amazingly efficient; pretty but demure girls in Stanfield blue wended their way through the crowds wherever delegates were gathered, giving out Stanfield matches, with the familiar dark blue diamonds and the red rectangles which proclaimed "The Man With The Winning Way". The technique was to persuade gently, never push, and it contrasted pleasantly with the aggressive buttonholing of the others.

The key area of the Stanfield organization — the combat information center — was completely out of sight. It was suite 355 of the Westbury Hotel, where Dalton Camp, in his favorite black loafers, glen-plaid slacks and a white, button-down shirt, sat like a modern Cyclops, television his single eye; a large Phillips taperecorder his memory; and a battery of telephones his arms, legs and weapons. Since Sunday, when he had attended the convention committee meeting to hear Dr. Johnston's complaints, Camp had maintained a low profile.

While Stanfield addressed the policy committee in the Royal York that evening, Dalton Camp and his wife Linda would be having a quiet dinner at Mr. Tony's. Throughout the convention, he would appear only when his presence was required as president of the national PCA. He would never be seen with or near Stanfield or any of his key aides. This was essential to the strategy of relieving Stanfield's candidacy as much as possible of the burden of public identification with Camp, and hence eleminate the hostility of key Western supporters. And so, quite truthfully, Stanfield could say that he did not know where Camp was, and that he had not seen him all week. Their consultation was done by telephone. Camp wrote all of Stanfield's speeches that week, as he had done for most of the key speeches in the campaign, but there was actually surprisingly little need for communication. Both men were on the same wavelength, their policy ideas identical. Stanfield might make a few changes in style or form, but nothing of substance. He had told Camp the general line he wanted to take in a speech, they had discussed the main points, and Camp wrote it. As he put it, "it's the same old crowd, we've worked together before."

An elaborate code was developed to maintain the secrecy of Camp's position in the Stanfield team. Stanfield was "Father"; Camp necessarily became "Mother", and when McCutcheon tossed in his support on Saturday, he became, appropriately enough, "Uncle".

As early as Sunday morning, the Stanfield strategists had acquired lists which told them at which of the voting machines each delegate would vote (Fulton and Hees committees also had the lists), and from the moment a delegate arrived in town, he or she was quietly cultivated by those members of the 20-man Stanfield team who were in the same line-up. In this way, all 2,412 voting delegates were tabbed. Results of this subtle pressure were constantly relayed back through team captains to command headquarters. Key people in the Stanfield team (and in several others) were issued "Bell-Boys", an invention of the Bell Telephone Company that slips into a shirt pocket and lets out a sharp beep whenever headquarters activates a small transmitter signal on its specific wavelength. The beep means that the individual must call in to receive instructions. Others had walky-talkies, though strategists in the Fulton team banned them for fear that they could be monitored or jammed by rivals. Such are the problems of electronic-age politics.

The policy committee meeting Tuesday evening was held in the Royal York's ballroom, and it was barely big enough for the 400 delegates and 300 supporters, newsmen and spectators, who came to watch. There were nine candidates for the leadership at that point. Most of the speeches were predictable. Alvin Hamilton hammered away at his theme that the Liberals were trying to sell Canada to the United States. Donald Fleming insisted on fiscal conservatism, warning that "the big spenders are in full control in Ottawa today". Senator McCutcheon spoke for the right-wing option in politics, but also was in favor of entrenching the Bill of Rights in the constitution. John Maclean attacked government spending and Michael Starr attacked special status for Quebec along with Dalton Camp's Montmorency proposal for a reassessment of Canada's NATO and NORAD obligations.

Davie Fulton took seven minutes beyond the ten allowed to talk in Kennedyesque terms, but without the style, about what the people could do for government, as well as what government could do for the people.

Roblin's campaign team apparently did not realize that a formal policy speech was in order, and their candidate came prepared with only a five minute statement which he figured would set the stage for questions. He found out too late that there would be no questions and even frantic rewriting on the platform couldn't disguise the fact that his speech was ill-prepared and windy.

George Hees, so flushed that he looked as if he had fallen

asleep under a Granite Club sun-lamp, stumbled through his statement at high speed, sweat running down his cheeks. Every policy
statement he had ever made seemed to be tossed into the speech,
along with every cliché, and the total effect was appalling. "It
sounded as if he were delivering the baccalaureate speech at Vic
Tanny University," said *Time's* Marsh Clark.

The man of the evening had to be Robert Stanfield, who spoke
clearly and to the point and got a standing ovation at the end.
He said nothing that he had not said before, many times. He
repeated his own clear understanding of what Canada should be
and of what French Canadians, in particular, wanted from the
rest of the country.

By the next morning, from being an also-ran, Stanfield began
to emerge as the strongest contender.

Wednesday afternoon in the *Telegram*, columnists Harry Crowe
and Douglas Fisher wrote bluntly that "if the Federal Progressive
Conservative party doesn't grab Robert Stanfield, they've got rocks
for heads. Davie Fulton and George Hees? They were unbelievably,
irretrievably bad." In Quebec, Claude Ryan announced his own
assessment of the Tory leadership candidates, based on the policy
speeches Tuesday night. It was an extraordinary moment, closely
noted in Quebec political circles and by the delegates in Toronto.
Ryan ran quickly through the list of candidates, rejecting Fleming
and McCutcheon as too Conservative, Hees because "one just can't
manage to take him seriously," Fulton because "he is too close
to Fleming and McCutcheon," and Roblin because he had shied
away from giving any specific meaning to "special status". That
left Stanfield, said Ryan, and he would carry *Le Devoir's* colors.

The important thing about Stanfield, according to Ryan, was
not that he supported special status — he did not, specifically —
but that he was open-minded. "The simple, spare and effective
style of this man appears to us to correspond to an indistinct but
real expectation of the Canadian people," Ryan wrote. "The
election of Mr. Stanfield would be the logical continuation of the
spirit of renovation."

Le Devoir has an awesome reputation in French-Canada, akin
to *Le Monde* in Paris or the *Times* of London, and Ryan's endorsement of Stanfield was a shattering blow to those whose hopes were
highest in Quebec — Roblin, Fulton, Fleming and Hees.

But for George Hees in particular, the unkindest cut of all came when he turned to the editorial page of the *Telegram* and read a signed editorial by his old friend, John Bassett, the publisher, who had been one of his staunchest supporters, which said, in part:

"Robert Stanfield, the Premier of Nova Scotia, came off best and George Hees was the most disappointing. The battle is joined. The issue is still in doubt. At the moment, this observer believes only Bob Stanfield can beat Duff Roblin."

For Stanfield's strategists, Bassett's editorial defection was a triumph, but they agreed with him that Roblin was the man to beat and refused to let their policy committee success blind them. Wednesday was an off-day for candidates; the party's policy committee was in session (as it would be Thursday as well) in the Royal York, hammering out the resolutions it would present to the plenary session delegates on Friday. But even if candidates were not making speeches, they were expected to court the delegates who were pouring into town in hundreds by Wednesday evening. Stanfield visited each of his hospitality suites in the Royal York, the Westbury, the Lord Simcoe and the King Edward three times during the day. He held a press reception at 12:30 p.m. on Wednesday, and was in a fine humor for the occasion.

Since it was a reception and not a press conference, Stanfield decided to have a bit of fun by giving a fake statement. So, as deadpan as the Sphinx, with his finger-tips in a steeple under his chin, he said dryly "when I become Prime Minister of this country, which I expect to be a year from now, I shall create the Canadian News Relations department.

"This department will be dedicated to the principle that no news is good news, and that suppression is the better part of valor. This new CNR will insure that no news henceforth will ever lack good news management."

But the major event on Wednesday was the arrival of John Diefenbaker, the X factor himself. He arrived from Ottawa by air at 9:45 a.m., and from the moment he stepped into the lobby of the Royal York, three quarters of an hour later, until balloting ended on Saturday night, he successfully dominated the convention, though his presence was more an omen than an outright threat. His entry into the Royal York came in brilliant sunshine, a flying wedge of policemen clearing a path for the old leader, his wife

Olive, and the ever-faithful Dr. Johnston, whose bald head looked so much like Dalton Camp's that one elderly spinster thought it was Camp, and belabored Johnston with her umbrella, shouting "You miserable man, you did it to him!" Ultimately, she was restrained and persuaded that Johnston really was a Diefenbaker loyalist like herself. The Diefenbakers then retired to their suite, and for the rest of the day, candidates practically lined up at the door to pay their respects. The first was Donald Fleming, certain that he alone had Diefenbaker's blessing. He emerged disappointed.

Alvin Hamilton was second — and Diefenbaker came out to wish him "all the best," as he disappeared down the corridor.

Roblin was third, staying for 41 minutes, newsmen noted, followed by Stanfield, Starr and of course Diefenbaker's closest Parliamentary ally, Erik Nielsen. Only Hees and Fulton did not pay courtesy calls on the old leader.

Few really expected Diefenbaker's support; indeed, it was becoming clear by Wednesday night that the old man intended to endorse no one, while mysterious hangers-on, whom nobody seemed to know, made wild predictions of up to 80% of the Quebec delegates favoring Diefenbaker if he ran. Other loyalists formed groups calling themselves "Youth for Dief" and "Friends of Diefenbaker", whose sole purpose seemed to be to feed the old campaigner futile, false intelligence about his popularity and support, despite the fact that all but the most myopic Westerners realized that Diefenbaker's day was ended. As Daniel Lawrence of Pine Lake, Alberta, put it to *Time's* Ed Ogle: "Look, I love the old guy. But I love my mother too. And she wouldn't make a good Prime Minister either."

But Diefenbaker believed the rumors and encouraged the sycophants who surrounded him, dreaming strange dreams in his aerie on the Royal York's 16th floor. And the party held its breath. If he ran, chaos was inevitable — the delegate counts of nearly all the candidates would go awry. He could cut most deeply into support for Roblin. "Half the Manitoba delegation are yahoos, and they'll vote for Diefenbaker if he runs," said one Tory observer. But the yahoo-menace also affected Hamilton and Fulton, and to a lesser extent, Hees, as well. Only Stanfield seemed to have a secure enough power base in the Maritimes to be sure of a good first ballot standing. It was a nightmare nobody liked to think about.

Besides Wednesday night was party night — a big bash was thrown by the convention co-chairmen, Goodman and Régimbal — and Robert Stanfield invited everyone into the ballroom afterwards to dance to the country-style music of Don Messer and His Islanders, with Quebec's top yé-yé group, Les Cailloux ("The Pebbles"), ringing the changes in fine bicultural style.

The day ended with candidates running in the same order they were that morning, with no gains and no slippage, except George Hees. It also ended with the policy committee's sparsely attended sessions (the sub-committee on culture even failed to obtain a quorum) producing a new draft on the constitution resolution which was almost word for word the version produced at Montmorency. So few were left at the end that it was voted through by 120 to 20. A constitutional tribunal was also recommended, as well as the granting to French Canadians throughout Canada the linguistic rights given English Canadians in the province of Quebec.

Thursday, September 7, was the day convention activities shifted into high gear, and moved from the big hotels into the huge Maple Leaf Gardens. The morning was taken up with delegate caucuses from the various provinces. Nova Scotia's delegates met at the Royal York. The other provinces held theirs in various downtown hotels, though most main events took place in the Royal York, King Edward, Westbury and Lord Simcoe.

Promptly at four in the afternoon, all delegates gathered at Maple Leaf Gardens to familiarize themselves with the surroundings and find out where they could go and could not go. Familiarization with the Shoup voting machines was regarded as so critical that two machines were set up in the lobbies of the Royal York and the Westbury so that delegates could practice voting and not slow things down when votes were cast on Saturday.

The formal opening ceremonies of the convention, and the welcoming address by the party leader, John Diefenbaker, were to take place that evening. The prospect of Diefenbaker's speech presented a number of dire possibilities, from a denunciation of the proceedings, to a walk-out that would split the convention wide

open. Dief had worked most of the previous day on it, between
visitors, and had handed it to his volunteer secretaries late that
night with instructions that a draft should be ready for him by
6:30 a.m.

He worked most of Thursday morning re-drafting his speech,
padding around the hotel suite, consulting friends and advisers.
Finally it was ready, and the Diefenbakers headed for Maple Leaf
Gardens, where pipers led them to their seats on the stage.

The arena erupted with warm, generous applause, very different
from the cold, semi-silence that had met him in the Chateau
Laurier's ballroom less than a year before. When he was seated,
the chairmen started the repetitious, tedious but necessary procedures which are followed on such occasions, notably the adoption
of a resolution approving the convention arrangements. This was
a formality, but organizers were aware that a dedicated provocateur
could foul up the entire convention if a debate started on the issue.
You could almost hear a sigh of relief as the resolution passed
without accident, and the convention swung into action, with
introductory speeches, reports and finally the keynote speech which
heralds the main event of the evening. While the formalities plodded
forward, the temperature in the Gardens rose steadily, delegates
melting in the heat and groaning at each new interruption. Peter
Lougheed, the keynoter, leader of the Alberta PC association, tried
to spice the fetid atmosphere with some drama, "Ladies and
Gentlemen," he said, "there's something going on in this country
of ours — you can feel it — you can sense it . . ." and some teenagers interrupted him from an upper gallery with the chant, "We
want Dief, We want Dief, We want Dief!"

Co-chairman Eddie Goodman wasn't taking the heat any better
than anyone else, and he wheeled on them with both barrels, like
the old tank commander he used to be, and shouted back, "Lookit,
kids, if you don't like it up there, go home. This is a private
meeting." But Lougheed got the message. He ended quickly and
Diefenbaker at last faced the party.

After all the excitement and tension, the drama and the drafts
that toiling secretaries turned out in the small hours of the morning, the speech which finally emerged was utterly baffling. On the
one hand, it was a familiar ramble along well-trodden paths of
exhortation and sentimentality and, on the other, it was a series of

sudden steeplechase hurdles over verbal thickets which left the baffled listener one jump behind, and sometimes more.

"Is he going to run, Eddie?" yelled a hog-calling voice from the gallery at the end, "that's all we want to know." But Eddie Goodman could only shrug his shoulders and bang his gavel.

"What did he mean?" became a plaintive refrain that night in suites and hotel rooms all over town — most particularly at the swish party Duff Roblin threw for supporters and delegates afterwards at the new Sutton Place Hotel.

Diefenbaker had clearly denounced "two nations", but he had done that before; he had also denounced the Liberals and urged the Conservatives to unify. But he never said whether he would run or not. And that, as it turned out the next day, was very significant.

In order to be a candidate for the leadership of the Progressive Conservative Party, a person had to have the signatures of at least two delegates on his nominating papers. Nominations had to be in by 10 a.m. on Friday, and Maclean, Stanfield, Fleming, Hees and Hamilton had all filed on Thursday.

On Friday, Mike Starr filed his papers at 8:58 a.m., Duff Roblin at 9:02 a.m., Mrs. Mary Walker-Sawka at 9:12 a.m., and Senator Wallace McCutcheon at 9:41 a.m.

It was at this point that the well-modulated baritone of Joel Aldred was heard in the corridor outside the Manitoba Room (heading the wrong way, as it turned out), calling out "These are Mr. Diefenbaker's Nomination Papers", holding the documents above his head, and generally behaving as if he intended to draw attention to himself. Re-directed into the Manitoba Room, he made the same momentous declaration to Lincoln Alexander, the elections officer, who accepted the news calmly.

Unabashed, Aldred then issued a statement that Diefenbaker had prepared to go with the papers. This did cause some consternation among the convention organizers, for it read as follows: "I remain unchanged and unswerving in my opposition to the two nations concept. I cannot consider being a candidate for the leadership of this party, if that concept remains a policy of the party. A question as vital as this should be placed before the convention delegates for a final decision before voting takes place."

It was what they feared most — a diversionary tactic over a

non-issue that could divide the convention. Goodman, Régimbal and Rhéaume went into immediate consultation. Then they called a press conference to announce that, since the recommendations of the policy committee were merely guidelines for the federal leader and the party caucus in Parliament, and not binding directives, there was no need to take a vote. "And we do not propose to call the policy committee to meet again." They also agreed to table the policy committee report and not to present it without debate as planned. Diefenbaker was satisfied with the solution, which he still regards as a major personal victory.

He says today that 17,000 "communications" came in to him about the proposed "two nations" formula. "I stopped it from being brought before the convention," he says. "They had it all nicely planned. I would put my nomination in, and then they would bring it before the convention and get it through. But I prevented it — and I would do the same thing again."

He says "the number of letters from Quebec exceeded the number of letters from every other province except Ontario" as a result of his speech about "two nations".

Almost unnoticed in the fuss over Diefenbaker's nomination, was Davie Fulton's entry at 9:51. Alexander then closed nominations and the die was ready to be cast.

There was a plenary session that day, and time passed slowly between the closing of nominations and the nominating speeches that evening. For the candidates, it was a day of polishing their final drafts and practising. Stanfield spent a long time correcting a tendency to lower the pitch of his voice when he spoke French during the speech. Tutored by Bernard Flynn, his Quebec expert, he worked most of the morning, reading the speech aloud in his suite. George Hees had his speech transcribed onto fourteen filing cards with key headings. John Maclean memorized his. John Diefenbaker wrote his on the back of an envelope in his box while the others were speaking. And so it went.

On Friday night, the heat was worse than ever in Maple Leaf Gardens, and the rumors that had been circulating all week buzzed through the audience like agitated flies spawning new progeny, while the interminable process of nominating, seconding, demonstrating for and finally listening to the candidates went on. Some of the scuttlebutt was prophetic, the rest rankest baloney. A Fulton-Stanfield axis had developed. McCutcheon's support would split. Hees would inherit Fleming's support. Hees's support was the least deliverable to another candidate. Diefenbaker would not run. Diefenbaker would resign and offer Prince Albert to whoever won the leadership, then run as an independent, whip the daylights out of the man, and declare portentously, "The People have spoken."

One of the best demonstrations that evening was McCutcheon's. It employed two statuesque blondes in thigh-slit Grecian dresses (fastened in the appropriate spot with a McCutcheon button) to provide a fanfare of golden trumpets along with nubile baton-twirlers and a skillful 'lighter-than-air' strategy which insured that helium-filled balloons with McCutcheon on them were left hanging from the ceiling long after the 20-minute limit was up. As for McCutcheon, he clearly enjoyed his girl-power, while his speech was dry and whimsical, his rasping bass voice blending perfectly with the bacchantic atmosphere. He spoke in favor of small "c" conservatism but allowed that "I am not afraid to say *deux nations*". He also added that "in a careful reading of the BNA Act, I've never found any provision that requires an audience to listen to me in French."

McCutcheon's speech ended with his supporters releasing a "rocket" filled with dozens of green, pink and yellow balloons, which floated up to the ceiling to remain there all evening as a souvenir of the fun-loving senator from Gormley, Ont.

Diefenbaker's demonstration was noisy but unexceptional, and his speech, to everyone's relief, was almost mild. He took only one crack at the two nations concept and repeated his wish for unity, "let us re-direct our attitudes of belligerence toward the other side," he said and concluded "with malice towards none and charity to all." (Sidelight: A couple of American tourists who noticed a "Dief the Chief" sign in the lobby of the Royal York were heard to ask: "What does Dief want to be chief of?")

Fulton's demonstration was faultlessly organized and his speech far better than his policy effort two nights before. He spoke articulately about *deux nations* "unhappily becoming a matter of confused words this week" and said that in his mind "confederation is based on the concept of two peoples coming together as equal partners, neither superior, neither inferior, each having a right to preserve its distinctive culture." Shifting smoothly into French, he said the concept of two founding nations and two cultures was a unique Canadian achievement, and he got a resounding reception.

Alvin Hamilton seemed determined to cram as much into his allotted time as was physically possible. But once again the thing he emphasized was Canada's survival as a free nation, while the Liberals were trying to sell it out to the United States. The constitutional issue, he concluded, was merely an excuse, a camouflage. (Sidelight: it was discovered during the week that Hamilton's 19 statuesque Go-Go girls had to share nine miniskirts. "They have to work in shifts," said a Hamilton aide, "but we are getting a lot of exposure.")

Hees's 14 filing cards improved his performance over Tuesday night, but the content still came through more as a between-the-halves pep-talk than a formal statement of intent. "I know I can lead this party to victory," he said. "Join me in the crusade for our party's sake!" He, too, commented on the *deux nations* controversy, concluding that he was "convinced that the people of Quebec do not want to separate from the rest of Canada. They want one country. The French merely want the rights they were given 100 years ago. This whole question is simply a matter of misunderstanding in translation. It shouldn't be an issue at all! Let's get going, and get on with building a nation for our two founding peoples!"

"Let's go, George," yelled an approving fan. But he went back to his box looking a bit dazed. "Win or lose, I've done my damndest. I couldn't have given any more."

Roblin had worked all day on his speech, while his strategists had worked on delegates. They had buttonholed hundreds of delegates and asked the same almost unarguable question: "If it comes to Stanfield and Roblin, and a general election is called, can Stanfield win in Quebec, and can he hold the West for the Tories? Duff Roblin — think it over." It was a question that must have given hundreds of delegates pause.

But in spite of all the effort, his speech did not seem to grab the crowd. Applause interrupted him 26 times, but it was light applause. His supporters, inexplicably, had been asked not to interrupt. On top of that, Roblin read the speech, and the lectern, he said later, was six inches too low for him. Roblin performs best when he's ad-libbing; using a text made it all sound too wooden.

The content, however, was good. He met the two nations issue head-on and openly challenged Diefenbaker. He argued that "recognition in 1867 cannot be the same as recognition in 1967 . . . the works of Macdonald and Cartier are not the laws of the Medes and Persians. We must not let words divide us. We must make their meaning clear so that they become a source of strength. When we hear the words 'two nations,' let Canadians of both languages mean the same thing." Politically, he repeated, Canada was one nation; culturally and sociologically, it was two.

Somehow Stanfield's appearance was different. The opening fanfare of pipers, the gold and silver helium balloons, and the now familiar Stanfield song ("Sing out for Stanfield, for Robert Stanfield" to the tune of "This Land is Your Land"), seemed to set it apart from all the others. While his speech, when it came, sounded more like an acceptance speech than an election speech.

He promised "no easy solution to offer for some of our profound problems — I shall only press on with the search for answers and solutions." He said the two nations issue clearly would not be settled immediately, and he would propose a policy convention to be held in 15 months' time to provide a definitive assessment for the party. He also challenged the audience on the leadership issue. "It is natural for you to be thinking as to what kind of a leader you want for your party, but as a leadership candidate I would like to reverse the process and tell you what kind of a party I want to lead."

It was a daring twist, and it was perfect after all the blather the audience had listened to that evening. Stanfield said he wanted a party that attracted the uncommitted youth of Canada — and said the open convention taking place was a vital thing in commending the party to youth. He wanted a party in which all "who consider themselves Progressive Conservatives will feel at home. I am not appealing for the support of part of the party, but all of it." And in the same sense, Stanfield promised that "I may not speak for all sides of every question, but I intend to speak to all sides and with all sides."

He did not intend to make the party "more united by making it more exclusive, but to make it greater by making it even more representative." And in ending, he asked the party to create a Canadian society "that will be recognized not merely for its affluence, for its comfort, for its power — but for its humanity, for its compassion and for its decency."

It was a tremendous speech, and it received thunderous acclaim. It was the highlight of an evening which had few other memorable moments. There had been the pathetic speech by Mrs. Mary Walker-Sawka, a grandmother from a Toronto slum district, who was determined to obtain a national audience for a point of view that would have received short shrift on a neighborhood open-line radio show. She had no supporters and no demonstration and in a nervous ten minutes told the convention that she was "100% against the 11% building tax," and for a 12% cut in corporate taxes. The only applause she got was on the last suggestion, which must have appealed to a few industrialists in the audience. The Hertz dealer from Brockville, John Maclean, who also had no demonstration, spoke clearly and without notes in both French and English, making a strong pitch for constitutional change. "I believe implicitly in the two nations theory," he said, getting some solid applause. Mike Starr, who disarmingly offered "no gifts to beguile you", talked about his own boyhood as the son of poor Ukrainian immigrants and said only in Canada could a boy from a background like his own get as far as he had. He spoke strongly for one Canada in the name of immigrants who were neither English nor French by origin. He said the *deux nations* theory should be thrown out.

If the evening seemed endless to delegates, wilting under the lights on the main floor, it was doubly so to co-chairman Eddie Goodman, who was obliged to keep his coat on, due to the sensibilities of television. As the evening lengthened, Goodman's fuse shortened. And at last waiting to introduce the final speaker, it happened: "Would you please take your seats," said an exasperated Eddie, "so that we can hear from the *last* of our great Canadians?"

The timing was perfect. The audience had an enormous belly-laugh and woke up for Donald Fleming's version of the *deux nations* theory.

At last the evening was over. Only the balloting remained — and the feverish pursuit of delegates.

Saturday, September 9, was obviously going to be a historic day, since a political party does not choose a leader very often. The amazing thing was that it would also be an exciting day. So often, leadership conventions become mere formalities, with the process of candidate elimination occurring long before the ballots are cast — and frequently before the convention even meets.

This time the drama had started nearly a year before and had heightened without abating, until the delegates stepped into the voting booths. At the start of the week, Roblin had seemed an almost certain winner. Wednesday, he had been strongly challenged by Stanfield who had been rated no better than fourth on most of the polls the previous weekend. Friday the old firehorse, John Diefenbaker, had confounded all pundits by plunging into the whirlpool himself, against seemingly hopeless odds.

As the delegates went wearily to bed that Friday night, there was no way of knowing what shifting alliances would lead to victory the following afternoon. Only time would tell. Balloting was due to start at 12:30 p.m.

X

The New Order

In a rebellion, as in a novel, the most difficult part to invent is the end.

— *Alexis de Tocqueville*

THE CLEANERS and maintenance men had worked from midnight to noon in Maple Leaf Gardens, cleaning up the debris of the Friday night nomination meeting and clearing away the chairs that had covered the ice area floor, scrubbing and polishing until the great, $16-million arena gleamed afresh.

Where the chairs had been, there was an open space roped off into lines with theatre barrier cords and chromium plated stanchions. The lines, 10 each side, led to voting booths lined up along both sides of the ice area. Inside the voting booths were 20 Shoup voting machines, a cross between a cigarette vending machine and a refrigerator, 7 ft. high and 5 ft. wide, weighing 600 pounds. (The two voting machines which had been available for delegate practice in the lobbies of the Royal York and Westbury, stood by as spares, in case one of the twenty broke down.) Each machine would handle 120 delegates who would enter the booths, pull a red lever which closed the entrance curtain and cocked the machine. They would then vote by tripping one of the levers beside each candidate's name. This would release the curtain and they would step out. It is the fastest and most foolproof voting system ever invented, and, though Dief would make a show of calling for assistance during his first vote, by the end of the afternoon men would be voting at an average speed of five seconds per vote. The ladies, perhaps exercising their divine right, took five seconds longer.

The over-all effect in the arena was one of brilliant primary color. At the north end, where the stage jutted into the ice area, a huge yellow map of Canada, picked out in spotlights, hung against a floor-to-rafters Tory-blue backdrop. In the center of the map was the monogram, CP, so familiar to Canadians as the initials of the Canadian Pacific that it took a moment for mental relays to snap to the fact that it really meant Conservative Party. To either side, tastefully set off by the dark blue curtain, were huge blue-tinted photographs of the ten Conservative leaders who had become Prime Ministers as well, from the legendary John A., with his bouffant hairstyle, to John G., each portrait framed ovally to give the impression of a gigantic cameo.

From the high roof girders, pink, yellow, orange, and blue banners, 20 to 30 feet long, hung down, bearing the crests of Canada's ten provinces. The banners swung lazily in the updraft of hot air which came from the batteries of arc lights below.

Finally there were the seats in the arena itself, 15,000 of them in red, blue, and grey, punctuated by pristine white entrance-ways. Gay advertisements for Toronto radio stations were stitched along balconies and, in dim recesses, the advertisements of sponsors who make hockey one of Canada's billion dollar industries reminded politicians that they were on sufferance in a temple of sport.

The voting booths were battleship-grey and arranged in numerical order, with top brass, officers and caucus, voting on machines 1 to 5, constituencies and delegates at large on the rest. Thus the machine-by-machine results would be highly significant, giving a sector break-down of support for each candidate — whether he was favored by the party sachems, whether his strength lay in parliamentary caucus, and so on.

Saturday morning was a time for sealing alliances, reaching the unreachable, and converting the converted. For the front-runners, it was a time to make sure that their support did not slip away before the first ballot that afternoon, while, at the same time, trying to add that extra margin of safety that would give them a commanding lead.

The calmest man in town was Dalton Camp. He had a late and leisurely breakfast in his Westbury suite and spent the rest of the morning talking about voting tactics with his assistants.

At 11:30, news came through that John Diefenbaker had

finally agreed to Goodman's solution of tabling the policy committee report on *deux nations* discussed the day before. This meant he would allow his nomination as a candidate to stand. Diefenbaker would be on the ballot after all.

It was what Camp had secretly prayed for, and to celebrate the news, he prepared a very cold, very dry, benedictory martini for all hands, serving it with priestly solemnity himself. And a silent toast was drunk to the end of the Diefenbaker era.

Everything had been done that had to be done. All that remained now was skillful team-work during the balloting, the right friendly persuasion at the right time, and Robert Lorne Stanfield would be the 12th leader of the Progessive Conservative Party of Canada.

As for the Stanfields, they were up a bit earlier than Camp in their suite farther downtown at the Royal York. They breakfasted with their two eldest children, Max and Sarah, and then they visited each of the Stanfield hospitality suites in town. At 11:15, they were ready for a light lunch and accepted an invitation to join Finlay MacDonald in his suite at the Royal York for drinks and sandwiches. By 12:45 (far too early as it turned out), they were in their seats at the Gardens.

Duff Roblin and his wife, Mary, were up and away by 8:45, after a light breakfast of coffee and rolls. He did a 15-minute interview for a French radio station shortly after nine, then headed over to the Sutton Place Hotel for a two-hour strategy meeting with delegates and campaign workers. For the first time since he came to Toronto, Roblin was behind, and he knew it. Hundreds of extra placards, white blazers and cheesecloth hats had been ordered to boost the Roblin demonstrations. At the meeting, the campaign strategy committee outlined how they would use an "ink-blot" technique to show how Roblin strength was growing among delegates. As each rival candidate tossed in his support for Roblin, a task force would sweep into the newly converted sections to offer delegates Roblin placards and buttons. It was important psychologically for the delegates to feel wanted, and it was doubly important for those not yet committed to see how fast Roblin's support was "spreading."

After the meeting, the cheering and the outward confidence, Roblin went quietly to his apartment in The Village Green, a new building not far from Maple Leaf Gardens, for a light lunch of vegetable soup, buttered bread and milk.

Voting was due to start at 12:45, but long beforehand, his spotters in the Gardens warned him that there would be a long delay getting started because the scrutineers' voting lists were not ready. Each candidate was allowed three scrutineers on the floor whose duty was to make sure that only those who were eligible to vote did so (they backed up the poll clerk and convention staff) and that the final votes were added up correctly. The lists were essential.

Finally, at 3:12 p.m., the chairman called the meeting to order and announced that the first ballot would start immediately.

For the average, still non-aligned delegate, voting day consists of long periods of boredom, interspersed with gratifying but fleeting moments of flattering attention. He sits, sipping coffee or a soft-drink between ballots and watching the rival candidates' supporters shouting it out in paroxisms of activity (Go Roblin Go!, Go Roblin Go!), getting hoarser and thirstier and wearier as minutes become hours, and afternoon turns to evening. Then, once every ballot, he gets up from his seat, very conscious of his importance, and walks down to the voting area to line up with the other delegates. While waiting, the aligned delegates take him gently by the arm and press him to see the virtues of X or Y. He nods knowingly, and minutes later, still uncommitted, votes for the man of his choice.

The aligned delegate, on the other hand, does double-duty, both voting and promoting. Between ballots, if he's in a cheering section, his job involves the increasingly hard task of getting the section to cheer at all, preferably on its feet. As the day wears on, the slogans get simpler, the pauses get longer, the standing chants rarer, and the placard waving less enthusiastic. If the delegate is "working the floor", on the other hand, balloting is a desperate time of chasing rumors, passing messages ("tell the candidate to stop picking his ear; he's on television"), fetching coffee, bromo-seltzer, a key strategist from another team, or working up and down the line of voters making a pitch, low-key or high, soft or hard.

Finally, for everyone, there's the anguished wait when the voting is done, the polls are closed, and the ballots are being counted.

The Tory Centennial Convention would go to five ballots to choose its leader and each would become more agonizing than the one before. And, despite an organization that was superb in every respect, there were inevitable snafus. When the duplicating machinery broke down at the company turning out the voting lists, on Saturday morning, it caused a two-hour delay.

But finally, at 4:30, Eddie Goodman rapped his gavel and announced the results of the first ballot.

Stanfield — 519
Roblin — 347
Fulton — 343
Hees — 295
Diefenbaker — 271
McCutcheon — 137
Hamilton — 136
Fleming — 126
Starr — 45
Maclean — 10

And Mrs. Walker-Sawka came eleventh with two votes.

A tremendous cheer went up from Stanfield's supporters: they were ahead. But the strategists huddled over their tally sheets. It was still going to be awfully close, and they would need all their considerable skills to bring in the support they needed to take them over the top. Stanfield himself radiated quiet confidence. "That's a good start," he said, munching a roast beef sandwich. "I had no particular figure in mind, but I hoped to lead — and I am leading."

To be ahead was a tremendous psychological advantage, even if it only represented 23% of the total vote, less than half the number they needed to win.

The first ballot revealed three fascinating facts. Stanfield's support was almost entirely in the Maritimes and in the party hierarchy — and practically nowhere else. The Maritimes produced almost 400 votes on the constituency level, a power base that would undoubtedly grow. But results from the first five voting machines, which tallied the votes of the officers and the high totems, showed that Stanfield had an overwhelming lead of 218 votes to Diefenbaker's 74, Roblin's 56 and Fulton's 40. On machine number one, which should have been almost solidly for Diefenbaker, Stanfield got 24 votes and Fulton 23, while the old

Chief got only 34. Clearly, if Fulton and Stanfield could combine, they would sweep the party hierarchy.

There was another encouraging statistical result. Stanfield led on seven machines out of 20, whereas Roblin and Fulton only led on four out of 20, tying on one. Fulton, a potential Stanfield ally, also led in the constituency votes.

And there was one very curious statistic: apparently, 181 of the registered delegates either spoiled their ballots, or couldn't be bothered with the heat and crowds, or couldn't quite find their way out of the hospitality suites.

John Maclean and Mrs. Walker-Sawka were eliminated.

Theoretically, there were to be 15 minutes between ballots for wheeling and dealing. In fact, the time available was nearly twice as long.

The most untutored layman could deduce from the first ballot that Diefenbaker was no longer a threat. There was no way he could possibly win. And, even before the results were announced, the old chief seemed to sense it, too. "The heat's abominable in here," he harrumphed. "It's a mess." He was upset about the voting machines. "If that be not complication, then I don't know what complication is," he said, non-plussed by assurances that they were simple, if one knew how to use them. He felt the whole convention was relying too much on gadgets and electronic equipment. The delay for the voting lists was lumped with the rest. "Nassar had all the modern instruments, but he didn't know what to do with them either," he said, to no one in particular.

He looked around, and his eyes glinted. "The Queen's picture! The Queen's picture is not even here," he repeated, in a doom-filled tone that indicated the gathering was clearly seditious and fit only for Liberals. A newsman gently steered him onto his favorite subject — fishing. He relaxed. He was going up to Lac La Rouge on a fishing trip just as soon as he could shake the treasonous dust of Toronto from his shoes. Would he write his memoirs? "I never think of memoirs," he said sternly, dismissing the impudent man. "I'm still making history."

But the line of his jaw hardened, when he heard that the Conservative Party considered his potential for future historical contribution worth 271 votes, out of 2,223 cast. Even with Hees and Fleming and Hamilton and Starr, were all to come over to him, and all their delegates were to dutifully follow suit, the maximum he could possibly muster was 873 votes — 239 less than he needed to win. Yet he stared on, perhaps in disbelief, or in the hope that at the last minute, possibly because of a multiple deadlock at the top, the wayward delegates would finally see the error of their ways.

For the leaders, there was work to be done. The key was Hees, with nearly 300 votes, which many felt were still monolithic. Fulton's support was equally solid, unbreakable, and it would stay that way until Fulton himself decided to release it. Hamilton, Fleming and Starr would help Roblin — and so would Diefenbaker, if he could be persuaded to withdraw. For the Roblin strategists, the problem was to persuade all of them to withdraw soon, so that their support would show a surge for Roblin that might pull in others.

For Stanfield's general staff, the trick was to keep the right-wing support from coalescing around Roblin, while at the same time encouraging a maximum erosion from the Hees, Fulton and McCutcheon groups who were sympathetic to Stanfield.

Camp, now very much present, was the first man to get to George Hees. They held a long, murmured conversation (Camp rarely speaks louder anyway) in the Directors' Lounge, John Bassett, an onlooker, noted approvingly, "George is cooking."

Roblin's reaction, when he heard the first ballot results, had been that "this is rather what I expected." But unlike Stanfield, who stayed calmly in his box right through the afternoon, Roblin soon found an excuse to duck under the stands to his tiny, 8-foot by 8-foot dressing-room headquarters, where he sipped ginger ale and discussed tactics with his strategy chief Harry Marden.

The second ballot was almost a straight-line projection of the first. No one had dropped out except Sawka and Maclean, but McCutcheon sagged from sixth to eighth. As soon as he heard the result, he gamely got to his feet in the row behind Stanfield, slapped a Stanfield sticker onto his lapel and shook his candidate's hand.

The vote was Stanfield, 613; Roblin, 430; Fulton, 346; Hees, 299; Diefenbaker, 172; McCutcheon, 76; Hamilton, 127; Fleming, 115; and Starr, 34.

Stanfield had gained 94 votes; Roblin, 83; Fulton, three; and

Hees four. All the rest had lost support, and Dief nearly a hundred votes. Once again, the game for the tacticians was maximize your own support and minimize haemorrhage to others. There were no withdrawals, except McCutcheon. Starr was eliminated.

The third ballot showed the same order, but a disturbing new trend appeared for Stanfield forces; Roblin was gaining support faster than they were.

The vote was Stanfield — 717, Roblin — 541, Fulton — 361, Hees — 277, Diefenbaker — 114, Hamilton — 106, and Fleming — 76.

Roblin had gained 111 votes; Stanfield, 104; Fulton, 15. Hees had begun to slip, and all the others had lost heavily except Hamilton. Fleming was eliminated and threw his 76 votes to Roblin.

The third ballot proved too much for Diefenbaker. And his wife, Olive, was weeping as they left the Gardens together for their suite at the Royal York. "Stay, stay," his supporters pleaded, but the Chief shook his head. And for a moment it was almost quiet in that vast arena, as time seemed to hesitate, and more than a few felt a tightness in their throats.

It wasn't long before a rumor was circulating that he had privately favored Roblin. His supporters denied it, but it did not matter; what left of the Diefenbaker vote was going to Roblin anyway. Gordon Churchill ended any doubts by prominently shaking Roblin's hand.

The second withdrawal was by George Hees who crossed over to Stanfield. Unfortunately, he never consulted his strategy committee beforehand, and his main Quebec organizer, Martial Asselin, was so angry that he led half of the Hees Quebec group into Roblin's camp. The Hees monolith was badly split.

More than 460 votes were suddenly floating with the Hees and Diefenbaker withdrawals and the elimination of Donald Fleming as low man, and the nagging worry was where the votes would wash up. Clearly, the bulk would drift to Roblin — and only 176 votes separated him from Stanfield.

Camp pulled out all stops to persuade Fulton to withdraw before the fourth ballot and shore-up the feeble potential that Hees was offering. Goodman, Bassett, and even Hees joined him in the Directors' Lounge to help persuade Fulton. So did the Ontario Premier, John Robarts, and the ex-Premier, Leslie Frost. Fulton was being asked to be a kingmaker. He listened, he argued, and he finally agreed that he would come in on the fifth ballot if Stanfield seemed to be in danger, but as far as the 4th ballot was concerned, he would take his chances.

Fulton's position was agonizing. On the one hand, his support would certainly win the contest for Stanfield, and his role as a king-maker would guarantee him just about any job he wanted on the front-bench. But like John Turner, at the Liberal convention six months later, and with about the same number of votes, Fulton found himself in a moral bind. His support was solid as a rock, and it had been increasing, albeit marginally. To withdraw at this point might be misunderstood — and in any case, he did not feel he had the right to do so without his supporters' approval. To wait another round was actually the best solution, since Roblin could not possibly win on the next ballot. Even if all 460 free votes went to him, he would still be short of a majority.

Moreover, if Roblin gained substantially, Fulton could still be a kingmaker — on either side.

The fourth ballot showed Stanfield's lead slipping further. The vote was Stanfield — 865, Roblin — 771, Fulton — 357, Hamilton — 167.

Roblin had been the big winner with a gain of 230 votes to Stanfield's 148. Fulton lost four votes. Now Hamilton was eliminated as low man, and his 167 votes would undoubtedly go to Roblin, enough to put him ahead of Stanfield for the first time.

Davie Fulton held the balance of power. Whoever he endorsed would be the next leader of the Progressive Conservative Party of Canada. He called his supporters together and explained what he was going to do. "I intend personally," he said, "without in any way trying to influence my supporters, I intend personally to support Mr. Stanfield." He told them they were free to vote as their consciences told them.

But there was never any real doubt how the Fulton support would go. A few of the Quebeckers for Fulton were sincerely convinced that, in his absence, a bilingual leader like Roblin would be more effective constitutionally. So they took their support to Roblin. But 80% of the others followed Davie Fulton all the way.

There was a dramatic moment as the 5th ballot was taking place. John Diefenbaker reappeared, he had returned from his hotel after a wash and change of linen, and he was going to say goodbye with dignity.

Roblin rushed to meet him in an eleventh-hour attempt to get a rallying endorsement. But Diefenbaker was no longer interested in the election. Crestfallen, Roblin returned to his box, flushed and chain-smoking cigarillos.

Marden, his strategist, looked dejected. "We've got all we can, and we still lose by 230 votes," he told a newsman. (As it turned out, they were 50 votes too pessimistic.)

When the ballots were announced at 10:20, Stanfield had 1,150, and Roblin had 969. (Incredibly, just since the first ballot, 112 more delegates had either voted for eliminated candidates, were sulking, or had simply wandered away.)

It was all over, and Roblin gamely led the cheering for the new leader. His face was dark and his smile strained, but he declared firmly "Let this great convention greet its next leader. Let the whole nation greet its next Prime Minister. Let the whole party greet and unite behind its new leader! With loyalty and support we shall go to victory united together."

It really seemed to be a time of unity. As the multi-colored balloons cascaded down from the ceiling and the bands played and the people cheered, Eddie Goodman asked: "that greatest Canadian", John Diefenbaker, to join them on the platform.

Diefenbaker took the microphone, and the audience went wild. He started with a variation on his famous opener, "My fellow . . . Conservatives . . . I join you in welcoming the new leader of this Progressive Conservative party, the next Prime Minister of Canada. . . ." He went on to reminisce a little. And now, perhaps with a twinge, they wanted to hear it. "My course has come to an end (cries of No! No!), I have fought your battles, and you have given me that loyalty that has led us to victory more often than any previous Conservative administration since Macdonald . . . now that I am taking my retirement, I say to you with the deepest of feelings that I have nothing to withdraw in wishing for our Canada that it will be one country, one nation. . . ." He hesitated, then concluded, "from the bottom of my heart, I thank you for giving me the opportunity to serve in my day and generation," and he wished his successor, Robert Stanfield, "success, wisdom and forebearance."

It was a remarkable farewell, unexpected and courageous.

For Stanfield and Dalton Camp, it was a masterly triumph of organization and imagination. Nothing had been overlooked, nothing had gone wrong. And as Stanfield promised in his brief and graceful acceptance speech, he would do his best "to get along with that fellow Camp."

The rebellion had a perfect ending.

Unshrinkable

IT HAPPENED several years ago, during the early days of the Stanfield legend in Nova Scotia. There had been a big Conservative Party reception one evening at the Isle Royale Hotel in Sydney, the coal-mining and steel-making town in northern Cape Breton Island, and things got out of hand. Exuberant Cape Bretoners tend to regard any unemptied bottle of rum as a personal challenge, and the result was that part of the hotel looked like a war zone by the time the party ended. And since the visitors had enjoyed themselves about as much as the hosts, it was a giggly but slightly sheepish group that climbed aboard the overnight train for Halifax, under the disapproving eyes of Stanfield himself. When all were seated, and the train had started, Stanfield came into the compartment where some of the group seemed determined to keep the party going all night.

There was a sudden hush, as the tall, stooped figure appeared in the center of the coach, waiting for silence. Then in any icy voice, he started, "There will be no more of that," he said quietly, adding that there would be full restitution to the hotel for all damage. "If you want to behave like thugs, leave the party." That was all, and he turned on his heel and went back to his berth. The shamefaced and suddenly sobered group quickly broke up and went to bed. And the next morning the Isle Royale was told that the party would make good all damage.

Robert Stanfield does not like thugs. "I dislike violence as a solution to problems," he says. The qualities he thinks important in a person are reliability and humanity. "There are a good many people that are interesting to spend an evening with, or something, but I really would not want to have much to do with them."

Robert Lorne Stanfield was born in the little Nova Scotia town of Truro on April 11, 1914. The Robert in his name is after

Sir Robert Borden, the Conservative Prime Minister at the time, a cold and cautious Nova Scotian lawyer who led the coalition that defeated Sir Wilfred Laurier's Liberals in 1911.

The Lorne is after the Marquess of Lorne who was Governor General of Canada from 1878–1883, and highly regarded by Canadians.

Of the two, Borden is best remembered for his tactless handling of the conscription crisis of 1917, and for his skillful foreign policy which insured that Canada would emerge from the First World War with an independent role in world affairs.

And that was not all that Stanfield had to live up to: his own family was swiftly acquiring eminence itself.

Grandfather Charles Stanfield was a weaver who had emigrated to Canada in 1856, from the Yorkshire mill town of Wakefield, not far from Leeds, and had settled in Prince Edward Island. He built a small mill at Tryon, on the south-west coast of P.E.I., married a local girl and set about proving that Canada could produce its own sturdy tweeds. A measure of how well he succeeded is that Stanfield's Limited is still in business today, specializing in woollen and rayon underwear, and hand-knitting yarns. It makes about half a million dollars profit a year and has a healthy cash position.

The family stayed in Prince Edward Island for about 10 years, buying their raw material from the island shepherds and building up a fine reputation throughout Lower Canada for their quality products. Then, in 1877, ten years after Confederation, they moved to Truro, Nova Scotia, a small town strategically located on the Salmon River north of Minas Basin at the head of the Bay of Fundy. Though only 60 miles from the bustling seaport of Halifax, Truro is close to the New Brunswick border, near the sea and today sits astride four main highways and railroads. Charles Stanfield clearly foresaw the growth that would take place with Confederation and by relocating his mill at Truro set fair to take advantage of it. He might have done even better, his descendants admit, if he had not taken such a Yorkshire scunner at advertising. He believed that a good product advertised itself. He also disliked portraits, and there is not a painting or photograph left in Truro to show what the founder looked like.

By the time Robert Lorne was born in 1914, the Stanfield family had become a force in Nova Scotia, if not yet a dynasty. His father, Frank T., would in time become a provincial deputy and eventually Lieutenant Governor of Nova Scotia. His brother, Frank T., Junior, would be a federal MP. His uncle John was already an MP and would earn fame in the war that started that year as the Colonel of the 193rd Nova Scotia Highlanders, a regiment he raised at his own expense, which was to impress — and mystify — its French allies with the proud nickname, "Stanfield's Unshrinkables".

The "unshrinkable" testimonial came unsolicited from the Klondike goldminers who wore Stanfield's long woollen underwear in the Yukon winter of 1898, and found they stood up to the most primitive if infrequent laundering. The miners also spoke glowingly of the patented trap-door that all Stanfield "long-johns" featured in the rear, to provide minimum exposure while meditating in cold outdoor privies, a sort of balaclava helmet for the rump. However, Stanfield's never featured it in their advertisements, contenting themselves with two buttoned-up wrestlers locked in combat in their underwear.

Childhood in Truro, as the second youngest of five children (three brothers, one sister), was as peaceful as it could be in any politically-active, industrially-oriented family whose fortunes were still being made. Nova Scotians tend to be warm, outgoing people who enjoy life and take only two things seriously — politics and education. And though the Stanfields were only one generation removed from Yorkshire, they adapted easily to the Scots ethic, turning fiercely Conservative and sending their children to the best private schools and then on to Dalhousie University, in Halifax.

But Robert Stanfield was exceptional even in that ambitious household. His brother Charles recalls that "he was a great reader and a good student, we called him 'The Professor' at home." He was also undemonstrative to the point that the night he banged a shoe on a table to emphasize something about international affairs to his sister is still remembered as "the night Bob was noisy".

He says his childhood was a happy one. He played baseball in summer and hockey (defenseman) in winter and, in between time, took an increasing delight in making things grow in the garden. At the age of 15 he was sent to Ashbury College, a smart private boarding school near Ottawa, where he learned to play cricket and became something of a gymnast on the parallel and horizontal bars. He won the Southam Cup for combined academic and athletic excellence and went on to Dalhousie to study economics and political science, graduating with honors and the Governor General's Gold Medal in 1936 at the age of 22. His aim at that time was to go on to the London School of Economics, but his professors at Dalhousie urged him to spend a year or two at Harvard reading law first. He went to Harvard Law School reluctantly but liked it so much that he stayed on to take his degree three years later. Harvard also liked Stanfield, by all accounts, inviting him to serve as an editor of the Law Review in his first year, along with such classmates as former Secretary of Commerce, John T. Connor; Federal Trade Commissioner, Philip Elman; and the late Philip Graham of the Washington *Post*.

"I didn't intend to practise law," he says. "When I took it, I was more interested in economics, and I thought of myself going on to LSE after a year or two. But in the Thirties there were very few openings for economists. You might get a post teaching but the staffs were not large. And unless you were interested in the government service or teaching, that was about it."

His interest in economics had been sparked at Dalhousie where his honors thesis was on the British banker-economist, Walter Bagehot, who shocked Victorian England in 1872, by pointing out that European supremacy existed not because of any innate superiority but rather because they had "the books, the utensils and the machines". Though he denies that any one political thinker has influenced him more than another, he still has a great fondness for Bagehot and the basic idea that education and tools can permit a people to control and improve their environment. Many years later, when his provincial government launched such projects as Voluntary Economic Planning and their industrial development corporation, Industrial Estates Limited, the essential idea was to apply Bagehot in the Nova Scotia context.

Almost ten years ago, Stanfield was talking about the role of a government development corporation: "(It) is not for assistance to alleviate a condition but rather with the implementation of a program which will raise the general economic level in Nova Scotia to a point where special assistance is no longer necessary."

Long before federal officials started saying that subsidies and grants would offer no permanent solution to the problems of under-developed areas, Stanfield was saying that under-developed regions did not want hand-outs or subsidies to maintain uneconomic industries, but rather that they needed seed capital to attract new industries to replace the old.

He graduated from Harvard in 1939, and went to work for the family-owned Acadia Trust Company in Truro for 18 months before joining the Halifax office of the Federal Wartime Prices and Trade Board. He had tried to join the army on the outbreak of war but was rejected on medical grounds for spinal curvature.

He also got married in 1940 to a Vancouver girl named Nora Joyce Frazee, and after the war they bought a rambling, gabled, clapboard house and four largely uncleared acres off Gorsebrook Avenue in the south end of Halifax. They called the house "The Oaks" and settled down in it to raise a family of three girls and a boy, Sarah, Maxwell, Judith and Miriam ("Mimi"). They also started a great informal garden of lawns and trees and shrubs and perennial borders which has continued to grow, change and evolve like all well-loved gardens. "It's the general effect and process that I enjoy" he says. "The general business of planning things and watching them grow. I've never had any interest in raising prize roses or prize anything. But it's a good place to grow things. Halifax has a reasonably good climate, milder than any other part of Canada except British Columbia, and you can grow azaleas and things like that and some of the hardiest sorts of rhododendron, which you could never grow in Truro although it's only 60 miles away. There must be a difference of ten degrees in temperature. The ocean holds back summer and holds back the winter too."

After the war, he formed a legal practice, MacInnes and Stanfield, which was dissolved when he became premier in 1956.

The postwar years were exciting ones for Stanfield. His law practice was just starting and so was his interest in politics. And there was also the delight of a boisterous young family to distract him.

Like any father, he takes a great pride in his family. But unlike most fathers, Stanfield has never permitted his work to come first or to interfere with what he feels are the private moments a man should spent with his wife and children. The need to spend a certain time with his family at home is basic to the man. It's an essential restorative to be alone with his children, rambling through the woods near his house in Halifax, or swimming in the sea which lies beyond them, or maybe simply pottering around his garden or even sitting, reading a book, in a garden chair under a tree.

When his first wife was killed in a car accident in 1954, Stanfield immediately asked to be relieved of the leadership. He felt that his first duty was to be with his four young children, the youngest, Miriam, only 11 months old.

But the Progressive Conservatives knew that they were on the verge of victory in the next provincial election, if only he could be persuaded to remain as leader. His friends and colleagues pleaded with him not to give up the leadership and ultimately, after long discussion and deep thought, he agreed to stay on, on the condition that he would be allowed to spend his evenings and weekends with the children.

The Conservatives won the provincial election in 1956, and Stanfield became premier, but for many years, except during election campaigns, it was understood in the party and cabinet that no demands would be made on him to attend evening functions or sacrifice his weekends.

The tacit understanding of Stanfield's need for privacy has some curious results. His telephone number has always been listed, and those who call him will, if he is at home, get the familiar, half-swallowed "hello" of Big Thunder himself — as Conservatives affectionately call him. But the main point is that only the brashest would dream of calling him at home. He answers his own telephone in the office, too, but that is not holy ground, which his home is to his loyal Nova Scotians.

There is no doubt that the privacy Stanfield has been able to maintain during more than 20 years in politics explains to a certain extent a political style which is unusual.

As Courtney Tower of *Time* once said: "Like Pearson, Stanfield may be more the fox than he appears. He is so very bad in the traditional political sense that you begin to wonder if he might not be very good."

Privacy served him well when he re-married on May 10, 1957, and managed to slip away to Bermuda with his bride, Mary Margaret Hall, the daughter of Nova Scotia Supreme Court Justice, W. L. Hall, without a single reporter or photographer knowing about it. "I don't want to do any talking now," he told a reporter who caught up with him at Boston airport. "I didn't pull off any coup."

But back in 1946, Stanfield was just another young lawyer who had left the government service to start out in general legal practice. And by most accounts, law held little appeal to the gangling young man with his scholarly stoop and uncanny likeness to Lincoln. ("I know only too well they say I'm a ringer for Abraham Lincoln. I can't help that can I? And you must admit I don't grow a beard to trade on the similarity," he told Oliver Clausen of the *Globe & Mail* years later.) Nor was money much of a temptation to a man with simple tastes and no expensive vices or pastimes. He rarely drinks and does not smoke. And in any case, there was more than enough money around with his shares in his father's Acadia Trust Company (sold to the Montreal Trust in 1961) and in the family firm itself. In short, he was, as he once told a reporter with characteristic understatement, "comfortably off."

So it was perhaps inevitable, with father, uncle and brother in politics, that he should get involved, too. No doubt family, friends and acquaintances encouraged him to play a role in the community and, as he remembers, he could not help noticing that "there were just too many damned Liberals around". So the Conservatives got his support.

The Nova Scotia Progressive Conservative association certainly needed help in 1946. They had been wiped out in October, 1945, and had been leaderless since then. The Liberals, in power since 1933, seemed as invincible as ever under their awesome leader, Premier Angus L. Macdonald, a lean, flinty, Bluenose lawyer from Cape Breton.

Macdonald was a formidable opponent. He was a brilliant organizer, fine orator and widely admired. Stanfield was a beginner politically, a dreadful speaker and, except for his last name, completely unknown.

The Conservatives held an organizational meeting early in 1947, in the little fishing village of Chester, on Mahone Bay, 20 miles south of Halifax, and elected him as the association president. A year later, in November, 1948, Robert Lorne Stanfield was elected party leader. He was 34.

One of the original members of that lonely group of PCs was Professor Graham Murray who remembered how they sold Stanfield to the rank and file. "The pitch was 'we are bringing a guy down to meet you, and he can't speak, but we think he's good.'" Sometimes the reception was non-existent. At one meet-the-leader gathering in Dartmouth, across the bridge from Halifax, only two people showed up, Stanfield and the organizer.

But slowly, in the same deliberate way that he talks, Stanfield built up his party organization. His first move as party president was to visit every town and village in Nova Scotia by car, meeting people, talking to them and above all, listening.

By 1949, when the Liberals called a June election, the PC's were ready to do battle. Unrestrained by a seat in the legislature, Stanfield had led the Opposition by speaking all over Nova Scotia, using a freedom of movement that the desk-bound party in power did not have. And when the votes were counted on June 10, his Conservatives had defeated eight Liberals for seats in the house. Macdonald's slogan was "All's well with Angus L.", to which the Stanfield supporters replied, "The tide has turned" and "Ride the Tide". However, with the Liberals still holding 27 seats to the PC's eight and the CCF's two, the tide was only an eddy.

But in 1953, Macdonald was seriously ill, and the PC's increased their seats to 12 out of 37 in the general election that summer. When Macdonald died in April, 1954, he was replaced briefly as interim premier by Harold Connolly, the provincial minister of Health and Welfare, and then by Henry Hicks, the new premier, in September, 1954.

Just before he died, Macdonald said of Stanfield: "he'll never do wrong by Nova Scotia." And in 1956, the people of Nova Scotia took him at his word, answering Stanfield's prophetic appeal that "it's time for a change," by sweeping the Liberals out of office.

Prior to the October election, party standings were Liberals 19, Conservatives 13, CCF 2. Afterwards, it was Conservatives 23, Liberals 19, CCF one. (Redistribution had increased the number of seats in the house to 43.)

Observers called it "the political upset of the year," and Conservatives across Canada took a close look at the young Halifax lawyer who had beaten the vaunted Macdonald machine.

"I think the people agreed that the Liberal government had been in power too long," Stanfield recalls. The Liberals under Hicks had promised to spend $100 million on roads over the next four years, as well as $30 million on electric power resources; they also promised to cancel the highway tax on municipalities. Hicks was so confident that he predicted that the Conservatives would not win a single seat in Cape Breton.

Stanfield replied that the Conservatives would pave every gravel road in Nova Scotia and would establish an industrial development corporation. And when the ballots were cast, Cape Breton, which had not elected a Tory for 25 years, handed five of its seats to Stanfield. And for good measure, Halifax South, Angus Macdonald's old riding, was won by Mayor Richard A. Donahoe, who had left city hall to run on the Stanfield ticket.

In the middle of the victory celebrations, Stanfield excused himself. "Tomorrow night is Halloween," he said, "and I have a date with some children. We are having a Halloween party."

It was a tradition of patronage in Nova Scotia, as it still is in some parts of Canada, that as the government went, so did the civil service. When a party came to power, it rewarded its friends with plum civil service jobs, and when the party was defeated, its friends lost their jobs, too.

And after the victory many Conservatives were looking forward to some lush rewards to make up for 23 years in the political wilderness. But Stanfield would have none of it. Those civil servants who were competent and who had taken no openly partisan part in the election were given tenure. And only a very few Liberal patronage appointees, in the provincial highway department and on the liquor board, were asked to leave their jobs. In turn, people appointed by the Conservatives to fill their places had to satisfy Stanfield that they were competent. While it might be going too far to suggest that patronage was abolished in Nova Scotia, a near impossible feat in any democratic society, government appointments were invested with a dignity and incumbents were treated with a humanity which had been absent beforehand.

In December, 1956, two months after taking office, Stanfield led the Nova Scotia delegation to the federal Conservative leadership convention in Ottawa, where he was asked to give the keynote address.

He spoke briefly, as befitted a young provincial politician, but he told the large partisan crowd in Ottawa's Coliseum that the party was ready for "new leadership and a fresh force in the conduct of its public affairs." Perhaps spurred by his words, the convention went on to elect John George Diefenbaker as its leader. If the national Conservatives were impressed by what they heard from Stanfield in Ottawa in 1956, they did not tip their hand. Several attempts were reportedly made over the next years to get Stanfield into federal politics, but who made them, and with what in mind, has not been revealed. Stanfield turned down all suggestions. He had no interest in going to Ottawa, and, as he often said himself, "that's it."

His first concern as premier of Nova Scotia was to get the administration running smoothly and efficiently. He approached projects calmly, slowly, matter-of-factly. He has always disliked snap judgements of people or events. "I'm tired of a tendency in this country to improvise some sort of response to a problem rather than working out a careful decision," he said recently. "I would rather run the risk of being accused of being indecisive or vague. I cannot over-emphasize the importance not only of policy study and research, but of discussions within the party."

In addition to the job of premier, Stanfield also took on the portfolio of minister of education, a post he held until he resigned as leader of the provincial party in 1967.

Education had played an important part in his own life, and it was to receive constant attention from his administration in Nova Scotia. The budget was tripled, and the province entered exciting new fields in educational research and innovation, becoming one of the first to use closed-circuit television to teach science courses when teachers were in short supply.

Stanfield also managed to get the Atlantic provinces to work together for their common good. In June, 1958, he went to Britain with the premiers of the other Atlantic provinces, Newfoundland, New Brunswick and Prince Edward Island, to open "Atlantic House" in London, where the four provinces share a joint industrial, immigration and tourist promotion center. While there, the Royal Family invited them to watch the Derby at Epsom Downs. Stanfield liked the look of a horse named "Hard Ridden," but he was called to the telephone on business before he could place his bet. It came home at eighteen to one.

In January, 1959, Nova Scotia introduced its free ward hospital plan with provides free public ward hospitalization to anyone resident in the province for more than three months. A 3% sales tax to pay for the plan was passed without trouble. At the same session, a budget of $110 million was voted for new highways, and a $12 million grant established the long-promised industrial development corporation, Industrial Estates Limited.

Stanfield settled easily into life as premier. His routine varied little. Up early, a light breakfast of half a grapefruit, cereal with fruit, toast, glass of milk and a cup of coffee, and then a 30-minute walk to his comfortable office in Province House, with its cream colored walls, green velvet curtains piped with gold and its perfect high-ceilinged Georgian proportions.

There would be mail to deal with, newspapers, and then perhaps a quick glance at the airmail copy of *The Economist* that he rarely keeps far from his desk. There was usually a light lunch at noon, at the Halifax Club or in a hotel, or sometimes at home in summertime, then back to the office again until 5:30 or 6, when he would walk back home again.

The first major coup for the Stanfield administration was the $40,000,000 chemical pulp mill built by Nova Scotia Pulp Limited, a subsidiary of Sweden's huge Stora Kopparbergs Bergslags mining company, on Cape Breton Island.

But almost immediately after this industrial success, Haligonians began to gossip about the government's $20,000 plan to rebuild the rotunda which overlooked Bedford Basin. The plan was to restore it to the condition it had been in when the Duke of Kent, Prince Edward Augustus, had built it in 1794 for his mistress,

Madame Julie de Mongenet de St. Laurent. Prince Augustus was 26 years old when he scandalized Halifax by setting up house there with lovely Julie, a girl he had met in France. But since he was, as a chronicler put it, "the fourth of George III's big, burly boys" there was not much that Halifax could do about it, except gawk. When Augustus sailed away again with Julie in 1800 (ultimately to father Queen Victoria in a reluctant marriage to a German princess), the prudes of Halifax allowed the rotunda to fall into disrepair.

Since then the building had been a point of contention between prudes, on the one hand, who wanted no part of Augustus's past, and historians, on the other, who felt that a unique link with the British royal family should not be allowed to disappear.

Whether it was an encouraging word from Prince Philip, who visited Halifax early in August, 1959, with Queen Elizabeth, or simply one of his well thought out projects, nobody will say, but soon after Philip left, Stanfield dispatched crews to set about rebuilding Augustus's rotunda. They say the original $20,000 estimate for repairs more than tripled before the work was finished, but by then nobody was talking about it anyway. And today the rotunda overlooking Bedford Basin is a respectable local monument.

By refusing to enter the controversy, and by quietly going ahead with the restoration, Stanfield managed to do what he felt should be done.

In 1960, it was election time again and on June 7 the Conservatives were returned with an increased majority, 27 out of 43 seats and 49% of the popular vote. The new legislature contained two major surprises: the first woman ever elected, and the first time in many years that the leader of the Liberal party was forced to sit in the gallery. Henry Hicks, who lost his seat in the election, led the Liberals from a public gallery until he resigned later in the year and retired to private life as Dean of Arts & Science and later president of Dalhousie University.

By this time people were beginning to notice that whenever Stanfield held an election, a quiet, stocky, balding man with a monkish tonsure named Dalton Kingsley Camp would set up shop in the Lord Nelson to direct Tory strategy. The 1960 election was Camp's third for Stanfield (though his first as head of his own company, formed in 1959). In the meantime, he had done well by Hugh John Flemming in New Brunswick in 1952, and again in 1956, and by Manitoba's Dufferin Roblin in 1958, and was soon to emerge as a kingmaker for the federal party.

But Camp and Stanfield were still a long way from the almost constant contact that would characterize the latter Sixties and goad Diefenbaker to say, as Camp flew from talking with Stanfield to confer with Roblin that "Camp is flitting from flower to flower".

The Sixties were years of impressive growth in Nova Scotia. In 1961, the government and its advisers took the first steps to implement a planning project for the entire economy of the province. Task forces were sent to see the heads of planning secretariats in Britain and France, and then they set about applying what they had learned to the open economy of Nova Scotia, which of course had none of the monetary and few of the fiscal controls of closed economies such as Britain and France.

Voluntary Economic Planning, as the project was called, divided the economy of Nova Scotia into ten basic sectors, from agriculture to transport and communications. For each sector, experts were recruited to study the problems and collect data.

And finally, by getting everyone concerned in the sector — labor, management, producer, customer — to discuss the situation, they discovered ways to do things cheaper or faster, and sometimes even more efficiently. They discovered where growth areas existed, and where there was over-production. As always, Stanfield refuses to take any credit for the success of Voluntary Economic Planning, but sees himself only as a catalyst who helped it happen. "I was just noticing what was going on in France and in England and I wondered if we couldn't do something along the same lines in Nova Scotia, the idea of planning for growth and encouraging people to think in terms of growth as a method for overcoming some of our economic problems."

If a moment could be chosen for Stanfield's emergence as a national figure in the Conservative party, it would not be 1956, when the young giant-killer from Nova Scotia was asked to keynote the leadership convention, nor the campaigns of 1957, 1958, 1962, 1963 and 1965, when he fought shoulder to shoulder with

Diefenbaker to deliver Conservative votes to Ottawa. The key date
for his debut, to many people, was Charlottetown, August, 1961,
when the premiers of all ten provinces met to discuss financial
matters, and to give their approval to a cultural center in Charlottetown to commemorate the 1864 conference which paved the way
for Confederation.

At that meeting, Stanfield did two things. He made a little speech
in French to honor the presence of Quebec's newly elected premier,
Jean Lesage, and he made an important speech about Canadian
nationalism and its reverse-face, anti-Americanism. "National
pride," he said, "properly tempered, is a worthy and constructive
force. A feeling of nationalism which comes not from a pride of
national achievement, but a self-conscious pose, is a sham. And a
feeling of nationalism which feeds upon distrust or jealousy is a
destructive and corrosive force." He said many Canadians were
keen for "Canada to be distinctive in every respect. They want a
distinctive Canadian culture, distinctive Canadian art forms. Insofar as this is a protest against mere imitation of what has gone on
in other countries, it is healthy. But insofar as it is mere self-
conscious desire to be different, it is barren, and it will do nothing
but harm." More serious still, he went on, "is the anti-Americanism
one hears about in Canada today. Maritimers are not anti-American.
We populated a good section of the United States, and I expect we
understand Americans better than most Canadians. We have little
of the fear of American industry which seems to prevail in some
parts of this country. We have never feared United States capital.
We have sometimes feared Canadian capital. We in the Maritimes
helped establish our country. We have not always been happy
about the treatment we have received from the country we helped
create. Our history has given us friendship and understanding
with our American neighbors. We have not inherited any hatred
or distrust, and our sense of Canadianism is based upon pride in
Canada and not dislike of others. We should encourage the
Canadian spirit to grow naturally, not to feed upon self-conscious
desire to be different for the sake of being different, not to feed
upon envy and distrust. After all, we fathered this country. We
have some responsibility for the way it behaves as it grows up."

By 1963, when elections came again, Industrial Estates Limited had attracted 40 new industries to the province and the premier was driving a Volvo automobile — a product of one of the industries that had arrived. This time the Conservatives won 39 seats in the legislature and the Liberal opposition was reduced to four. And for the first time, Stanfield was asked publicly if he would be interested in the leadership of the federal party. "I'm not interested," he said. "I am very happy here. Those fellows in Ottawa have a tough life, and it doesn't interest me. I have no intention of entering federal politics. Of course, it's always foolish to say you would never do anything, I used to say I would never get into politics."

The election had also seen the end of any pretense that the government was seeking a mandate as a team. Under Camp's deft directives, the emphasis had been changed. It was a one-man campaign and the candidates offered themselves as "Your Stanfield Man".

Stanfield himself had become slightly less formal. He addressed reporters he recognized by their first names and found time for interviews that would never have been granted in earlier years. It seemed that as Nova Scotia had warmed to him, so he had warmed to the people. In January, 1964, Frank Lowe wrote in *Weekend* about "his uncanny ability to take a political disaster area and cultivate it until everything comes up roses — Conservative roses, of course."

And it was true. Yet for those around him who are not motivated by pure, blind devotion, serving Stanfield can be a thankless task. One of his oldest supporters and organizers has had just two notes of appreciation from him in the 20 years they have worked together. Yet those two notes are so heartfelt that they make up for all the others that were not sent. "He's a patrician," says a long-time associate in Halifax. "And there is no way that this guy is ever going to come up and gently punch you in the shoulder and say 'Gee, what a swell job, great work'. He just does not punch shoulders." He is inarticulate to the point of embarrassing reporters who have followed him main-streeting in a campaign and have watched while a long, limp and rather boney hand is thrust at a passerby with plummy, croaked cordialities, to the frequent astonishment of the person accosted. His repartee also leaves something to be desired, particularly when, summoning an answer from some verbal cavern within, his mouth opens and shuts wordlessly while waiting its arrival.

In April, 1964, long before the flag debate reached its bitter end, Stanfield was one of the first premiers to urge the adoption of a new national flag, as he put it, "to reduce much of the tension in the language and culture of our country. If our grandfathers could agree upon the principles of confederation, surely we are sufficiently Canadian 100 years later to agree upon a national flag or anthem."

His growing concern for the state of the nation was evident long before he made any move to enter federal politics. And though his public statements frequently disagreed with positions taken by Diefenbaker, his loyalty to the national leader was unwavering, not that Diefenbaker appreciated the subtlety.

Stanfield also started travelling further afield politically. That April, he went to France and addressed the national chamber of commerce. In early 1965, he was asked to run for the leadership providing Diefenbaker could be persuaded to step down. Diefenbaker did not step down and when somebody asked Stanfield in February whether he had ever considered running for the leadership he answered: "Yes, in much the way I have considered ski-jumping."

He also endeared himself to Torontonians in one service club speech by reminding them that "we were voting down there in Nova Scotia long before Toronto was even marked by the first rude hut."

In the General Election campaign of October and November 1965, once again, he spared no effort to support Diefenbaker in the Maritimes (at one point making 12 speeches in 13 days) and received the ultimate compliment from the national Liberal organizer, Keith Davey, who said, when Pearson was denied a majority: "The Stanfield machine creamed us. This was Stanfield's bid for the leadership, and he came through." Through Stanfield (and Camp, the Tory national organizer) the Conservatives held 11 out of 12 Nova Scotia seats. As usual, Stanfield gave the credit to Diefenbaker: "He ran a fine campaign." Diefenbaker made no comment.

Nova Scotia passed the first half of 1966 quietly. And by mid-year two things happened which showed how prosperous the Stanfield decade had been. In August, Industrial Estates investments topped $50,000,000 and it opened offices in Montreal, Toronto and Paris. And towards the end of the month the big fight with Mother Bell took place.

The story is a simple one. The Bell Telephone Company decided that it would like to have effective control of Maritime Telephone and Telegraph Company, the Nova Scotia telephone utility, in which it already owned a percentage of stock. So an offer of three Bell shares for five MT&T shares was made in an attempt to get 51%. Despite Bell denials, which were not too convincing, the Nova Scotia government saw the Bell takeover as an attempt to reserve MT&T's equipment purchasing for the Bell manufacturing subsidiary, Northern Electric. And since Industrial Estates Limited had invested in a new plant for Phillips Cables Limited, plus other facilities for electronics suppliers, they naturally discouraged the project. Premier Stanfield took exception to Bell's "aggressive campaign", as he put it, and called the legislature into special session to pass an act limiting the voting rights of any MT&T shareholder to 1,000 shares, no matter how many shares he actually owned. The draconic measure was hardly necessary, as it turned out, since Bell failed to obtain enough MT&T shares for control in any case.

However, the story did draw attention to Stanfield's successful attempts at industrialization and few financial analysts failed to note that MT&T's business had nearly doubled in ten years along with its assets, and the company was enjoying a better return on invested capital than Bell did.

By year's end, as Camp's re-election to the presidency of the Conservative party set the seal on a leadership convention, Stanfield's out-of-province speaking engagements doubled and tripled. From October to December there seemed hardly a week when the by-now familiar, high-beaked face of the Nova Scotia premier did not appear above some speaker's lectern in Ottawa, or St. John's or Toronto or Montreal. And perhaps presciently, after the bloody annual convention in Ottawa's Chateau Laurier, Stanfield allowed that he reckoned Diefenbaker would run again.

"That would present a problem," he said. "Anyone running against him would know that even if he won, he would be taking on a badly split party. I would have to be convinced that it was a matter of real urgency before I would take it on."

XII

A Few Powerful Men

"The worst folly we could commit, at this time, would
be to accept the premise that the Tories will not have
the will to sell their *deux nations* policy."
— *secret Liberal Party memorandum*
September, 1967

THE LIBERALS did not need Gallup to tell them that the advent of
Robert Stanfield on the federal scene put them in serious trouble.
Liberal scouts had hovered around the periphery of the Progressive
Conservative campaign and convention, and the smoke signals
they sent back to Liberal Federation headquarters on Cooper
Street in Ottawa were not encouraging.

As soon as Stanfield won, their strategists were ready with
position papers for the party hierarchy. The consensus: Roblin
would have been worse, but Stanfield was bad enough. "The
Progressive Conservative party is no longer old or tired," wrote
one Liberal sage. "It has become a viable political force . . . a
contemporary party, contemporary in thought, in language and
in policy . . . We are no longer the exclusive home for the intellectuals and the political thoughtful of Quebec . . . We must not
consider Stanfield a patsy because he is a neophyte and has an
intellectual bent . . . national unity is uppermost in people's minds
. . . we need to attract superior French Canadian candidates . . .
Liberals must fight on two fronts now: bringing Confederation
to Quebeckers and opposing separatism; and also opposing the
Tories."

The Liberals were impressed with the efficiency of the Centennial Convention, and advisers warned the party hierarchy against
continuing the Liberal habit of riding with a loose rein; if the
horse stumbles you get thrown.

Yet worried though they were, the Liberals had one great advantage over the Tories: they were in power. And no matter how heady the Conservative euphoria became, the Tories could not capitalize on it until the Liberals gave them a chance — a defeat in the house or an election.

For there is no question that if the Progressive Conservatives had been able to go to the country between September and February, the result would have been an overwhelming victory for Robert Stanfield.

In every way, the Tories seemed to be more in tune with the times, from the bicultural realism of their *deux nations* policy to the handsomely rejuvenated image of their front bench. Moreover, the country was seething with ideas for constitutional reform, ideas which were not to be rendered down to their real substance until the Confederation of Tomorrow Conference sponsored by the Ontario government of John Robarts in Toronto at the end of November, and the Constitutional Conference in Ottawa two months later. The constitutional debates of 1967 were the ladder which Pierre Elliott Trudeau used to climb to power. If there had been no constitutional crisis in the fall of 1967, making national figures of the proponents of each option; and no constitutional conference in February, 1968, it is doubtful that Trudeau would be anything more than Minister of Justice today.

Of course, it was not all fortuitous. Trudeau and his allies wanted a show-down on the constitutional issue. For months, they had planned in detail ways in which they could exploit a show-down to their own advantage. In addition, to the key plotters in the Trudeau "conspiracy" — Marc Lalonde, Gérard Pelletier and Jean-Pierre Goyer — there was never any doubt about the ultimate objective — to make Pierre Elliott Trudeau the Prime Minister of Canada, succeeding Pearson if possible, but waiting one turn if necessary.

Since early in January, 1967, with the Quebec caucus under control, Marchand, Pelletier, Trudeau, Goyer, Lalonde, Maurice Sauvé and Maurice Lamontagne had been meeting in Marchand's office after caucus on Wednesdays to discuss strategy in fighting separatism in Quebec and, to a lesser extent, the question of a French-Canadian candidate to succeed Pearson. Later in the Spring, they had moved their meetings forward to Tuesday noon. They called their group, *La Taverne*, though the strongest brew around was coffee from the parliamentary cafeteria. It was a strange triple conspiracy.

All seven men were united on the question of defeating separatism, but the leadership was another matter. Maurice Sauvé, for instance, was publicly opposed to any French Canadian trying to succeed Pearson. Today he thinks he may be wrong — "I certainly was on the short term; for the long term, we'll see."

Jean Marchand and Maurice Lamontagne were inclined to share Sauvé's opinion at the start, though there are indications that Marchand was starting to regard himself as a candidate for the leadership. In any case, the basic hostility that existed between them and Sauvé was enough to make them highly suspicious of Sauvé's motives.

Lamontagne, urbane, handsome, and silver-maned, was to go to the Senate soon after Trudeau's appointment as Minister of Justice, and his role at last became what it should have been all the time — the *éminence grise* of the Liberal Party, freed from humdrum ward politics, the supreme strategist and confidant, a role he played brilliantly. Lamontagne took the young activist, Jean Pierre Goyer, under his wing, and the two of them (directed by Marchand, Pelletier, Lalonde and Trudeau), set about organizing two key happenings: the two-day Quebec Liberal caucus in Ottawa, June 27 and 28, and the four-day "thinkers" conference it led to at Maison Montmorency, September 14 to 17. There is evidence that Lamontagne had his suspicions about the Trudeau plot, but he made only one token objection when it was far too late.

Finally, there was Trudeau's own position on the leadership question. For his part, while Trudeau knew that Lalonde, Pelletier and Goyer wanted him to have a crack at succeeding Pearson when the time came, he would not even consider it until the leadership became an issue. Moreover, Trudeau has impeccable manners, and quite apart from a deep personal affection for Pearson, until the Prime Minister actually announced his resignation, Trudeau literally refused to allow his friends to discuss the possibility of his candidacy in his presence.

There was also a very pragmatic side to Trudeau's reluctance to discuss the leadership (though significantly, he did not object to Lalonde, Pelletier and Goyer promoting his candidacy). The concern uppermost in Trudeau's mind during the summer and fall of 1967 was justice. Putting it bluntly, he considered his job as Minister of Justice much more important than the leadership issue. There were two reasons. The Minister of Justice was going to be on the hot seat that year. Major legislation was being prepared under his aegis to reform Canada's archaic divorce laws and its out-dated Criminal Code. This legislation was political dynamite. The Minister would also be responsible for piloting the federal-provincial constitutional conference through some tricky reefs in February, 1968. It was crucial that he should not prejudice the success of the conference by becoming involved in the leadership issue. If he were known to be a leadership candidate during the conference, his credibility as a participant would be reduced.

Nobody realized the awkwardness of Trudeau's position better than Marc Lalonde, Gérard Pelletier and Jean-Pierre Goyer. And naturally, it was vitally important to their strategy that Trudeau succeed brilliantly as Justice Minister. A mistake in the divorce or criminal code amendments, or at the Constitutional Conference, could blow his political future to bits. Success, on the other hand, would provide an unparalleled launching pad. It was to be the ultimate gamble.

They also knew that they needed to start a ground-swell moving for Trudeau, controlled by just a few powerful men . . . for unless he became a credible national figure, quickly, the other potential leaders would be far better identified as candidates in the public eye. So, while they respected Trudeau's position and protected him as much as they could, they had to fight to keep his options open. It was very important that he should never reject the possibility of his candidacy.

Meanwhile, the plotters had to conceal their intentions from Marchand, Lamontagne and Sauvé, because there was absolutely no doubt in their minds that the trio had their own private ambitions and would strongly resist any attempt to impose Trudeau on the Quebec caucus. During the fall and winter, they stage-managed several events to give Trudeau maximum national exposure.

Marc Lalonde was responsible for the Canadian Bar Association invitation which gave Trudeau one of the most distinguished platforms in the country for his historic speech on the need for a constitutional Bill of Rights. Next, Gérard Pelletier helped publish a collection of Trudeau's essays and speeches — the original French version of *Federalism and the French Canadians.* Then Goyer organized the press conference by Trudeau on federalism at Montmorency, September 14, well calculated to take full advantage of the aftermath of the Bar Association speech 10 days earlier.

The strategy employed to contain and control separatism was modified during the year. Initially, the plan was to make speeches whenever and wherever possible which denigrated separatism, questioning its influence, promulgators and rationale. However, it became clear, particularly after de Gaulle's visit and the prestige given to separatism by his statements, that a far more subtle approach than ridicule was needed to combat the threat effectively.

La Taverne accurately perceived the extent of the threat and the enormity of the potential consequences. And so, while it seems almost melodramatic now, by August, 1967, Marchand's group had actually begun to employ every known weapon in the arsenal of psychological warfare on the separatists, even coming up with a few original innovations. People who were (and still are) involved in the strategy are understandably reluctant to talk in specifics, or for the record, but they do reveal enough of what happened to permit an observer to sketch in the outlines.

Psychological warfare is basically the technique of sowing doubts among enemy forces, while bolstering the morale of your own. Doubts are created in a number of ways — through deliberate infiltration and the dissemination of false rumors, by stimulating rivalries and disloyalty, through sabotage of documents, plans and events, by sandwiching true and false information. One of the most effective methods is the police technique of infiltration. It is also the most dangerous, if the infiltrator is caught. Much the best way to create doubt is to make some startling conversions among those who are prominent in the enemy camp and then put them to use for propaganda purposes. Another technique is to upgrade your own forces, dumping those sympathetic with the opposition, so that doubts are not created within your own camp.

In this light, the promotion of such provincial figures as Eric Kierans, who wrote a book during the summer of 1967 called *Challenge of Confidence: Kierans on Canada* (McClelland and Stewart), could be attributed in some part to the new strategy of the federalists in the Quebec wing of the Liberal Federation. But this is not to say that Kierans had no federal ambitions of his own. One sure way to attract Ottawa's favorable attention was to write a book which took the federal option.

Kierans' decision to act as René Lévesque's eliminator at the Liberals' provincial convention in October was also a role he admits he sought out. Both things were highly desirable in terms of the federal party. The book, by a well-known, pro-French Canadian Quebecker, told Quebec that distinguished men still believed that Confederation could work. The removal of Lévesque, on the other hand, cleared the way for the re-orientation of the provincial party — a re-orientation which has now taken place, it might be noted, something which certainly could not have happened if Lévesque were still a member. Thus the friendly camp was purged. What all this did to Kierans' career was of no interest to the key strategists in the federal party. Indeed, he had to fight every inch of the way on his own, before clawing his way into cabinet in the thankless job of Postmaster General.

René Lévesque's own decision to "stand up and be counted" in September, 1967, opting for Quebec's 'sovereignty', was another development that may have been encouraged or even manipulated by the federal strategists. Lévesque is very naive and transparently honest, and after all, Quebec is a village, as they say.

Two things happened in the fall of 1967 which tend to confirm the effectiveness of the psywar strategists. The first was the speed with which the credibility of the Estates General was demolished. The second was the coup which brought in Pierre Levasseur as the executive director of the Quebec wing of the Liberal Federation, clearing the way for the January finesse which slipped Claude Frenette in as president.

The nationalists' Estates General of French Canada was a parody of democracy, drawing nearly all its 2,700 participants from a handful of separatist and sporting groups and associations, notably the St. Jean Baptiste Society (which openly favors associate statehood for Quebec). The gathering was depressingly corporatist, strongly representative of the *corps intermédiaires* beloved of the National Union party, and it was not that surprising to learn that Premier Daniel Johnson's party had subsidized them, to the extent of $60,000.

There is no doubt that Premier Johnson intended to use the Estates General to goad the other premiers at Robarts' conference in Toronto. The timing was too perfect. The Estates General met in Montreal's Place des Arts on the weekend of November 24 to 26, and the Confederation for Tomorrow conference opened in Toronto on November 27. President de Gaulle's "Second declaration of Paris" the day before was also too much of a coincidence, indicating that Premier Johnson's flunkies in Quebec's Delegation Generale in Paris had also been busy.

If the National Union had taken as much trouble to maneuver the meeting of the Estates General as it did to sponsor it, Johnson's position in Toronto that Monday morning would have been much more comfortable.

As it was, the Estates General became a source of considerable embarrassment to Johnson, since reports of Western Canadian delegate walk-outs and of National Union financial backing got wide publicity in English Canada, making his position in Toronto 'difficult,' to say the least. For here was the premier of the Province of Quebec, piously attending a conference on the future of Confederation, while his government picked up the tab for another, suspiciously packed conference in Montreal which openly espoused secession. Whose side was he on? Since this was not the first time that Johnson had been caught in an ambiguous position, his much-acclaimed "moderation" at the conference was probably the best face-saving solution that could be found; certainly his attitude was in marked contrast to the contents of the Quebec position paper tabled at the start of the conference. In short, the Estates General meeting was beautifully exploited by the federal Liberals, effectively neutralizing Johnson until the federal-provincial Constitutional Conference in February.

Finally, throughout the fall, there was the Liberal propaganda itself, which followed the classic technique of repeating a simple message over and over again. The Liberal message was the need for a Bill of Rights, entrenched in the constitution, that would, as Trudeau put it, "guarantee the fundamental freedoms of the citizen from interference, whether federal or provincial, and that would have a high degree of permanence, in that neither Parliament nor the Legislature would be able to modify its terms by the ordinary legislative process." Trudeau's proposed Bill of Rights would guarantee the familiar, universal freedoms of speech, press, religion, and assembly but would, in addition, protect the linguistic rights of Canada's two main language groups. This, the Liberals argued, should be the first step. Once all the provinces had guaranteed basic rights to all citizens, without the right of disallowance and reservation, then they could start talking seriously about other problems in the BNA Act.

It was a simple and logical proposal. So simple that it sounded almost colorless beside such ringingly complicated concepts as "Renewed Federalism", "Restrained Special Status", "Broad Special Status", "Associate Statehood", "Canadian Union", and "Secession". (These titles come directly from a chart prepared by the followers of René Lévesque to show where he stood in the colorful spectrum of French-Canadian political thought.)

The federal message got through slowly. People started to discuss and think about a Bill of Rights and, early in 1968, Trudeau's own lucid, 30-page discussion of "A Canadian Charter of Human Rights" was produced by the Queen's Printer.

It is often pointed out that Canada already has a Bill of Rights — and why does it need another? The answer is simple enough. The Canadian Bill of Rights of 1960, the pride of the Rt. Hon. John Diefenbaker, was not derived from the constitution, and as a result, it has been almost useless in the courts. As Trudeau put it, rather more diplomatically, "there have been some conflicting opinions in various lower courts, but there has, on the whole, been a strong judicial tendency to assume that Parliament did not intend by the Bill of Rights to alter specific, pre-existing, inconsistent statutory provisions. The courts have said instead that Parliament would have made an express amendment, had it intended to alter its own previously enacted laws . . ." So he concluded that in order "to overcome these shortcomings while preserving the essential purpose of the Canadian Bill of Rights, a constitutionally entrenched version is required which will declare invalid any existing or future statute in conflict with it."

Trudeau's proposal made a great deal of sense in terms of bilingualism, but critics were to point out that it should not inhibit the Government, while waiting for provincial ratification, from adding some of the specific judicial rights to the Criminal Code (the right to counsel during interrogation, etc.). There was also criticism about the Government's sensitivity over making federal-provincial agreement unanimous, since unanimity is not required under the constitution except by convention.

The Bill of Rights as proposed to the Constitutional Conference in February, 1968, was so sensitive about unanimity, in fact, that it permitted provinces to "opt out" of clauses with which they disagreed. Premier Ernest Manning of Alberta had two basic objections to it. First, it seemed to him that the charter would be a carte blanche for extremists, an ultra-conservative position that was almost unique at the conference. Second, he felt that opting-out was the wrong way to go about constitutional reform, and here he found wide support. Daniel Johnson, for his part, objected to the Bill of Rights in terms of priority rather than content and said that it "put the cart before the horse." Though the Quebec nationalists' feelings were perhaps more accurately summed up in secessionist René Lévesque's statement that he was all for human rights "but Quebec could never respect human rights voted by Trudeau . . . you don't respect that deeply something that is not yours in that field." In other words, why didn't we think of it first?

The Constitutional Conference failed to achieve any major changes, but it did reach a consensus on the need for reform and a continuing federal-provincial committee to study the subject. From a federal viewpoint, the conference was a modest break-through.

In terms of the few powerful men backing Trudeau, however, the conference provided an ideal opportunity. For three days, on the right hand of Prime Minister Pearson, the Minister of Justice was transported in living color into the living rooms, perhaps even bedrooms, of nearly four million Canadians.

Behind Trudeau, puffing his pipe whenever he could, sat the kindly owl-figure who had presided over nearly fifty government

inquiries, mediations and commissions, H. Carl Goldenberg, Q.C.
— law professor and political scientist extraordinary, collector of
books in general and Disraeli's in particular, a protegé of
Mackenzie King and a protector of Liberalism ever since.

Behind Goldenberg, bringing up the line, was Marc Lalonde,
lay Pope of the Privy Council, as impassive as a medieval tapestry,
the closest to an alter ego that Trudeau has yet found.

These two were at the core — publicly detached but privately
so deeply involved in Trudeau's candidacy that they were willing
to lay on the line combined careers of 55 years as key government
consultants.

Neither man had anything to gain by supporting Trudeau, except
personal satisfaction. In fact, to work with Trudeau meant a considerable financial sacrifice, for government work has rarely made
an honest man rich. At 60, after a remarkable career that had
seen him at the center of power for 36 years, Goldenberg might
have been expected to look for quieter pursuits than commuting to
Ottawa three days a week. Lalonde, only 39, was prepared to
give up an enormously lucrative private practice, if Trudeau won,
and he had no independent income to fall back upon.

What was it that motivated them? Lalonde and Goldenberg had
known Trudeau for years. Since 1961, they had worked in tandem
creating the University of Montreal's Institute of Public Law, and
few men knew him better, both as friends and as intellectual peers.
And yet they were as impressed by his harnessed genius as the
most feather-brained teeny-bopper would soon be dazzled by his
"swinging" life style. To this day, Goldenberg will quite matter-
of-factly tell anyone who asks, that Pierre Trudeau is one of the
most brilliant men he has ever known. Lalonde will say no less.

The academic fan club is by no means small. When Goldenberg
was named special counsel on the Constitution, in May of 1967,
his associate counsel was a young law professor from the University of Alberta named Ivan Head. He, too, as Trudeau's candidacy
emerged, became a member of the confidential "brain trust" who
met with Gérard Pelletier in his apartment on Monday nights to
discuss policy and plan strategy. Still another alumnus of the
Institute of Public Law was Professor Jean Beetz, whom Trudeau
himself described as "the very best expert from French Canada"

on constitutional law, joined the Privy Council during the Lalonde-Trudeau regime and became head of the provincial secretariat.

On May 12, Lester Pearson confided to his cabinet ministers that he thought he might step down as Prime Minister, as soon as the Centennial celebrations were over. To some of the cabinet who had been campaigning more or less discreetly for the leadership for months, Pearson's philosophizing had the effect of a starter's pistol. And so, Trudeau's press conference three weeks later, to announce the appointment of Carl Goldenberg and Ivan Head to the constitutional task force, was something of a ho-hum happening. The Minister of Justice felt constrained to insist that in spite of appearances there were still a few constitutional problems kicking around, but Canada was surfeited with Centennial bonhomie and in no mood for a lecture. He spoke of a "crisis," then decided to withdraw the word, because he didn't want to create a "crisis psychology". Nevertheless, he remained deeply concerned about the recklessness of some people and their approach to constitutional reform. "People don't seem to realize what a delicate mechanism a federal form of government is," he said somewhat wistfully. "Some of the provinces would be surprised if they knew their power to bust it up . . . and not only Quebec could do this."

But Canada was not listening. The Conservative leadership race was half run, and the Liberals were just starting (with Revenue Minister John Edgar Benson an improbable early candidate possibility). Expo was a huge success, and Walter Gordon wasn't — he'd just called Vietnam "a bloody civil war which cannot be justified on either moral or strategic grounds" and been rebuked by Pearson.

Since the spring, members of the Quebec federal caucus had been taking every opportunity to undermine the "special status" position of the National Union. The three principle targets were Daniel Johnson, Marcel Masse and Jean-Noël Tremblay, and most of the shooting had been done by Jean Marchand and Jean Chrétien.

By May, however, the return flak was getting thicker and the new Minister of Justice, now exposed as the commander of the federal offensive, was catching most of it. Johnson managed to enrage Marchand by implying that Quebec MP's in Ottawa were little better than traitors. While Liberal Opposition leader Jean Lesage (who had failed to persuade Pearson not to make Trudeau Justice Minister) stuck his knife into Trudeau over the Bill of Rights and again invited the National Union to fight Ottawa arm-in-arm with the Liberals. Several times later that fall and winter, Lesage would repeat his suggestion for a bipartisan approach to the constitution, but Johnson always ignored him.

Towards the end of June, as the summer recess approached, the Quebec caucus was called together for a two-day seminar, organized by Jean-Pierre Goyer and Maurice Lamontagne, the final session in the educational series that started during the winter of 1966. Its purpose was two-fold: to brief Quebec members thoroughly on the federal constitutional position before they went into their ridings on vacation, and to make detailed plans to take control of the party's provincial organization, which was still in the hands of the Old Guard. This two-pronged strategy would ensure that MP's would be able to convince their constituents back home that the federal option was the best course for Quebec. And that, in turn, would have the effect of bringing prospective convention delegates over to the federalist point of view, as well as adding support for the new slate of officers that the reformers intended to present at the December meeting in Montreal (for example, presidential candidate Claude Frenette).

The two-day seminar also prepared the way for a more ambitious four-day meeting at Maison Montmorency in September, where the federal MP's would be able to review the work and problems of the summer and refine their position on federalism still further with the help of outside experts from the universities, corporations and civil service (Lalonde and Goldenberg among them).

It is interesting to note, in view of the constitutional furor that developed in the wake of de Gaulle's visit, that the mood of the time was so relaxed. On June 27, for instance, Trudeau told the House of Commons that he did not think it was time to redraft the constitution because a consensus did not exist on what was needed to replace it. "If there were a specific constitutional issue, I would be glad to give it high priority, but this is not the case." He said ideas for constitutional reform were legion, but the fact that some governments were using the issue to divert attention from their own problems shouldn't permit it to become a football.

Nevertheless, it became a football a week later, when Pearson agreed to a request from the provincial premiers to hold a constitutional conference early in 1968. Invitations were sent out in August, and by mid-November Pearson was echoing Trudeau's line of thought by suggesting that a bill of rights would be a good start to constitutional reform.

Parliament recessed for the summer on July 7 and the members scattered to a belated enjoyment of the Centennial summer. For some, it was brief. Only four days after recess, the former Quebec leader and Minister of Justice, Guy Favreau, died in hospital in Montreal. The tragedy of Favreau's political career, the slanders of him by the Tory opposition, and the unequal workload given him by the Prime Minister, all spilled out again in the eulogies that filled Canadian newspapers.

Favreau had been ill since the previous fall, and he had hardly attended the spring session as his kidney disease worsened. He resigned from the Cabinet on April 3 and accepted an appointment to the bench in the Quebec Superior Court, but he was never able to hold court as his kidney ailment soon deteriorated into fatal uremia.

Jean Marchand, his successor as Quebec leader, was generous in his tribute to a man who had sponsored him, later opposed him, and had finally been defeated by him. "Guy Favreau was a good man, yet attempts were made to give him an image of wickedness. He was an honest man, with the kind of honesty that does not even suspect the bad intentions of others." Yet the most eloquent comment of all was Guy Favreau's own, in his letter of resignation to Pearson: "Whether my contribution has been successful or not, at least no one will be able to deny that I have given it all my heart."

His death was a personal blow to Pearson. "I have a deep and tragic feeling of regret about Guy Favreau who is one of the men I admired most and whom I persuaded to go into politics," he recalled a year later, after his own retirement. "I had picked him to be the leader, and perhaps my successor, and I begged him to come in. Even in those days, I knew I was going to retire before long, because I had always made up my mind that I wouldn't stay on after Centennial Year." Pearson said he did not know Favreau at all well, when he persuaded him to run in 1963, but the people who recommended him knew him. "I had great faith in their judgement, and Favreau made a wonderful impression on me," he recalls. "So I thought what I must do now is push him ahead as fast as I can. And if he's strong enough, he'll be able to take it." Pearson paused. "But he wasn't, and he wouldn't tell me. Oh no, if only he'd said, 'Look, you are giving me too much, I really don't know about Parliament. I need some time.' But he didn't. He did everything I asked him to do. And his back broke under it. But I don't feel in any way, shape or form that I was unfair to him. Not at all. And I have been pilloried for this. But we talked about it and he didn't feel that."

Pearson is severely critical of Opposition Leader Diefenbaker's attitude towards Favreau, Tremblay and Lamontagne. "What he did to those fellows was unforgivable," he says quietly. "Two of those men are dead, and though they didn't die of parliamentary attacks, that hastened their death. There is no doubt about it in Tremblay's case . . . This was the worst part of my period in office."

Pearson's regret is that he was not tactician enough to protect them all. "I was not a tough enough parliamentary politician to tell them what to do," he says.

With the death of Guy Favreau, the French-Canadian Old Guard in the party knew that there was no one left to protect them from the reformers. Favreau had been neither old guard nor new, and while his effective power in caucus had long since vanished, his power in the party had remained. Throughout July and August the Old Guard watched desperately for a chance to counter-attack, not the counter-attack of a wounded but still dangerous adversary, but the piteous, terrified counter-attack of the baboon at the leopard. For Marchand and the reformers were moving in for the kill, and the Old Guard knew the inevitable outcome would be merciless. All they could hope for was that it would be quick.

As it turned out, it took some time.

The arrival of de Gaulle, the controversy that followed, and the final stages of the Conservatives' leadership campaign took the spotlight off the federal Liberals for August and part of September.

Meanwhile, the Liberal leadership marathon was well under way, with Defense Minister, Paul Hellyer, running hardest.

Hellyer spent the month of August at Arundel Lodge, the hotel he owns on Muskoka Lake near Gravenhurst in the Southern Ontario cottage belt, flying in anyone and everyone who would consider him as Prime Ministerial material. He had persuaded his executive assistant from the Department of Defense, Bill Lee, a man of great charm and awesome efficiency, to run his campaign for him. And from mid-July until Labor Day, there were few weeks when the Hellyers' big Buick did not visit Gravenhurst Airport two or three times to fetch or dispatch incoming and outgoing Liberal Party brass. The Hellyer faithful ranged from Senator Keith Davey and David Greenspan of Toronto, to Bob Andras from the Lakehead and George Van Roggen from Vancouver.

While the tacticians were plotting his campaign, the power-brokers were treated to water-skiing exhibitions by Paul Hellyer himself. "He'd go water-skiing, showing he was virile and young," recalls Lee, "and also in order to get across to the public that he was only 44. At one point, we had the biggest pizza pie ever baked for his 44th birthday (August 6) and held it in a public park with thousands of balloons with '44' all over them. "There were Italian and Polish groups all doing their native dances and songs, and as a finale we brought out this huge, 92-pound pizza with '44' spelled out in pepperoni. We made the front pages of the newspapers and got on television, too. And this wasn't even an election campaign, just trying to get people to believe he was 44. This is unlike Trudeau who looks 38, when he's 48; Hellyer looks 54 when he's 44, and it's terribly unfair. We had real trouble with people on the prairies who were astounded that he had 20 years of experience, and he's only 44. They'd say 'Aw, don't give us that baloney: he's been 44 for the last 10 years . . . he was around when St. Laurent was there.' "

The upshot was that Pearson got so annoyed with his ambitious cabinet ministers that, on August 18, he announced publicly that he would probably stay on until 1968, and maybe longer. But Pearson's pique had no noticeable effect on the campaigners and their carelessly cloaked ministerial hustlings.

Finance Minister Mitchell Sharp, 56, was polishing his image of fiscal reliability and moral rectitude with as many television appearances as his able executive assistant, Michael McCabe, managed to muster. McCabe, who used to sell soap, did a brilliant soft-sell on Sharp whose homely honesty on the screen and guileless platform personality almost disguised his lackluster political performance in the House.

External Affairs Minister Paul Martin's problems were rather the reverse. A superb tactician in Parliament, in which he was a 32-year veteran, he never quite lost his strangled bull-frog look on video, nor a certain credibility gap on the hustings. But the untiring, 64-year old minister bustled around collecting political IOU's for the leadership race and took advantage of all the stately occasions that Expo and world crises offered.

He went to Chancellor Konrad Adenauer's funeral, caught up with French foreign minister (now Premier) Maurice Couve de Murville, and visited Poland to look at Auschwitz, all in the month of April. He briskly investigated powdered milk-bag scandals involving Canadian aid to India, tried to keep the Israelis and Arabs from each others' throats, and told President Lyndon Johnson how he could solve the Viet Nam problem. He disagreed with his parliamentary secretary, Gérard Pelletier, who said that Canada did not want to be an international fire brigade, when Martin was already wearing his firechief's hat. He talked about Canada recognizing Communist China in September and seemed to contradict himself in October. He boasted to the NATO conference in Brussels that Canada would be stronger than Britain and France within 15 years, and wrote an article in Le Monde saying how well Canadian bilingualism was doing, too. He also published a book of his own speeches (Paul Martin Speaks for Canada) in December, which one critic said was "very hard to pick up, once it has been put down." And, appropriately enough, he rounded out the year by playing the trumpet at the MP's Christmas Party.

A synopsis of Paul Martin's busy, busy year would be incomplete without mention of the five times he scolded the United States about Viet Nam, an average of once every two months, which always got good play in Canadian newspapers to whom sanctimony is a way of life. This displeased the United States, of course, but at least Dean Rusk, the Secretary of State, had the comfortable knowledge that whatever Paul Martin said about Viet Nam, he had never actually been there and this tended to weaken his position. And in any case, the needling used to be worse when Chester Ronning was around. Ronning, a 73-year-old Canadian diplomatic corps veteran of Kuomintang vintage, used to go to Viet Nam (generally Hanoi, which made it worse) at Martin's behest in earlier years, but he had started scolding the U.S. all on his own after his last trip in 1966, and Martin had been forced to can the competition for "indiscretion".

The other candidates were conducting their campaigns on a somewhat cooler scale. The Minister of Trade and Commerce, Robert Winters, 57, was not running at all, and it was an open secret that he was thinking of returning to private life because he disapproved of the spendthrift ways of the Pearson administration. The Minister of Health, Allan Joseph MacEachen, 46, who was also house leader, had the potentially glamorous job of bringing in Medicare, but at that point it had been postponed until July 1, 1968 — a bit remote for anyone with immediate leadership ambitions. While the Registrar General, John Napier Turner, 38, had the somewhat easier job of sounding like the champion of the underdog in consumer and corporate affairs, without actually throwing a real scare into the big corporations.

Throughout the summer and fall, all five potential leaders in the Cabinet kept platforms occupied across the country, dreamed up new ways of getting their pictures in the paper (the press didn't mind; it was great copy), and deluged all the media with advance copies of their texts.

In Quebec, major events took place. On September 4, at the Chateau Frontenac in Quebec City, Pierre Elliott Trudeau delivered his first important speech as Minister of Justice to the 49th annual convention of the Canadian Bar Association. His topic was the Bill of Rights and the speech had been reproduced widely and with reason. It is one of the most lucid documents Trudeau has ever written, and it put the case concisely for making a Bill of Rights the cornerstone of Canadian constitutional change.

The nationalist reaction was immediate and unfavorable, but

the real uproar was caused by Trudeau's free-swinging press conference on September 5, the day after the speech. Provoked by newsmen, he referred to the "special status" demanded by the National Union and others in Quebec as *une grande fumisterie intellectuelle* (a huge intellectual practical joke) and later on, described it less delicately as a *connerie*, which is very vulgar and perhaps best left untranslated.

This enraged the high priest of special status, Claude Ryan, the director of *Le Devoir*, who is not a man given to *conneries*, in print or in person. And he tore into Trudeau for his "arrogant, intransigence," his "detestable tendency to judge from ahigh and afar problems which he does not understand", his "destructive rigidity, hostility and dogmatic lack of serenity."

Nevertheless, Trudeau went serenely on. When the Federal Liberals gathered at Maison Montmorency on Wednesday, the following week, their mood was not a happy one. Thanks to Trudeau, the show-down between federalists and nationalists had arrived a lot faster than many had wanted. Some of the MP's, notably Jean-Pierre Côté, the Postmaster General, who had no love for the men who had dumped his old friend Favreau, asked for a vote of censure on Trudeau for his special status position. Jean-Pierre Goyer, Maurice Lamontagne and Jean Marchand spent most of Wednesday and Thursday soothing the ruffled feathers of the Quebec members. They persuaded Trudeau to stay away until Friday so that things could get back to normal before he arrived. He agreed. And sure enough by Friday, Côté's vote of censure had been abandoned, and, although the Justice Minister would be asked to explain himself, it was going to be done tactfully. The solution was a press conference that afternoon, which the MP's could attend along with newsmen, where Trudeau explained very carefully why he rejected special status. It was a masterly performance, and he got a standing ovation. Goyer, with his eye on late-comers, had the wisdom to tape-record the entire conference, complete with applause, to be played back to others in the evening.

As it turned out, the Liberal policy conference at Montmorency wound up as a resounding success for Trudeau's position. Nonetheless, Marchand and Lamontagne went to great pains to mollify nationalists by giving the impression that some sort of special status could be accommodated inside the federalism they were talking about. Trudeau kept silent.

The controversy over Trudeau's position on special status had maneuvered Jean Lesage (at this point, a power-broker with no power to barter) into a position of total support of the National Union. "By these declarations," said Lesage casting about for support — any support, wherever he could find it "Mr. Trudeau has proven that he does not accept the soundness of certain great principles to which the great majority of our compatriots adhere."

The principles, he said, were recognition that two nations existed in Canada, something, he added, "which I have been preaching for years." And secondly, that Quebec was the national homeland of French Canadians and therefore "should obtain the maximum autonomy required to safeguard its economic, social and cultural interests in North America."

Lesage asked the National Union to form a constitutional coalition on the matter. "We sincerely believe that the two main parties in Quebec have shown that in the constitutional and national questions they have identical views . . . and that it would be possible to explore fully and define precisely these views in the constitutional committee."

But within days it was Lesage's turn to look worried. On September 18, in Montreal, the most charismatic minister in his shadow cabinet, 45-year-old René Lévesque, declared that the only solution for Quebec was independence — but he was careful to avoid the separatist label. Lévesque saw Quebec as a sovereign state which would maintain very close bonds with the rest of Canada, such as dual citizenship, a common central bank and currency, tariff-free frontiers — in general, a position he preferred to liken to that which existed in Scandinavia.

The effect of Lévesque's announcement was sensational. Long suspected of favoring independence, Lévesque now admitted that he had been convinced about it since 1963. As the Toronto *Star's* able Quebec correspondent, Robert McKenzie, wrote the next day. "Partisans of Quebec independence waited seven years for René Lévesque. He arrived last night."

Lévesque's conversion to separatism made the movement

respectable at last. Until a credible political figure was prepared to lead the movement, separatism was fated to remain a splintered, shifting maelstrom of alliances and petty rivalries. With Lévesque it got a chance to coalesce, reach a broad cross-section of the people, and become a viable political movement.

Claude Ryan was inclined to see the developments with dismay. On September 21, he said the effects of the Trudeau and Lévesque moves could only increase Quebec nationalism, harden English Canadian reaction, and slow up constitutional reform. He was also dismayed by the planning fad. "We excel in setting up organizations on paper, without putting into them any dynamic content."

So, it was not surprising that when Parliament resumed on September 25, the constitutional question dominated everything else. While the new Tory leader, Robert Stanfield, watched from the public galleries like some appropriately Gothic ornament, Lester Pearson told the House the situation was very serious.

October was another month dominated by shifting constitutional moves in Quebec. While Robert Stanfield went about winning an unopposed by-election in his family's old Nova Scotian riding of Colchester-Hants, the Quebec provincial Liberals headed for a show-down between Lévesque and Eric Kierans. In his book, Kierans examined confederation from an economist's point of view and concluded that bilingualism and equal opportunity would go a long way to ending French-Canadian discontent. As mentioned already, it put him squarely on the side of Trudeau, Marchand and the reformers. Moreover, as president of the Quebec Liberal Party, Kierans directly challenged René Lévesque's thesis that a "Canadian Union" (the name *Mouvement Souverainété-Association* came later) was the solution to Quebec's problems.

His main point was that it was very doubtful that the rest of Canada would be prepared to enter into a common market arrangement with a Quebec that had just ruptured Confederation, and he painted a grim picture of the flight of capital and know-how that would take place, if Quebec did secede in such a way. He said it would cost Quebec $2.3-billion in its first five years and lead to a 20% drop in the standard of living.

Others joined Kierans in persuading Lévesque against the idea. One was a fast rising young Quebec Liberal lawyer-economist, Robert Bourassa, heir to a famous name. Another was Douglas

Fullerton, a former bond dealer, now treasurer of the Canada Council and one of Canada's better known financial experts, who wrote a "Dear René . . ." letter backing up Kierans' contentions. "The consequences, economic and financial, of the separation of Quebec would be catastrophic for the province in the short term, without discussing the long term . . ." Fullerton wrote in his open letter, published by *Le Devoir*.

The nub of Fullerton's argument was, as he wrote, "capital hates uncertainty and, while one can easily be cynical about the motives of capitalists and entrepreneurs and say that they are more interested in profits than political gambles, nobody likes to jump into a financial crisis or political troubles." Fullerton said that Quebec had been seeking long-term capital funds increasingly during the previous five years, with annual borrowings running at about $500-million. This had flooded the bond market and "today Quebec provincial and municipal bonds are practically impossible to sell in Canada outside Quebec." Issues had been cancelled because institutions were stuffed with Quebec bonds and the ability of the Quebec Pension Fund to absorb them was stabilizing at about $130-million a year. The resistance to Quebec paper had driven interest rates for prime credit borrowers in the province up to 7% (it was to go much higher during the winter). This had depressed the market for older Quebec bonds with lower interest yields, many of them selling at 20% discount. And if it were not for the Quebec Pension Fund being ready to provide a market, many Quebec debt securities would have been unsaleable at any price.

"American buyers are tending to become a little less ready to buy Quebec bonds," wrote Fullerton, "or, if you like it, perhaps a bit more on their guard in relation to Canadian political problems." While international tight money had much to do with it, along with Quebec's high borrowings in the 1960's to finance badly needed capital investments, he said "one cannot minimize the importance of the political factor, the fears of the investor on the subject of nationalism, and the uncertainty that reigns over the future of Quebec are also important factors." As a member of Quebec's economic Advisory Council, with both Lesage and Johnson, Fullerton was no willful denigrator. He meant it.

Fullerton analyzed the results of Quebec independence as follows: an immediate sell-off in Quebec bonds and a sharp, steep drop in provincial credit; a more serious, almost panic-stricken out-flow in private funds; the cut-off in equalization payments from the federal government, estimated at about $500-million a year. This last would force Quebec taxes up to compensate for the reduction in tax revenues (equalization payments, in over-simplified terms, make sure that each have-not province has the same *per capita* tax revenue as the richest provinces), and as a result reduce spendable income, lowering the standard of living and increasing unemployment. This, in turn, would put off investors — and so the vicious circle would spiral downward.

Lévesque retorted that equalization payments only amounted to about $350-million. He said many expenses incurred by the federal government's establishment in Quebec would be eliminated since Quebec had already duplicated most of them in any case. He thought Quebec would be able to continue to borrow at about $450-million annually, because it would not scare away investors — though he did not say how and hardly refuted Fullerton's point about capital psychology. Lévesque's main argument seemed to be that Canadian business had a large investment in Quebec and a profitable market there for everything from insurance to shoes, a market it would not want to kiss off. And in order to do business, institutions, such as insurance companies, would be required to invest a percentage of their premiums in the province, as required by most sovereign states. He also felt the common currency, central bank, dual citizenship and tariff-free, customs-free frontiers would stabilize things.

The economics of separatism is an argument that continues to this day. It has to be one of the most futile exercises in Canadian politics because nobody can know for certain what is likely to happen until it actually happens. But it is significant that so few economists side with Lévesque, who seems to get almost all his support from the nationalists of Montreal's Ecole des Hautes Etudes Commerciales and precious little from the schools of London, Boston and Chicago.

The furor surrounding Lévesque was like gasoline on the embers of the "Great Canadian Debate". The results in federal terms were a return barrage of speeches by Members of Parliament, favoring the federalist option. One of the most important was a speech in Quebec City on October 5, by Maurice Sauvé, in which the Minister of Forestry said that the constitutional conference in 1968 would be open for discussion of all constitutional options. The speech had been vetted beforehand by both Pearson and Trudeau, and it specifically emphasized that the federal government no longer considered the discussion of a Bill of Rights a *sine qua non* to constitutional amendment. "It is not the policy of the federal government to place any restrictions on the extent or subject matter of a constitutional conference," said Sauvé.

There could be no doubt about it. Ottawa was softening its stand. Clearly a trend established the day before by Daniel Johnson's National Union government.

Premier Johnson, by design or accident, always seemed to be out of Quebec when the worst political storms developed and in September, as it happened, he was in Hawaii, recovering from a mysterious ailment. (After his death in September, 1968, it was revealed to have been a preliminary heart-attack.) At any rate, on October 4, Johnson assured the rest of Canada, greatly alarmed by Lévesque, that "in June, 1966, the National Union Party did not receive a mandate to build a Great Wall of China around Quebec."

From his $85-per-day cabana at the Kahala Hilton in Hawaii, Johnson dictated a long statement to the Montreal afternoon newspaper, *La Presse*, in which he said quite clearly that what his government wanted was a new constitution, made in Canada, which would let all citizens, irrespective of origin, feel at home everywhere in Canada.

"Quebec, as the hearth of the French Canadian nation, has a major role to play in the search for the equality we want, but each and all of the other provinces, as well as the federal government, have their responsibilities." He saluted the "better understanding" that was being shown towards constitutional affairs and described Ontario Premier John Robarts' Confederation of Tomorrow Conference as "a real turning point in our history". But he warned the federal government to realize "that federalism can be built only with the provinces and not against them. It's a disservice to the country to describe as separatist those who are seeking with peaceful and democratic means the full-flowering of the French Canadian nation."

Trudeau greeted Johnson's statement with the comment that he would only have to add "and vice-versa" on the end, and he would almost be able to sign it himself, while Pearson, for his part, said he was "happy to learn that Mr. Johnson did not want to isolate Quebec," and pointed out that it was the federal government, and not the provinces, which had been taking all the initiatives in constitutional matters in recent years.

There was a slightly snappish edge to Pearson's comments, as well there might be. If Johnson, lounging luxuriously in Hawaii, thought he was going to play Solomon at the Constitutional Conference after doing his best to damage federal-provincial relations for 16 months, Pearson was going to put him in his place, which was as one of Canada's 10 provincial premiers, and one who, by all the laws of representation, had no right to be premier in the first place.

Besides, Johnson was not the only burr under Pearson's saddle that fall. Pearson disliked brawls and never really understood the furious dog-fight that was taking place between the old and new guards in his party's Quebec wing. In fact, the whole sound and fury of Quebec politics was really beyond the ken of an Ontario United Church minister's son turned statesman. And to hear his own Minister of Justice describe the Quebec constitutional option as a bit of *connerie* must have curled the hair on his toes.

Then there had been Lesage, never one of Pearson's favorites, trying to push him around still almost as if he was the deputy premier of the Province of Quebec, instead of the ass who now led the Opposition as a direct result of his own pomposity.

There had also been the silly business with Paul Martin, who couldn't stop scolding the United States, disagreeing publicly with his parliamentary secretary; there had been Paul Hellyer and his wretched pizza race for the leadership; Mitchell Sharp; Allan MacEachen; John Turner and all the other over-ambitious party members who did not have the decency to let a 70-year-old Prime Minister live out Centennial Year in peace and then quietly retire.

To cap it all, there was the Centennial Convention of the Conservatives and the huge success of Robert Stanfield. Columnists were already describing Stanfield as a "credible" leader as though Pearson had somehow become incredible, which was rather hard. Like the old Diefenbaker-Pearson political canard. "You see John Diefenbaker is supposed to be the great parliamentarian, the great political tactician of our time," he reminisced a year later, "and I was supposed to know nothing about politics. John Diefenbaker won an election when almost anyone could have won it and with a majority of whatever it was, in 1958, the biggest we've ever had. But in five years he was finished. Now if he really had been a good political leader, he would still be in office. I came in with 40-something members, inexperienced myself, and most of them inexperienced too, and inside five years, with a good deal of help from John Diefenbaker, we were in office."

Lester Pearson had virtually rebuilt the Liberal Party, re-launched it, set a course through some of the toughest legislative reefs in Canadian parliamentary experience and wound up in safe harbor, maybe miraculously, but still afloat and still in command — only now faced with something akin to a mutiny. It was decidedly unfair.

Columnists wrote that there was talk in party circles that the government would be defeated in the next election, while back-benchers were petitioning him to stay; leadership candidates were suggesting that the time had come. And everyone was saying that it was *Pearson's* indecision that was hurting the morale of the party.

There was also trouble in Cabinet over spending cuts. The bond market was in bad shape. The new Canada Savings bond issue was not selling. And so it went. It was not Pearson's indecision that was so amazing, in retrospect, as his forebearance.

Yet there was a lone compensation in all the trouble. As noisy and rude as they were to each other, Pearson's Quebec members were standing by him with unparalleled loyalty. Trudeau in particular had become one of his closest confidants. It had been a natural enough development, yet the relationship was always a professional one, always correct. "He's not an easy man to get along with very well," Pearson says, "and I didn't want to get too chummy with him because that would increase suspicion that I was grooming him. But I did get to know him, and the more I got to know him, the more I respected his abilities, his toughness and his pragmatism. This fellow is not only an intellectual, he's really a tough Tammany politician."

There was one typical anecdote in Cabinet. "We were all arguing about whether or not we would bring in Medicare. Walter Gordon got pretty deeply involved. So Trudeau took over with his calm, sort of objective approach, weighing the pros and cons from a political point of view. And he came to the conclusion that we had to bring it in, because if we didn't, we'd be ruined." Pearson was astonished by Trudeau's political flair. "That's part of him, he does understand that you have to make concessions, he's not doctrinaire. He didn't say very much in cabinet, but when he did, it commanded attention. He was a well-balanced party tactician as well as a good minister — and a very brilliant man."

Pearson will always remember Judy LaMarsh's quarrel with Trudeau about a judicial appointment she wanted made in Cochrane, in Northern Ontario. Trudeau turned it down and Judy appealed to Pearson. "She thought that I would reverse his decision, but we both told her to go to hell," chuckles Pearson. "Of course we didn't say that. But Judy is pretty impulsive, an emotional person. And out she swept!"

But nobody was concerned, because sweeping out was a normal LaMarsh routine. "Oh, she used to do that regularly," Pearson says. "We never knew if she was just going to the bathroom or what."

The Quebec Liberal Party did some sweeping itself at its annual convention in Quebec City in mid-October, which took some of the attention off the federal party. It was at this meeting that Kierans' show-down with Lévesque reached its conclusion with Lévesque's resignation as a Liberal. But the relief of the purge was cut short by the appearance of the Provincial Liberals' own background paper on the constitution, produced by Paul Gérin-Lajoie's special committee, which, to all intents, proposed a special status for Quebec that was even more extreme than the National Union had demanded. (However, by the time the National Union got around to producing its detailed proposals in November, the ante had been bumped up several notches, and there was little to choose between the two parties.) Gérin-Lajoie's proposal went under the general description of "broad special status" which reduced federal powers, or required joint-jurisdiction, in such things as international agreements, financial institutions, offshore mineral rights. It also demanded that Quebec become a republic but, at the same time retain its rights to Canadian citizenship and, of course, full representation in the federal parliament.

The Lajoie proposals never came to a formal vote but they remained a threat for the next twelve months. It was not until October 6, 1968, when the Quebec Liberals met again for their annual convention (this time in Montreal), that they decided to drop the republican "special status" label and adopt an elastic constitutional position which gave the French language priority in Quebec, while guaranteeing English minority educational rights, and also left an escape hatch which would allow a future Quebec Liberal government to demand provincial jurisdiction in such currently federal sectors as international affairs, immigration and broadcasting. As a lone dissenter put it, the constitutional position was a blank cheque giving the executive the right to adopt any stand it pleased without further consultation of members. But it satisfied both federalists and nationalists, which was the main objective, and insured the party's unity in case the National Union decided to spring an election.

Back in October, a year before, however, the Quebec Liberal party seemed to be on the verge of turning separatist and only the polls indicated otherwise. On October 7, a poll by the Toronto *Star* and *Le Soleil* of Quebec City established that only 2.6% of the members of the Quebec legislature were ready to accept the status quo, while 83.3% wanted "Special Status," 28% were for "Associate Statehood," and 32% wanted total Independence (Associate Statehood is one step closer to independence than special status; it includes such things as an elected Senate to deal with customs, defense and foreign policy, the only things that remain in common between the two nations.)

On October 24, the results of a poll commissioned by CBC Newsmagazine from the Opinion Research Corporation showed that only 7% of Quebeckers themselves favored independence, though 64% wanted to have a new Constitution, and 77% wanted French to be Quebec's working language. The desire for French priority was quite understandable. The poll found out that 41% of those sampled spoke no English.

Other findings were that 57% of French Canadians felt they

were less well treated in Canada than English Canadians; the bitterest group were people over 55 years of age, with the 18 to 24-year-old group next. However, in the 18 to 24 group only 9% wanted independence against 33% for special status and 30% for the status quo. Seven per cent of the Quebec population said they would leave if it became independent. The survey also backed up economists' claims that more opportunity would solve most problems, by reporting that by far the largest group among separatists were primary school drop-outs.

The October polls offered some surcease to the troubled Liberals, but the climate soon worsened again, and by November they were reporting that 47% of the public wanted Pearson to resign while only 35% felt he should stay on. Maybe on the strength of it, news leaked out that the Pearson's had asked the tenants of their house at 541 Montague Place, in Rockcliffe Park, Ottawa, to move out by May 1, 1968.

There was an immediate, tumbling rush of Liberal leadership candidates to the Alberta Liberal Association convention in Edmonton on November 10, when Paul Martin, Paul Hellyer, Mitchell Sharp and John Turner all promised to appear on a panel discussion. Coming on top of Judy LaMarsh's celebrated "rotten management" row with the CBC, the Edmonton rally was too much for Pearson, and he ordered his cabinet ministers back to Ottawa, to the fury of the Alberta Liberals.

As Newfoundland MP Richard Cashin said, the Liberals seemed to be suffering from Murphy's Law: "If there is any trouble, we'll get into it."

The only show of Liberal unanimity all month was the vote for total abolition of the death penalty on November 23, which passed by 114 to 87, with Judy LaMarsh the only prominent Liberal voting for retention.

In mid-November, René Lévesque founded his Mouvement Souveraineté-Association, whose initials, M.S.A., (which sound like *aime ça* in French) were quickly turned into a slogan, *"J'aime ça"* by young Montreal separatists. The November 23 to 26 meeting of the *Etats Généraux du Canada Français* proved to be their first major work-out and, in separatist terms, a considerable triumph.

Of the 17 resolutions voted at the meeting, only four passed with less than 90% majorities, and their contents ranged from such things as Quebec autonomy in external affairs to provincial control of broadcasting and monetary policy. The Confederation of Tomorrow Conference opened the following Monday in Toronto, under ominously grey skies, light snow and a chilly 30-degree temperature. So much had been said on every side about the constitution by the time it opened, on the top floor of the Toronto-Dominion Center building, that the televised meeting did little more than add an interesting visual dimension to the debate, as Robarts, Alberta's Premier Ernest Manning, Saskatchewan's Ross Thatcher, Johnson of Quebec, Louis Robichaud of New Brunswick, Alexander Campbell of Prince Edward Island, Ike Smith of Nova Scotia and Newfoundland's inimitable Joey Smallwood became real people, familiar faces in Canadian living rooms.

It was the first major constitutional conference in 100 years at which the federal government had not taken part (it was not invited) and, in its absence, the provinces were forced to evolve their own strategy along unfamiliar egalitarian lines. This had fascinating results, with the Atlantic premiers, Smallwood, Robichaud, Campbell and Smith, emerging as articulate co-equals; Ontario's Robarts and Quebec's Johnson as cautious progressives; while the Westerners, Thatcher, Manning and the deputy ministers of Manitoba and British Columbia, came through as the only alienated Canadians, ultra-conservatives with little tolerance for change and no compassion for the desires that motivated it.

By removing the federal government as a common scapegoat and thereby reducing provincial bigotries to their basic regional elements, Premier John Robarts' conference provided a greater service to the central government than he probably intended. For it became quite clear to Canadians by the end of the televised sessions that, in much that ailed Confederation, Pearson's administration was more sinned against than sinning. Federal observers, including Marc Lalonde and Carl Goldenberg, were delighted by what they saw and heard. The federal-provincial Constitutional Conference scheduled for February would be the more realistic for it. "Nobody closed the door to anything," said Lalonde happily.

In *Le Devoir*, on December 1, Claude Ryan noted that the conference had produced "a distinct rapprochement but no conclusions" and had indicated "a timid acceptance of a constitutional revision . . . by progressive stages." Ryan said the basic recognition of a French Canadian's unsatisfactory position outside Quebec and the resolution to continue working on the problem in committee was a pretty small achievement. "For separatists, avowed or disguised, this rather slim balance sheet is excellent. They will find there a new confirmation of their opinions." But there was hope, he said, and he gave Daniel Johnson an alpha for effort, adding that "if he maintains in Quebec a language similar to that which he held in Toronto, and avoids undoing, by some intemperate declarations aimed at a local clientele, the trust he has won, he could exercise a decisive action on the course of events in the months to come." It was a faint hope; Johnson soon returned to his old habits of adjusting his tone to suit the audience.

Only eight days later, on December 9, Reuters News Agency in Paris would monitor an interview by Johnson for Radio Luxembourg in which he told Frenchmen that while many of his Quebec "compatriots" were ready "to sacrifice the French Canadian nation", he would defend it. "On the contrary, I say that we absolutely must work not only for the survival but also the expansion of the French Canadian nation — even at the price of Confederation."

Johnson went on to say Quebec demanded a new constitution that recognized a French Canadian nation as an entity and added, in words that must have been underlined in red by the constitutional task force clip desk, "We are not very far from that theory of sovereignty and an economic union."

What of de Gaulle's inflamatory press conference on November 26 (in which he looked forward to Quebec as "a sovereign state and master of its national existence")? Johnson was full of praise for the General: "President de Gaulle has done us an enormous service, lifting the inferiority complex of 200 years." So much for Premier Johnson as a modern Father of Confederation.

By December, the Marchand, Trudeau, Lalonde, Sauvé, Lamontagne and Goyer strategy had made considerable progress. As president of the policy commission of the Quebec section of the Liberal Federation of Canada, Goyer had been involved in the arrangements for the annual convention. The convention had been postponed twice and was now firmly scheduled to take place on the weekend of January 26 to 28 at the Hotel Bonaventure in Monreal.

The postponement was at the request of Marchand, the leader of the Quebec caucus, because it was felt that the convention should take place as close to the federal-provincial Constitutional Conference as possible — for tactical as well as practical reasons.

Marchand (and Goyer) were worried that the influence of "special status" thinking would be too strong if the convention took place as originally planned in December, right after the Estates General and its quasi-separatist theme, and the Confederation of Tomorrow conference when Daniel Johnson would be pitching for special status. If the Quebec wing of the federal party endorsed special status it would wreck the work Trudeau had been doing to make a Bill of Rights the prime constitutional requirement. It would also finish him as a credible spokesman for French Canada and potential candidate.

In short, it was vitally important that the Quebec wing should reject "special status" and give a ringing endorsement to the Marchand-Trudeau position.

Therefore they selected a date which would come as close as possible to the Constitutional Conference on February 5. In fact, there is evidence that the dates for both the Quebec meeting and the Constitutional Conference were chosen by the same people — indeed, it would be surprising if they were not.

Having settled the date, Marchand and his team had to make sure that this time they succeeded in getting their man elected as president of the provincial association. Convention organization was the key. Claude Frenette was an active member of the policy commission but there was nothing he could do about making sure that the party secretariat, in Montreal, the permanent staff, did not sabotage the convention. Clearly the Marchand team needed their own man to run the thing. Frenette found just the person.

One of his closest friends at Laval as a student had been Pierre Levasseur, an MBA from the University of Western Ontario, fluently bilingual and a convinced federalist. Levasseur had gone to work for Paul Gérin-Jajoie in the Quebec Department of Education, after graduating from Western in 1965, and had stayed on, after the Liberals were defeated, to work for his National Union successor, Jean-Jacques Bertrand. Working for Bertrand had been fine, and they are still good friends, but Levasseur had fallen afoul of the government's civil service commissioners who refused to put him into the salary-bracket his job demanded, on the grounds that at 29 he was too young. So Levasseur was vaguely looking for another job, when Frenette bumped into him at a mutual friend's stag party. Frenette told him that the Liberal Federation wanted an administrator for its Montreal office, and with his qualifications, he would be the perfect candidate. The next thing that happened was a historically brief, 10-minute coffee counter interview with Jean Marchand at 9 a.m. one Sunday morning in November, which went something like this.

Marchand: "You want to work for us in Montreal?"

Levasseur: "Yes".

Marchand: "It's going to be a rough job. But I've been asking about you, and people say you can do it."

Levasseur: "Well, you don't know me, and I don't know you. Maybe I should let you know something about myself."

Marchand: "I'm not interested. You'll get a phone call from somebody else."

And he was gone.

The next man to vet Levasseur was Maurice Sauvé, who treated him to lunch, discussed salaries and so on.

The third caller was Marc Lalonde, "M" himself, who phoned from out of the blue and asked Levasseur and his wife to come and have dinner with him at his house in Montreal. Trudeau was at the dinner party. "He froze me completely," says Levasseur. "He was too cool for me. I felt he over-powered me. I could play it cool with Marchand, and I could play it cool with Sauvé, and no problems with Marc. Marc and I ticked off right away, as soon as we saw each other, that was it, we knew we could function together. But Trudeau just froze me. Luckily my wife was sitting beside me and she's even cooler than I am, besides being very pretty."

So Trudeau talked to Levasseur's wife all evening, and when they were about to leave, he came over to Levasseur and said:

"It's going to be a tough job, but you look pretty strong. People say you can pull this through. Well, let's see what you can make of it."

The selection of Levasseur was less casual than it appeared, because his role would be critical in getting Frenette elected president and in seeing that the convention ran without a slip. But it was also, for Lalonde and Goyer, part of their two-pronged strategy. It was essential that the executive director in Montreal should become a Trudeau man not only for the constitution but for the leadership race. The extent of his loyalty could make the difference between a candidate that Quebec delegates would support and one they would ignore. Very quickly, the executive director achieves a position of unchallenged power in the party structure, and in Levasseur they wanted to be sure that they had a man who would not betray them.

It was coincidental that the same day Levasseur started work in the federation office in Montreal, Justice Minister Trudeau introduced his first major piece of legislation in the House of Commons. It was Bill C-187, "An Act respecting Divorce".

The Divorce Bill had been long awaited, and by general consensus it satisfied those who wanted changes in the country's archaic divorce laws. Just how archaic those laws were became clear during second reading, December 5, when Trudeau told the House some of the history of Canada's divorce legislation, all of it drawn from English laws written before 1870, and some of them older than Confederation. "Therefore, with laws dating back to 1870, in a society which has moved so quickly and so far in the intervening 97 years, it is not astonishing that the present divorce laws and the way in which they govern our society is highly unsatisfactory and indeed produces some very evil results."

New grounds for divorce under Trudeau's bill covered not merely adultery, the only previous ground under Canadian law, but a wide range of other causes. The prime ones included such perversions as sodomy, bestiality, rape and homosexuality; criminal offenses such as bigamy; and also "physical and mental cruelty of such a kind as to render intolerable the continued cohabitation of the spouses". But that was not all. The bill permitted additional grounds in the very broad category of "marriage breakdown";

desertion was included, with the deserted party getting slightly kinder treatment than the deserter; imprisonment and drug addiction for more than three years were also new grounds.

He talked about grounds for divorce and how evidence had become a sham and a hypocrisy in many cases. He also said that many people in Canada (500,000 was the figure he quoted) were living in common law relationships due to obstacles to remarriage. "The remedy we envisage is first to preserve marriage, and second to make better marriages possible by weeding out the legal impediments which now prevent remarriage and the formation of happy couples . . . As I said earlier, I think one of the fundamental tasks we must achieve in this parliament is to avoid mixing the sacred and the profane. We must realize that we are living in a pluralistic society, and even though some laws may be repugnant to the morals of individual members, they must realize that we are all here to legislate not our own personal morals upon the country but to seek solutions to evils which arise in a civil society and which must be solved by civil or criminal laws."

This was to be a theme that he would repeat again and again in the next six months.

Trudeau spoke during second reading that Tuesday evening for barely 40 minutes, but his eloquence, in French and English, his calm, lucid argument, and his patient replies to questions, seemed to captivate the House and galleries. Here was a Quebecker, a devout Roman Catholic, and a bachelor, quietly and undramatically proposing legislation that would be violently attacked in his own province. Here he was, talking about a new sort of Canada that many of the Members could barely perceive, a pluralistic Canada where Catholics, Anglicans and dour United Church Presbyterians were no longer the guardians of the nation's morality, nor even the majority.

Who was Trudeau? The next day, that question was being asked from coast to coast, in newspapers, radio editorials, and by television pundits on their panels. He was suddenly 'discovered'. A fresh face had been introduced to the Canadian "pop" scene. It was not true of course. He may have been Minister of Justice for only seven months, but his name and sometimes his picture too had graced dozens of learned articles on the Constitution opposite the editorial pages in better newspapers and journals. His thoughts and style were widely admired in legal and political science circles. Now the men of law and letters were going to have to share him with the public; he had reached the front page.

As the Trudeau bandwagon started to roll, the academics gave a hearty heave-ho, and their friends in the newsmedia did the rest. Several key figures emerged in rapid succession. Ramsay Cook, a young author and professor of history at the University of Toronto, had known Trudeau well since 1964, when he published the Lalonde-Trudeau Manifesto in *Canadian Forum* at the same time as it appeared in *Cité Libre*. He had contributed frequently to *Cité Libre* in the years since then, and Trudeau and others had responded with their contributions to Forum.

Cook had entered the constitutional debate that fall with a strong supporting brief for Trudeau's Bill of Rights and had taken a close interest in the Confederation of Tomorrow Conference in Toronto. He had run into Marc Lalonde at the conference, and they had talked about the possibility of Trudeau becoming a candidate. He had also discussed it with John Saywell, the peripatetic Dean of the Faculty of Arts and Science at Toronto's York University, who is also an active participant in CBC Public Affairs.

They also discovered an ally in Donald Macdonald, Liberal MP for Toronto-Rosedale, who had first met Trudeau in the fall of 1966, when they were both members of the Canadian delegation to the United Nations General Assembly. Trudeau had been a delegate on the special political committee, and Macdonald had been on the economic and financial committee. "We naturally saw quite a bit of each other in the professional sense," Macdonald remembers. Both felt strongly that Canada should recognize Communist China. When Trudeau became Minister of Justice, it was natural that Macdonald, also a lawyer (Toronto, Harvard and Cambridge), and parliamentary secretary to the previous Minister of Justice, would bring some ideas to him. "This bilateral contact became multilateral," Macdonald recalls. And he was one of several MP's appointed to a Liberal caucus committee to discuss the Criminal Code reforms.

"I guess I started considering him as one of the possibilities as leader in the fall of 1967. It became increasingly evident that a decision would have to be made in this regard. And as I ran over in my mind the qualifications of some of the more likely individual possibilities in this, I arrived at the conclusion that the most obvious people for the role, who would declare themselves as candidates, would not be acceptable to me as leader for a variety of reasons. I think probably the most important one was the fact that they didn't have the same capacity as Trudeau did to relate to the two main language groups: there was nobody who had the same facility in both languages and was *modern*."

To Macdonald, someone like Paul Martin, though fluently bilingual, was "still thinking in terms of the Roosevelt era . . . he had not moved with the times." Trudeau, on the other hand, "was a reformer and was prepared to smash a few icons for the purpose of bringing in a more up-to-date system of law — and not just law but of government generally. And in the fairly rapidly moving era that we are in, it seemed to me that this was one of the requirements of a new leader."

Trudeau's newness in politics did give him pause. "It was a hesitation that everybody had," he says, "to use the old advertiser's slogan, 'Will it sell?' I might think he's a great guy, but in hard political terms, can I persuade enough people to do the same thing? I think I originally formed my views in October, November and December, 1967, on the basis that, well, it would be a noble losing effort!"

The rallying point for the Toronto group seems to have been a Christmas party given by Toronto artist Mashel Teitelbaum and his wife Ethel, who knew Ramsay Cook and introduced Macdonald to him. Cook put him onto Marc Lalonde who told him that the Montreal group for Trudeau was centered around Jim Davey (Levasseur being fully occupied with Liberal convention at that point) and Jean Pierre Goyer.

They found out later that yet another Torontonian had been taking an independent tack towards Trudeau — Professor Allen M. Linden, an expert in International Law at Toronto's Osgoode Hall Law School. Linden had been on the panel of legal experts consulted by Trudeau, Goldenberg and Head for the work of the task force on the constitution. He was soon to become vice-president of the Ontario Liberal Party and had been active in the party policy councils since the Kingston Conference of 1960. A tall, dark, ebullient man, Linden represented what might be called the party's young Ontario activists, a group that included Martin O'Connell, Mark McGuigan and Jerry Grafstein. Linden had met Trudeau for the first time in Ottawa at the convention of Canadian Law Teachers (ACLT) at the Chateau Laurier in June, 1967. He took to Trudeau immediately. "I liked him. And he was a hell of a good Justice Minister," he says. But the young professionals around Linden were under heavy pressure from the other would-be candidates. Some got sucked in long before Trudeau declared himself. And Linden himself was in a quandary. He liked Hellyer ("he's really a mild, pleasant, sweet, simple, gentle man," but Hellyer's campaign manager, Bill Lee, "turned me off"). He found John Turner exciting. And, surprisingly, Paul Martin quite compelling. "But the nation was yearning for something else."

Everyone knew the leadership race was officially going to start soon. But when? Pearson made no move, and everyone assumed that he wanted to stay on until after the Constitutional Conference. So there was still plenty of time, or so it seemed.

Linden and his group wanted to try to persuade a French Canadian to make a commitment before they made up their minds. At that point, they hoped it would be Marchand, though Trudeau was being talked about more and more frequently since the Divorce legislation had been tabled. It was finally decided that John Munro, MP for Hamilton-East, should write to Jean Marchand and ask for an appointment for himself, Linden, and the group to go up to Ottawa to talk about the leadership question.

The date set was December 15. It was never kept.

At 11:55 a.m., on Thursday, December 14, Lester Bowles Pearson told his cabinet that he was retiring, and at 12:25, in a black Homburg, heavy overcoat, blue suit and with a white carnation in his buttonhole, he walked from the East Block across to the National Press Building on Wellington Street to repeat the announcement to the world. Four days later, Senator John Nichol, president of the Liberal Federation of Canada, announced that a national leadership convention would be held in Ottawa from April 4 to 6.

The race was on.

XIII

Waiting For Trudeau

It is time for a new generation of leadership, to cope
with new problems and new opportunities. For there is
a new world to be won.

— *John F. Kennedy*

RETIREMENT, like marriage, seems to require a ritualistic observ-
ance of ordinary events so exaggerated that the day quickly
becomes extraordinary. Prime Ministers, unfortunately, do it in
public and Lester Pearson's day of decision was no different. Every
humdrum detail of an event which greatly relieved both Pearson
and the Liberal Federation of Canada was recorded for posterity,
from his arrival at the East Block, as usual, at 8:15 a.m. in his
4-year-old Buick to the fact that he went home, as usual, shortly
after 4 in the same Buick, to continue working into the night at
24 Sussex Drive.

But one detail of the day was different. At 6 p.m., Jean Marchand and Pierre Elliott Trudeau were summoned to Sussex Drive.
They were there for nearly an hour and they refused to say what
had been discussed.

It was the first of several private discussions, and it wasn't too
hard to deduce the purpose: Pearson felt strongly that there should
be a French Canadian candidate at the Liberal convention, and
he was determined that one of the two should run.

There was no question that Trudeau was the candidate Pearson
wanted. Yet he needed all his enormous diplomatic skill to achieve
his objective. "I was most anxious, like everyone else, that Marchand should not *feel* that he was being replaced by Trudeau as
the French-speaking candidate," he says. Trudeau and Marchand
were a delightful pair and Pearson was very fond of both. So he
called them in together and put his cards on the table. " 'We must

have a French-speaking candidate' I told them. 'This is a tradition of the Liberal Party — and he may or may not win. But he must be a good candidate and get a lot of votes, and we must show that although the Tories can't, we can always come up with the alternative from Quebec.' " The decision was to be theirs. Pearson did not expect any answer from either of them that night and would have a second and third session with them, alone together, during January, before events proved out.

Pearson had made his move masterfully. As the senior MP, it would be up to Marchand to decide whether he would run or not. Marchand had spoken to Pearson about his health on other occasions. Pearson also knew that Marchand's wife had refused to live in Ottawa, "and she hated the possibility of moving into Sussex." With luck, time would persuade Marchand against the idea of running for the leadership, and he would then be able to turn his immense ability into a wholehearted campaign for Trudeau, the only other possible candidate.

But the taste of absolute power does strange things to men, and Pearson would have to wait it out for nearly a month.

"When Marchand decided that he couldn't do it (in mid-January), I think there were three reasons," Pearson says. "He was very worried about his health; he's not a strong man physically, and he works and plays so hard — he plays as hard as he works. My wife tells me he's a wonderful dancer! But he is very hard on himself, and he uses up a lot of nervous energy. Secondly, I think he was really worried about his ability to get his stuff across in English Canada. He was very conscious of this, even though he speaks English far better than I speak French. But this is a handicap, in my mind. If I had only realized I was going to be a politician in Toronto 50 years ago, I would have become fluent in French, too. I always felt that a tremendous handicap — and I think Marchand felt it a bit, too. And then of course his wife did not want to live in Ottawa. So he bowed out."

The way was clear for Trudeau — but would he go?

Pearson decided to call him in, with Marchand, to explain what Marchand had decided, putting it bluntly to him that he was now the only possible candidate.

"I think he was genuinely surprised by all of this," Pearson says. "I haven't got the chronology very clearly in mind, but it was after he got back from Fiji or wherever he'd been." Trudeau's reaction was interesting. "One of Trudeau's assets is that he can conceal his feelings very well and he gave the impression of being surprised. I remember, many years ago, when I was at Oxford, there was a young English girl who got into the finals of the Women's golf championships against one of the great Americans of that era — and I remember reading in the papers that this girl said 'Apparently, I'm England's last hope, what a lark'. She may have been as nervous as hell, and this may have pertained to Trudeau. You know, 'Well, I'm Quebec's last hope — what a joke'. But I think he was thinking about this alright. And this was probably the right way to react. With all the mistakes we make, we Liberals are, as a party, far better politicians than the Tories are. We have never had anybody in the leadership who hasn't given the impression that he didn't particularly want it but that everybody wanted him . . . So Trudeau is following along in the tradition of being dragged to the Speaker's chair, as it were, reluctantly but not too reluctantly."

The announcement of Pearson's retirement had plunged the party into frenzied activity. Two other events that day were significant. In Montreal, Jean-Pierre Goyer was driving his wife Michelle to an afternoon seminar at the University of Montreal when he heard the news about Pearson over the car radio. His immediate concern was to make sure Trudeau kept his options open. As soon as they reached the U. of M., he dashed to a payphone to call Trudeau's executive assistants, Eddie Rubin and Pierre De Bané, at the Ministry of Justice in Ottawa. He told them to let Trudeau know that he would be on the next plane to Ottawa and not to say anything about his candidacy until they had a chance to talk.

In Ottawa, Gordon F. Gibson, Jr., the executive assistant to the Minister of Northern Affairs, Arthur Laing, put through a call to his friend Marc Lalonde at the Prime Minister's office as soon as he heard the news. Gibson, like so many of the executive assistants, had a brilliant background but had found that his skills were barely employed on Parliament Hill.

He had graduated in mathematics from the University of British Columbia, got an MBA from Harvard and had been half-way through a political science diploma at the London School of Economics (running a Chelsea laundromat on the side), when he was called back to Vancouver in 1962, to lend a hand in the family business — a multi-million dollar holding empire with interests that range from timber and mines to a radio station and a motel in Hawaii. He started yet another business on the side, manufacturing "Paneloc" prefabricated buildings, but politics remained his passion. His uncle had been an Independent Liberal MP in the late 1940's, and his father was an MLA. It was inevitable that he would get involved in provincial politics, campaigning for Dr. Pat McGeer (now leader of the B.C. Liberals) in the provincial riding of Vancouver-Point Grey and, soon afterwards, federally for Arthur Laing in Vancouver South (his uncle was Laing's finance chairman). This led to a job offer from Laing, and Gibson went to Ottawa in 1965. He ran into Marc Lalonde in the spring of 1966, and they met regularly since then. Gibson was full of ideas for reorganizing government administration, and Lalonde enjoyed listening to them. By September, 1967, Gibson knew Lalonde well enough to say that he would like to work in the Prime Minister's office, if Lalonde knew of any vacancies. He also told Lalonde that he thought Trudeau would be the ideal man to succeed Pearson.

Suddenly, Lalonde was assessing Gibson in quite another light, as a potential partisan. He pumped him for ideas as to how they could promote Trudeau's candidacy. He also asked Gibson if he would be interested in working for Trudeau if he became a candidate. Gibson immediately worked out a detailed strategy for the West, while Lalonde did the East. By the time Pearson's retirement was announced, Lalonde and Gibson were ready to roll.

Jean-Pierre Goyer managed to catch the 3 p.m. plane to Ottawa that Thursday afternoon, but he missed caucus, and when he arrived on the Hill, it was over. Rubin and De Bané met him with the depressing news that Trudeau had just told newsmen that there was no question of him being a candidate. Goyer was furious. "You can't slam doors like that!" he insisted when he caught up with Trudeau. "You are the only valid candidate." Trudeau disagreed; what else could he say? He had the Criminal Code Omnibus Bill coming up and then the Constitutional Conference — obviously there was no time to even consider the leadership question until after it was over.

"You can always say there is nothing to be said until after the Constitutional Conference," he replied. "Say, 'I have no time to think of it now' when the newsmen ask."

Trudeau agreed reluctantly. It was the least he could do for Goyer and Lalonde and all the others who had the idea that he should run, or at least consider it. Yet he was not at all sure. As he confided to friends, he had so little parliamentary experience, so little time in the party itself. Could he honestly delay a decision he felt sure would be a negative one? Raising everybody's hope and putting a lot of people to considerable trouble?

But Trudeau was tired, and he did not want to fight about it. He tires quickly, in spite of a careful regimen of diet and exercise and sleep. He has to sleep eight hours each night, or fatigue affects him badly. Life had not been peaceful at the Justice Department with the Divorce Bill going forward, the Omnibus bill running into half a dozen new drafts, and the Bill of Rights documentation for the Constitutional Conference being made ready for the printers. A gifted writer himself, in French or English, Trudeau is unreasonably demanding in his speeches and documents. Ottawa's mandarins were not used to being told to go and do something over again when it was not good enough — but they were growing used to it under Trudeau.

Trudeau's two assistants, Rubin and De Bané, had been walking on eggs for weeks while the boss worked furiously, cancelled all engagements, and refused to receive anyone (and that meant anyone, as a few tycoons found out, when they tried to beard him in his den). Occasionally, when they least expected it, he would burst into one of their offices with a suggestion like, "who's for a walk?" or "who's for Chinese food?" and they would struggle into their coats to follow him out into the raw and frequently snowy night, to walk rapidly around Parliament Hill, just for the exercise, before heading to the Canton Inn at 205 Albert Street.

But the past-midnight drafting sessions were draining him. Normally Trudeau is miserable in the morning, better in the afternoon and in top form in the evening. By mid-December, he was miserable all the time.

Fortunately, he ran into his old Nigerian beach-buddy, Tim Porteous, then executive assistant to Industry Minister C. M. Drury, at the Chateau Laurier one day and learned that for $589, all-in, he could spend two weeks on the Tahitian island of Moorea, at the Club Mediterranée, including air fare from Los Angeles, during the Christmas recess.

Nobody likes a bargain better than Trudeau, to whom parsimony is a way of life, and he immediately decided that he would go to Tahiti, too. But the Club Mediterranée organizers in New York were "desolated" — the trip had been booked solid for months. Trudeau let on that he was Canada's Minister of Justice, and almost immediately the club discovered that it did have one small place left, after all.

The news of his vacation plan was a relief for everyone. After two weeks of skin diving in Tahiti, Trudeau would be his old self again. And he could use the time to think about the leadership. Until the trip, he would take Goyer's advice.

Meanwhile, Goyer was hustling for Trudeau supporters. One of the first people he sounded was Pierre Levasseur, who was in Ottawa talking to Quebec MP's about the January convention. Levasseur was enthusiastic, but he was snowed under with convention work. Goyer also spoke to Marc Lalonde, who was being cagey and felt they would have to wait until they could get a better evaluation of support in caucus.

Lalonde probably knew through Trudeau and Pearson that nothing could be decided until Marchand had made up his mind, and that would not be until after he got back from his Christmas vacation in Miami. If Marchand decided to run, they would have to support him and that was that. Goyer also called Walter Gordon in Toronto to ask what his plans were. Gordon said he was going to support Marchand but he agreed, reluctantly, not to do so publicly until Goyer had a chance to talk to him. As it turned out, he couldn't wait for Goyer and came out in favor of Marchand during the Christmas recess.

It was a frustrating period for Goyer, but he had strong allies in Montreal with Levasseur, Davey, Frenette and a young Montreal lawyer named Harold Gordon. Moreover, he knew that Lalonde would pass the word when the time was right.

While the would-be Trudeau groups tried to keep cool and inconspicuous, the other teams organized briskly. Transport Minister Paul Hellyer was well ahead. Finance Minister Mitchell Sharp and Registrar General John Turner were also busily lining up their support. Robert Winters, the Minister of Trade and Commerce, had indicated that he did not intend to be a candidate at all, but would talk with his Toronto advisers before deciding. Paul Martin had been told personally about Pearson's decision in a transatlantic telephone call to Brussels, where he was attending a NATO conference. Wags on Parliament Hill said that he had offered to fly back to Ottawa immediately, with or without an aircraft.

The 23 members of the Liberal Federation executive met in Ottawa and decided that the convention would take place in Ottawa's new civic centre, an indoor arena which was located underneath the new Ottawa Rough-Riders football club grandstand, at Lansdowne Park, beside the famous Rideau Canal. The arena would hold 9,300 people, and it could be turned quickly into a convention complex by lifting out a block of seats, and by taking over some of the nearby exhibition buildings, such as the Ottawa Coliseum.

The executive also approved plans for several provincial Liberal conventions which were scheduled to take place before the leadership convention in April. This was important news to candidates, for the provincial conventions would afford key opportunities to meet delegates, and no serious contestant could afford to miss them.

Meanwhile, the House was proceeding towards the Christmas adjournment. The leadership race was on everyone's mind, including the Opposition, as one intervention in the divorce debate indicated. Second reading was in full spate when a New Brunswick Tory named Gordon L. Fairweather entered the debate to say that he wished it were possible to hear "professional and other criticisms of the bill," before Parliament had to vote on it. "I do not blame the Minister for what has happened," he added. "Clearly, a change in the parliamentary setup is needed. Perhaps in a few months the minister will have the opportunity to lead a government that will bring about such an interesting innovation."

At which point *Hansard* notes:

"Some hon. Members: Hear, hear.

"Mr. Fairweather: Speaking for myself, I can think of no more distinguished person on the government side to lead such a government."

"An hon. Member: Why not support him?

"Mr. Fairweather: No. I will stick to my own man.

"An hon. Member: Join us.

"Mr. Fairweather: No, I have no interest in joining. I shall give you the files to show you what can be done." His reference was to Tory Centennial Convention files which the Progressive Conservatives had offered to loan the Liberals to help plan their April convention. It got a laugh because Fairweather's role in the Stanfield campaign was widely known.

Opposition parties are not often complimentary about members of the Government, and Fairweather's comments about Trudeau were sincerely made, indicating that the Minister of Justice was already considered a leadership candidate by some of those sitting across from him.

But a lot of Liberals needed a lot more convincing than Fairweather did.

There was strong opposition in Cabinet that week to the Prime Minister's plan to introduce Bill C-195, the well-named "Omnibus" bill, a thick, 72-page wad of amending legislation that was officially entitled *An Act to amend the Criminal Code, the Parole Act, the Penitentiary Act, the Prisons and Reformatories Act and to make certain consequential amendments to the Combines Investigation Act and the Customs Tariff.*

Like the divorce bill on December 4, the amendments were long overdue, and half of them were routine updating of archaic law. The bulk of the remainder dealt with such ho-hum things as breathalyser testing for drunk drivers, lotteries and a mild tightening of Canada's gun laws to require registration of rifles and shotguns.

But these clauses were of only marginal interest to the Cabinet. Their main concern was with clauses on pages 12 and 24 of Bill C-195.

Section 147: Every one who commits buggery or bestiality is guilty of an indictable offence and is liable to imprisonment for 14 years.

Section 149: Everyone who commits an act of gross indecency with another person is guilty of an indictable offence and is liable to imprisonment for five years.

The Omnibus bill would simply add section 149A, to exempt from such draconic justice, acts committed in private between husband and wife or between any two persons, "each of whom is twenty-one years or more of age, both of whom consent to the commission of the act."

It went on to define what was not private as being an act committed in a public place, or if "more than two persons take part or are present."

It also said that "a person shall be deemed not to consent to the commission of an act i) if the consent is extorted by threats or fear of bodily harm or is obtained by false and fraudulent misrepresentations as to the nature of quality of the act, or ii) if that person is, and the other party to the commission of the act knows or has good reason to believe that that person is feeble-minded, insane, or an idiot or imbecile."

The point made, of course, was that section 149A would not only protect married and adult heterosexual couples from legal entanglements, but would protect adult homosexual couples, male and female, as well.

The second clause, on page 24 of the Bill, amended Section 237 of the Criminal Code to permit abortions under certain conditions (danger to life or health) in an accredited hospital after approval by the hospital's therapeutic abortion committee, with a majority of the members present.

This was a major piece of humanitarian legislation. It was also, like section 149A, political dynamite.

Even before its release, Pearson's cabinet ministers argued long and loudly over it. One was so strongly opposed to the legislation that he declared bitterly that it would make a great slogan in the next election: "How about this? For abortion, homosexuality and easy divorce — Vote Liberal!"

But Pearson overruled the dissenters. The amendments were controversial, and they did cause a sensation throughout the country — but the timing was perfect, and so was the spokesman for the bill. His argument was the same as it was for divorce: Canada had become a pluralistic society and "even though some laws may be repugnant to the morals of individual members, they must realize that we are all here to legislate not our own personal morals upon the country but to seek solutions to evils which arise in a civil society and which must be solved by civil or criminal laws."

More colorfully, he quipped later that "The Minister of Justice has no place in the bedrooms of the nation" and on yet another occasion, "you may have to ask forgiveness from God, but not from the Minister of Justice."

Blasphemy or not, the intention of the Omnibus bill was consistent with the spirit of Christmas, of goodwill and tolerance towards all men. It was legislation of compassion, and the man responsible for it suddenly became an object of national fascination.

A cynic might observe that it's doubtful whether any legislation in the history of Canadian Parliament could have been timed as perfectly to launch a political strategy. But the point is, the Omnibus Bill on December 21 and the Divorce Bill on December 4, these twin rockets which carried Trudeau's candidacy into orbit, could have easily misfired. They were daring, imaginative and superbly handled (the Omnibus Bill was simply tabled and went into committee and died with the 27th Parliament, though the Divorce legislation was passed into law by springtime) but they were also fraught with danger for Trudeau. If there had been an error in the drafts, if he had failed to defend the legislation skillfully either inside or outside the house, his political career would have been stopped dead or been gravely compromised. The risk was colossal. But the gain was enormous.

Did Pearson plan it deliberately?

"Well, I put him in the Department of Justice as soon as I could," he says. "And I told him to go ahead with the criminal code. Some of my older colleagues disapproved, in fact the majority did not want to go ahead with the code. But I insisted, and besides, I had a Minister of Justice who was interested in it. I could have dropped it, put it off, because I did not want to get Mr. Trudeau into too much trouble. But I knew he could handle it alright, and it had to be done by a Catholic if at all possible."

Trudeau tabled the Omnibus Bill at 2:40 that Thursday afternoon, and three and a half hours later the House of Commons voted to adjourn until Monday, January 22.

Soon afterwards, Ottawa was deserted, Trudeau was in Tahiti, Marchand in Miami and at parties from Christmas to New Years Day, and for two weeks after that, the speculation mounted. Would Trudeau run?

The pace of events speeded up considerably in the third week of December. It became clear that two groups were emerging, Trudeau supporters and Marchand-Trudeau supporters.

In Montreal, Bob Giguère, chief federal organizer for the province of Quebec, headed the Marchand supporters outside the party caucus. Giguère and Marchand took their Christmas golfing vacation together in Miami Beach and reports soon filtered back that Giguère was introducing Marchand to members of the French-Canadian community in Florida as "the future Prime Minister of Canada," and that Marchand was basking in the attention.

In Toronto, Allen Linden's group were also Marchand backers in principle, but it never became more than a tacit understanding with people like Walter Gordon that, if Marchand decided to run, they would support him.

In both Montreal and Toronto, of course, the Marchand men were in close contact with the Trudeau people and promised that if their candidate did not run, Trudeau would have their active support. It was not necessarily a reciprocal understanding.

As for the Trudeau group, their campaign organization was already taking shape. In Toronto, the Donald Macdonald faction had made contact with Ramsay Cook, John Saywell and William Kilbourn, another well-known public figure and academic who is chairman of the Department of Humanities at York University. Kilbourn had known Trudeau since their student days in Europe, in 1948, when they met in Budapest, and their friendship had continued ever since. In Montreal, Jean-Pierre Goyer and Jim Davey were coordinating their efforts closely with Marc Lalonde and Gordon Gibson in Ottawa.

Lalonde's position was difficult. Officially he was a civil servant working for Pearson. Unofficially, he was the supreme commander and tactician of the draft-Trudeau movement. Pearson was still Prime Minister and would remain so until his successor had been picked in April. Lalonde was his special constitutional adviser and confidant and had committed himself to remain with the Prime

Minister's office until April. So Lalonde worked all day for
Pearson and most of the night for Trudeau.

"I could not use my ordinary working hours," he says. "I had
to be very careful to be honest and fair to Mr. Pearson. I couldn't
allow Mr. Pearson to be dragged into this and I couldn't allow
anything to intimate that Mr. Pearson was behind this. So I would
not talk about it to Mr. Pearson and he would not talk about it to
me. It was a kind of silent understanding."

Lalonde began to rely heavily on Gordon Gibson for most of
the person-to-person work, Yet, in spite of all his work for Trudeau, Gordon Gibson did not actually meet the man himself until
December 20, at the Liberal Caucus's Christmas party.

"I told Marc Lalonde I thought it would be a good idea for me
to meet the man I thought should be Prime Minister," says Gibson. Lalonde agreed, and the introduction was arranged. Gibson
told Trudeau that he should be a candidate but remembers that
"while he listened courteously, he didn't say yes or no."

Another important figure in Trudeau's campaign was Gérard
Pelletier. He had been out of Canada on External Affairs business
from September until December 22. When he left he was convinced that Trudeau would not be able to run with any chance of
success and had felt it would be best if no French Canadian ran.
Nevertheless, before he left, he had written the preface to a little
book of essays and speeches that Trudeau had been putting
together for Claude Hurtubise of Editions H.M.H. Ltée in Montreal. It was to be published in October as a study of federalism
titled "Le Fédéralisme et la société canadienne-francaise". It
appeared in October, 1967 in a limited $3.50 hard-cover edition
of 3,000 copies and had sold rather poorly.

In December, therefore, Pelletier was surprised to learn from
Hurtubise that the book had sold out completely, and a $2 paper-
backed edition was being prepared. Then, Hurtubise told him that
Macmillan of Canada had acquired the English translation rights
and were preparing a $2.50 paper-back edition for publication in
the New Year, thanks to a chance discussion between the company president, John Gray, and Ramsay Cook, Trudeau's main
booster in Toronto.

It was obvious to Pelletier that Trudeau had become the sensation of Liberal politics in his absence. He rapidly assessed the situation and came to two conclusions: there would have to be a French Canadian candidate, and Trudeau should be the man Quebec put forward.

Pelletier's influence on both Marchand and Trudeau has always been considerable, and, as soon as they returned from their vacations, he set to work to convince them. "I had changed my own mind, I suppose," he says. "I reminded myself that we got into politics in the first place because we felt that if Quebeckers concerned themselves only with Quebec, and not with Ottawa, then Canada would fall apart by default. It had become very important, particularly since the Conservative Convention, for the Liberal leadership convention to be relevant to French Canada. A French Canadian had to take part in it. Quebeckers would not support something that did not concern them."

Marchand had returned from Miami before Trudeau got back from Tahiti. Giguère's efforts to persuade him to run had failed. He had decided he could not, as he would explain to both Trudeau and Pearson. "Giguère and the others in Miami did their best to make me consider it," he recalls. "I thought about it very seriously. And in my heart I said no, though I was always ready to accept right up until the end if no one else was found — and I must say, I didn't think they *would* find another one. What I wanted to do was reintegrate Quebec in Confederation — as a Quebecker — and this could be done best as a minister, I felt, without being Prime Minister, without having to cut your roots in Quebec. I am not the least interested in being Prime Minister, in Quebec or Ottawa! I never looked for a job, I have never sought a job, all you can accuse me of is seeking power! And that's true, I did seek power. But in December, the miracle happened, Pierre started to produce his divorce bill, his Omnibus bill — and he became a national political figure. He became a possible candidate. I did my damnedest to make him accept before he went to Tahiti — and when he went without accepting, I said he'll accept when he comes back."

Miami was just an interlude to Marchand. "I had already made up my mind to push Pierre. That's why I had asked him to prepare a paper for the Quebec Liberal congress.

Trudeau arrived back from Moorea on January 12, sun-tanned and delighted with his new prowess as a game-fisherman. He had taken a day off from snorkeling and scuba-diving to go fishing — and had caught a 150-pound marlin almost on his first trawl. Within 40 minutes the big fish had been gaffed and stuffed into the hold, half the time it usually takes to boat a big one. It seemed a good omen.

Would he run? "I won't do anything until I know what Marchand is going to do," he said. "And in any case, I'm not giving the leadership a thought until after the constitutional conference, I wouldn't even toy with it until after the conference."

But he had thought about it. He couldn't help it. Among the people at the Club Mediterranée on Moorea were the Honorable James Sinclair, former Minister of Fisheries in the St. Laurent Cabinet, his wife and five lovely red-haired daughters. And though Sinclair himself was backing John Turner, his wife and daughters flipped for Trudeau — urging him to run and promising to campaign for him if he did. They did.

During the first weekend back in Montreal, Trudeau dined with Marchand and Pelletier at the Castel du Roy, on Drummond Street, two blocks from his bachelor apartment at Cantlie House on Sherbrooke Street. It was a long dinner and seems to have been the decisive one. They talked about the need for a French Canadian candidate, about the relevance that Pelletier had mentioned, and they agreed that one of them should be the candidate. Pelletier nodded to Marchand, and Marchand looked at Trudeau. "Good," he said, "we are all agreed. It's Pierre who must run."

Trudeau was genuinely astonished. "He had always felt it should be Marchand," says Pelletier. "He was completely taken aback. There was silence. Then he said, 'I agree that a French Canadian should run. And I won't say no. But I'll have to consider the thing.' "

The dinner ended, as it always did, with each of them carefully dividing the bill and paying their own share. It was the way you always did it with Trudeau. If he went out with a married couple it was the same. He'd pay his share, carefully itemized on the bill; he would never offer to split the tab. He had a phobia about check-rooms, too, and would do anything to save a 25¢ hatcheck tip. It was one of the less attractive habits of a bachelor and one that his friends tried to ignore, along with the fact that he never reciprocated any hospitality he received, lunches, dinners or parties. Like many old bachelors, he is socially under-developed in some areas.

His friends swear he never gave a party in his life — although he loved going to them — until he became Prime Minister and could throw them at state expense at 24 Sussex Drive. Prime Ministers never have to check their own coats, either, which must be a relief.

Once Marchand had decided to back Trudeau, his main problem was "trying to get Pierre to stop saying that he wasn't interested." As Goyer had before him, Marchand persuaded Trudeau that he should not make any statement until he was sure. He, too, understood Trudeau's concern for the Constitutional Conference and did his best to hold back the Quebec caucus from committing themselves to other candidates until after the conference was over.

There was also another issue. Earlier in the year, some of the Quebec members had wondered if they should not support Paul Martin, even if it meant defeat, since no French Canadian candidate had emerged. The theory was that Martin would be a short-term candidate, soon to retire, by which time a French Canadian of stature would have emerged. Both Marchand and Lalonde fought this theory. "I attacked this with as much strength as I could muster" says Lalonde. "I could not see any sense in a strategy developed towards going into Opposition. It was such a long-term, defeatist strategy. It was all very well to say that Mr. Martin would do a turn and then gracefully retire — but who knows? They said that about Pope John and they were all surprised for the better, I admit, but it was a risk. My advice, and I made no bones about it, was that Trudeau should be the one to run."

Marchand and Trudeau were called in by Pearson a few days after their dinner with Pelletier. Marchand told him that they had decided it should be Trudeau, and Pearson was delighted. He was also pleased to know that if Trudeau did not run, for any reason, Marchand would step in, and the Quebec caucus was keeping its options open.

"I was very pleased," Pearson recalls. "I thought that (Trudeau) would be a very appealing candidate to young people. I thought he was a reflection of the new age in Canada — new ideas, new people, all of that. I thought he would have great appeal. But I did not realize then that it was going to extend so far or go so deep."

Lalonde and Gibson started planning in mid-January on the basis of a February 19 entry — the date was two weeks after the Constitutional Conference and would permit a 45-day campaign. There was little they could do beyond blocking out weekly itineraries, since actual dates could not be established until they knew Trudeau would enter for certain. (Before Trudeau entered, Gibson would go through seven draft itineraries.) There were obviously certain places a candidate would have to go if he wanted to meet delegates, it was as simple — and as complex — as that. Later, after Trudeau entered, they would simulate an itinerary using Air Canada commercial flights and decide that it would be far more convenient, at marginal extra cost, to hire a seven-passenger De Havilland. The cost? $36,000 as against $24,000 by Air Canada, but a computer analysis showed that the added flexibility of the private jet would permit much better coverage of the country.

"We knew it would be a late entry into the race, and there was nothing to be gained by getting in early," says Lalonde. "So we decided to get as much publicity as possible before he entered. The idea of having him tour the provincial premiers was certainly very worthwhile in terms of the conference itself, and it should have been done anyway, but we certainly had another reason. I think I planned that part of the campaign in December!"

Lalonde got the idea from his own trips across the country on constitutional missions for Pearson, and he felt the contacts with provincial officials were a tremendous help. "It was quite clear that Mr. Pearson could not do it, so who did it leave?" he said with a Gallic shrug.

Pearson knew what Lalonde was up to. And, of course, he privately approved. But he was under suspicion already in the cabinet for promoting Trudeau's candidacy by arranging such a convenient schedule for the Divorce and Omnibus bills, as well as the Constitutional Conference.

If he then sent Trudeau off in the Prime Ministerial Jetstar to visit the Provincial Premiers, some of the leadership candidates might get upset. He thought about Lalonde's plan during his two-week vacation in Florida over the New Year, getting back to Ottawa the same weekend that Trudeau returned from Tahiti. After his talk that week with Marchand and Trudeau he told Lalonde to go ahead, discreetly.

"The planning went through without fanfare," says Lalonde, "we had to be very careful for it not to appear a leadership tour. We knew the news people would catch up with him somehow, and so they did, picking him up from capital to capital."

Trudeau's trip took place over a two week period. Without warning on Friday, January 19, Trudeau, Goldenberg and Eddie Rubin left on a Department of Transport Lockheed Jetstar for Edmonton. The departure came so suddenly that Goldenberg, who lives in Montreal, was caught without his pyjamas, as he had only intended to spend the day in Ottawa.

"You don't need pyjamas," said Trudeau, "I never wear them myself."

"Now, now Pierre," said Pearson, "you follow your style, and let Carl have his — if he wants pyjamas, he'll have some." And a clerk was sent out to buy Goldenberg his nightwear, at government expense.

The team spent the morning in Edmonton with Ernest Manning and the afternoon with W. A. C. Bennett in Victoria, British Columbia, where they stayed exactly two hours before heading back East to Regina for a visit the next day with Ross Thatcher. They saw John Robarts in Toronto the same day on their way back to Ottawa.

The following week, on Thursday, January 25, Goldenberg, Trudeau and, this time Pierre De Bané headed to St. John's, Newfoundland, to see Joey Smallwood, came back to Halifax that night to see Ike Smith of Nova Scotia and were grounded by freezing rain. They saw New Brunswick's Louis Robichaud on Friday, had to miss Prince Edward Island because of weather, and dashed back to Montreal in time for the Quebec Liberal Party's convention Friday night, Saturday and Sunday.

The calls on the premiers were designed to brief them on the agenda for the Constitutional Conference and in particular to seek

an agreement on such amendments for the BNA Act as the Bill
of Rights, a constitutional court and the just-published recommendation of the B & B Commission that provincial government offices
and schools be bilingual where the French or English minority
amounted to 10% of the population.

It was very important that the Constitutional Conference be a
success. "We could not afford to have a failure," says Lalonde. "If
the conference had failed, Trudeau would not have run. We saw
all the other candidates priming their pumps and we knew that we
could not win on the same basis. We had everything to win by
staying out of the race. We had the constitutional conference well
planned. We had the Liberal meeting in Montreal well planned.
We wanted success in all these things."

In mid-January the Gallup poll had shown the Tories still well
ahead with 43% popular support to 32% for the Liberals. The
NDP had 18%. But the Liberal leadership race was beginning to
heat up. The first entry had been Lloyd Henderson, a perennial
nuisance candidate. The second, to the surprise of many, was Eric
Kierans, the Quebec MLA who slew the separatist giant, René
Lévesque, and was clearly determined that the Liberals should give
him his quid pro quo, even if he had to run for the leadership to
get it. The third was Transport Minister Paul Hellyer.

On January 12, the Minister of Trade and Commerce, Robert
Winters, called a press conference in Toronto to say that he would
not be a candidate. It had been public knowledge that he did not
intend to run, and the announcement was hardly surprising. What
was a surprise was the sharp criticism of the government's financial
policy which seemed to be implied in his remarks at the news
conference.

"I was getting increasingly restive about the handling of financial
affairs, and I made several public speeches on the subject," recalls
Winters. "I felt the country was heading for a financial crisis —
and we did. And when someone asked me what I looked for in the
next leader, I said I hoped he would be motivated by a desire to
restore the fiscal integrity of the country."

The Toronto *Star* bannered Winters' remarks as meaning that
the government "lacks integrity," and on January 22, the Minister
rose in the House on a point of privilege to correct the *Star*.

"Mr. Speaker, I said no such thing," he declared. "In fact, I said nothing which could be considered as meaning that the government lacks integrity, fiscal or otherwise. In replying to a question I said that whoever becomes the new leader must attach great importance to fiscal integrity — the fiscal soundness of the country as a whole. In this, of course, the role of the federal government is just one part of the national fiscal structure. I was speaking of the country, not of the government, and in any event, I did not say anything which would justify the attribution to me of a quotation such as that which appeared in the newspaper."

Some hon. members: Hear, hear.

Whatever he meant, Winters' exit speech struck a responsive chord in thousands of Canadians. "The letters started coming in at the rate of 40 or 50 a day," he says, and this ultimately led to his decision to re-enter the race. He ignored the pleas for awhile, and he had to go to India for the UNCTAD conference in February, expecting the fuss would be over when he got back.

"But when I got back (February 9), I was very surprised to hear of all the letters, and all the "Draft Winters" moves, and people writing and telephoning in. But the burden of it was 'You've expressed what we feel, now give us a chance to vote for you'. We finally felt that we did have an obligation and I did it." (There is some doubt about Winters' surprise at it all, since he raced back from India to attend the Ontario Convention.) Thus, seven weeks later, Winters was back in the contest again and running hard.

Meanwhile, the fourth candidate, Health Minister Allan J. MacEachen, had become convinced that he had a bastion of support as a favorite son in his native Maritimes. The support turned out to be as insubstantial as a Nova Scotia morning mist, and when the luckless MacEachen chose the Nova Scotia Liberal Association meeting on January 13 to announce his candidacy, he found himself upstaged by the Minister for External Affairs, Paul Martin. When MacEachen unwisely allowed that he "wanted to declare my candidacy for the leadership of the Liberal Party of Canada", he was quickly one-upped by Martin, who quipped: "I don't *want* to be the Prime Minister, but I'm going to be." (At that point he still had not announced his candidacy.)

The fifth man into the ring was Registrar General John Turner;

the sixth the Finance Minister, Mitchell Sharp (both declared themselves on January 18); the seventh was Agriculture Minister Joe Greene; the eighth, the man who didn't want to be Prime Minister, Paul Martin.

"I am seeking the leadership of the Liberal party at this time — almost at the same age that Mr. Pearson did, as Mr. St. Laurent did — and while I don't want to compare myself with the great personalities of our time, the great men of our age have gone into public life when their experience gave them a special reason to assume the responsibility of office." As he walked away after the news conference, a CBC cameraman caught some memorable footage of Martin asking his executive assistant, Duncan Edmonds, how he'd done, with all the anxiety of a stage-struck housewife.

"Well, do you think I got over the main points? It's so hard, you know. If you go into great detail then they criticize you, and if you give just quick short answers they're never satisfied. It's so hard to please them, you know . . ." his voice trailed off.

By the end of January, all the main candidates were in except Trudeau. A petition to Trudeau from the academic community, originated by Ramsay Cook, was sent out on January 10 and had obtained 150 signatures by January 22.

Meanwhile, a clear picture was developing about Provincial intentions at the Constitutional Conference. Premier Bennett had announced on January 15 that he did not intend to budge on the BNA Act. "It's a solid thing," he said. "It works well." In Alberta, Premier Manning was still cautious. And in Saskatchewan, Premier Thatcher stuck to his December position that if there were 100 problems facing Canada, the constitution would be the 102nd. "There are too many bread and butter problems in Saskatchewan," he said.

Quebec's Daniel Johnson dimmed the probability of consensus still further. He waited until January 20 to publish a list of sixteen changes that the province considered essential. He demanded exclusivity or provincial veto or drastic changes in manpower policies, immigration, bankruptcy, health and welfare, international agreements, resources, marriage and divorce, the administration of justice (making Quebec courts the last court of appeal for matters under provincial law), corporate and securities legislation, mining companies, education at every level, taxation by all means except customs and excise and, finally, that all residual powers be vested in the provinces.

It was an outrageous brief in federal terms, locking the central government into the limited fields of monetary policy, international trade, defense, external affairs, criminal law (except juvenile courts), post office, citizenship, transport and fisheries beyond the territorial limits.

Quite clearly, Johnson was out to torpedo the Constitutional Conference and Trudeau with it, if his brief came close to the demands Quebec would bring to the table. As one senior Quebec civil servant aptly put it: "We are not administering a province, we are building a homeland."

There was not much comfort for the Federal Liberals in the position of the provincial sister party in Quebec. At about the same time, the party's constitutional expert, Paul Gérin-Lajoie, produced a refined version of his October document on constitutional reform which included demands for a new Supreme Court for Constitutional matters; bilingualism; provincial exclusivity in social welfare, manpower, immigration, broadcasting, professional training and cultural affairs. It demanded a share in economic and monetary policy; abolition of the monarchy and reform of the Senate. It was approved by the party MLAs on February 2.

But if Trudeau was worried about the fate of the conference, he certainly did not show it in a long interview for CBC's "Newsmagazine", on January 23, when he was questioned by Correspondents Norman DePoe and Ron Collister.

". . . I think the accommodation we are looking for is not in the entrenchment of two nations, as it were, one of them to be represented by the Quebec government and the other by the other governments, this is a conception that we completely repudiate. We feel that there are two languages in Canada and that they should be entrenched in the constitution, that they should be considered as the official vehicles of communication. That's all. I don't think this leads to the existence of two nations, and we certainly deny any one government in Canada . . . the right to say it speaks for one nation. This is not so."

Trudeau said he had nothing against re-writing the BNA Act

completely, but he didn't think it necessary. "I think the essential thing is to ensure that French speaking Canadians are not locked into the Province of Quebec and that therefore no one Provincial government can say 'I speak for the French and you other governments speak for the English'."

Why a Bill of Rights first? Just a question of basic values, he said. "How do you look at a new constitution? Do you throw it out of the window and start with Article One? Obviously not ... the most logical approach would be to look at those basic values which all Canadians stand for ... such as the various freedoms and linguistic rights, these are the ones which normally you find in a Bill of Rights ... and if we can't agree on that there's not much point looking at the mechanics of amending the constitution".

DePoe and Collister ended their interview with a question about "the speculation that you will declare your candidacy for the leadership of the Liberal Party in Montreal this weekend . . .?"

Trudeau laughed. ". . . that speculation is completely false". But he paused. "You shouldn't have added 'this weekend' there, you might have had a different answer."

He left them hanging on his words.

For two weeks, in fact, Canada had been waiting for Trudeau. Hardly a day had gone by without front-page pictures of him greeting one premier or saying goodbye to another. And in the evening, on television, there was always the wintry figure of the Minister of Justice, striding purposefully through the snow from a steaming jet in frigid January weather, bundled in his father's old coonskin fur or wearing his own ankle-length leather greatcoat, reminiscent of newsreels, old Mercedes-Benzes, and *déclassé* Wehrmacht generals. Only his hat — a crushed, black leather trilby from Paris, (needed to keep the thinning Caesar-cut warm) added an appropriate touch of frivolity. It wasn't really Phillips Oppenheim, it was a joke, and the people loved it.

When Newfoundland's Joey Smallwood, who had never clapped eyes on Trudeau before, pronounced him "the most brilliant member of the House of Commons . . . and I say that without qualification. . . . He will be known as the one great political intellectual of Canada!" the country knew that Trudeau was approaching apotheosis. What did it matter that Joey didn't really know Trudeau? Or that Joey had monopolized the conversation so completely at lunch, that he hadn't let him say a word? Or that his entire knowledge of Trudeau was contained in the hasty, whispered aside of an aide? Joey knew politics. And by politics, Trudeau was it.

Saturday, January 27, was another triumph for Trudeau, in person and in absentia. A poll of Liberals in the Toronto suburb of Scarboro showed Trudeau far ahead of everyone for the leadership, and he was not even a candidate. While at Montreal's Bonaventure Hotel, the meeting of the Quebec section of the federal party almost became a love-in, as Trudeau in a well-cut soft brown tweed hacking jacket, light grey flannels, suede shoes, blue striped, button-down shirt and maroon knitted silk tie, sauntered down the escalators to the ballrom, followed by a crowd of pubescent youth, "Oohing" and "Aahing" every word.

"I think this guy's the greatest," said one shocking-stockinged micro-bopper to her similarly decorated companion, as they happily trailed the jaunty figure along the corridor. They gambolled around him like puppies, laughing too hard at his jokes, asking cheeky questions and loving the firm put-downs they got.

Yet it was easy to see why Trudeau had won their affection. He listened to them, paying the same serious respect to their intellect as he demanded in return, expressing disagreement with a shrug and a gesture and a smile. Would he run? Please, sir?

"I'm not playing hard to get," he said. "I'm not playing a game. Three months ago I was the scum of the earth as far as Quebec was concerned. And I'm not sure about the leadership question. I may fall flat on my face at the constitutional conference. And the criminal code — let's see what happens to those amendments. We might be swept from power because of Trudeau's amending formula."

Students in unison: Oh, sir!

"It's nice to know students feel as I do," Trudeau said, his shy little-boy smile flashing again. It was a masterly performance. His hands thrust nervously into the pockets of his jacket, not trousers, a less arrogant stance somehow, less cocksure, disarming. Occasionally, he would fiddle with some loose change, listening, then a smile, and a nod to an adult friend on the edge of the crowd would accentuate the monkish tonsure effect of the bald patch on the back of his head.

An over-eager Liberal public relations man tried to barrel in with an introduction and Trudeau straightened, withering the man with slightly narrowed eyes. Great presence. Not a man you take liberties with. For a moment, something of the other, earlier Trudeau, perhaps the real Trudeau, emerged. The man who, only two years ago, had no time for people who did not do their homework — impatient, irritable, very didactic. What did he think of topic A? Nothing. Next question, please. Topic B? Read what I wrote ten years ago in *Cité Libre*. It's all there. Next question?

He had mellowed markedly in two years of political life, and who would not. But the same man was still there, underneath the new political veneer, a man with a mind like a precision instrument. Some insist it is a closed mind. An old friend, who admires the brain but not the theories, says "He's programmed, just like a computer, no matter what the question is, there's a set answer — and it comes as fast and as flawlessly as a computer's. It's a beautiful machine, but it's rigid. He's a jurist and a theorist. He knows his law well, very well, but he has all the rigidity of a theorist. For him what is written is more important than what is felt. The law goes before all else. If something is not written down it means little to him. But he is also a brave man and a sensitive man."

Brave and sensitive he was that weekend. Jean Marchand, Jean-Pierre Goyer, Pierre Levasseur and Jim Davey had done a superb organizational job on the convention. To protect Trudeau's option, Marchand had even banned all leadership candidates from taking part in the discussions except as observers. Platformless and unhappy, they skulked about the hotel; Paul Martin, polishing his French Canadian ancestry; John Turner, surprising everyone with his impeccable French; Eric Kierans, an anathema so recently to so many Quebec Liberals in Ottawa, nervously making friends again; the rest of the candidates staying discreetly in the background. They were not wanted. And if they failed to grasp the fact beforehand, the discussion groups, almost entirely in French, brought home the point bluntly that, if they could not speak French, they need not bother to leave their cards. A vote to abolish the monarchy was passed without incident, and Claude Frenette won the presidency of the party handily.

But the most important session for the Trudeau strategists was the panel on federalism on Sunday morning. Meticulously planned by Goyer and Davey (who prepared the audio-visual aids for the panelists), it was a distillation of two and a half years of lectures and thoughts. It had its origin in the caucus lectures of 1966, proved itself at Montmorency and was now being used to persuade the entire membership of the Liberal party in Quebec that federalism was relevant, indeed essential, to French Canada's aspirations. The panelists, apart from Trudeau, were Paul Tellier, Professor of Political Science at the University of Montreal; Maurice Lamontagne; and Maurice Sauvé.

There was one awful moment of crisis. Towards midnight on Saturday, after all the delegates had left the Bonaventure's ballroom, Goyer, Giguère, and the four panelists met for a brief rehearsal. All were tired and some of them had heard much criticism in the hospitality suites.

Suddenly, Lamontagne announced that he would not go ahead with it.

"It's just a platform for Trudeau," he said bitterly. "We do all the work, then he'll arrive and we'll just be pedestals."

"He was right, of course," Goyer says, "Trudeau was going to be the star, and that's the way we had planned it. But we couldn't let him wreck it at that point. But Maurice has started something. Next thing we knew, Sauvé had seen the door open, and he was ready to bolt too."

Sauvé started asking about the question period, how would it be handled? Simple, said Goyer, each would answer his own, according to his expertise.

"And if all the questions are on federal options?" Sauvé asked, pointedly, since that would be the part handled by Trudeau.

"Trudeau will answer them all," said Goyer.

Why couldn't everyone answer the questions?

"Because it is not a debate, it's a panel," said Goyer.

Sauvé and Lamontagne said they would not take part.

"Alright," said Goyer, "if you want to walk out, go ahead. In any case you are not essential. We will work all night to replace you."

Trudeau tried to be the peacemaker. "Let's be realistic," he said quietly, "let's be practical."

Tempers cooled slightly.

"I'm going to call a press conference right afterwards to protest," Lamontagne grumbled.

"If you do, then I'll call one right after yours and really fix you," shouted Goyer, who, as president of the policy commission, had the weight to carry out his threat. Bob Giguère stepped in as the peacemaker at this point, leading Lamontagne away to soothe his feelings. The next morning, everything went ahead as scheduled.

It was a triumph. And at the end, leading a standing ovation for Trudeau and the panel, was the MP for Lotbiniere, Auguste Choquete, an avowed opponent of the Minister of Justice who shouted out as the applause died away, "There's our future Prime Minister!" (Four weeks later Choquette would come out in support of Robert Winters, but that was another story.)

In his editorial in *Le Devoir* on Monday, January 29, Claude Ryan said this about Trudeau. "Several delegates always considered Trudeau as a distant, abstract, cold intellectual. They were astounded to find out that the Minister of Justice is capable, on the contrary, without any oratorical artifice, of rising to a degree of lucidity and simplicity which is perhaps the most eloquent of our era."

For Trudeau supporters in Toronto, Ottawa and Montreal, it was the sign they had been waiting for. On Wednesday, January 31, Gordon Gibson, Jim Davey and Donald Macdonald attended a key meeting in Toronto at the house of former Scarborough MP Maurice Moreau on Markham Road, and the Ontario draft-Trudeau committee was formed. Two other MP's who had committed themselves to Trudeau along with Macdonald were present at the meeting, Robert Stanbury, a lawyer, who succeeded Moreau in Scarborough when he retired, and Russell Honey, also a lawyer, the MP for Durham. Stanbury and Honey had come out for Trudeau publicly in mid-January, a move that literally put their political careers on the line.

About 28 people crowded into Moreau's basement playroom for the meeting on January 31. Most had met already at previous events at Scarborough for the Liberal poll, at Linden's house on Chaplin Crescent, in the Teitelbaums' or at the Macdonalds'. Some had been Marchand men, but now the two groups were united for Trudeau. Davey and Gibson brought a simple message.

Trudeau was nearly ready. He had been delighted by the Montreal meeting and pleased by the Scarborough poll. But he did not want to commit himself until he was sure that he had enough support in Ontario, the major bastion of delegate strength. How could they persuade him that there was no longer a risk in Ontario?

After a long discussion the meeting decided that they would have to devise a strategy which would let him exploit the Ontario Liberal Association convention at the Royal York the following week. All the candidates would be there on Friday, February 9, to give eight-minute speechlets. Trudeau was not a candidate, so he could not give a speech. How about a news conference? It was a brilliant idea, particularly as it would take place before the speeches.

By the time the Markham Road meeting broke up, Donald Macdonald had been put in charge of the committee organizing Trudeau's appearance at the Royal York the following week, while a finance committee had been started under the chairmanship of Martin O'Connell to start raising the funds needed for Trudeau's campaign.

Finance is the most critical area of political organization after the candidate himself. Without adequate funds — and it is estimated that it costs a minimum of $150,000 to run for the leadership of a party in Canada — a candidate simply cannot operate. Bob Giguère, the chief Liberal organizer in Quebec, breaks down the costs: transportation and accommodation, $50,000; publicity and advertising materials of all sorts, $75,000; convention expenses, $25,000 (phones, messengers, walky-talkies, etcetera). And these are minimum figures. The Trudeau strategists estimated the executive jet at $36,000 (60 hours at $600 per hour). But on top of this, there are charter fees for light aircraft and helicopters (fearfully expensive but essential in certain time and terrain situations), cars and buses, hall rentals and receptions. There is also the bill for his hotel accommodation, at about $40 per day per head for room and food, for six weeks. This all makes Giguère's $50,000 figure realistic.

Publicity costs are appalling and campaign chairmen are convinced that printers rub their hands with glee every time a political campaign or election comes around. Some, of course, are straight profiteers, but most printers do heroic work, since publicity is nearly always produced at the last minute against contributions received the day before (hardly any of the candidates operate a successful cash-flow accounting system).

This runs the print shop into over-time, costs soar, and the job comes in at about twice what was budgeted. But printing is only part of it. There are photographs to be paid for, secretarial services to be purchased, as well as costumes, hats, bands, songs, public relations men, tape-recordings, and, in some cases, the use of the creative department of a major agency (Young & Rubicam handled the National Union election campaign in Quebec in 1966). It all becomes very expensive.

Martin O'Connell was the presiding genius of Trudeau fund-raising in Ontario. At the outset, the province was divided into 75 zones, each with a target, and the most stringent procedures were instituted for remitting funds back to headquarters.

As a result, Ontario exceeded its quota substantially ten days before the convention. Furthermore, the funds came from the people themselves, not just from a few large corporate donors. More than 85% of individual contributions were for less than $100. Some of the group donations were imaginative. O'Connell had started a "500 Club" for Trudeau for all who gave $500 or more, and one canvasser, Mrs. Marianne Duncan, solicited $5 each from 100 people in order to join the club.

While the Ontario committee raised money and prepared for Trudeau's arrival on February 9, the Montreal and Ottawa groups re-organized themselves. The end of the Montreal convention immediately freed Goyer, Levasseur and Davey for other work in Ottawa.

Meanwhile, the Constitutional Conference arrived at last and was duly recorded in livid color by the television networks, whose cameras remained baffled by the contrasts of the tarted-up Confederation Room, glittering with public works department gilt and specially-imported Victorian chandeliers, where ten scarlet and white Canadian Maple Leaf flags clashed shrilly with the muddy-maroon flocked wallpaper.

But if the decor was novel, there was a *déjà-vu* quality about the cast, whose performance had changed remarkably little since their last three-day constitutional stand at Robart's Confederation of Tomorrow conference in Toronto. Except for Bennett of British

Columbia, of whom *Time* wondered "if he had wandered into a hardware dealers' convention by mistake", the show was stolen by the new headliners, Pearson and Trudeau.

It started out as high drama with Pearson's statement that "what is at stake is no less than Canada's survival as a nation" and ended as tragi-comedy with the rather less urgent decision to let a continuing committee to carry on the work. Pearson made the best of it by recalling the story of St. Denis, the martyred Bishop of Paris, who walked five miles after his execution with his head under his arm. Upon hearing the story, a French peasant remarked: "The distance is not important, it was the first step that counted."

Between that beginning and that end, however, television viewers were entertained by repeat performances from Manning and Smallwood and, more importantly, between Trudeau and his would-be nemesis, Daniel Johnson, who referred to each other tartly as "the Member for Mount-Royal" and the "Deputy for Bagot".

When Johnson argued that Quebec needed more power for its "special role" as the guardian of French Canadian culture, Trudeau retorted that if the French language and culture are constitutionally guaranteed by a bill of rights, why would Quebec need any special powers? "The inevitable, logical conclusion would be that people of ambition in Quebec would not be interested in Federal politics. And that would lead to separatism because Quebeckers would feel that nothing is being done for them in Ottawa but only in Quebec," said he.

Or as Smallwood put it, more bluntly, "The Quebec MP's — what are they? Dummies?"

"The matter cannot be solved with an aspirin!" Johnson harrumphed. "It goes deeper than that. If we want to make progress at the conference, these matters should be discussed in committees, in an atmosphere more favorable than this one."

Pearson then intervened, diplomatically suggesting a coffee break. But Johnson was heard huffing on for television cameras in the corridor "that if Mr. Trudeau's policies are followed, it will mean the end of Canada." Trudeau, who caught the remark, shot back, "if Mr. Johnson's policies are followed, it will mean the end of federalism." But peace was restored ultimately.

On Tuesday, February 6, Pearson threw a dinner party for the premiers which seemed to be saying something about culinary confederation. The eleven men sat down to spinach soup, weiner schnitzel, fried rice and a mousse of chocolate and rum, all washed down with Portuguese *rosé* wine and Bollinger champagne.

Editorialists were perplexed by the conference. On reading the federal position paper, Claude Ryan said he felt that "this text is about a country which isn't quite Canada. The whole is impressive, but it lacks one essential thing — a political dimension." He found it too coldly logical and rational. "The very existence in Quebec of a distinct society is in itself a political fact of the highest importance," he pointed out. Two days later, however, he decided that the conference's endorsement of the B & B commission's linguistic proposal did show "a will to oblige that would have been unthinkable a year ago."

In truth, the conference was a flop. The bill of rights proposal got nowhere, while the B & B endorsement had no legal guarantees. But at least there was no loss of face on either side, and that, as a pre-conference briefing seemed to indicate, was all that anybody could hope to achieve. It would be up to the new federal leader to resolve the basic issues of jurisdiction at some later date.

For now, the country had other things on its mind. In the *Globe & Mail*, Scott Young wrote that the winter madness seems to affect Canadians as the Baltic winter does the Finns, with ferocious NHL hockey games substituting for Finnish candle-light moose hunts. "This winter Trudeau is our Chinook, our friendly groundhog, our Peter Pan come to make us fly, make us fly, make us fly," he wrote.

Quebeckers were less complimentary. René Lévesque called him "our Negro King in a sports jacket" and Hamilton's CHCH-TV kept the feud going by airing Pierre Berton's program "Under Attack", taped on December 13 at Carleton University where Trudeau made the statement that French Canadians spoke "lousy" French. He also pointed out that education had been under Quebec jurisdiction for 100 years so it was hardly the fault of the rest of Canada.

"Lousy" was promptly translated by anti-Trudeau forces in its literal *pouilleux* (verminous) meaning instead of its idiomatic sense *moche* (poor), which didn't burnish the Justice Minister's image in Quebec.

The Ontario Liberal Party annual convention at the Royal York February 9 was another triumph for Trudeau. He flew in the night before, on Thursday, February 8, with Stanbury and Goyer, to attend the first executive meeting of the Ontario for Trudeau Commitee, which had replaced the Draft-Trudeau committee, and which was under the chairmanship of Russell Honey.

Trudeau's visit to Toronto had only been confirmed definitely on Thursday morning, due to the Constitutional Conference, and as a result the only reception room Macdonald could get for the news conference on Friday was the "Ontario Room", a huge salon nearly the size of a small ballroom.

"Frankly, that morning I can remember being scared to death," says Macdonald. "I kept thinking 'what happens if we get these notices out, and the press turn up, and all we've got is a brave group of 25 gathered in one corner? We'd really lay an egg.' But we went ahead on that basis."

When Trudeau arrived, they whisked him in a side-door and up to Macdonald's suite on the sixth floor. About 50 "insiders" were there, from the Teitelbaums, Lindens and Robert Kaplans (the man who would defeat Dalton Camp in Toronto-Don Valley), to such people as Merle Shain, social worker and smashing W5 hostess who would become den mother to the "Pierrettes," the lovely girls in orange shifts who looked after Trudeau hospitality suites at the convention. Bill Kilbourn was there and so was Ramsay Cook, whom Trudeau hailed as the newest convert to Liberalism after himself. "And Eugene Forsey," replied Cook. It was a gathering of the faithful from all over Ontario and a good place to build up courage before venturing into the possibly echoing emptiness of the Ontario Room.

At 5:45, Macdonald took Trudeau down to meet the press, with some trepidation. "We were to have a press conference at quarter to the hour, and then the general membership were invited to come for 6:15," recalls Macdonald. "I'll never forget my surprise when we took him downstairs, and we found that over 200 people were lined up around the newsmen. At that point, my worries ended. The press conference became a sort of Roman Games. Trudeau would say something, and the crowd would cheer, and the newsmen would crane to hear what the answer was! It was very successful. This was my first experience of these phenomenal situations, where people came crowding in on him. Reid and Stanbury and myself had to physically pilot him from the crush of the crowd."

After a time, the newsmen gave up trying to compete with the delegates, and the crowds closed in.

Trudeau was spirited away before the other delegates started delivering their eight-minute statements at 7:30 p.m. and went back to Montreal that night. But there was no question who would get the front page in the morning.

The final hurdle was the Quebec caucus. Goyer flew back with Trudeau from Toronto, and he remembers that "the gestation had started. Montreal had been a reassurance, but Toronto had been the key. If it had been a flop in Toronto, it would have been all over, he wouldn't have run," he says. "It was essential to have a success, and Toronto was above our expectations."

Goyer and Macdonald had both noticed Trudeau's detached acceptance of crowds. "There was this strange way this guy could go into a huge crowd and be pushed and pulled everywhere, and then minutes later, in that quiet little room upstairs he would be talking with Ramsay Cook as if he had been reading in a library all day. I think I noticed it first in Toronto. And I knew then that there was no danger of the adulation reaching him. It's reassuring, you know, because he could become a dictator otherwise."

It would be Goyer and not Marchand who would stage manage the Quebec caucus show of support. The Quebec MP's were not in a good mood, and it was mostly because of Marchand's methods. He had become more autocratic since he took over the leader's job, and his old, union-boss tactics had tended to reassert themselves. Marchand can be as kind and as persuasive as anyone, but he can also be brutally blunt, particularly when he is busy and tired. On the whole, the Quebec MP's were in favor of Trudeau, but they felt that Marchand was being too cavalier with their support, taking it for granted. If he had spoken to each member, privately, and told him why he was supporting Trudeau, there's a chance the caucus would have been almost unanimous. As it was, it was badly split. "There was not a majority," says Goyer, "and there was a lot of indecision. And those who were sympathetic had been badly handled. It was a pity, because he could have had two thirds of the caucus."

As it was, only 20 of the 56 members came out for Trudeau.

"Trudeau told me that if you have no majority, I won't run," Goyer remembers. "And I had to persuade him to go on the basis of what we had and what was possible."

The caucus met on Wednesday, February 14, and was far from unanimous for Trudeau. Lalonde and Trudeau discussed it that night in Trudeau's office. The final decision was up to Trudeau.

"It was genuinely touch and go," Lalonde remembers. They met for three hours and finally he left him walking, alone, in his coonskin fur coat around Parliament Hill.

"The question was, could we carry it?" Lalonde recalls. "Would he carry it to the extent that he would not come in 4th or 5th — because this would mean a complete discrediting of everything we stood for, and the defeat of the reformist element in the Liberal Party. In that case, it would be much better to support somebody else, instead of being thrown to the wolves. Even if he came third, it would have been a serious situation, if not exactly a set-back. Well, we were convinced we could carry it. I was sure in mid-January that we could get 700 votes on the first ballot. We could not but do fairly well — and I also had a very strong feeling that he could not *not* run, it would have been a letdown for all the radical, reformist elements in the party. Not in a boasting way, but the type of people who did not feel attuned to the other candidates, the young people attuned to the new style in politics, would have had no opportunity to express their voice or their support for any candidate. And I felt we would let down a whole new generation of people, I felt that extremely strongly. We could not send him to the butcher, but we could not, at the same time, let go of an opportunity for a more progressive element in the party to express itself. If we had a convention without someone like him, the party was bound to go down."

One of Trudeau's last requests before making up his mind was to ask for a commitment from Lalonde. "He wanted to be sure it was a commitment for others too," Lalonde remembers. "I promised him one year, doing anything, and I committed a few other people who did not know it at the time!"

That was good enough

"Well," said Trudeau, "it may all burst, but it's going to be a bloody big one."

And with that he went off into the night to walk around Parliament Hill alone.

XIV

The Man to Beat

"Dear Senator Nichol:
After much thought I have decided to offer my candidature for the position of leader of the Liberal Party of Canada. In view of your position as president of the Liberal Federation, I thought it appropriate to advise you of my decision. (Signed) P. E. Trudeau."

PIERRE ELLIOTT TRUDEAU was the man to beat from the moment he entered the Liberal leadership race with a note to Senator John Nichol, at 9:30 a.m. on Friday, February 16.

As the voting machine test poll at York-Scarborough had shown, he was far ahead of the rest of the field. In delegate strength alone, he should come in with between 700 and 750 votes on the first ballot, or close to 30%, and on the second ballot, strategists knew he was the second choice of so many delegates that the figure could soar to between 40% and 50%. A third ballot victory seemed probable, a fourth ballot victory certain. He was ahead and the strategy was to keep him there. The organization structure had changed substantially in the first week of February, with Gordon Gibson taking a leave of absence from Laing's office to work full time on Trudeau's campaign. One of the first things he did was to go looking for office space, because the evening meetings in Lalonde's East Block office had been getting suspiciously crowded. The search ended with Trudeau's executive assistant, Eddie Rubin, taking an option on space just vacated by the Centennial Train staff, at O'Conner and Laurier streets, at $1,000 a month for three months.

The next problem was how to pay for it — and that was also solved by Rubin, with a personal $1,000 loan which opened an account at the Bank of Montreal branch on the corner for "Gordon

F. Gibson-in-Trust". Rubin's loan was later replaced by a $10,000 demand note from the bank, co-signed by Gibson, Levasseur, Goyer, Davey and the man they hired from management consultants, P. S. Ross and Associates, Bob Brouillard, a bright, 24-year-old MBA, who had been a classmate of Levasseur's at Western.

Until Trudeau came into the race there was a good deal of trouble getting leases signed, loans made, and furniture supplied, because, as everyone said, understandably, "who is Gordon F. Gibson-in-Trust?" Toughest of all was not the loan, apparently, but Mother Bell, who had never leased a telephone to anybody-in-trust and was not about to start.

Another man to take a leave of absence in the first week of February was Jim Davey, a project manager with Chemcell Limited of Montreal when he was not organizing Liberal conventions.

Levasseur started commuting to Ottawa from his job with the Liberal Federation in Montreal. He also continued to give business school lectures at Laval in Quebec City, on Mondays. When Trudeau entered he quit the Liberal Federation with Claude Frenette's blessing.

With Trudeau's entry, Marc Lalonde felt his role had changed. He became the coordinator of the brain trust with Pelletier, Kilbourn, Cook and many others who wanted to help within the limitations of jobs in universities, civil service or sensitive professional connections with government.

The day-to-day running of Trudeau's campaign was handed over to the troika of Gibson, Levasseur and Davey. Jean Pierre Goyer was active in liaison with the Quebec group, which was run by Bob Giguère, and with the Ontario group under Russell Honey, Donald Macdonald and Mo Moreau.

Gérard Pelletier became, as he puts it, the "desk man" to the publicity side of the committee. Towards the end of February, he countered a slander campaign in Quebec by splicing together tapes of Trudeau's answers to certain key constitutional (bilingualism, *deux nations*) and legal (divorce, abortion) questions, plus many small, nagging ones. Example: "Are the English supporting you 'against' Quebec?" Trudeau: "People who think about me as a good candidate for Prime Minister because they believe I'll be tough towards Quebec, would do better not to vote for me." The transcript of the tape was edited quickly into a 128-page book titled *Réponses de Pierre Elliott Trudeau* and published on March 21 by Jacques Hébert's Editions du Jour. Pelletier's other job was vetting speeches and news releases for style and accuracy. He knew from old experience with Trudeau at *Cité Libre* that there were certain things he would not say. And of course he was impossible about speeches. "He's a nice man the rest of the time," sighs Pelletier, "but when it comes to speeches, he's a finicky bastard."

Trudeau had a succession of speech writers before he settled down with Tim Porteous, the man who has that thankless job today. His writers during the campaign ranged from Pelletier himself to Don Peacock, one of Pearson's writers, Porteous, who had left Drury to work for Trudeau, and Ramsay Cook, who spared what time he could during the campaign but really only became a major contributor during the general election which followed.

The main trouble was not the style of the speeches, it turned out, but Trudeau's own inability to deliver a text. In fact, one of the most startling transformations — and one which pleases Trudeau most — is the way he has forced himself to learn to read effectively. There was no comparison, for instance, between the stumbling, bumbling Trudeau who read a turgid speech to party faithful (at $1 a head) in Toronto's Queen Elizabeth Theater on March 29, and the smoothly polished orator who went from text to improvisation and back again before 18,000 people (free) at the Hamilton football stadium on June 14. Yet both speeches were largely the work of Tim Porteous.

The written word played a prominent part in the leadership race. Eric Kierans, Paul Martin and John Turner all had books out to back up their platforms. Kierans had his work of the previous summer. Turner's and Martin's were both dressed-up excerpts from old speeches. But the sensation of the spring was the English translation of Trudeau's *Federalism and the French Canadians*, put out by Macmillan in a $2.50 paperback, which turned into a best-seller. This started a chain-reaction on the French original and by the end of the summer the two editions had sold a combined total of nearly 50,000 copies. (Even "Réponses" sold 13,000 copies.)

"That's not bad for a collection of essays and speeches," said

Claude Hurtubise, of Editions HMH, who has made arrangements with the distinguished French publisher, Robert Laffont, to produce the European version in Paris, presumably just in case de Gaulle might want to read it.

After Trudeau's entry, Levasseur, Davey and Gibson set about creating an effective management team. "First," says Levasseur, "we sat around a table, and we hired each other. Then we started hiring other people." Initially it was friends, then friends of friends. "Part of the success I think was that nobody was hired with a specific job description," says Levasseur. "I think the organization chart changed four times during the campaign." Essentially what did not change were the roles each man played. Levasseur was the anchor-man, in charge of operations at the headquarters on O'Connor Street and the publicity; Davey was in charge of regional development and chairman of the campaign coordinating committee; while Gibson became Trudeau's executive assistant.

Davey insisted that the financial controls of the campaign committee should be good enough to reveal at any time how much had been spent, how much was left, where it had gone, and what percentage of budget it represented. All bills were approved by Brouillard, who was the financial comptroller, and by one of the troika.

The committee was divided into seven responsibility areas by Brouillard and a budget established for each area — management, comptroller, press analysis, public relations and publicity, policy research, convention planning, and candidate. When all the bills were paid and all business wound up, Brouillard found that the entire operation had come within 10% of budget, an amazing tribute to the administrative skill of everyone involved.

Politics is a selfish game for the most part. Every political organizer secretly believes that he or she played a key role in their candidate's success, that because of some idea they proposed, speech they wrote, tactic they devised, publicity they created, color they chose, demonstration they staged, the miracle suddenly happened. And if the campaign fails by some chance, as most do, obviously, it is equally swiftly blamed on a failure to accept one of their ideas, tactics, suggestions, and so on.

This was where the Trudeau people seemed to be different. For them, living vicariously was enough. There was an almost religious dedication to the cause — the election of Pierre Elliott Trudeau. There were clashes of temperament and ideas and furious arguments, but little jealousy and practically no sniping. There was a rational acceptance that if someone could do a job better, then give him or her the job.

Few of Trudeau's committee workers were over 30 and many were under 25, but there was an extraordinary maturity in their teamwork. It was quite striking to outsiders. When Gordon Gibson had a motorcycle accident shortly before the general election, and Paul Hellyer's assistant, Bill Lee, came in to act as Trudeau's tour manager, the old Trudeau hands accepted him calmly. "There was never any resentment," says Lee. "And I don't know that I would have been nearly as generous in welcoming a Trudeauite into our midst as tour manager if we had won."

It was partly that the Trudeau team were amateurs in politics, but more significantly perhaps, that none of them depended on politics for their livelihood any more than their candidate did. They were all highly educated, skilled in several fields and unconcerned about their personal future. Gibson, Davey, Levasseur, Lalonde and the others did not have to worry about security, about who would offer them a job if the project failed. Their skills were in constant short supply. And besides, Trudeau certainly seemed a winner.

". . . in a sense he is the man we would all like to be," wrote Tony Westell in the *Globe & Mail*, "charming, rich, talented, successful." Westell saw Trudeau's apparently facile entry into politics and seemingly effortless rise to fame as something that appealed to the Walter Mitty in everyone.

The carefully created illusion that no plot had prepared the way was assiduously maintained. Although Trudeau had made up his mind on February 14, he went through another session of make-believe Hamlet-like indecision in Jean Marchand's office on Thursday night, ending it with a careless toss of a coin, to the delight of the large audience present. Two days later, at his press conference, he pretended that it was all a joke by newsmen. "I have a suspicion that you people had a lot to do with it. I think it started out as a huge practical joke on the Liberal party," he

said, ". . . We dare the Liberals to choose a man like Trudeau . . ."
The newsmen grinned with pleasure.

The pleasure would be short-lived. A sound-proof curtain was about to be rung down on the newsmedia. An essential strategy of the campaign was to be Trudeau's visual personality, his physical difference from the other candidates, his natural charm, his boyish smile. "We decided to take advantage of any television opportunities offered us," says Davey. If this meant that a three-man camera crew wanted to ride in Trudeau's 7-seater jet, that would be just fine. Kick out the newsmen. When delegates asked for closed meetings with Trudeau, his organizers would approve readily, but would manage to slip a cameraman into most meetings to catch the crowd scenes.

The Trudeau people put up with local press conferences with impatience, but interviews were discouraged, and depth reporting virtually eliminated. The CBC's cameraman-director Grahame ("Wojeck") Woods trailed Trudeau for three weeks in order to get just 15 minutes of comment on his Nagra tape-recorder to mix in with the wild footage he had shot for a documentary. Reporters for *Time*, the Toronto *Star* and *The Telegram* would tell the same story. Even Patrick Watson, a Trudeau favorite, waited weeks for his famous interview. Long-promised interviews would slowly vanish as Trudeau slept with his leather hat over his face; or gazed out of the DH-125s narrow portholes into 32,000 feet of cloud; or boned up on a brief, munching cookies and drinking milk. All the publications who accepted a seat on the Trudeau jet paid their way, though it must have seemed at times that they were paying his, for all the benefit they received.

Why? There was no direct answer. But there were several clues. The strategists felt that Trudeau had said so much during the previous three months that he hadn't anything to add or to gain from interviews, on the contrary, it was felt that the wrong phrase, misquoted or out-of-context, could do great harm. It seemed advisable to avoid interviews altogether.

Then there was the undeniable fact that during the leadership convention, the people who counted were the delegates, not the general public. Trudeau could achieve more by meeting delegates person-to-person than he could by giving interviews. Wild television footage (of Trudeau in a crowd of delegates, getting off a plane, sliding down a bannister) would keep him well exposed to the public without wasting his time or putting him into political danger.

Finally, though always understated, was Trudeau's long and quite active dislike for the newsmedia, particularly newspapermen. In private, he often talks about public opinion, as represented by the news media, being "the last tyranny" in the Western world. He has slightly more time for radio and magazine people than he has for newspapermen and frankly enjoys television as a performer, though he claims he never watches it for pleasure. He finds many newspapermen ignorant and boring and does not conceal his contempt for some of them or for their publications. He is apt to say he "never reads" certain publications, and the statement is generally hyperbole, particularly if there is something in a paper which concerns him. While he believes strongly in the freedom of the press and would fight any attempt to reduce that freedom, Trudeau does not necessarily share the conventional political wisdom that the newsmedia must be denied nothing.

Trudeau's campaign entry was timed perfectly. The day before he declared, 200 French Canadians of prominence signed a petition asking him to run, and *Le Devoir's* Ryan noted that the list included "a good number of names who count." The same day, Dr. Desmond Morris, author of *The Naked Ape*, paused on his way through Montreal to say that he had "certain animal leadership properties — as a zoologist, I'm tremendously impressed with Trudeau. He has an intellectual virility which is exceedingly important . . . His anatomy, his gestures, his facial expressions are animal qualities that set him apart and bring him to the top of the heap."

On the day he declared, Brother Jean-Paul Desbiens, better known as "Frère Untel", author of the book which gave *joual* (a French Canadian saying "cheval") to the Canadian lexicon, wrote a long endorsement.

"What is the paradox of Pierre Elliott Trudeau? It is to be a man who lives in his liberty to the limit instead of whining about alienation. It is to adopt deliberately the comportment of an aristocrat among men who have contempt for superiority or even differences from the norm. It is to aim at reason rather than play on emotions."

Desbiens saw Trudeau challenging his opponents as John F. Kennedy challenged Lyndon B. Johnson. "Canada of 1970 will take on the face that it gives itself at the April Liberal convention. *Qui Potest Capere Capiat* — let him take who can. All things considered, I am more concerned about Canada than I am for Quebec."

His entry also flushed out some of the opposition. "I don't want a New Democrat as leader," growled Ralph Cowan, the Anglo-Saxon separatist from Toronto's York-Humber, who would stoop low in fighting Trudeau during the campaigns ahead.

No sooner had Trudeau's campaign started, however, than a parliamentary crisis brought everything to a full stop.

The defeat of the Liberal government on routine, third reading of a tax bill, on February 19, was much more serious at the time than it seems in retrospect. The question which roiled the House for the next nine days (effectively preventing all campaigning) was whether the Liberals had lost a vote of confidence or not. The Liberals said they hadn't and of course Robert Stanfield's Tories said they had, with John Diefenbaker playing his favorite role as Gabriel.

"This last week we have witnessed the ravishment, if not the rape, of Parliament" he thundered. "Parliament, Mr. Speaker, has been emasculated," he added, with a hilarious mixture of metaphor.

Trudeau, in light brown sports jacket and dark brown trousers, led the reply: "The question is quite simple. We have to know, Mr. Speaker, if the government should continue to govern or should call an election . . . two opinions prevail. It is the opinion of the Opposition that, last Monday, we lost the confidence of the House. It is our opinion that we did not lose it."

At 3:42 p.m. on Wednesday, February 28, the Commons divided on the Question: "That this house does not regard its vote on February 19th in connection with third reading of Bill C-193, which had been carried in all previous stages, as a vote of non-confidence in the government."

There were 138 yeas and only 119 nays. The Créditistes had supported the government.

The nine-day moratorium on campaigning helped Trudeau more than it hurt. He had managed to get in three solid days of campaigning before the crisis came. And since he was in his seat in the Commons the night of the defeat (unlike several other candidates), he was not hurt personally. The delay also allowed his youthful organization time to shake down. A whole raft of new people came on board during the second half of February: comptroller Brouillard, speech-writers Porteous and Peacock, PR-man, Hal Kroeker, press analysts, André Massé and Jean Haché, plus many others, like lovely Jennifer Rae who took over PR from Kroeker; Suzanne DePoe (Norman's daughter) who started on the switchboard and ended up running the production department; Merle Shain who came to decorate the office and ended up choosing 20 "Pierrettes" and their stunning dresses and seeing to everything from dress production to rotation plans at the convention, Gwen Clark, who became a Girl Friday with a flair for political organization that included persuading the P.E.I. cabinet not to sit the night Trudeau came to Charlottetown, Allison Gordon, who designed the "Pierre" and "Trudeau" placards and buttons; Judy Holland, and others who deserved to be remembered, too.

On the whole, the crisis in confidence left the opposition in worse shape. Robert Winters, who had hurried back from India to the Ontario Liberal convention on February 10, had planned to announce his re-entry the week of the 19th. But he could hardly enter while the government was in danger of defeat, and had to wait until March 1 for the propitious moment.

Mitchell Sharp, who had been deputy Prime Minister (Pearson was in Jamaica) at the time of the defeat, lost a lot of credibility as a result of the government's handling of the money bill vote. He tried to regain his prestige later by staying in Ottawa to fend off the international gold crisis that lasted most of March, but it was too late. Fate was cruel to a dedicated man.

Paul Martin had been encouraged by a Gallup poll putting him ahead with 26% of popular support, but he had been caught in Three Rivers without a "pair" (a mutual agreement with an opposition MP, not to vote) in the government's defeat, and had lost ground as a result.

Only John Turner still seemed to be going strong. He had been paired during the government defeat and unlike Paul Martin and Joe Greene, he had told the Liberal Whip Bernard Pilon who his pair was.

It was a strangely disjointed campaign. Unlike the Conservatives, who had swept in stately style around the country, the Liberal candidates were forced into the jet age with a vengeance, streaking away from Ottawa's Uplands Airport at 600 mph for a meeting and then back again the same evening or following morning in order to be in the House. But Pearson had made his decision to keep Parliament in session and the House sat until the evening of March 27, a week away from the opening of the convention, when it finally adjourned for the Easter recess, planning to reconvene April 23. Dragging out the session meant that all candidates (except Eric Kierans who was not an MP at the time) had to crowd all their travels into weekends and weekday evenings when the House was not sitting.

To cope with the difficulties, nearly all the serious candidates rented private planes, many of them jets, which were lined up at Uplands like some super-posh flying circus, ready to streak there and back again at a moment's notice. The aircraft ranged in size from Joe Greene's ill-fated Beechcraft (it failed to get airborne at Woodstock, Ontario) to Robert Winters' private Douglas DC-9, an enormous aircraft which he chartered from Air Canada for lack of anything smaller. Trudeau, Sharp, Martin and Turner had a variety of executive jets and turbo-props.

Campaign speeches were thin, since by March, most of the candidates were starting to make the same speech for the third time. Besides, the rules of cabinet solidarity prevented anything which sounded like deviation from the party line. This left Kierans in an enviable position for any Irishman — being able to say anything that came into his head and not really having to worry where the shafts landed. It also made him refreshingly original.

News on Trudeau was so sparse at one point that papers were reduced to speculation about his age. He said he was born on October 18, 1921, his brother was sure it was 1920, while his sister said it was really 1919. Trudeau himself did not help matters by admitting "it's somewhere around there".

Which date was correct? Since nobody bothered to dig, the subject lapsed until *Time* checked it out in the Montreal Superior

Court records and revealed to the world on April 15 that Trudeau was born on October 18, 1919, and baptised two days later at St. Viateur's Church in Outremont.

Canadian Press news agency was apparently so ashamed of its lack of enterprise that when it "matched" *Time's* story, two days later, it unaccountably failed to give the source of its information.

On March 6, Trudeau said he saw signs of French meddling behind the "Gabon Affair", and warned that if France itself "were ever to do that, to invite Quebec as an independent state to sit among independent states, we would have to react in the same manner." Canada had broken off diplomatic relations with tiny Gabon over its gratuitous insults to the Canadian ambassador, Jean Thibault, and for its decision to seat Quebec as a sovereign state at the February meeting in Libreville of the 14-member *Commune Africaine et Malgache.*

On March 11, evidence appeared that although Trudeau seemed to have cornered the market on academics, not all of them were go-go for Pierre. Reviewing *Federalism and the French Canadians* in the Toronto *Star*, political scientist Paul Fox wrote: "Well, bravo, Edmund Burke! Whether or not Trudeau likes it and despite the fact he considers it all a silly exercise, Quebec is on fire with nationalism and passionately involved, like a new nation, with fulfilling itself . . . the truth is that beneath his dashing image, Pierre Trudeau is a conservative." Fox concluded that Trudeau's conservatism "is the source of his appeal to English Canadians."

On Wednesday, March 13, Quebec's separatist RIN party came out in support of Trudeau "Because he'll bring about separatism quicker than anybody else."

The president of the four-year-old Rhinoceros Party, Dr. Paul Ferron, said his group was in hibernation and hence inactive, but felt that Trudeau was a likely affiliate. "He fits the party symbol better than any other candidate," said Ferron, reminding people that "the rhinoceros is a thick-skinned, clumsy, stupid animal which loves to wallow in the mire but can move fast when it senses danger. In other words, it's a perfect symbol of the Quebec MP in Ottawa."

And on the same day an enterprising Ottawa haberdasher named Herb Gosewich produced the first batch of his "Go-Go Trudeau" sweat shirts in a fetching purple, priced to match at $4.25.

Trudeau's foray from Parliament Hill that Wednesday night

was to the safely middle-class community of St. Basile-le-Grand which, despite the imposing Norman name, is a once tiny farming village on the wrong side of the tracks off the main southshore highway, 10 miles south-east of Montreal. It was to be Trudeau's first test of Quebec opinion as a candidate.

St. Basile has become an exurban sprawl of heavily-mortgaged, split-level, ranch-type "homes", gleaming with the aluminum storm windows and doors which are the penalty for insisting on Californian architecture in the Canadian winter. It's neighbors, if it ever wandered from its conservative course, are the wealthy suburbs of St. Bruno and Beloeil, not the sort to encourage radicalism.

In short, if Trudeau had really wanted to test his appeal in the mainstream of Quebec political thought, St. Basile-Le-Grand was hardly the place to do it. The fact that the Trudeau committee picked it, and the audience, which was "by invitation only", was clear proof that his Quebec organizers wanted to do everything possible to avoid a public confrontation for their man in Quebec.

The meeting was held at the Hotel Maranda, no better than its name, a sprawling, one-storey motel self-advertised in violent neon signs, with a huge, tavern-like cocktail bar which the Trudeau organizers took over.

Trudeau got a warm but not enthusiastic welcome when he arrived, nearly two hours late, and with becoming diffidence introduced himself as one of several candidates seeking the leadership, expressed his admiration for the others, and his appreciation for being able to meet the riding association delegates *en famille* with no reporters present. Instead of making a speech, he asked to hear their questions, a pattern that would repeat itself through his campaign.

There was no shortage of questions but they were surprisingly mild. The delegates asked about the guaranteed minimum wage, about Canada's role in NORAD, in Viet Nam, in NATO (reflecting the residents of the nearby Canadian Forces Base at St. Hubert), and on defense spending in general. A persistent young man kept asking Trudeau what he felt about the emotion of separatism. Trudeau replied that he liked talking about it, because it reminded him of the discussions he had had as a university professor, but that he felt the audience was interested in more important questions — and urged the young man to read what he had already written about separatism. He did it so nicely that it would never have caused offense, unless the questioner was familiar with Trudeau's technique for brushing off questions he does not like.

The other questions were predictable — but there was a curious absence of interest in either divorce or criminal code amendments, such as abortion, homosexuality or other topics which were popularly regarded as a threat to the Catholic church. One observer explained later that "these sort of people never feel that they'd be in a position to want a divorce or an abortion — so the question doesn't touch them."

Trudeau's press conference, which followed, was stern and swift. How about the audience? "I go to as many delegates as I can and ask them to assess me. My assessment of them really doesn't matter very much. I know I have considerable support in Quebec and several other provinces." The Gabon situation was discussed briefly — and he was gone.

Paul Martin also campaigned hard that week, including a turn around his native town of Pembroke, Ontario, where he recalled how he worked for a lumber company for $1.50 per 10-hour day and his sister Lucille went to work as a telephone operator to help put him through school. There was also one of those well-meant introductions by a boyhood companion who got a little tangled in his quotes as he introduced Martin declaring: "And as that great man Mackenzie King used to say, 'you don't need brains to be Prime Minister'."

The following week, the executive jets were buzzing faster than ever as the convention was only two weeks away, and the Trudeau committee rooms were in a state of disarmingly attractive confusion. Nobody, it seemed, knew anything about the press conference on Monday morning to announce that Jean Marchand and Edgar Benson were to be Trudeau's national co-chairmen.

Trudeau had been campaigning in the West over the weekend and had happened to mention that the French Canadian claim to linguistic equality was no less valid than, say, a Chinese claim to similar equality would be, if Canada ever had a population of 10 million Chinese. This prompted Claude Ryan to accuse him of speaking with forked tongue. Trudeau said Ryan was being "intellectually dishonest" in his criticism. "I pride myself on never reading *Le Devoir*," he said, "but for other reasons I did read it today, and I did see Ryan's editorial. I shall now go back to my previous resolution of never reading it."

By the following week, with a blockbuster launching for *Réponses* to cheer him up, Trudeau was well braced to receive the slightly less welcome support of economic nationalist Walter Gordon. On Tuesday, March 26, his old friend, playwright Roger Lemelin, came out with an open letter to Quebec's *l'Action* and Montreal's *Le Devoir* entitled, "Why I support Pierre Elliott Trudeau". Lemelin would also pay Montreal's Channel 10 television station, *Télé-Métro*, to air an interview he did with Trudeau, a gesture which would earn him a seat on Trudeau's jet between Quebec City and Sherbrooke that week.

The week started in Newfoundland, where the unpunctuated sign at the provincially-owned Holiday Inn declared "Welcome Hon Pierre E Trudeau" on the airport side but yielded to its commercial instincts on the other to say "Welcome to NCRs Release of The Century" (National Cash Register was in town too.) However, the Inn's goodwill did not prevent Trudeau from having to carry his own bag due to an absence of bellboys.

Trudeau was in Newfoundland at Joe Smallwood's special invitation to address the provincial legislature, in session, an unparalleled honor, of which he was reminded several times during the day by his host.

It was a day filled with tableaux.

There was Trudeau nervously reading his address beside the Speaker's chair in the legislature, a backdrop of curtains shutting off the magnificent 10th floor view of St. John's harbor. There was Joey beaming proudly from the disproportionately packed government benches, (all physically moved to one side of the house, leaving the four Opposition members in terrible isolation), as if he were somehow the parent and architect of Trudeau's career. Joey had done everything, significantly, except actually endorse Trudeau, which prompted one crusty Newfoundland delegate to say "Joe spends so much time sitting on the fence, he's got splinters in his arse." Smallwood, like several other Atlantic premiers, did not want to be on a losing team in Ottawa.

There were other scenes during the day, Smallwood introducing Trudeau to the Liberal Ladies Association at the Laurier Club, reading a letter he said he had received that day ("I swear it came in the mail that very morning," said executive assistant, Ed Roberts) from a lady in Toronto who thanked Smallwood for backing Trudeau, ending her note with an emotional triple benediction, "bless you, bless you, bless you."

Then, at the Legislature, Joey just happened to have a young lady in the public gallery who had won a provincial essay contest on "the person I would like to meet most." The person? Who else?

At a private dinner for Trudeau and cabinet ministers at his house on Roaches Line, irreverently nicknamed "The Ponderosa" by Newfs, Smallwood underlined his familiarity with both culture and the world of high finance by serving a Chateau Mouton Rothschild which he had obtained through his good friends you know who.

Joey's vinic panache faltered on the pronunciation of Chambertin, whereupon he decided it was time for a French lesson. And having perfected his own pronunciation with Trudeau's help, he forced each unhappy, unilingual cabinet minister to say "Chambertin" until he got it right, bullying them mercilessly until they did.

Tuesday was to be spent in Quebec. It's a two hour flight from St. John's to Riviere du Loup, and the moment the DH-125 lifted off the runway, Trudeau was deep in reading matter, a speech, a brief on local and regional problems from one of the black, looseleaf ring books his staff prepared for every leg of the trip. Occasionally he would drink a large glass of milk or orange juice, munch a sandwich, oblivious to the conversations around him. The plane was noisy and drowned out all sounds. Trudeau never fastened his seat belt, kept his bulky leather coat on until well after take-off so the cabin had time to warm up. It was cold, wet, Irish spring weather in Newfoundland, but in Rivière du Loup the snow-banks were four feet deep and it was still winter — a bleak, lonely landscape on the south shore of the St. Lawrence river, which could be seen swirling malevolently under its ice-floes.

He was made an honorary citizen of Rivière du Loup (the Mayor was a Liberal), then it was back to the jet for the 100-mile, 20-

minute flight to Quebec City. The speed of the jet was astonishing.

Quebec Liberal leader, Jean Lesage, refused to be photographed with Trudeau, which was understandable in view of the background, but he shook hands with him while flunkies guarded the door to his office in the legislature.

There was a tremendous reception at Quebec's Reform Club, where 300 people jammed into three small rooms, wearing scarlet carnations and acting like good Liberals should. The women were enraptured by Trudeau's weathered features, shrieking with nervous laughter at every joke. His effect on women is extraordinary and most don't know why they like him so much. In Prince Edward Island, the next day, a level-headed housewife in her thirties persuaded her baffled husband to drive 40 miles from their home in Summerside across the island to Charlottetown, to a Trudeau reception. She waited for two hours for Trudeau to appear, went to within five feet of him, but refused to go closer, and stared for a full two minutes, devouring him, (he was unaware of the scrutiny). Then, with a triumphant grin, she rejoined her husband in the hotel lobby and they drove 40 miles back to Summerside. "I just love that man," she said as she left. "Oh, I just love him." There was no further explanation.

Roger Lemelin was on the jet that evening to Sherbrooke, wrapped in his faded green Italian trench-coat, carrying a little tin of tooth-whitener that he had asked his dentist to make up that morning for Trudeau. "It sounds funny, I know," said Lemelin, "but these little tricks all help." He advised Trudeau to use the powder twice a week, and gave him the benefit of other wit and wisdom until the candidate put his seat back, tipped his leather hat over his face — and went sound asleep. Lemelin beamed like an indulgent uncle. He told the other passengers he had bought 150 copies of Trudeau's *Réponses*, which he was having "distributed to the poor." He had also been to see the Bishops about Trudeau. "I told them he's okay," he said. "They will be behind him," he added, only half in jest.

At Sherbrooke, it was the Reform Club again, where the party had started three hours earlier for Robert Winters, and the bilingual audience was getting into a third language. Winters' plane was leaving the ramp, when Trudeau arrived. "I hope you haven't messed things up for me," joked Trudeau to Winters, whose reply is lost, but whose coolness was best reflected in Mrs. Winters expression.

At the club Trudeau's speech was memorable only for the absolute refusal of the toastmaster to shut up. He went on, and on, and on, impervious to hoots, shouts or even insults. The meeting lasted until well after midnight.

Wednesday was another early start, this time for Saint John, New Brunswick, where Ross and Harrison McCain of the frozen food family business were in charge of Trudeau committee arrangements. A delegate meeting and lunch were at the Admiral Beatty Hotel where a choice of chicken à la King or lobster à la Queen was the first real food Trudeau had seen that day. He had missed breakfast and made do with two-day-old orange juice aboard the plane.

At Moncton in the afternoon there was another closed meeting. The McCains had flown delegates in on chartered DC-3's from as far away as Charlo, up near the Quebec border.

Last stop on Wednesday, March 27, was Charlottetown where Premier Alex Campbell led a crowd of 200 to the airport to meet the jet with "Go Go With Trudeau" sweatshirts, signs, flags and balloons. "I want you to meet the future Prime Minister of Canada," said Campbell to one family, giving the Toronto *Star* reporter, Jack Cahill, a front-page story. He was the first premier to commit himself to Trudeau.

Nearly 300 people turned out for the Trudeau reception at the Charlottetown Hotel that evening, filling the ballroom and overflowing into the lobby. Even the Conservative leader, Walter Shaw, was there to wish Trudeau well. It was a triumph for pretty, 24-year-old Gwenneth Clark, daughter of P.E.I.'s health minister, William Clark, a Trudeau volunteer from the administrative staff at Queen's University, Kingston, who had turned out to be a crackerjack organizer. She even persuaded the P.E.I. cabinet not to hold its regular Wednesday evening session in Trudeau's honor.

Gwen flew back to Montreal with her hero and there was a look of pure bliss on her face when Trudeau said good-bye to her at the airport, thanking her with a gentle kiss on the cheek. It was not a cab that carried her away to the airport hotel, just a cloud.

Thursday was Montreal, committee meetings and conferences, a taping for *Les Couches Tards* with Roger Baulu and Clémence Desroches; a race to Rosemere, off the north end of the island, for a dinner with delegates at the Thorncliffe restaurant; a dash back to Mount Royal town hall for an evening rally with his own constituents, open, at last, to the press.

By this time there was no doubt Trudeaumania had caught on. He did a gay buck-and-wing onto the stage to the tune of "Maitre Pierre." The crowd cheered and started singing "*Il a gagné ses épaulettes*", the French equivalent to "He's a Jolly Good Fellow", which they also sang.

A large group of fellow MP's were on stage. "Almost enough to put a bill through third reading," he cracked.

Friday, March 29, was Toronto's day and the Toronto *Star* announced its endorsement. ". . . we think Mr. Trudeau is right on the biggest question before the country, and that he clearly has the potential to offer Canada fresh, stimulating and able leadership. He is the best of a strong field." It was another busy schedule of meetings, taping, press conferences.

It was also the night of the rally of 1,350 people at the Queen Elizabeth theater, where 800 paid $1 each for the privilege of hearing why Trudeau wanted to be Prime Minister of Canada. No one had ever heard of anyone paying to attend a political meeting before, but Mo Moreau was right, 200 were turned away, and the organization even made a small profit.

Rumors were rife in Quebec that Jean Marchand had been twisting arms to persuade delegates to vote for Trudeau. Marchand denied it angrily in public, less so in private. "It's not true," he told his old friend Gérard Pelletier. "I haven't twisted anybody's arm. But of course I might start twisting some next week."

Saturday, the Trudeau jet lifted off from Toronto's island airport bound for Three Rivers. It was the last swing of the campaign. He was relaxed. The *Star's* Cahill had been a scuba diver in his native Australia, hunting sharks, and Trudeau was fascinated. He had learned to scuba dive himself at the Cousteau school at Cap d'Antibes and had gone as deep as 200 feet. But he had never hunted sharks.

At Three Rivers the delegate meeting was at the Castel des

Prés Motel, but the local organization seemed keener on Paul Martin than Trudeau. At Arvida, the Manoir du Saguenay was an elegant, chateau-like site for an afternoon reception. Trudeau was asked about the Criminal Code amendments. He replied easily, sipping a glass of milk. Someone asked about homosexuality. He told them about Canada becoming a pluralistic society. And then it happened.

"What about masturbation?" asked an apparently sensible man. The audience gasped.

Trudeau shrugged. "Well," he said, "I suppose everyone has his problems."

The crowd roared with laughter. The bomb had been defused. *Bon Jour. Bonne chance, mon p'tit Pierre.* And he was gone.

It was the last leg. Halifax. Saturday night. It was over. It was Winters' country, or MacEachen's, and there was no interest in Trudeau. He shook hands, nodded, smiled a bit more tautly. He was exhausted. He would rest in Montreal. They had to fly back that night if possible. No newsman would be allowed on board because Trudeau wanted to lie down on the bench seat, Gibson announced.

The campaign was over. The court was dismissed.

XV

The Fifteenth Prime Minister

"The immense advantage of federalism is above all the contact between State and Individual, permitting legislation on the local level for local needs, regionally for regional needs, and on the Federal level when it's a question of facing problems generally."
— *Pierre Elliott Trudeau, April 2, 1968*

TRUDEAU SPENT Sunday and Monday of convention week at home in his one-room bachelor apartment on the 10th floor of Cantlie House, in Montreal. He visited his mother, who is crippled with arteriosclerosis, and held convention strategy sessions with Marc Lalonde, Jean-Pierre Goyer and others. The Trudeau committee had decided the convention strategy would continue the campaign policy of making the candidate appear different from the others. There would be no organized demonstration, no cheer leaders, and no bands. Anything that suggested gimmickry was suppressed. The Trudeau presence and support would be made to appear natural and spontaneous. And spontaneity is the hardest of all things to organize. Westerners would complain bitterly about the lack of pizzazz, they would fight to permit the use of the band they had brought with them, and they would lose ungracefully.

On Tuesday evening, at the Queen Elizabeth Hotel, Trudeau made his final and perhaps most important speech of the campaign to a special banquet of the Richelieu clubs of metropolitan Montreal. Richelieu is an international French-language service club, analogous to Rotary, but with a membership that extends beyond commerce into the fields of finance and the professions. Marc Lalonde had "arranged" the invitation through some good friends in the club. It gave Trudeau an unequalled opportunity to address the elite of French Canadian society on the eve of the convention.

His speech was a brilliant plea for French Canadians to accept the federal challenge, "to plunge into the federal game today." He told the audience it was either incompatibility or federalism. "We are thus faced with a clear choice. The first hypothesis, incompatibility, or whatever you want to call it, points towards separatism, to which it will lead us sooner or later, if we accept it. The second hypothesis is federalism, approached with a new resolution and new tools, the new resources of a modern Quebec. A choice must be made between the two. The worst attitude we could take would be to hesitate, wavering between one and the other, and letting events decide for us."

The speech was long, but it was a summary of everything that Trudeau, Marchand, and Pelletier had been working for since that same springtime exactly twenty years ago. This was what it was all about, the essence of their commitment. It was a passionate appeal to French Canadians to give federalism a real chance, to participate, to seize the opportunities a truly bilingual federal state could offer.

Le Devoir judged the speech important enough to run the full text in its next two editions.

On Wednesday, Trudeau and his aides left for Ottawa by railroad, a private car was attached to the regular noon train. Marc Lalonde, who left with them, was not on board when the train arrived at 2:15 p.m. at Ottawa's Alta Vista station. Discreetly, he had slipped off at an earlier halt and continued the journey by car. For the rest of the week, he would be the Dalton Camp of the convention, active but unseen, to emerge on Saturday to watch the balloting with Lester Pearson and his wife in their private box.

Ottawa had been invaded.

At the airport, in the hotels, even on the streets when April showers permitted, the capital seemed to echo to a cacophony of campaign sounds.

"Paul Martin's the Man, Hey Martin's the man, Say Martin's the Man for Ca-Na-Da," sang the satin-tunicked followers of the Minister for External Affairs, supremely confident that their man would be lucky the third time around.

"So *everyone* here, kindly *get up and cheer*, and let a *Hellyer* lead the way," came the brassy reply from the Minister of Transport's bosomy sweater girls, in red and white, proud possessors of the tune from Broadway's "How Now Dow Jones", which cost the Hellyer committee a cool $2,000 when they bought the rights way back in the fall of 1967.

But there was something rather adolescent about it all compared to the lovely Trudeau girls in their persimmon shifts from Susie Kosivic's *Poupée Rouge*, who sauntered elegantly past the demonstrators, shepherding some delegates, assured, mature, fluent in both languages, and definitely not children.

Among the onlookers, men's eyes would widen and ladies' narrow, and the "Pierrettes" would pay no attention to either. For in spite of their worldly looks, few were really that old and all were *jeunes filles bien élevées*, which meant that they were all boarded in pairs in the homes of families known to the Trudeau committee, all had to be home by 1:30 a.m. at the latest, and up again at 7, or their bunny-mother, Miss Shain, would hear about it.

"There was a great deal of sexual tension, of course; all the boys were walking the fence for those pretty girls," says Merle Shain, who is an extremely pretty girl herself. "I've directed summer camps and social workers, but I'm telling you there is nothing like handling 50 kids, when all the boys want that blonde in the front row to notice them."

She had chosen them from Montreal, Ottawa and Toronto. All had to be over-21 and "sensible." The Trudeau committee "felt it should be a sort of Peace Corps thing, keeping away from the hysterical teenager type," she says. Each of the 400 who volunteered had to be bilingual and had to have a reason for wanting Pierre Trudeau as Prime Minister. The hardest to pick were the boys (dressed in white turtle-necks, persimmon jerkins and dark flannels), where the quality of volunteer had been markedly lower than among the girls.

Officially called "hosts" and "hostesses", the Trudeau kids were divided into teams under a captain and were rotated between hotel hospitality suites and the civic arena by squads of volunteer drivers all planned and coordinated by Merle herself. Her emergency contact with central headquarters, like the other senior staffers, was a Bell-boy call unit. Unlike others, however, Merle had no pocket and kept the Bell-boy clipped to her bra, a source of several hilarious scenes, notably one when she forgot to zip-up again after a call and bumped, poitrine-to-poitrine, into the future Prime Minister, as he strode round the corner just as she was leaving a call box.

"There I was, with my dress undone to my navel, and all he could say was 'Where have you been for the last three weeks, Merle?'" she recalls.

The big news on Wednesday was Mitchell Sharp's withdrawal from the leadership race and his decision to endorse Trudeau. "My conversations with Liberal delegates across the nation in the last few days have convinced me that there is one man who . . . can command the broad support that will be necessary to our leadership in these dangerous times and that is the Honorable Pierre Elliott Trudeau," said Sharp at his press conference. He had called Trudeau at 11:30 on Tuesday night to tell him. "I met with my principal workers this morning at breakfast, and without exception they will follow my lead and support Mr. Trudeau," he added.

Sharp's withdrawal was a blow to his supporters, but it had become inevitable. The defeat of the tax bill in February had started it, campaign funds had dried up, and Sharp was on the verge of pulling out of the race even then. Jean Chrétien urged him not to. "You can't quit when you're down," he had said and Sharp's strategists supported him. For the next three weeks, Sharp had stuck close to home, getting maximum exposure out of "defending the dollar". His executive assistant, Mike McCabe, did a masterly job of getting Sharp on as many TV shows as possible to counter the effect of his decision not to campaign. ("Plus about three unnecessary press conferences," he recalls.) After his trip to Washington, to obtain exemption for Canada from the latest U.S. balance of payments protection program, Sharp's support started picking up again. Campaign contributions began to flow once more. And they decided to put down $20,000 to rent a Jet-Commander aircraft for the last 10 days of the campaign.

By this time the Red-smear campaign by the so-called Canadian Intelligence Service had started against Trudeau, and so had a persistent series of even more scurrilous, gutter calumnies in the province of Quebec. The Sharp group, who regarded Trudeau as their second choice, became increasingly concerned. Trudeau was clearly gaining ground but the opposition to him was getting uglier by the day. Paul Martin's supporters seemed to be the most concerned, according to Sharp's intelligence, but the right-wing of the party as a whole was taking on a "let's stop Trudeau" atmosphere.

"The factor that really put the blocks to us was Winters coming in," says McCabe. "I was keeping the books, and we weren't adding any numbers."

By the Sunday of convention week, it looked as if Sharp would be lucky to squeak into 4th place with about 350 votes. But on Monday the Sharp team got bad news from Opinion Research Corporation, in Toronto, who had been asked to double-check Sharp's support in a survey of eight provinces (Quebec and New-foundland were not included). "Sharp turned out to be in a very bad way," McCabe recalls, with at least half of those who were down as committed Sharp supporters by now voting for somebody else. "They were all over the lot," he says.

Clearly, Sharp was not going to win, and on the basis of the poll, he was not even going to be a king-maker if he went into the ballot and received only about 150 votes. On the other hand, Sharp's reputation, particularly in the West and in Toronto, was such that he could lend an air of integrity to the Trudeau bench if he came in early enough.

"So we decided that it would be best not to have our strength measured and to take our workers, our expertise and the moral force of Sharp himself over to Trudeau right away," says McCabe.

And that is why Sharp moved when he did, a sensibly pragmatic step which did both parties good, helping Trudeau and saving face for Sharp at the same time. Unstated, as always, was Sharp's personal antipathy to Winters, and his determination that Winters would not benefit from any first ballot indication that Trudeau did not have the support he expected.

Trudeau pronounced himself "flabbergasted and delighted" with the news. "If a man of Mr. Sharp's ability and judgement and experience can support me, then perhaps I'm not that bad a risk," he said. He hardly had time for more, since a seemingly inexhaustible and endless crowd of supporters had engulfed him at the railroad station, sweeping him off to the Skyline Hotel, on to the

Party Headquarters, and onward again to the Chateau Laurier, chanting "Tru-deau," "Tru-deau", "Tru-deau" all the way. Finally, that evening, the crowd swept him all the way to Aylmer, Quebec, and into the Chaudière Golf and Country Club, on the banks of the Ottawa river, for the most tumultuous event of all. Nobody will ever know how many people there were for the party thrown at the Chaudière Club by the Quebec Caucus. The place was jam-crammed with people, and it was impossible to park within half a mile. At the clubhouse, the sound-system had failed, newsmen piled onstage, so did the television crews, nobody could see or hear anything — but as everyone was having a marvelous time, it hardly mattered. Even Trudeau finally judged the situation irremediable and beat an early retreat, hopefully to get a good night's sleep before the convention proper started on Thursday.

If Wednesday's love-in for Trudeau was a fluke, there was no mistaking the genuine article on Thursday. From the moment he arrived, at 10:15 a.m., his hair freshly barbered by Bob Barton, his Caesar-cut stylist, Trudeau was the calm epicenter of a tumult. He wore a series of flowers in his buttonhole (he kept on giving them away to girls, and a rose would be replaced with a carnation, a daffodil, and then another rose). Everywhere he went, starting out at the delegates' breakfast at the Skyline Hotel at 8 A.M., a phalanx of photographers, cameramen and reporters traveled with him.

There was something sad about John Turner, in the neighboring box, sitting beside his pretty wife, Geills, and a Kennedy-like display of tiny blonde children. While in the next-door box sat Trudeau, who did not care about being Prime Minister, surrounded by six cabinet ministers, Bryce Mackasey, Jean Chrétien, Jean-Luc Pepin, Mitchell Sharp, Bud Drury and Edgar Benson.

The main purpose of the morning session was a welcoming address by Prime Minister Lester Pearson, to which no one seemed to listen, and a great deal of preening by the candidates themselves.

Paul Martin hustled over to Trudeau's box at one point, leaving his bench of beetle-like men in black homburgs, shaking hands and declaring in French, "It's going to be a good fight" as if he really was looking forward to it. (Maurice Sauvé was in Martin's box, a move Marchand and Goyer would never forgive him for.

"He doublecrossed us royally," said Marchand, "one day he says we are all in the same team and have a job to do, and the next day he joins Paul Martin.")

The Trudeau benches rustled with rumors. That Allan Mac-Eachen was pulling out, that Kierans was, that Greene would. Joe Greene squelched that rumor himself, ambling over in his country-handsome manner to, as he put it, "Say 'Hello' to the second-best choices for Prime Minister."

Two things set the Liberal Convention apart from the Conservatives Centennial Convention six months earlier: the leader being chosen would become Prime Minister of Canada as well as head of the Liberal party, and the Conservative Party organization was about 200% better.

On just about every count, except nominating and seconding speeches (the Liberals eliminated them, wisely), the Liberals managed to ignore all the good advice that had been put at their disposal by the Tories. The site, the Ottawa Civic Centre, was handsome enough for a minor league hockey team, but with only 9,500 seats, which was about half the seating capacity of Toronto's Maple Leaf Gardens, it left something wanting for a national political convention which would have 2,481 delegates, 795 alternates, a like number of wives, girlfriends, children and hangers-on. Plus a press corps of more than 1,000 that would include a CBC crew of 275, and a 55-man team for the leaner, commercially-oriented CTV network.

Apart from the small arena, the adjacent buildings were woefully inadequate to the task, made up of such elderly barns as the Coliseum, best known as the annual site of the Ottawa Valley Farm Show.

Then there was the capital itself, quite incapable of producing the 7,000 hotel and motel beds required for the convention, so that delegates were bunking down three to a room on rollaway cots for five days; braving seedy rooming houses; or gratefully accepting sanctuary in some of the 700 private homes which offered to ease the accommodation crisis.

Perhaps the worst goof of all was the Liberal Federation decision to pass up the successful Conservative experience with Shoup voting machines and instead use a contraption from IBM called

"Votamatic", which required delegates to punch a hole in a computer card with a stylus and then drop it into a ballot box. In theory, the ballots would then be stacked into an IBM 2030 processing unit and the results flashed in seconds by a mated IBM 1403 printer. Somehow, the magic words "please do not fold, spindle or mutilate" did not register on the delegates, as well they mightn't in the excitement of a vote, and the IBM computers choked repeatedly, taking nearly eight hours to process four miserable ballots. Those who sold their IBM shares first thing Monday were probably over impetuous, but they had the sympathy of everyone who sat through the Saturday vote.

Voting was done alphabetically, at 37 scarlet booths, which made the results of the individual polls meaningless statistically and complicated floor management for the candidates. The confusion during voting was heightened by an almost total lack of control on the floor of the arena. Delegates, alternates, newsmen and anybody's aunt could wander pretty much at will if they borrowed the right colored button, for unlike Toronto, credentials were interchangeable. At times the number of unauthorized people in restricted areas became hilarious — for everyone except those who had to work there.

Security service was abysmal. The only time the Ottawa City Police acted decisively was when they cleared a path for the newly elected leader through a crowd of supporters and newsmen, a job they tackled by knocking down anyone who stood in their way, then trampling over them. But in spite of it all, the typical Liberal bumbling remained good-natured, the crowd stayed friendly, the police were called off, and it all ended happily.

The convention was estimated to have cost $3,150,000 including the campaign expenses of the candidates ($2,000,000), delegates and guests ($1,000,000) and the Liberal Federation itself ($150,000). Registration fees were $25 per delegate, the same as Toronto, and it was expected that everyone who attended the convention spent about $200 while there, in addition to transportation.

To bring everyone to Ottawa and take them away again, the Liberals laid on 16 charter flights, 60 buses but no private trains.

To entertain them, there were hospitality suites for most of the candidates in the main hotels. Trudeau had eight suites, and the strongest refreshment was orange juice and coffee. Mitchell Sharp had planned a keg party, but canceled it when he pulled out and the beer went back to the brewery.

Allan MacEachen had his own private television network, AJM-TV, with a production crew of 35, which broadcast, among other things, the poolside party he threw at the Skyline Hotel (before someone sabotaged his cables).

Joe Greene had no hospitality suites and little campaign literature, but he did send around boxes of Laura Secord peppermint candies to all the delegates.

Paul Hellyer and Robert Winters had suites in all the main hotels and so did Eric Kierans. Hellyer and Trudeau both published newspapers. Trudeau's was bilingual, rushed up from Montreal by truck at 4 a.m. every day to be under delegates' doors by 7 a.m. Delivery failed only once, when the truck driver overslept.

Television played an even bigger role at the Liberal convention than it did at the Conservative event. Each network had between 15 and 20 cameras on the floor notably CTV's highly portable "creepy-peepy" camera which put its snout and boom mike into the most intimate conversations, like an alley-cat investigating ashcans, with equally alarming results. People who stayed home in front of their television sets generally wound up knowing more about the convention than those who were there, forced by human limitations to cover just one segment.

But television did not win all the games. One ambitious television experiment that failed was a Thursday morning trans-Atlantic interview for BBC between Pierre Trudeau and the Canadian political scientist, Robert Trelford McKenzie, Professor of Sociology at the London School of Economics. McKenzie, an old class-mate of Trudeau's at LSE, was to ask his questions from the studio in London, while Trudeau's answers were taped in video in Ottawa, to be flown over to the BBC later. But the vagaries of the British GPO Telephone department defeated them, and the BBC program "24 Hours" did without its first depth exposure to the man behind Trudeaumania. It is still waiting for a re-ask.

Communications were less of a problem at the Thursday afternoon policy workshops. This was an ingenious idea which kept everyone circulating between three auditoriums to hear the 10 candidates speak for 25 minutes on each of three subjects, "Our Life", "Our Country" and "Our Economy". All topics so broad that, as someone said, it really meant they could talk about anything they wanted. Also, the three-ring idea kept things informal and delegates had a chance to check all candidates without causing offense by leaving in the middle of a speech.

The styles were as different as the candidates. Allan MacEachen wandered around the audience like some Nova Scotian Johnny Carson, asking the delegates questions. "What do you think is the biggest problem in Canada today, Madam?" he asked one lady delegate.

"Trudeau", she replied.

"You mean you're not close enough to him?" asked MacEachen.

Robert Winters was suavely handsome but text-bound. After rapping out his theme of fiscal integrity, he invited questions from "the panel", which turned out to be a carefully prepared group of Winters' supporters, whose "provocative" questions he answered vigorously and eloquently — from his text.

Paul Martin was unusually vigorous and concise, and his speeches drew good crowds and applause. His theme was what it had been since January, national unity, and how he would ask for a total review of the Canadian constitution "in a spirit of flexibility". He would overhaul Parliamentary procedure, reform election financing, implement the Glassco recommendations on government administration. He knew everyone, answering questioners by name: "Yes, Mrs. Mackenzie . . ."

Each of John Turner's sessions was packed with bright, eager, young supporters in their attractive pale yellow jackets and those strange white construction helmets which looked as if they were a huge survey crew come to look the property over. He did best in the main auditorium, with a rock-jawed speech about Quebec, where the problems would not be solved by pure logic and intellect, "but by the heart and gut — because that is what Canada is all about," he thundered. The construction workers loved it.

Eric Kieran's policy speeches were frank and original. Asked if he would stop arms shipment to the U.S. that were bound for Viet Nam, he replied, "My answer to this," he paused, "is I would." But he still had his old tendency to get bogged-down by syntax and side-tracked by trivia, a bad habit he probably picked up over the years with René Lévesque.

Paul Hellyer also remained Paul Hellyer, as precise, energetic, as he always was. But no new frontiers were opened and no old territory lost.

The big winner of the policy sessions was Trudeau once again, followed by large crowds wherever he went, from the main arena to the Coliseum to the smaller convention hall. His first workshop was on "Our Life" which started him off about his concern for individual freedom and how the amendments to the Criminal Code would protect it. He talked about "legislation of tolerance," a catchy phrase he used often, and the idea behind it of "permitting the other man to have his own belief," without State interference. The Hudson Institute had said Canada would soon be one of five "post-industrial" countries, he noted, and freedom from poverty must surely be one of its aims.

Yet, turning conservative, he said that Medicare would "put a floor" of social security under all Canadians, and the country should not be afraid of means tests or needs tests in applying future social programs. The crowd of 500 was enthusiastic.

His second workshop was on "Our Country". There again, he talked about the "basic fundamental rights" and how a Charter of Human Rights would protect them. He said that all levels of government must cooperate "so that Canadians will be well governed on all levels. . . ." Tension between federal and provincial governments was inevitable and good, so long as "it shall be a creative tension." He talked about the importance of "extending to French Canadians all over Canada the rights constitutionally guaranteed to English Canadians in Quebec. If we can solve this, we shall have a basic Canadian consensus. And once we have settled the problem of basic rights, then we can talk about the division of powers, the Senate, the Supreme Court, and the establishment of a National Capital that reflects the whole country."

Again, he nodded to the conservatives present by admitting that he was one Cabinet minister who was not very enthusiastic about giving the vote to 18-year-olds. "This was not one of my priorities," he said, "though when I see the support I am getting from the young people, the more I could live with it."

The final workshop was on "Our Economy", a topic Trudeau

had pretty much skimmed throughout his campaign. "We must solve the problems of economic disparities, which means we must end the disparities." Regional desks and other government reforms would help keep the grass-roots in touch. "We cannot go on waiting to see every four years whether the public approves what we have done as a government."

He talked about "investing in the future, not buying back the past" and praised the verities of a balanced budget, stable economy and developing economic structure. Performance in world trade would depend on excellence in a few fields: "we can't do everything, we are a little country in terms of the world." For the farmers he offered better research, diversification of products. He talked about immigration ("I am not for protectionism in trade or immigration") and Canada's duty to welcome the people of the world. "There are new peoples all over the world coming onto the edge of the stage of history, and it is our duty to open our doors to those people. We have an immense land and we should offer to accommodate some of the peoples of the world here."

He was superficial on foreign relations. He talked about "recognizing" Communist China while maintaining recognition of Taiwan, which is a contradiction in terms; about U.S. draft-dodgers in Canada being "a problem for America but not for Canada"; about wanting to join the Organization of American States — but not until Canada had a credible hemisphere policy of its own. "I don't want to be in the OAS as a parrot of the American government."

Trudeau was walking a political tight-rope during the policy seminars. His strategists had already detected a surging undercurrent for Turner and Winters. Sharp had gone to Trudeau.

Turner sounded appalling on television. "It disturbs me very much that what I hoped was going to be an open convention on Saturday is being taken away from a good many of us by deals that are being made behind closed doors," he said. "It's going to take John five years to get over that little outburst," said a top Liberal organizer. "It sounded much too much like 'somebody just stole my apple' and it did him a lot of harm."

On the contrary, in terms of the convention, Turner's statement was a shrewd move, recommended by his able campaign manager,

Jerry Grafstein. For the delegate reaction was quite different. In the steamy partisan atmosphere of the convention, the indignation on the right at what they felt was a left-wing plot expressed itself in a polarization towards the two men who represented the conservative option, Turner, who offered the advantage of youth, and Winters, who had experience and style.

Trudeau's tactic during the seminars was to appear a solid middle-of-the roader. Radical enough to keep the converted warm to him, but conservative enough to ease the anxiety of any middleground delegate who might be tempted to take a chance.

Partisan politics ceased momentarily on Thursday night for Lester Pearson's farewell speech to the party he had led for a decade. It was one of the best of his career, a sensitive balance of wit and irony and justifiable pride.

The new party leader, he said, would be "expected to be a combination of Abraham Lincoln and Batman — to perform instant miracles," and he gently counseled the party against expecting any such paragon. "Liberalism must help Canada to come to terms with the new age," he said. "If it doesn't, it will cease to have much relevance to the issues and the people of 1968." He looked back with justifiable pride on a record of social welfare that was unequaled by any other political party in Canadian history. He talked also about unification of the armed forces, foreign aid, transportation, the GATT agreement, and, of course, about the flag.

"We have, in short, changed the face of Canada," he said. "And I hope and believe we have made it better."

Pearson received a thunderous applause — and the gift of a West Highland terrier puppy, so that he could meet John Diefenbaker and his labrador on equal terms when they met on strolls through Rockcliffe Park.

It was a night of emotion and sentimentality. And afterwards, in the hotels around Ottawa, the candidates kept delegates in mellow mood with a catholic assortment of entertainers. Paul Martin offered Quebec's "Feux Follets" folklore group; Robert Winters had the entire "Tommy Hunter Show" from CBC; Paul Hellyer hired Denny Vaughan and his orchestra for dancing; John Turner had the Montreal chanteuse, Danielle Dorice; while folksingers Ian and Sylvia played at the Chateau Laurier for Trudeau.

Trudeau had two other things going for him that night. One was an hour-long interview with Patrick Watson over Ottawa's CJOH-TV station, channel 13, which had been taped two and a half weeks earlier. Produced by Roy Faibish, the former executive assistant to Alvin Hamilton, the interview was a gentle but probing interrogation in which seemingly innocuous questions led Trudeau deeper and deeper, like a shelving beach, until he found himself making such visceral statements as "I honestly like people. People don't always think I like them, because I like solitude, too, I like to be alone. . . ." And again, "I like to test my limits all the time, both physical and mental. I get fun out of new experiences. I like to feel alive. I like to taste new fruit or to dive into new waters or parachute from new skies. . . ." It was compelling propaganda.

The other Trudeau event was not for public consumption. It was a crisis. The Quebec caucus had revolted.

The story was long and complex, going back to the original caucus anger with Marchand the week Trudeau entered. Resentment had smouldered fitfully, and with the entry of Robert Winters on March 1, the disaffected Quebec MP's had a rallying point. Jean-Pierre Côté, Auguste Choquette, Ovide Laflamme and Jean Charles Cantin, aided by Senator Maurice Bourget, started a campaign to persuade Quebec MP's that Winters was their man. Significantly most of the Winters' supporters were from the Quebec City area. Their efforts had little effect on the bulk of the Quebec caucus until convention week, when the Quebec MP's and their delegates arrived in Ottawa to find that they were expected to meld into a national group working out of the Trudeau headquarters on O'Connor Street.

The Quebec provincial caucus was not used to the idea of being treated as a caucus *comme les autres*. Even within the Liberal Federation, Quebec's MP's had a special status which operated more on a Montreal than national axis. While Trudeau might change it ultimately, he had not changed things yet. Besides, the French-Canadian MP's felt lost in the seething Anglo-Saxon mob at O'Connor Street. So they left their buttons and notebooks in their sealed cardboard boxes, and the placards stacked against the wall, and quietly went away to watch the proceedings passively in the arena or wherever their inclinations took them.

Late on Thursday afternoon, someone discovered the unopened Quebec boxes, the stacked placards and untouched notebooks and an emergency call went out for an executive committee meeting. Marchand, Giguère, Gérard Loiselle, Bryce Mackasey, and some aides held their emergency meeting at the Skyline Hotel at 7 p.m. The threat was real and immediate. Unless the Quebec MP's were persuaded to take part, there was an excellent chance that the Winters' group would grab a hefty parcel of votes by default. Winters organization was lean and professional, and it would be only a matter of hours before they found out about the disaffection in Trudeau's group. There were 25 key MP's involved, each controlling about five delegates for a total of 125 votes. It could be very serious.

Marchand looked around for the hardest-nosed politician he could find. "Bryce," he said, "you handle it." Mackasey quickly formed his own committee with Giguère and Loiselle and went in search of Jean-Pierre Goyer, the national committee co-chairman, who was sitting in Trudeau's box listening to Pearson's speech. Goyer was completely nonplussed at the news, and they all dashed back to O'Connor Street to summon a meeting of Quebec MP's for 11:30 that night in the committee suite at the Chateau Laurier.

Meanwhile, Mackasey got on the phone to set up a special Quebec caucus committee room at the Skyline — for the MP's to have a place of their own away from the confusion of O'Connor Street — and by not always gentle persuasion arranged for a suite to be set aside and special telephone lines installed.

At 11:30, Marchand met the MP's in the Chateau with Mackasey and Giguère, and the new arrangements were announced. The MP's were happy again. Mackasey got to bed at 5 a.m. that night.

Two hours and one resolved crisis later, Mackasey was up again to shepherd Trudeau to the second of three vitally important delegates' breakfasts, events which the candidate was understandably reluctant to attend, since all his nights had been late ones and his fatigue quotient was becoming critical. Somehow, Mackasey managed to get him to each breakfast on time, to the Skyline the day before, the Talisman Seaway Motor Inn that morning, and the Chateau Laurier the next day. The breakfasts were vital, because they were the only opportunities Trudeau would have to meet the delegates personally before the balloting. "Of course he was terrific, once you got him there," Mackasey recalls. "He has this fantastic memory, and it was just great. But oh boy, trying to get him there was quite a problem."

Trudeau does not like getting up early in the morning.

Mackasey's third major contribution of the week was his work as a member of the floor committee on Saturday, when he hurtled through the crowds time and again to tackle some delegate or persuade Hellyer supporter Keith Davey to come over to the Trudeau team (successfully).

By Saturday night Mackasey was reeling with exhaustion. On Sunday, he had a heart attack which took him to Ottawa's Civic Hospital for six weeks and forced him to convalesce most of the summer.

There were many heroes in the Trudeau team, few gave as much though as Mackasey. On Friday, each province held its caucus. Mackasey had persuaded the Quebeckers not to hold one — just in case the Winters group decided to work on their newly restored loyalists. "Eighty per cent of the caucus supported Trudeau, so why expose them to Winters' group?" he says.

In the arena, most of Friday was taken up with routine Federation business, attended by a handful of delegates, while candidates raced around Ottawa looking after special interest groups. Trudeau had a coffee and sandwiches lunch with lady Liberals at the National Library, spent the early afternoon closeted with farmers in the West block outlining his wheat policy and other agricultural matters. His approach to the farmers was disarming: "I am not very knowledgeable about agriculture, and if any of you are wondering what the devil does Pierre Elliott Trudeau know about farming, I can't blame you." He won them.

Then it was back to the hospitality suites to press the flesh and later home to change for the big event of the evening, the wind-up speech by each candidate, their last chance before the vote on Saturday.

Watching the speakers, as Peter Newman put it so well, "it was fascinating to contemplate the difficulties Lester Pearson must have had keeping together a cabinet of such widely disparate men."

Trudeau was seventh in the line-up, and it was a long wait for the other six to get through their performance, nearly all of them accompanied by a deafening demonstration.

First was Paul Martin, punningly nicknamed "Oom Paul" after the Afrikaner statesman, Oom ("Uncle") Paul Kruger, who united the Boers.

"Paul Martin's the man, hey Martin's the Man, say Martin's the man for Ca-na-da!" shouted his teenagers, stumping their man up the center aisles.

"I believe that my affiliation with the two communities of this country, with my experience in the federal service, I am the man to deal with our current crisis, over the next few years, when this problem will be resolved!" he said, leaving a dazed audience two sub-clauses behind, the thick, convex lenses of his glasses glittering as he swung first left, then right, then left again. His voice had the unnatural, nasal rhythm that in Quebec instantly identifies a former seminarian. In Martin's case, maybe it was a relic of his days at St. Alexander's College, in Ironsides, Quebec. At 65, he was an old style politician, in a three piece suit, with a thick, gold watch-chain looped across his tummy. Even his hair was grey again.

Robert Henry Winters is tall and distinguished, his blond hair turning almost imperceptibly white at the sides. His father was a humble Nova Scotia fishing captain, but years at the Massachusetts Institute of Technology, in big business and bigger politics left little trace in him of the bright, eager boy from Lunenburg High School.

"Winters is as solid as St. James Street. Just look at him: he looks like a prime minister," said one Quebecker, subtly indicating that Trudeau did not. And many others from *la belle Province* would be echoing his sentiments before the week was out. Besides, Winters had been a first rate Minister of Trade and Commerce, and if everyone said that he let others do all the work, so what? At lease he was able to delegate authority. It was a pity other Liberal cabinet ministers could not take a tip from him about managing their own departments.

Permanently sun-tanned, healthy (he's still a fine tennis player at 57), and immaculately dressed, his orotund statements about the crying need for balanced budgets and fiscal responsibility were as calculated to please Bay Street as they were to infuriate the Ottawa establishment, whose dislike for Winters seemed to reach a new peak during the leadership campaign. He denied being a Bay Street tycoon, and the parliamentary guide listed P.O. Box 459 in Lunenburg, Nova Scotia as his only address. But within weeks of the convention he would be president of the Brazilian Light and Power Corporation, with an office at King and Bay Streets and a mansion to match on Russell Hill Avenue.

Perhaps the truth about Winters is that the Ottawa mandarins were jealous. A man who has made money is under suspicion in Liberal circles, if his political ambitions do not stop at a Senatorship or a tame role as the party satchel-man. With a Horatio Alger background and a thing about balanced budgets, Winters was doubly suspect in the corridors of power. Besides, he also wanted to be Prime Minister and, as Pearson has mentioned, Liberal Prime Ministers are expected to display a certain gentlemanly reluctance. "There can be no greater honor than to have the privilege to unite and lead this party and this country," he declared that night.

Perhaps if Winters had turned Conservative and Dalton Camp had stayed Liberal, after that summer convention nearly 20 years before, Canadian political history would have been very different.

The third speaker was Joe Greene, 47, a Torontonian born and bred, who had won a DFC as an RCAF pilot during the war, and had later settled down to practice law in the quiet country town of Arnprior, Ontario, not far from Ottawa. Tall and lanky, with a habit of tugging his lapel that looks like a farmer snapping his galluses, Greene had turned into such a folksy countrified character by the time he reached Parliament in 1963, that they called him the Ottawa Valley Lincoln. His success as Minister of Agriculture was assured from the day he let Westerners know that Ottawans could hate the CPR just as hard as they could in Winnipeg. In fact, it was largely on the strength of his Western support that he entered the leadership race in the first place.

But on Friday night it was not Abe from Arnprior who stood beside the lectern, without a note to prompt him, but a scared young pilot of 21 who was finding out what being a Canadian was all about. He took that great crowd back with him to 1942 and an air force base somewhere in Britain where a *maudit Anglais* from Toronto and a "fat frog" from Quebec found out that they had more in common than they had ever dreamed. And as they kidded each other, they also told each other what they would do when they got back from war. Except that Greene came back, and his friend from Quebec did not.

Greene switched effortlessly from French to English throughout his speech, and when he finished there were few dry eyes in the arena. The applause was deafening. It made them laugh, it made them cry and at the end it made them stand up and cheer themselves hoarse. "It was a personal triumph for Joe Greene," said Turner organizer, Mel Rothman. "The best speech of the evening."

Greene's speech had unexpected results for the others. The next day nearly 100 delegates who were committed to Hellyer decided to pay Greene the compliment of a first ballot salute. "We had him down for about 58 votes," says Hellyer's campaign manager, Bill Lee, "and he came out with 164. He stole 106 ballots just with that speech. They came right out of our hide, in Alberta, Saskatchewan and Manitoba."

Paul Hellyer knew he looked faintly ridiculous. Not even Judy LaMarsh, in miniskirt and kneeboots, could help him as they came prancing up the aisle together to that tune from Dow Jones. Hellyer is not built to prance. He is so big that his knees simply cannot reach elevation quickly enough. So he finally gave up trying and did a sort of silly little shuffle instead, agonizingly conscious that he was making a fool of himself.

To cap it all, his speech was dismal. Bill Lee had pleaded with him to continue their successful campaign technique of letting the real Paul Hellyer stand up. "But he was under the influence of a couple of friends of his, a Toronto lawyer whose name I can't remember, and they had convinced him that they had written the world's greatest speech," Lee recalls.

"Well, it was a good treatise, but it was not a speech."

But Hellyer was not about to give it up.

"This, then, is my message to you fellow Liberals," he intoned, "and I believe it must be the message of the Liberal Party to all

Canadians. There is no country in the world where there is a better chance to create a truly great society, a society which welcomes the civilizing values of adventure, and of truth, and of art and of peace, a society which nourishes the spirit of unselfishness and generosity."

Allan MacEachen was deft, eloquent, liberal and unexceptional.

Eric Kierans was earnest, but at least he had lost his habit of adding an "eh?" to every sentence. He was nervous, and when he's nervous, he tends to plod. He plodded. "Vote," he said, "but vote with your conscience. And if you vote for me, I can promise you a future and a Canada that will mean courage and confidence, a Canada of which you and I and all of us will be very, very proud."

Trudeau was next.

The plan called for no demonstration, just a single spotlight that would pick him out in his box and follow the lonely figure through the crowd where he would make a "hand of destiny" speech suited to the drama of the moment.

But the Trudeau committee had not counted on the total lack of security arrangements and chaotic floor management. There had been a mob in front of his box for two days, and a spotlight could only worsen things. He might never reach the platform at all.

Hence the placard "strategy", which was no strategy at all, but brilliant improvisation on the part of a young Toronto lawyer named Bob Kaplan, aided and abetted by members of the Quebec caucus. Quietly, before the speeches started, Kaplan and his henchmen, along with as many kids as they could round up, distributed nearly two thousand placards throughout the arena. So that when delegates arrived to take their seats, there was a placard waiting on it, ready for them to wave. With luck, when Trudeau himself came to the platform, they would wag the placards close at hand, but not even Kaplan anticipated the total effect.

Senator Nichol was ready. "I now call upon the Minister of Justice, the Honorable Pierre Elliott...TRUDEAU!" the crowd bellowed the name before Nichol could finish. And suddenly, with a tremendous whoop, the entire auditorium erupted with a forest of Trudeau signs. It was the most fantastic spectacle. Veteran politicians can remember nothing like it in Canadian politics.

One Trudeau delegate happily turned to his companion. "That's the ball game," he said. His friend could only grin and nod.

The placards and the cheering took attention off Trudeau long enough for him to slip from his box and walk slowly to the platform where 20 hostesses, in their orange and white knitted dresses and berets had formed a guard of honor on the steps. He climbed up to the podium slowly, humbly and stood there alone, looking rather sad and small and frail, his bowed head and shy smile seeking the mother in every woman present.

It seemed at that moment that destiny really had touched him, that it was all somehow inevitable, and that he had been chosen.

But the moment passed and he became a candidate again, gently quieting the crowd with palm-down motions of both hands. He spoke softly, reading his text carefully but well. He sounded tired and sincere, fatigue adding sybillance to his consonants.

"For many of us the world of today stands on the threshold of a golden age. Yet for many people, the only reality is war and famine. We know that millions remain in poverty, in ignorance, in hunger and in sickness, and we know that even the most favored people suffer from external conflict and internal division."

He reminded the Liberals, and was the only candidate to do so, "of the tragic events that began last night in the assassination of Martin Luther King and which have degenerated today into strife and arson, hate and murder, are a tragic reminder of that reality."

He shifted smoothly, in mid-sentence, into his flawless French, now slightly more colloquial, more "joual," and less of the *Académie Française* than it was when he was not a politician. He never insulted the intelligence of his audience by repeating what he had just said in the other language.

"As Canadians, 20-million heirs to half a continent, are we not beset with doubts about our economy, about our society and about our independence? Where wealth is equitably distributed to all groups and to all regions? And where every citizen has an equal right and an equal opportunity to self-fulfillment?"

Some people give up when faced with these problems, he said, "but Liberals reject this counsel of despair . . . as Liberals, we rely on that most unlikely bulwark, the individual, you and me, the individual citizen, the young and old, the famous and the unknown, the Arctic nomad and the suburbanite. It was this confidence in the individual which set me on the road which has led me to my present quest. For many years, I have been fighting for the triumph of logic in politics over passion, for the protection of individual freedoms against the collective tyranny and for a just distribution of the national wealth. It was this concern which led me to join the ranks of the Liberal Party."

He talked about Liberalism, about national unity, about federalism "Canada will be a strong country when Canadians of all provinces feel at home in all parts of the country, and when they feel that all Canada belongs to them. We want nothing more, but we will accept nothing less. Masters in our own house we must be, but our house is all of Canada."

When he finished, in French, his last audible words were some he used many times, in many places, "*et c'est ca le Canada!*" The cheers, the shouts, the clapping drowned out the rest and as he inched his way back to his box to the left of the platform, combed by clutching hands and arms, the chants could be heard, louder and clearer, "We Want Trudeau", "*On Veut Trudeau*".

Someone wrote later that Trudeau's speech sounded like an acceptance speech, and so it was. It was a challenge rather than a promise, a profession of faith and determination which saw no easy solutions, no panaceas, offered no comfortable generalities.

To follow Joe Greene was hard enough. To follow Trudeau was impossible. And it was John Turner's luck to have that role. Under the circumstances, he did extraordinarily well. Never before had Turner appeared to be so positive, so decisive, and so gutsy, as he was that night.

"I'm not just in this race so you will remember my name at some future date," he said. "I'm not here now for some next time. I am not bidding now for your consideration at some vague convention in 1984, when I've mellowed a bit. My time is now, and now is no time for mellow men."

He bit into his monosyllabic words with an angry rhythm that evoked the Kennedys (who else?). And yet they were definitely his own, deeply felt, as if at last, after doing all the right things all his life, Turner was ripping apart the politician to expose the man he really is, in private — a tough, sincere, honest fellow who has a passion about Canada which demands and deserves respect.

Whether he wants them to or not, the delegates will remember John Turner warmly next time around. And next time, who knows, it may be his turn? He emerged from that evening with new stature in the Liberal Party of Canada, and in Canada as a whole.

And then it was Saturday.

Voting was meant to start at 1 p.m., but it was delayed 45 minutes by an unexplained snag, and when Senator Nichol finally announced that the 37 booths were open, some delegates had been sitting in their grey and red seats for nearly two hours.

Most of the candidates did not get to the arena until around noon. But Trudeau was there shortly after ten, carefully dressed in a new, dark grey three-piece suit of Italian silk, with a grey knitted wool tie, one of his familiar horizontally striped shirts with a white Edwardian cutaway collar. His shoes were black monk-strap loafers in Italian calf. It was a warm but showery April day and he wore his favorite tan trench-coat.

He had stayed all week in a friend's apartment at the Champlain Towers, on Rideau terrace, because his normal suite at the Chateau Laurier would have lacked privacy with boisterous conventioneers on every side and, besides, the noise would have been impossible.

He was up at 7 a.m. on Saturday morning and over at the Chateau by 8 a.m. to have breakfast with 600 delegates. For the second day running, he delighted photographers by sliding down the banisters at the Mackenzie street entrance. The Newfoundland delegates were badly split between following Joey Smallwood to Trudeau (he had endorsed Trudeau on Wednesday night at the Chaudière Club), or following their consciences to Robert Winters, who had done much for the province as president of the British Newfoundland Corporation (BRINCO). Many were at the Chateau that morning, and Trudeau did his best to persuade them to stay together in a block. But the split was deep, there was little Trudeau could do.

The Smallwood loyalists were mostly the older delegates who would follow him right or wrong. Typical was colorful Ross Barbour, 67, a former stevedore, MLA for Bonaventure South, who would tell anyone who'd listen how the Newfoundland delegates felt about True-dough. "Oh, they was just jubilant. They was so excited, and so happy because our great Premier of Newfoundland, the Honorable Doctor J. R. Smallwood has played such an important part — and I'm sure because Smallwood said Trudeau was the man for Newfoundland, and because Smallwood has been in Newfoundland for 19 years as premier, we respect, we honor, we love him, and when Smallwood advises us, we take his advice!"

But in the end, more than 30 of Newfoundland's 84 delegates ignored his advice to go over to Winters. Smallwood had lost control of his fiefdom and the revolt would grow in the following months. It was a sad irony that in opting for the new, the exciting, the challenging, Smallwood would wind up sacrificing his own position.

The other candidates spent Saturday morning quietly encouraging their own supporters, meeting delegates and handling all the little crises which occur as tension mounts.

The ballot took more than an hour to cast and count. Finally at 3:16 Senator Nichol had the results. He read them alphabetically. Joe Greene, 169, living proof that oratory still counts for something; Paul Hellyer, 330, far below what was expected; Lloyd Henderson, the nuisance candidate, zero, since not being a delegate he couldn't even vote for himself; Eric Kierans, 103, a respectable showing in light of the odds, but plainly a disappointment to his supporters since each vote had cost him about $1,000; Allan MacEachen, 165, a poor showing for a man who was meant to have a major power base in the Maritimes; Paul Martin, 277, a shattering disappointment; Pierre Elliott Trudeau, 752, almost exactly what his strategists had predicted, and the audience went wild. When they quietened, Nichol continued. John Turner, 277, tied with Paul Martin, and a decent vote considering everything. Robert Winters, 293, about what was expected.

Kierans withdrew first. "I am not having any discussion other than a friendly one with the other candidates," he said firmly.

Paul Martin was scribbling something, puffing hard on a cigar. "I have been at many elections, and I've learned how important it was to be generous in victory and generous and serene in defeat. I pledge my whole-hearted support and cooperation to whomsoever shall become the new leader of our great party and the next Prime Minister of Canada."

He had withdrawn. He would endorse no one, and he would retire to the Senate, more puzzled than bitter at why his time had passed him by.

Allan MacEachen would withdraw too late, but conspicuously led into Trudeau's box by two Nova Scotian pipers.

Maurice Sauvé would dash to Trudeau's side, too, blundering across the feet of those on the front bench beside Trudeau, pinning on a large "Trudeau" button (the organization went through 70,000 buttons, and the big ones cost 40 cents, the small ones, a dime) and, when it was obvious that no one was giving him a place in the front row with Trudeau, reluctantly heading into a seat behind.

Little Martin support came to Trudeau with him. Hellyer and Winters organizers were busy. Hellyer wanted to persuade Winters to come with him, but only 37 votes separated them and there was not a chance. Turner was hanging tight, too. The second ballot would tell. There would be 545 votes loose for someone to pick up. It was every man for himself. Even Joe Greene was hanging on.

Two hours later, the second vote result came through. Greene sunk to 104 but he still would not withdraw. Paul Hellyer got 465, an increase of 135 and something close to what his strategists had hoped for the first ballot. MacEachen, who had withdrawn too late, got eleven votes. Trudeau soared 212 votes to 964. John Turner gained 70 to 347. Robert Winters jumped to 473, putting him into second place and becoming a major threat to Trudeau.

Winters was over to see Hellyer in a flash. Someone once said that he moved around Ottawa like a big, elegant cat; that afternoon he was purring, with just a hint of menace. Hellyer was dazed, bewildered.

Winters: "Anything we should do, Paul?" he asked.

Hellyer: "Well, Bob, I think we have to. I don't know. I think we have. I really don't know what we should do."

Winters: "Want to think about it and talk some more, Paul?"

Hellyer: "Might do. All right."

Winters: "I'll be available."

Hellyer: "Alright, Bob."

Winters: "You've done well, Paul."

Hellyer: "Thanks very much, Bob."

Through the prying eye of television, the whole intimate moment was captured.

Judy LaMarsh had already forsaken Hellyer and was called in to persuade him to join her in the Winters Wonderland. "You know him, Paul, and he knows you," came her familiar bullfrog voice out of the huddle. "You're alright with him. It's tough, but what the hell's the point of going down and letting that bastard be there! Come on Paul, you're 44, and we've still got lots of time."

Hell has no fury. . . .

Bill Lee tried to save the situation for Hellyer in a vain attempt to persuade John Turner to join forces so that they could vault ahead of Winters. "Turner wouldn't budge, so I told Hellyer squarely what the situation was. 'Turner's not going to go, and Winters certainly isn't going to go. He's now ahead of you. I think we're finished, and if we are going to stop him, it's Winters.' "

But Hellyer was not ready to drop out.

"We can't get any more until either Turner or Greene go out. If we slip this time, then we'll go because we've got a reason to. We're not letting our people down."

Judy LaMarsh interrupted: "I think it'll be too late, Paul." She was right.

"I don't really think so," said Hellyer.

"It's up to you," said Judy. "I'm with you to the end if that's what you do. But I don't think it's good. . . ." And she took off her Winters' button.

There was another airing of the Bob and Paul Show.

Winters was getting irritated. "I'm ahead. You can't stop when you're ahead. There's a whole psychology to this. . . ."

The third ballot was quicker. Soon after 6:30 the results were in.

Trudeau, 1,051. Winters, 621. Hellyer, 377. Turner, 279. Greene, 29.

Joe Greene finally withdrew, joining the Trudeau benches, by now so full that there was a rotation system to accommodate all the cabinet ministers who wanted to be photographed close to Trudeau.

Nichol read a note from Hellyer. "I wish to announce my withdrawal from this Liberal leadership contest and thank my wonderful loyal supporters."

But Hellyer would not be able to deliver his full block to Winters.

Bryce Mackasey, "the fighting Irishman from Verdun", was there ahead of him. Time and again, his eyes glazed with fatigue, sweat pouring down his cheeks, Mackasey would dash down from his command post on the Trudeau benches, barrelling his way through the crowd on an emergency mission. One such mission was to see a friend the moment Hellyer slipped behind. The friend was Keith Davey, loyal to Hellyer but an opponent of Winters. Mackasey quickly talked him into the Trudeau camp. "I just couldn't see him there on the Winters bench with all the old party reactionaries like Laing and McIlraith," says Mackasey. "And he couldn't see it either."

Trudeau made a rallying trip around the arena, trailing newsmen, photographers and aides like a sea turtle trails seaweed.

The fourth vote would see the complete polarization of the party, left and right. Only John Turner would stick it out, some say to keep right wing votes from going to Winters, others say to keep young people from going to Trudeau. His campaign manager, Jerry Grafstein, said this at one point: "Our young people will not back either Mr. Hellyer or Mr. Winters, so that we cannot transfer mathematically our young support to either. . . ."

Winters and Hellyer made a joint appeal to Turner.

Winters: "We'd like you to join us, John."

Turner: "Gentlemen, I'm staying in the ballot."

Hellyer: "It's your decision, John."

Turner: "I respect yours."

Just before 8 p.m. Nichol announced the results of the fourth ballot. Trudeau, 1,203, the crowd roared, and Nichol's scores for the others never were heard (they were Turner, 195, and Winters, 954).

In Lester Pearson's box Marc Lalonde was grinning and clapping and trying hard to suppress an instinct to cheer.

Winters took the news with calm relief: "Ah, he's got it," he said, and that was all. Mrs. Winters was positively delighted: "Oh I'm *so* relieved," she said, smiling really happily for the first time in weeks.

Trudeau had leapt to his feet and was being hugged by everyone. The long hours were over; the agony of uncertainty, of toying with a carnation with studied insouciance, of conducting his own cheering section, teasing his assistants, needling the press — it was all over.

He would be the 15th Prime Minister of Canada.

XVI

"A Solitary Sort of Fellow"

AS AFTERNOON turned to evening, on that final day of the leadership convention, Trudeau seemed to withdraw into himself. To newsmen clustered around the front of the box, notebooks poised, he was barely civil; to other candidates and supporters who joined him on the front row seats, he smiled, exchanged pleasantries, but swiftly withdrew again into himself, silent, his nose buried into his orange and yellow carnation, his eyes looking out into the cavernous arena. As the day grew longer, his hair matted a bit, his silk suit became rumpled, and the carnation lost most of its petals — by the end, in fact, it was a limp memory of a boutonnière.

At moments of crisis, it's said that a man's life flashes by in his mind. Was this what Trudeau was thinking about? Not with regret ("I seldom have remorse or regret about having made the wrong decision") but perhaps in wonderment, perhaps with a little humility, that the highest office in the land was almost his.

So many things dovetail to form the structure of a man's life, both controllable and uncontrollable. Where Trudeau could control events, he did ("I never let myself be pushed into things, or let people make up their minds for me"), and if there is one quality he personifies, it's discipline, in work, in play and in everything he does.

Robert Truteaux was born in Marcillac-Lanville, 18 kilometers from Angoulême and he moved to La Rochelle, on the Atlantic coast of France, in the early 1600s. A son, Martial, was born in 1611 and his son, Estienne, sailed for New France in 1659, settling at Ville Marie, now Montreal, and marrying Adrienne Barbier. These people, according to the archivists of Angoulême, were the ancestors of the Prime Minister.

In 1889, in St. Rémi de Napierville, Joseph Charles Emile Trudeau was born. The Trudeaus had farmed in St. Rémi for generations — and cousins farm there to this day. They were well-to-do farmers with ambition for their children. Charles Emile, or "Charley" as he was always called, and his brother, Cléophas, ten years his senior, were both clever boys and they were sent to College St. Marie, Loyola and to the University of Montreal. There was also another brother who became a dentist.

His closest friends at college were fellow law students, Georges Beauregard, Charles Edouard Guérin (who became his law partner and married his sister), and Maurice LeNoblet Duplessis. The four of them were such pals that they used to study together at Beauregard's house. It was the start of a life-long friendship, Guérin and Beauregard becoming distinguished lawyers and Maurice Duplessis the founder of the National Union and premier of Quebec.

Charley Trudeau was a short, slim little man with dark hair, penetrating eyes and a little toothbrush mustache. His speech and movements were quick and nervous. He adored practical jokes and had a great zest for life, which his oldest son Pierre inherited. Trudeau was a compulsive gambler and he would play bridge or poker for hours at the St. Denis Club in Montreal, sometimes the games would last all night and the pot would be $18,000 and more. The club membership consisted entirely of wealthy French Canadians, and the drinking was as heavy as the gambling.

Trudeau practised law for 10 years with Guérin and Ernest Bertrand, then went into business on his own as the founder president of the Automobile Owners Association, established in 1921.

AOA was conceived and flourished on a basic truth: in the 1920's, cars and trucks were unreliable, prone to frequent breakdowns, which, at 20° below zero in mid-winter could be dangerous as well as annoying. For $10 a year, Trudeau offered members 24-hour-breakdown service within a 25-mile radius of Montreal and cut-price rates on gasoline and oil at his two big service stations, on Sherbrooke and Girouard Streets in the West end, and on St. Denis Street, north of Mount Royal Boulevard.

AOA was immensely profitable, and when Trudeau sold out to Imperial Oil in 1931, it was worth $1.4 million dollars. Imperial also bought Loyal Oil & Gas Limited at the same time, from J. Romeo Gauvreau, a close friend of Trudeau's, and both companies were molded into Champlain Oil Products, one of Imperial's wholly-owned subsidiaries.

Soon, Gauvreau, Trudeau and two friends of theirs, Hector Racine, the president of Racine, Hodgson and Greenshields, a brokerage house, and Jean Beauchemin, president of Sullivan Consolidated Gold Mines, started to wheel and deal together. Their earliest joint venture was Belmont Park, a 26-acre amusement park on the north end of Montreal island, which is still in existence, though suffering badly from competition by Expo's La Ronde amusement area. Belmont Park was estimated to be worth $4 million four years ago, mostly as real estate. The company is 30% owned by the Trudeau family to this day.

Trudeau and the others made large investments in such mining concerns as Sullivan, Hollinger and others. The Trudeau family owns extensive amounts of real estate in Montreal and particularly in the Laurentians. Most of the family fortune is in a trust, J. C. E. Trudeau Succession Ltée, and the exact value is impossible to assess accurately. However, under prudent management, the value should have doubled each decade. When he died in 1935, Trudeau senior left something in excess of $2 million, according to his associates, which would put the total at about $16 million today, divided between the four members of the family, or income from invested capital of about $4 million per person. However, since the money was handled by trustees for a number of years, it is quite likely that investments were conservative and capital appreciation was much less than $16 million. Nevertheless it is hard to see how the Prime Minister would have a private income of less than $40,000 a year.

One of Charley Trudeau's investments for amusement was the Montreal Royals Baseball Club, which he bought in 1933 with Racine, Gauvreau, Beauchemin and Alfred Paradis, the owner of another oil company bought by Imperial, Joseph Elie Ltée.

Buying a ball club was not the huge investment that it would be today. The club franchise cost $75,000 and they rented the stadium. The surviving partners finally sold the club to the Brooklyn Dodgers in 1939 for what they had paid for it. It had been fun, and that was all they wanted.

Trudeau was vice-president of the Montreal Royals and the principal shareholder. He adored sports all his life. He used to hunt and fish and was passionately interested in hockey, boxing and baseball. He gave future hockey great Phil Watson a job in his gas station and backed a lightweight boxer named Leo "the Kid" Roy. His interest in boxing was so great that he insisted that both his sons be taught to box, and since there were no boxing lessons at Brébeuf College, the two youngsters were whisked away by the family chauffeur once a week to a nearby gymnasium for private instruction in the manly art. The boys still remember being awed one day by the visit to their home of the bantamweight champion of Canada.

Charley Trudeau was married during World War I to Grace Elliott, whose mother was French and father Scots, and the Trudeau home was to become a model of bilingualism. Though their mother spoke fluent French, the children talked to her only in English, to their father only in French. Trudeau père's French was not the polished tongue his sons would acquire. It was earthy and colorful, and nobody at AOA could out-cuss the boss, when he set his mind to it, which was frequently enough. But he was enormously kind-hearted and his workers adored him. Politicians found him an easy touch, up to a point. He was an active Conservative party fund-raiser and was known to subsidize the perennially penniless but colorful Mayor of Montreal, Camillien Houde, whose requests for "oxygen" (his word for a hand-out) at Trudeau's gas-station office were never refused. But even Charles Emile's generosity had its limits. When the Conservative Party offered him a Senate seat in return for a $40,000 donation to party coffers, he told them to do some colorful things with the senatorship.

He died in April, in Orlando, Florida. He had spent his Easter vacation with his partners at Orlando Beach, where the Royals were in spring training camp, and he had stayed on, after the others went back to Montreal, to see how the team was shaping up. He apparently caught influenza which turned to pneumonia, and died within the week — he was only 46.

"Charley Trudeau didn't really have a chance to achieve what he could have done," says Brigadier Guy Gauvreau, the son of the late J.-Romeo Gauvreau, Trudeau's friend and partner in many projects. "I saw my Dad cry three times in my life; one of them was when Charley Trudeau died," he says.

His death had a profound effect on his older son, Pierre, who was fifteen and a half, and who had worshipped his father. He told Roger Lemelin, years later, that his initial reaction was one of numbness and that the realization of what it would be like not to have a father through his critical late teens only grew on him later. His sister Suzette, three years older, was grown up, and his brother, Charles ("Tippy"), 13, too young still to fully appreciate the loss — and in any case, his hero was always Pierre.

Mrs. Trudeau's role was clearly a remarkable one in the years after her husband's death. Though now crippled with arteriosclerosis, and quite elderly, she was able to provide the emotional stability the children needed and yet still stimulate them, so that the absence of a father in their formative years did not cause any adjustment problems in college or university. Mrs. Trudeau has been described by her friends as a very quiet, shy sort of person, yet with such warmth and sure judgement that she has a circle of devoted friends.

Left well-provided, she changed the family's life as little as possible, living in the same, modest, brown-brick house on McCulloch Avenue that they bought in the 1920's, and continuing to make the visits to Europe and to the United States that her husband had encouraged. (He was an inveterate traveler, something that combined well with cards and gambling, since he would play cards on the train and bet on the size of the population of each new town he came to.)

Trudeau seems to have started styling himself Pierre *Elliott* in his late teens, deliberately emphasizing the maternal grandfather's Anglo-Saxon heritage.

Not part of his surname at all, it is but one of no less than five names he received when he was christened in October 1919, Joseph Philippe Pierre Yves Elliott. He probably got away with this because he was, by then, the unchallenged leader of his group at his exclusive private school, the Jesuit-run Brébeuf College.

One of his close friends then, as now, was Roger Rolland, who was director of programming for Radio Canada in Montreal until he decided to become a freelance producer.

Rolland recalls that he used to be called "Toto", the usual nickname for someone called Trudeau, which is a common French-Canadian surname. One day Trudeau told his classmates that he would not be called "Toto" anymore. Immediately, one of them shouted, "Toto!"

"What did you say?" Trudeau asked in cold fury.

"Toto" said the boy.

And Trudeau knocked him down with a backhanded swipe.

He was never called Toto again.

But Trudeau seldom provoked fights, even though he was often drawn into them to defend his friends. The familiar tale of how Trudeau beat up an (Anglo-Saxon) tough on a street-car is incorrect. As Trudeau remembers it, his friends, but not he himself, were lolling around as teenagers are apt to do, when the individual told them to colorfully move their feet. Trudeau told him to watch his language (his own strongest swear-word is a British "bloody") and the tough asked him to step outside. They did, and while Trudeau was donning his gloves, the man hit him in the face breaking two teeth. Trudeau finished pulling his gloves on and proceeded to give the man an awful thrashing.

It went on until the man begged him to stop — and apologized — whereupon the incident was closed.

There is a sort of clean-limbed Victorian sportsmanship about so many of the anecdotes involving Trudeau that they sound as if they must have been devised by John Buchan or Frank Merriwell with the imprimatur of the Boys' Own Paper. Yet they are very much in keeping with Trudeau's code of behavior.

He learned judo quite late, in his 30's, and has been known to use his skill as a brown belt (1st Kyu) to help defend people less well trained than himself. But he has misjudged on some occasions. On a visit to Tokyo in the early 1960's, he decided to have a work-out with the Kodokan Club, the *crème-de-la-crème* of judo experts, including some of the greatest teachers of the sport. They did not appreciate his request and put him through the toughest series of put-downs he has ever experienced.

In the opinion of some people who knew him at Brébeuf, his pounding from the Kodokan came years too late, since Trudeau and his small clique of rich boys were known as poisonous little snobs. Brébeuf was divided into boarders (*internes*) and day-boys (*externes*); Trudeau was in the latter group, as were nearly all the students from the wealthy bourgeois families of Outremont. To the *internes*, Trudeau was quite the most unpopular, clannish, fearfully clever and awfully arrogant — yet a boy who refused to do any team sports despite the fact that he was a superb athlete in boxing, skiing, swimming and diving.

At the monthly *lecture des notes* when the austere Jesuit principal read out the report cards of the best students, awarding prizes to the top five, Trudeau never failed to lead his class. His brother Charles was even more brilliant intellectually, though painfully shy and withdrawn.

The two boys would arrive at Brébeuf each morning in their chauffeured car, and be whisked away by the same car each night. But Trudeau swears that the car also used to pick up other neighborhood kids and was more of a school bus.

A girl who knew him as a young man says that there is a strong streak of classical idealism in Trudeau, a pursuit of Juvenal's dictum, *mens sana in corpore sano*, which can be detected in his passionate quest for mental and physical excellence. There is something classical in his unconscious Graeco-Roman style, the Caesar hair-cut which accentuates his finely sculpted face, and also, perhaps, as some women claim, in his rejection of women as intellectual equals.

Trudeau denies there was any classical idealism involved. As far as school-work was concerned, he says "I liked to know, there was a desire for knowledge. I was never satisfied with reading eight chapters, I had to read twelve. I was in competition against myself more than the others."

His teachers remember him as a brilliant student, and several have been picked out as major influences at that period. But the only teacher Trudeau will admit influenced him is Harold Laski at the London School of Economics.

He breezed through Brébeuf and then through a law degree at the University of Montreal. He was at the U. of M. during the war, from the fall of 1940 until 1943, when he graduated. He was a law clerk with the Montreal firm of Hyde and Ahern until called to the Bar, then stayed on with the firm until he went to Harvard in 1945, to take a joint degree in political economy and economic theory.

The fact that Trudeau decided to go back to university, after having settled down to practice law, marked the first of several important shifts of direction in his career. From 1940, until he passed his Bar exams in 1944, Trudeau seemed to have been little different from the rest of his contemporaries, caught up in the anti-conscriptionist agitation of the *Bloc Populaire*, campaigning for Jean Drapeau in the Outremont by-election against General LaFlèche, in 1942. Trudeau recalls his opposition to conscription wryly: "It was perhaps the only time I got involved in local politics and perhaps my motives were not too noble. I think I just wanted to irritate the government."

Less charitable observers have concluded that he simply wanted to avoid doing military service, a desire which was rather widespread in Quebec at that time. University students who maintained certain grades and served in the Canadian Officers Training Corps were exempted. And by the time Trudeau's exemption ended, the need for soldiers was not so pressing.

His activities during the war are subjects that Trudeau prefers to avoid discussing and, when forced into it, treats the matter with condescending boredom. After the war, of course, he seemed to pursue danger, ranging the world from one trouble spot to another, and it is tempting to see some sort of compensation being made, though that probably oversimplifies the situation.

At any rate, Trudeau's wartime activities were hardly the stuff of which statesmen are made — silly pranks in German uniforms (World War I vintage) in the Laurentians; horsing around the countryside on expensive 1,200 c.c. Harley-Davidson motorcycles; and generally making life difficult for a training sergeant at military camp in Farnham, Quebec. The Farnham episode preceded Trudeau's expulsion from the COTC for indiscipline and his transfer to the *Fusiliers de Montréal*, a tough outfit that knows exactly how to handle bolshy recruits.

Harvard came as a shock. Suddenly, Trudeau realized how backward Quebec education really was. "The majors in political science there had read more about Roman Law and Montesquieu than I had as a lawyer," he recalls. "I realized then that we were being taught law as a trade in Quebec and not as a discipline." As a graduate student, the pressure of work was enormous, and there was little time for students to get to know each other well.

A Canadian who shared some classes with Trudeau was Dr. Fred Gibson of Queen's University, who remembers "a very articulate, independent-minded, critical, amusing, detached but very interested person." Trudeau also had "a nice ironic sense of humor" which was a pleasant change, Gibson said, since "graduate school tends to be frightfully earnest."

Yet there was no clue then, "no nucleus or matrix" which would indicate that Trudeau would become a statesman. "He showed an independent purchase and judgement," says Gibson. "And you had the feeling he had other interests; he had a point of view that was his own and not likely to be the result of a particular set of circumstances, or the environment of a particular school."

Trudeau did not appear to have any close friends, nor did he seem to be unusual in his style. "His style of life was very similar to the others, rather penurious and not very prudent young bachelors," says Gibson.

Gibson and Trudeau were to meet again in Ottawa as young civil servants in 1949, and even then, in the wake of the Asbestos strike, there was no new assessment. Still the same detachment. "It wasn't so much a feeling that he might leave next month as there was a certain intellectual detachment, or an insistance of maintaining his own intellectual identity that I recall. Plus a pretty wide margin of curiosity. He was a good listener. He didn't hit you with his opinions. If he disagreed, he implied it with a shrug."

The professors at Harvard in those days were people like Karl Friedrich, the political theorist; Merle Fainsod, Charles MacIlwain, and W. Y. Elliott, in politics and government. Trudeau himself remembers being introduced to Harold Laski, Keynes, Hansen, Leontieff and Schumpeter. He would, of course, meet Laski in person two years later, at the London School of Economics and Political Science.

From Harvard he went to the *Ecole des Sciences Politiques* for a year, 1946-1947. Post-war Paris was not the gay City of Light it is now, but Trudeau and Roger Rolland, who was reading for his Ph.D. (D. *ès lettres*), shared a room at the *Maison Canadienne* and created their own Canadian world.

Trudeau's uncle, Gordon Elliott, had been a pilot in World War I and had crash-landed his plane at a place called Varengeville, near Dieppe, in Normandy. He liked what he saw so much that he had settled in the village in the 1930's and became well-known as a landscape architect. Two close friends who also lived in Varengeville were the late Georges Braque and his wife. Over the years, their friendship let the Trudeau family acquire a number of superb Braques, which now hang in 84 McCulloch Avenue, plus a unique collection of Christmas cards which Braque used to paint himself for close friends.

Gordon Elliott had returned to Canada during the Second World War to look after the RCAF base at *Cap de la Madeleine*, now the airport serving Three Rivers, and had renewed acquaintance with his nephews and niece. When Trudeau arrived at the Sorbonne in 1946, Elliott was back in Varengeville and invited him down whenever he could. Rolland went, too. The two young men had brought their Harley-Davidsons over to Paris, to the admiration of every small boy who saw them thundering down the boulevards, though what the French adult population thought was another matter.

Most of their time was spent working, Rolland recalls, with Trudeau regularly putting in 16-hour days. They also looked up François Hertel, the classical scholar who had taught them both at Brébeuf before he left the priesthood to go to live in Paris, writing and acting as a consultant to publishing companies. Many of their Canadian friends of those Paris days are still members of their circle, though Trudeau had long ago shown a tendency to compartmentalize all but his closest friends. His sports friends and his literary friends, his legal and his political friends, his artists and his canoeists — are all kept in separate boxes.

"I am inclined to look for good things in people," he says. "A good skier, a good poet." And if he compartmentalizes them, it's not deliberate, he says.

Sharing with Rolland brought out Trudeau's taste for practical jokes again. One of the most successful was the night one of their friends, Marcel Blais, went to London, and they grabbed a bust of Philippe Roy, the former Canadian ambassador in Paris, from its plinth downstairs and laid it in Blais' bed, its greenish-brownish bronze contrasting horribly with the white pillow. They then told everyone that Blais had met with the most awful accident on his way to London, and would they mind taking turns staying with the body until the undertaker could come in the morning? So, all night long, the other students at *la maison Canadienne* took their turns kneeling in the darkened room, lighted only by candles. Only when dawn broke did they discover the truth.

Trudeau came down with appendicitis that winter, barely two weeks before he, Rolland and some other Canadians were due to go skiing in Megève. It meant an all-night journey from Paris in a third-class (wooden bench) coach, and his friends did not expect him to make the trip. Not a bit of it. Trudeau joined them on the train for the long ride and promptly went skiing as soon as they got to Megève, stitches and all.

In the spring, Rolland decided that life in the *Cité Universitaire* prevented him from getting the most out of Paris, and he moved into rooms in the city.

At about the same time, Trudeau decided that the Sorbonne had nothing on Harvard, and he switched to the London School of Economics.

London, in 1947, was even more austere than Paris, but Trudeau found the academic atmosphere far more stimulating. One of his friends was Robert T. McKenzie, now well known as a broadcaster and Professor of Sociology at LSE, who came from Vancouver and had taught at the University of British Columbia before war broke out. He was going back to school to get his Ph.D., after serving in the armed forces. McKenzie remembers Trudeau well and they have remained in touch over the years.

"He wasn't carrying a field marshal's baton in his knapsack visibly," he says. "One thought of him far more as ending up in some literary, political, journalistic-cum-academic activity. But there was never any surprise that, once he set his mind to it, he became an outstanding figure in the literary cum political world of French Canada, and then moved on as he did. But there was nothing about him to suggest to any of us that he would end up as a serious politician in one of the old-line parties."

Harold Laski was their supervisor (as he had been Dalton Camp's the year before), and both McKenzie and Trudeau used to go to the open house Laski held every Tuesday evening at his home in Fulham. There were generally 30 to 40 prominent people of the Left there to meet each other and exchange ideas.

The question of Trudeau's wartime activities was never raised ("it was bad form to say 'what did you do during the war' "), and McKenzie can never remember Trudeau discussing it.

Trudeau had an ancient MG in London, McKenzie says, and was generally regarded as being rather well-to-do. "Maybe I've got it wrong and it was the next time he was here, as he was back and forth a number of times," says McKenzie. "But I associated this slightly rakish, raffish business with him — having a car was quite a thing with rationing and everything else." In London, as in Cambridge, Massachusetts, Trudeau kept his private life very much to himself.

"This seemed to be a consistent thread, when one looks back on it," says McKenzie. "This slightly aloof quality — but he was certainly well liked, even though I don't remember anybody being his particular friend.

"I can never recall that anybody knew how he spent his time, really. But he stood out in retrospect as a very lively, colorful sort of student in the rather physically drab set up of London in 1947. He was a very lively participant in the kinds of discussion that students had. We were mostly ex-servicemen and therefore fairly hard-headed and Pierre was one of the enormously scintillating, congenial people around the place."

Trudeau remembers London primarily for Laski and his infectious enthusiasm for Lord Acton, notably Acton's essay on *Freedom and Power*. He was strongly influenced by Laski's own *Grammar of Politics*, and he remembers Laski's admiration for Cardinal Newman. "Paradoxically, for me as a Catholic, Laski's respect for Newman was for his logic and insight — rather than for his Catholicism." London also brought him back to Plato, Dupire, Montesquieu and de Tocqueville.

The world was seething with revolution in 1948. So much so, in fact, that many likened it to the great surge of democratic upheaval 100 years earlier. At any rate, Trudeau decided that the opportunity for case study was too good to be missed and set off to gather material for his Ph.D. in political science.

He traveled light, with literally only a knapsack on his back ("hence very few souvenirs") and an ability to blend into his surroundings ("you can't do it by being conspicuous"), despite shorts, a weird jungle hat from an army war surplus store, and a burgeoning blond beard.

Old Baron Montesquieu would have approved. "It is always the adventurers who accomplish great things" he once said. Also, "to succeed in this world, one must have the appearance of a fool and be wise."

The story of his first trip around the world, on $800, between May 1948 and April 1949, has been told many times. But it was not mere thrill-seeking. It was a serious studious journey; he took copious notes (but never did write his Ph.D.) and lectured at colleges along the way.

First he went to Germany, obtained faked papers (anyone could in those days) and slipped into Hungary by way of Austria. In Budapest, in August, he met a 21-year-old Canadian from Toronto named, William Kilbourn, ("There weren't that many Canadians in Budapest that summer"), today a professor at York University. "He was looking like a bearded ragpicker," says Kilbourn. "He seemed to have an uncanny instinct for being where the action was, and I guess that's why he is where he is today." He signed on as a French-English interpreter for a free trip to a Trade Fair in Poland with the Communist International Union of Students ("in those days the Communists did anything for students"). From Poland, Trudeau managed to persuade the Russians to fly him free via Aeroflot to Belgrade, having convinced them that the Yugoslavs (about to break away from the Soviet bloc) had given him a visa. They had not.

Once in Belgrade, bearded, unkempt and visaless, the Russians refused to take him back, and the Yugoslavs refused to let him in. They finally compromised and threw him in jail until the Canadian chargé d'affaires got back from a long and leisurely holiday in Switzerland. When the Canadian diplomat showed no signs of coming back, they relented and gave him an exit visa to Bulgaria. There Trudeau's ability to speak Spanish endeared him to a group of Sephardic Jews who entertained him and sent him on his way to Turkey.

Naturally, he swam the Bosphorus. "It wasn't that hard, but it was cold and had a bloody strong current." From Turkey, he went to Syria, Lebanon and Trans-Jordan. His arrest as a spy was innocent enough. When some hard-drinking journalists at the bar of the Philadelphia Hotel in Amman told him that it was impossible to get to Jerusalem, Trudeau smilingly picked up the challenge, wandered out of the hotel and down to the bazaar, where he climbed aboard a truck filled with Arab irregulars heading for the front at Jerusalem. Once in the city, the soldiers went about their business, and Trudeau went sightseeing. "All the others had somewhere to report to and after three or four hours I suppose it must have been obvious that I didn't have anywhere to report." So the Arabs jailed him until he could prove he was not an Israeli spy.

Free again, he was visiting Ur of the Chaldees when two brigands decided to try to rob him. They fled when he started making wild gestures and spouting a mixture of joual and any verse that came into his head. He traveled across the Persian Gulf to Karachi, arriving in the chaos of post-partition Pakistan. He went up into Afghanistan, via the Khyber Pass, spending a few days with the Khyber Rifles and sampling goat's milk and wild bee honey. He then went down into India and spent most of his time traveling on third and fourth class Indian trains — fourth class Indian train travel is so bad you do not just stand, you generally hang onto the train from the running board outside.

He made a point of looking up all the newspaper editors and university teachers he could find — and paid for accommodation in Istanbul, Turkey, and Lucknow, India, by giving political science lectures. He went to visit the Holy Cross Fathers mission at the mouth of the Ganges and Brahmaputra rivers, infested with crocodiles, and helped them re-supply their mission with rice. Pirates attacked them on their way back, but fog rolled in, and Trudeau, who was in the rice boat, managed to get lost. "When we found the other boat after the fog lifted, we found they had all been robbed and stripped," he remembers.

From India, he went into Burma overland, by way of Chittagong, in Assam, and on down the Burmese coast to Rangoon. Burma was, as usual, in a state of uncontrolled civil war, movement impossible, and Trudeau went on to Thailand and Cambodia, visiting Angkor, of course, and joining a French military convoy carrying bound and gagged prisoners to Saigon.

He wandered around Indo-China, took a ship to Hong-Kong and then used a Nationalist Chinese visa he got in Ankara to slip into China itself, then in the final throes of the civil war. He wisely changed his money into large silver coins beforehand as inflation was driving the yen down so fast that paper money had become worthless. He wound up in Shanghai, tried to get into Yenan but was not allowed to cross the Yangtse. When the Communists and Nationalists called a truce, he felt that the stalemate was likely to last for years and decided to take a ship back to Canada via Japan. Less than a month after he left, the Communists crossed the Yangtse and captured Shanghai, and within months the war was over.

Back in Canada, he estimated that the entire trip, less $300 for the passage from Shanghai to Vancouver, cost him $500.

The Asbestos strike was his next involvement, then the Privy Council, from 1949 to 1951. The foundation of *Cité Libre* in 1950; the French-Canadian Institute of Public Affairs in 1954; *Le Rassemblement* in 1956; various literary activities — *Les Ecrits du Canada Francais* in 1954, with Claude Hurtubise, an annual anthology of the best essays, short stories and verse of the year. He helped a little with labor union problems; practised a little law. He made frequent trips abroad — went to Europe almost every year. He was in Moscow in 1952 for a world economic congress. This was the occasion when he threw the famous snowball at a statute of Stalin (not Lenin) and talked his way out of it by explaining that he always threw snowballs at the statues of famous Canadian politicians, too, the revered Laurier in particular. Less well known was his insistence, during that same visit, on being able to attend mass on Easter Sunday in a Moscow church.

In 1960, he returned to China with his friend Jacques Hébert; Dr. Denis Lazure, a psychiatrist; Micheline Legendre, the puppeteer; and Madeleine Parent, a labor organizer. The trip was arranged by a pro-Communist paediatrician named Dr. Daniel Longpré, the president of the Canada-China Friendship Committee, at the request of the government of China. Longpré was told to select several groups, mixing Communists and non-Communists, but generally making sure that they would be sympathetic towards Communist China. *Cité Libre* was an obvious place to look, and the editorial board was invited to send three people — Trudeau, Hébert and Lazure. Miss Legendre and Miss Parent (an avowed Communist) were selected from other groups. The five of them toured China for six weeks and were the first white Westerners to be admitted since the revolution.

Hébert was amazed at how many people remembered Trudeau

from his last visit in 1949, and he was constantly being told how tough Trudeau had been. Trudeau was the delegation chief, largely on account of having been to China before, but rebelled against the restrictions. As Hébert remembers it, the party-line palled for all of them after awhile, even for the lady comrade, and he will never forget Trudeau, bracketed between two Chinese pedants, walking ahead of the group during some commune-inspection, suddenly doing a somersault, then resuming his step. The Chinese, says Hébert, remained completely impassive, paid no attention whatever.

Soon after he came back from China, he started work at the Institute of Public Law at the University of Montreal, specializing in civil liberties. His entry into politics followed naturally.

Trudeau is a very private man, and in respecting the privacy of others, he expects them to respect his. He likes solitude, ("I am a solitary sort of fellow") and the loneliness of high office does not concern him.

Yet he defies categorization. He likes solitude but he adores parties, though he never gave any himself before becoming Prime Minister. He loves beautiful things — art, music, literature, women — but he has an almost ascetic abhorrence for possessions. He is publicly rather stingy but privately tremendously generous (and because his generosities *are* private, few are ever discovered), particularly with his time and talent — defending Jacques Hébert in the law suits that followed publication of his book, *J'Accuse les Assassins de Coffin*, for instance.

He would like to think he is as knowledgeable about food and wine as he is about the other sensual pleasures. He banished Canadian wines from his campaign plane in preference to French and makes quite a performance of the selection and tasting of wine. Yet he cannot tell chicken from pheasant, as one Montreal grande dame would testify, and his best friends admit that he is basically indifferent to what he eats and drinks, is more conscious of the dietetic quality of a meal than its culinary perfection. Food is a fuel, except for Chinese food, which he adores, and Trudeau's dinner is usually a small, medium-rare steak, green salad, no vegetables, and a glass of milk, and occasionally just oatmeal cookies and milk. He loves ice cream and fruit, never touches hard liquor, sticking to beer and wine.

His clothes are a combination of conservatism and ostentation. He once possessed leopard-skin swimming trunks, but generally he favors greys and browns, striped shirts (horizontal rather than vertical), knitted ties, in silk, leather, or cashmere wool, lightweight shoes. His suits are all made-to-measure and emphasize his trim figure, of which he is justly proud, and are usually ventless in the Italian style, with tapered trousers, no cuffs, no waistcoats. He is 5 feet 10 inches tall and weighs 158 pounds and is in excellent shape for a man his age, well-muscled in the shoulders and chest. He used to work out once a week in judo with Roger Damblant, a French judo expert living in Montreal, but he says his attendance record has slipped badly during the last year. He does setting-up exercises every day. During his session at Vic Tanny's Health Spa in Oshawa on June 22 he went through a vigorous work-out that included 50 sit-ups and 20 thigh-extensions with 30 pound weights.

He does not smoke and regards the habit with distaste. When he can't ski or swim, in spring or fall, his favorite weekend activity is jogging through the woods. "It's very important to me. I like to go into the woods. I like to explore parts of the Canadian north that have no roads. I like to leave my car and go off with a map, discovering undeveloped lakes and mountains. I'm by myself half the time — or with an enterprising young lady who does not mind bushwacking and climbing mountains." If he can go for a weekend, he likes to pitch a tent in some wilderness and spend a Thoreau-like 48 hours with a pile of books.

In Ottawa, he has tended to exercise as best he can by swimming in the Chateau Laurier or the Skyline. He will also surprise visitors to his office by leaping to his feet and saying in a tone that expects no refusal, "let's go for a walk". And he'll bound out without hat or coat for a brisk 10-minute walk around Parliament Hill, bringing his visitor back, teeth chattering, with the comment: "Fresh air does you good."

His acrobatic skill as a championship caliber diver gives him some athletic advantages. His brother-in-law, Dr. Pierre Rouleau, once watched aghast as Trudeau climbed onto a neighbor's trampoline and started doing double somersaults first time up.

He seeks adventure quite consciously, testing himself, driving fast, riding a parachute on water-skis, learning to fly (he soloed

in six hours), snorkeling and skin-diving. "I like to test my physical and mental limits all the time," he told Pat Watson in that
superb interview on television just before he won the leadership.
"I get fun out of a new experience. I like to feel alive. I like to taste
new fruit or dive into new waters. This is to me what is good about
life. It's making sure that you are using yourself to your limits.
That's why I like sports. That's why I like to keep in shape
physically. It's because I don't really feel happy if I'm run down.
I don't feel that I'm quite alive."

Trudeau has hundreds of acquaintances but few close friends.
He has chosen his friends wisely, counting on their discretion, both
men as well as women. He has not been disappointed. Most of the
people who have been most prominent in claiming to know him
well, have turned out not to know him at all, or very slightly. The
amount of actual information released about his private life
remains very small. To learn more a reporter is sworn to discretion
and thus becomes part of the protective conspiracy — not that
there is anything in the least scandalous but because his friends
do not want to disappoint him, they value his respect and friendship so much that they will not dream of betraying his trust.

This is particularly true in regard to his relations with women.
His sexuality has been discussed on a number of levels, from the
entertaining interpretation by Dr. Joyce Brothers, the psychologist,
who concluded that he personified "machismo" but that the teeny-
boppers liked him because he was remote — sexy but safe: to the
gratuitous testimonials by women of a certain age who are keen
to jump aboard the Trudeau bandwagon. Significantly, however,
none of the four women who have been very close friends of his
in recent years are the kiss-and-tell type. Moreover, it is inconceivable that they ever will say anything about their relationship
with the Prime Minister unless it leads to the logical conclusion —
marriage, when there will be nothing more to be said anyway.

How likely is marriage? The question is in the minds of millions
of Canadian women. A better question would be 'How permanent
is bachelorhood?'

Unpleasant though the thought may be to women, who prefer
to regard marriage as the natural state, there are many men who
can see no great advantage in it. A great many normal, virile men

who are extremely fond of women find bachelorhood a happy and self-sufficient state. It helps to be rich, of course, because then you can take advantage of the freedom from ties or responsibilities that bachelorhood permits. It helps to be almost universally attractive to women, which improves the hunting. The Prime Minister seems to fill all of these requirements admirably. Why should he get married?

His friends say they would not be surprised if he never married — or if he were married impulsively next week, to the next woman he falls in love with. But at present there seems to be every indication that he is enjoying his bachelorhood.

An element of bachelorhood that seems to be unappreciated by Canadians, certainly by most Canadian women, is that as Prime Minister a single man can devote himself completely to his work — which is demanding — and that the country is fortunate not to have to share Trudeau with a wife and family.

Trudeau's entry into politics came willingly and naturally, as discussed already. "There was no reluctance — it was basically what we wanted to do," he says. The reluctance was on the Liberal side — and only Marchand's insistence on a "package" deal got them in.

Trudeau adapted quickly to life in Parliament after a frustrating first year. He wanted to intervene in the Spencer debate and also when Lucien Cardin was under attack, but he only got the Speaker's nod once. "I only made a mark when I became a minister," he says. Though he denies that the atmosphere of the House of Commons has quietened him. "I am just as raucous and noisy as I used to be in the days of *Cité Libre.*"

To gallery watchers, Trudeau did not really become a parliamentarian until December 4, 1967, when he introduced his Divorce Bill, and the House was able to take his measure in debate. Until then, his slim stature and high-pitched voice did not come across well in the chamber. It may be unkind to say so, but until December, 1967, the only remarkable thing about Trudeau to most of his fellow Members were the clothes he wore. Since December, his brilliance has been appreciated better.

He has very decided ideas about the role of a Prime Minister. "The Prime Minister has to act with the limitations he has. He can direct and orientate but he cannot create. Look at Harold Wilson, a man of the Left, and yet he has had to adopt policies which even the Conservatives wouldn't take. The Prime Minister's mandate is to be himself, as much as possible, he is the leader of his party and gives work to his ministers. He needs decisiveness and firmness. He always knows what cabinet ministers positions will be — and he needs to be well-informed to make good decisions.

"As Liberal leader, what will I do? I'll bring a bit of clarity into the debate — perhaps because I have been studying and speaking and writing about this area, I can speak with clarity — but I don't think the opposition (from the provinces) will be fundamentally different whether some other person is Prime Minister of Canada or whether I am. There was just as much tension between Mackenzie King and Mitchell Hepburn as there was between Godbout and King. There was a great deal between Duplessis and King. It's not a new thing today. Except that in the past Quebec tended to be quite negative — to say no to everything — and Quebec is now being constructive, trying to test the Federal government. Until 1960, Quebec did not really concern itself with the 20th century. I think it's a good thing for Quebec to find firm opposition in Ottawa . . ."

As Prime Minister, Trudeau can be expected to apply some of his own economic ideas, decentralized planning ("economic policy decisions from Ottawa should not be made to fit like a mould on the rest of Canada") and some sharp pruning of federal programs which seem to compete with each other rather than help the individual or area concerned. "There's too much of a piecemeal approach to regional development. You have ARDA and FRED and the ADB, and four or five ministries applying eight or ten programs — it's not as coordinated as it should be."

Provinces will be asked to plan properly ("they must decide the priorities, planning has to be done on two levels and incorporated into the whole infrastructure of the provinces").

Subsidies will be questioned constantly. "I am against subsidies if they promote inefficiency. I am against any resource never paying its way." He will probably order a major re-evaluation of what Canada does best and where the greatest growth opportunities lie. He has mentioned transportation, mineralogy and he has often pointed to the success of Sweden and Switzerland in adapting themselves to the technological age. He will seek growth areas for Canadian capital without discouraging foreign investors. "Let's put our capital into the future and not into the past," he says. "Let's be the best in something."

"My liberalism is not the liberalism of big business, but to help the individual fulfill himself to the utmost. At times we shall encourage big business; at times we shall encourage labor; and at times the individual. Liberalism is to seize the temper of the times."

XVII

"Trudeau Is A Happening"

What of soul was left, I wonder, when the kissing had
to stop?

— *Robert Browning, 1855*

THE KISSING STARTED right after the convention on a bright Spring
morning outside the Center Block, and it hasn't stopped yet.

From Mildred's Catering, in Red Deer, Alberta, where regulars
hailed Trudeau's victory with drinks on the house, to the teeny-
boppers on Parliament Hill, pursuing the object of their osculation,
the apotheosis of Pierre Elliott Trudeau became a major national
ambition.

Politics were relevant again. To the great mass of Canadians who
had forgotten, or never known, the excitement of a charismatic
national figure, here, at last, was a politician who was articulate,
candid, without pomposity of any sort. They could identify with
him. He spoke their language, used their idioms, seemed to understand their anxieties and hopes.

Of course there had to be a general election. How else would the
people be able to express the pent-up need to say yes — yes to
change, to excitement, to honesty and to all the other shining
virtues they were sure he possessed?

In retrospect, it is incredible that the Liberals should have
doubted the wisdom of an election. But doubt they did, and for
17 days they agonized over the problem.

A Liberal organizer John de B. Payne fired off a list of 32
reasons he could think of for calling a general election — but still
they procrastinated.

From a legislative viewpoint, the election would provide a
majority to let the government push through such important but

politically tricky bills as the new Labor Code and the Drug Bill. The election would test the strength of the NDP, prime opponents to the Labor Code, and the pharmaceutical manufacturers who were vehemently opposed to some of the Drug Bill proposals.

Another factor was that redistribution had taken place and a new parliament would be more representative of the country.

Then, of course, there were the psychological advantages of an election in consolidating Trudeau's victory over the "old guard" of the Liberal party. And there's nothing like uniting against a common enemy to heal sectional rifts. As one Liberal strategist wrote: "His victory had roots far deeper and more significant than the mere triumph of the reform wing over the conservative wing of the party. He is the symbol of change. His support extends beyond the churchyard of the party. He is the breakthrough that the dominant generations of the electorate have sought in national politics. His success complements the achievements of his contemporaries in business and labor. He now commands the energies of those generations which, for so long, had been dissipating in restlessness."

A mandate would give Trudeau complete freedom to pick his own cabinet, unswayed by the nuances of a minority government, or obligations of a past regime. He could attract new candidates who would complement his existing team. He would be able to get a personal mandate from Quebec, cutting the ground out from under Premier Daniel Johnson's feet, and killing the argument that he was out of touch with Quebec.

Not to call an election would mean continuing in a minority government and facing the possibility, though not probability, of a defeat. Delaying an election would waste the enthusiasm that had built up, which would probably dissipate by the end of summer, when some strategists were urging an election. His popularity was likely to peak in June and July.

Trudeau's lack of experience had been pointed out by those who felt he needed 'an apprenticeship'. Yet experience had been no bar to the delegates, who knew that they were electing a Prime Minister as well as a leader, and there was no reason to suppose that what did not concern 2,500 astute politicians at all would concern the public any more.

Then there were the other parties to consider. The NDP had cut into Liberal strength badly in 1965 and it was a continuing threat in towns and suburbs, particularly in the industrial areas. The election of Trudeau, a former NDP supporter, plus the conversions of numerous actual NDP members, such as Ramsay Cook and Eugene Forsey, had hurt NDP morale badly. The Liberals felt they could capitalize on this effect to win back some of their previous losses.

The Progressive Conservatives were still suffering from the wounds of their leadership campaign and convention. John Diefenbaker had been both discourteous and unhelpful to Robert Stanfield during the winter months. He had refused to introduce him to the House after his election in November, 1967, on the grounds, as he put it, "that it might be misunderstood". After the defeat of the government on the tax bill in February, he had been openly contemptuous of Stanfield's handling of the matter. He would rumble on for months, "we would have swept the country, nothing more, nothing less, if they had listened to my advice . . . but that's not my funeral."

Instead of strengthening his party through the loyalists who supported him, Stanfield made the tactical error of trying to make friends with the Diefenbaker wing. Thus the Conservatives were in no better shape than they had been in September, 1967, in terms of grass-roots reorganization.

Under the Canadian election act, general elections must be held on Mondays, unless the Monday selected happens to be a public holiday, in which case it can be held on a Tuesday. There is also an archaic convention which requires between 56 and 60 days campaign time to be required between the dissolution of Parliament and the holding of an election. It's a convention (not a statute) designed for an era when 56 to 60 days were indeed the minimum a man needed to travel the breadth of Canada by train — and visit the places beyond the rail-head by horse and buggy.

There are also other conventions, no less archaic, which say that an election should not be held in July or August, or in the winter, or before the harvest is in, or until the crops are sown. They, too, are relics of an agrarian Canada which ceased being dominant shortly after the turn of the century.

Today, with jets and helicopters, national television and instantaneous communications of all sorts, there is no reason why a politician should spend more than a month putting his case before the electors. Some students of politics even say three weeks would be enough.

But, bound by the 56/60 day gentlemen's agreement, the longer the Liberals delayed in April, the later the election would be in June.

Hopes for an immediate election were dimmed on April 10 when it was revealed that Trudeau would be going away for a short holiday "in the Laurentians." But alert reporters picked him up the next day at the Beach Club Hotel in Fort Lauderdale, Florida, where he was registered in a $34 a day room as Revenue Minister Edgar Benson's son, and performing like a teenager from the high board at the hotel pool.

He got back from Florida on April 17, and for the rest of that week held a series of meetings with his cabinet ministers-to-be or not-to-be. Judy LaMarsh could hardly have stayed after her nationally expressed opinions of April 6; the Minister of Labor, John Nicholson, was retiring too; and so was the Solicitor General, Lawrence Pennell. This left the Secretariat of State, Labor, Solicitor General and Justice (Trudeau's old post) portfolios vacant.

Two more posts would become vacant during the week. Paul Martin was offered the Justice portfolio but refused it and became the government leader in the Senate. This left External Affairs open.

The second post was Trade and Commerce. Trudeau had a long session with Robert Winters on April 10 and reportedly offered his runner-up no new post but asked him to keep the same ministry with increased responsibilities. The truth was somewhat different.

Winters felt very strongly that there should be no St. Laurent-Howe arrangement which would tend to fractionalize the government and his basic inclination after losing was to step down and out of politics. There was no bitterness in this. He was thinking of leaving anyway and admits "I was willing to leave it to the delegates. If they wanted me to be the leader, I would have responded. But I was not seeking it. So when they responded otherwise, I was quite happy." He also felt that because of the great backing he received he ought to offer his services, which he did. But Trudeau wanted Winters to tell him what job he wanted. Winters told Trudeau the job was up to him.

"If I had won on Saturday, I'd be telling you what I wanted you to do," he said to Trudeau. "Now you tell me what you want."

The upshot was that a newsman friendly to Winters, in good faith, mentioned to him that he ought to be in the government. "I'm not sure," said Winters, "that's a matter for Trudeau." The newsman wrote a story which suggested that Winters ought to be in the government but the only way he would stay would be for something pretty big. This in turn was blown up to mean that Winters was "demanding" the deputy Prime Ministership.

Winters' wife called him from Toronto in Ottawa to say "I didn't think you'd be buying power."

"Don't worry," Winters replied. "I'm going to play it right and honorably, but when I come to a decision with Trudeau it's got to be the right one."

On April 17, Trudeau saw Winters again, and they had a friendly discussion. Towards the end, Winters said: "Pierre, we have been talking for two hours on two successive days, and I still don't know if you want me in your government or if you don't?"

Trudeau said, "Well, it's a decision you will have to make."

"Well," said Winters, "if you are leaving the decision to me, I'll make it, and I'll let you know tomorrow." So Winters returned to Toronto and held discussions with friends in business and politics, notably the late Grant Glassco of Brazilian Light & Power. And on Thursday, April 18, he called Trudeau from Glassco's office at 25 King Street West, in Toronto.

"I said 'Pierre, I have decided not to be a member of your government.' And for the first time he really did seem to be concerned. He said he was sorry and that he hoped I would reconsider. He hoped there wasn't any lack of warmth in his invitation. And I couldn't tell. If he had said 'Now look here, Bob, we had a great fight and you got almost half the votes of all the delegates, and what we need now is a strong team. You and me together. We could do things for Canada', I wouldn't have been able to resist. I think I would have stayed until the next election, as I said. Though I think I would have got out then, if I could have done so honorably — because this was what I wanted to do. But after that there was no point in my staying in the government."

Yet he is philosophical about it all.

"When you get to a position like I have had in business and in government, where do you go? There's only one logical job you can do, there's only one more promotion. But back in business I could do many things."

The departure of Robert Winters disturbed Trudeau but it did not distress him. In retrospect, it must have been what made him decide to go to the country right away. The logic is clear. With Winters stepping down, under such cloudy circumstances, his supporters would quickly conclude that he had been torpedoed like Paul Martin. And no number of denials would disabuse them of that opinion. To unify the party was essential. And as many politicians have discovered before him, there is nothing so unifying as a common enemy. Winters departure must have tipped the scales.

At 4:20 p.m., on April 19, the telephone rang in the office of Guy Robillard, press attaché at Government House, to tell him to get ready for a swearing-in ceremony the following morning, a Saturday. It was most unusual. It could mean only one thing: a June election. The swearing-in was not expected until Monday, April 22, which would have allowed Prime Minister Pearson to conclude five years in office. It was not to be.

At 8:25 Saturday morning a blue Ford custom sedan drove up to Rideau Hall with Pearson inside. He entered quickly. He was out again not long after. "You can call me Mike now," he joked with reporters. He climbed into his car and was gone.

At eleven the same morning, the Trudeau administration was sworn in and the great seal of office passed into the hands of its 15th keeper. The cabinet was a caretaker affair, as interesting for whom it left out as it was for who got in. The newcomers, Ontario Trudeau strategists, Donald Macdonald, 36; John Munro, 37; and Trudeau's old Cité Libre friend, Gérard Pelletier, all became ministers without portfolio. The rest of the cabinet jobs were divided up among existing members: Trudeau kept Justice; Sharp took External Affairs; Benson moved into Finance. Drury, Pépin, Marchand and Turner were asked to take on the additional ministries of Trade and Commerce, Labor, Secretary of State and Solicitor General respectively.

Three days later the House of Commons met and the proceedings were to fill only 68 lines in Hansard. The Commons was called to order at 2:30 p.m., and the Speaker gave notice of "the following vacancies in the representation": Pennell and Martin had resigned.

There was also a note that Mr. J. Gordon Dubroy had been appointed Clerk Assistant to the House.

The Prime Minister then rose on a point of privilege to express his thanks for "the messages of congratulations and encouragement I have received from all parts of the house." He spoke in French. "In a democracy, the people's representatives have the privilege to disagree on the best ways of governing the country. However, we are all prompted by the same desire to make Canada a greater and a stronger country. The best answer I can give to that generous tribute is by undertaking to serve the house and the country to the best of my ability."

Then, switching to English, Trudeau told the house that "In view of the announcement I am about to make, Mr. Speaker, I feel any further comment by me on any other subjects would be improper. This afternoon I called on the Governor General to request him to dissolve parliament and to have writs issued for a general election on June 25."

The election, once announced, was something of an anti-climax. Everybody was expecting it. Only the week before, on April 16, Dalton Camp had thrown an off-the-record dinner for Robert Stanfield at the Albany Club. Tommy Douglas, the leader of the NDP, was spoiling for a fight too.

For several weeks, while nomination meetings were organized and strategy laid, nothing much happened. Everyone seemed to have picked the week of May 20 as the kick-off for their campaign. To start much earlier meant a risk of peaking too soon.

So with little hard election news to talk about, and Parliament no longer sitting, national politics left the front-pages of the newspapers for a little while, leaving the field for such regional events as the founding convention of René Lévesque's *Mouvement*

Souveraineté-Association in Montreal. (It had a short life, merging with Gilles Grégoire's Ralliement Nationale in October, 1968, to become *le parti Québecois.*)

There was also renewed tension between Ottawa, Quebec City and Paris over Quebec Education Minister Jean-Guy Cardinal's statement that Quebec was thinking of sending aid to Gabon. He also indicated that France intended to treat Quebec as a sovereign state at an upcoming educational conference.

Quebec's persistent truculence over international relations was beginning to embarrass the National Union's allies in the Progressive Conservative Party, notably Marcel Faribault, who was on the verge of announcing his candidacy in the June 25th election. The word went out to Cardinal to cool off the controversy a bit.

On May 4, Trudeau moved into 24 Sussex Drive, noting that he had lived in hotel rooms for so long that he could put all his possessions into one suitcase.

On May 8, he indicated that he had more than housekeeping on his mind with the release of a 73-page White Paper showing that Quebec's attitude had been little more than boorish over the Gabon incident. It showed that Prime Minister Pearson had written three letters to Premier Johnson on the subject, all of them conciliatory in tone, but Johnson had deigned to reply but once.

Trudeau's strategy was a bold one. He was taking his case to the people. He had provided evidence that the Canadian government had done everything possible, short of giving up its own sovereignty, to give Quebec a face-saving solution.

Furthermore, the Conservatives suddenly found themselves on the defensive, an unusual position for the party in Opposition, but one in which they would find themselves increasingly as the campaign went on.

With the appearance of the White Paper there seemed little justification for Stanfield's criticism of the government's handling of the Gabon affair. And, as a result, given their stated opposition to Quebec representing Canada in international affairs, the Tory position became remarkably weak, while their criticisms seemed seldom more than nit-picking.

The *Globe & Mail* felt that "Prime Minister Trudeau must be applauded for the firmness with which he asserts the right of the federal authority to be the only authority which determines the course of Canada in international affairs . . . he now turns the ball game, for this particular inning, over to the Conservative Party, which must clarify its position on the issue . . . (and) it is difficult . . . to believe that the Conservative Party would be party to such a significant degree of decentralization."

The change in tactics pushed campaign plans forward. Trips which might have been routine, suddenly became campaign tours: Trudeau headed West for a swing through British Columbia, the Yukon and the Northwest Territories, while Stanfield suddenly found something very important to do down in the Maritimes.

The West has seldom seen such crowds and enthusiasm as Trudeau drew in New Westminster and Edmonton, and up in Yellowknife, the weekend of May 11. Crowds mobbed him wherever he went — and Westerners showed that they could pucker up just as quickly as they did in the East, when it came to bussing the Prime Minister. Yellowknife, kissing aside, was probably the highpoint of the Trudeau trip: nearly 1,000 people, or 20% of the population, were out to welcome him at the airstrip at ten at night, and 600 of them stayed up to attend a special welcoming ceremony at the local elementary school.

They gave him mukluks, a 248-gram gold brick, and a huge polar bearskin rug — which he promptly threw over his head and started to play bear. When he took it off again, one of the weighty paws clonked a little girl on the head, making her cry. But when Northwest Territories commissioner Stuart M. Hodgson comforted the child with a kiss, Trudeau took him by the arm and said jokingly, "Hey, that's my line!" However, he beat a strategic retreat later in the evening when a lusty group of local damsels named the Daughters of the Midnight Sun entertained him with a floor-show and then, with meaningful glances, to such ditties as "Cigareets and Whusky and Wild, Wild Women" and less familiar local ballads such as "Out Behind the Barn."

The pace of the campaign was speeding up. There had been rumors in Quebec that Daniel Johnson would throw his party organization behind Stanfield during the election campaign. The rumor seemed to have been sparked by Marcel Faribault's entry as a Conservative candidate in the new Montreal riding of Gamelin. Trudeau told newsmen he doubted Johnson would "risk a humiliating defeat." "After all," he said, "Mr. Johnson is the leader of a party which has always made it a point of pride not to take part in federal elections." It looked like a long needle to many observers. Was Trudeau trying to draw Johnson in, making him commit his prestige?

Stanfield clearly thought so.

On May 17, still touring the Maritimes, Stanfield said Trudeau was "playing a dangerous partisan game with the future of Canada." He said he was trying to destroy Johnson. "Even if Mr. Trudeau were able to destroy Mr. Johnson, as he wants to do, he would be left to face the provincial Liberals, who go beyond the position of Mr. Johnson, or the separatists who are most extreme in their views. Nothing will be settled, except that the gulf will become wider, the attitudes of both sides more rigid, the climate inflamed, and the chances of working out solutions to all the problems more impossible. I cannot believe he fully understands the consequences."

But the day he spoke, Trudeau and Johnson were both taking part in a cold, wet, but enjoyable afternoon in Montreal, helping Mayor Jean Drapeau open Terre des Hommes or, as the wags called it, "Son of Expo." Trudeau, dressed for the weather in his elegant Valstar trenchcoat, grinned at Drapeau, Johnson and the other dignitaries huddled in their emergency plastic coats. It didn't look as if anyone was out to destroy anybody, which is often the way in French Canadian politics, where form and substance are two very different things.

Meanwhile, Stanfield's position was being weakened by the publicity given to Marcel Faribault's interpretation of the Conservative Party's constitutional stand. In a series of interviews in the weeks since he had entered politics as a candidate, Faribault had shown a remarkable reluctance to be pinned down on specifics. But the specifics which did emerge were somewhat chilling to a Tory policy strategist.

Faribault felt that Quebec had to be recognized as the homeland of French Canadians and that it needed the powers of a nation in "the psychological sense." However, he would add, hastily, that Quebec needs "very few more powers". Repeatedly, he would declare "I don't want any particular powers for the province of Quebec which are not given the other provinces."

Things needed, he said, were small, such as new sources of taxation, "modernization of the constitution" and having residual rights assigned to the provinces and not to the federal government as they are at present. It was studiously vague, and of course far more complex than he was prepared to admit. Residual rights, for instance, are a constitutional mare's nest.

About the only thing Faribault was frank about, in fact, was Trudeau.

"I don't intend to let this man raise the spectre of racism by pitting English Canadians against French Canadians."

Every time he opened his mouth, it seemed, Faribault would provide Trudeau's strategists with more ammunition.

It was beginning to tell. At Conservative Party headquarters, calls were already coming in asking what Stanfield thought he was doing with a fellow like Faribault, going soft on Quebec or what? "I'm scared to death," said Eddie Goodman. "Trudeau's got a neat little issue here. Backlash? I've had calls from all over. But maybe in the long run we can come out alright."

The Trudeau team had yet another surprise in store for the Opposition the next day with the first appearance of the Trudeau jet, a stretched DC-9 chartered from Air Canada, with 78 economy seats and 16 in 1st class (for the Prime Minister), which came right on top of Tory H.Q.'s decision to lease an elderly DC-7 (1959 vintage) from Transair Limited in Winnipeg.

(Campaign chairman Goodman admits the jet helped Trudeau's image, and "we probably were wrong to get the DC-7. But we thought we would have a great deal more efficiency with it." He says the DC-7 could get into shorter fields than the DC-9, and offered more comfortable accommodation — beds for the candidate to sleep on, more office space for staff. But in fact it took too long to get from place to place, at half the speed of the DC-9, and proved a poor campaign tool.)

The Trudeau jet made its appearance for the first time at Toronto on Saturday, May 18, when the Prime Minister made a rapid two-an-a-half hour sweep through four city ridings, meeting people in shopping centers and being seen with the candidates, notably former Toronto Mayor Phil Givens, the candidate in York West, and Walter Deakon, who had defeated Trudeauphobe Ralph Cowan for the nomination in York-Humber.

By the following Tuesday, May 21, the official campaign was off in earnest.

In Winnipeg, a grand rally of Conservatives at the Civic Auditorium brought together the likes of Ontario's John Robarts, New Brunswick's Ike Smith, Duff Roblin and Marcel Faribault. They did their best to get things off to a lively start: Roblin had at the government for the high mortgage interest rates saying that "at 9¼% that's not interest, it's usury." Alvin Hamilton scorned Trudeau's "kissing campaign" and said "I think of 908 million bushels of (unsold) wheat, and you can't kiss that away."

But the sensation of the Conservative meeting, if such a listless event could be said to have a sensation, was a speech by Faribault, who seemed to have got the message that a declaration on national unity was required. "There is no square inch of this land that I shall ever renounce," he said and he defended his constitutional position as one based on "one country under a federal system of government, two languages officially recognized and many cultures." He told the delighted Prairie audience that his Grandmother was "born Mary Kelly in Dublin" and his wife's grandmother was the daughter of the Canadian explorer, Alexander Mackenzie.

Then the meeting passed to Stanfield who, in the words of one observer, "quickly cooled it down" with a doggedly read 30-minute speech, devoid of humor or anecdote.

About the liveliest things at the Conservative campaign opener were the hecklers and placard-wavers who showed a cool disrespect for both Liberal and Tory. One sign read "A vote for Trudeau is a vote against Stanfield" but viewed from the other side it said, "A vote for Stanfield is a vote against Trudeau."

In Montreal, meanwhile, Trudeau's nomination meeting at the Town of Mount Royal town hall the following day was more of a love-in than political accounting. For one thing, unlike the last time around, he was unopposed, and the 750 people who jammed the hall were matched by a like number who waited outside with their signs, "Un Vrai Canadien", and "Trudeau is a Happening", or "Do it, Trudeau, Do it, Trudeau."

Trudeau had his eye on the English morning papers as he attacked both Stanfield and Johnson ("We believe in one Canada, in one nation"), ridiculed Claude Ryan of *Le Devoir* for suggesting that constitutional matters should not be made the topic of electioneering. "Are people stupid?" asked Trudeau. "No, I don't agree. I'm not raising any new subject. We've said we want to examine all aspects of the constitution."

He urged his audience to participate in national affairs, to get involved in the community. And he left them shouting for more.

Crowd control was becoming a problem. In Ottawa, that afternoon, Trudeau was besieged by schoolchildren as he left the East Block to walk across the 10 ft. sidewalk to his Cadillac. Pinioned by the crowd of touchers, kissers and autograph-seekers, there was nothing he could do when a souvenir-hunter behind him decided to grab the closest keepsake to hand — his hair. Three scarlet coated Mounties, who had been watching the scene indulgently, finally heard the cry of alarm from Trudeau's assistant, Eddie Rubin, and hurried to detach the Prime Minister from the children. It was a scene that would repeat itself frequently as the campaign reached its end. Trudeau was so anxious to meet people, to let them shake his hands and touch him if they wanted to, that it was difficult for police to judge when things were going too far.

Trudeau was in Winnipeg on May 23 for a press conference at the International Inn, a speech to the Canadian Club and a tour around city ridings, including St. Boniface, across the river, where the Mayor, Joe Guay, had defeated the incumbent, Veterans Affairs Minister Roger Teillet, for the nomination, by 91 votes.

Teillet's defeat had been a sensation. Incumbent members rarely get beaten and cabinet ministers never. But Teillet would not be the only cabinet minister to go down that month. In Montreal, Forestry Minister Maurice Sauvé would lose his bid for the nomination in the new riding of Gamelin to an underwear salesman named Arthur Portelance.

It became clear in Winnipeg — with Toronto as precedent — that Trudeau's campaign style would be radically different to any of his predecessors. There would be maximum emphasis on exposure, minimum on content beyond a few simple themes. The main strategy would be to be seen — hence favored treatment to television camera teams who would be able to keep just about any sized crew they wanted on his plane. Shopping centers, plazas, parks and malls would be put to maximum use both visually (camera angles were checked by the advance men before the platform location was decided) and aurally. Speeches would be of minimum length, rarely more than five minutes, in which Trudeau would talk off-the-cuff, juggling around the basic themes of unity, participation, mutual help, specialization, efficiency, education, equality, justice and bilingualism.

Questions were encouraged, so was heckling. Trudeau's performance would soar whenever he was heckled. In Oakville, right at the end of the campaign, bleary eyed from too many long days and short nights, he urged the crowd to heckle him. "Come on, ask me some questions, wake me up," he said.

His formal speeches would be carefully written and the site chosen with precision. In Winnipeg it was the Canadian Club, 900 of Manitoba's more influential citizens. "If you identify one nation in the sociological sense with one province and its government, you are well on the way to admitting that that province speaks for French Canada. Then you've gone a long way towards special status, associate statehood or independence. If you start with two nations, you end up with two states."

During question time, he said frankly that he had no solution to the wheat surplus beyond more aggressive salesmanship. He also told them that he saw no point in keeping Air Canada's maintenance base in Winnipeg in order to service obsolescent Viscounts — but he did think some other solution should be found. They cheered his candor.

In St. Boniface, he said he was proud to speak in "a place where French Canadians have proved they belong to Canada and not to just one province." He touched on President de Gaulle (facing down student and other riots in Paris at the time) gently. "I don't want to be hard on the General. He seems to be rather busy. In fact France seems to be having more difficulty with itself than with French Canada."

As for Marcel Faribault, he told a news conference that someone should ask him where he stood on reform of the Criminal Code. He also mentioned that Faribault had been secretary general of the University of Montreal at the time when he was turned down for a professorship himself. (Faribault later denied having anything to do with this decision, apparently made by Paul Emile Cardinal Léger, the chancellor at the time).

While Trudeau and Stanfield were fighting it out in suburbia, the NDP was struggling to consolidate its hold on the industrial areas of Canada. The arrival of Trudeau on the national scene had put the NDP at a great disadvantage. Here was a man who had supported the NDP and the CCF before it (though never a card-carrying member of either) who had broken with the party over its special status position for Quebec, and was leading a fairly widespread defection to the Liberals. If the NDP could show itself as modern and concerned as the renewed Liberals and Conservatives, there was a good chance they would make the break-through, particularly since the election would be fought on redistributed boundaries, giving the urban-based parties a better break.

But it was hard to be modern when the leader, Thomas Clement Douglas, 63, was not only the oldest of all the national party leaders but had been a power in Canadian socialism since 1934, and a member of Parliament off and on since 1935. Born in Falkirk, Scotland, he had come to Canada with his parents at the age of six, graduating with a BA from McMaster University and an MA from the University of Chicago, before becoming a Baptist minister in Weyburn, Saskatchewan, in 1930. He had been a member of Parliament for nine years, when he resigned in May, 1944, to lead the CCF Party in victory in the Saskatchewan provincial election, becoming Premier of Saskatchewan on July 10, 1944, a position he held for 17 years. When the federal CCF Party allied itself with the national trades unions in 1961 and changed its name to the New Democratic Party, Douglas, as the most famous socialist in the land, was elected national leader.

Thus, Douglas was hardly new to the electorate.

But there were other problems, too. There was the constitutional bind, for one thing, brought on by the decision of the party to endorse "special status" for Quebec. This might never have happened if the Quebec wing had not been allowed to run loose in constitutional plays, adopting whatever new whim its mercurial leader, Robert Cliche, came up with. Cliche, an excitable country lawyer from the Beauce region of Quebec, finally faced up to his incompatibility in October, 1968, and resigned from the NDP, admitting a strong attraction to René Lévesque and his separatist *parti Québecois*, founded that month.

Nor did that end the litany of NDP problems.

There were also two tactical errors in the early moments of the election, when Douglas told a national television audience: the NDP could not expect to win power that time, and that he would not lead it again in another general election.

Suddenly, in addition to its other worries, the NDP was stuck with a no-win label and a lame-duck leader. The seriousness of that mistake did not become clear for several weeks. Throughout May, and for most of June, Douglas concentrated his efforts on a holding operation in existing NDP ridings. On weekends, he dashed back to Vancouver to campaign in his own riding of Burnaby-Seymour, where the leader of the British Columbia Liberal Party, Ray Perrault, was fighting an uphill battle against him.

Perhaps typical was the week Douglas spent in Northern Ontario, from May 20 to 24, a once solid bastion of Liberalism that had been won over first by the CCF and then the NDP, starting in 1957. With the appearance of Pierre Elliott Trudeau on the national stage, the heavily French Canadian populations of such towns as Timmins would clearly be tempted to revert to one of their own, particularly if he showed any conception of regional problems faced by an isolated French-speaking community.

Trudeau was not scheduled to visit Timmins until June 12, and when Douglas flew into the town on May 21, Trudeaumania had as yet shown no sign of taking hold.

Northern Ontario is a bleak country of dark spruce woods, rocks, little lakes and wild rivers which the hand of man has done little to tame. Instead, sensing the hostility of nature perhaps, man has reacted with like emotion, exploiting and moving on. The Hollinger mining interests took over half a billion dollars worth of gold out of its Timmins mine, but the town has little to show for it.

The tailings from the mine ruined the prettiest lake in the town until an outcry forced Hollinger to turn it into a park, tatty and unkempt, but the only park in town. With the closure of the Hollinger mine, in 1967, the park was sold to real estate developers for a shopping center site.

But Hollinger was no villain. It had behaved just as every large industrial group has behaved in the northland, where governments turn a blind eye, and speculators lick their lips in anticipation of easy profits.

Look at Sudbury, surrounded by a wasteland of defoliated countryside, caused by the noxious gases of the once uncontrolled International Nickel Company smelter operations. What was once a sylvan wilderness is now a moonscape. Look at Kapuskasing, sadly nicknamed the "model town of the north", where the Spruce Falls Paper Company mill (controlled by the Kleenex people, Kimberley Clark) spews the white foam of pollution into the river.

Each town and village in Northern Ontario, it seems, has erupted at one time or another into the hideous violence of labor war, when angry men raced down the dirt roads in battered cars, baseball bats on their knees, looking for other angry men to battle.

Why? It is not hard to see why. It's a country where ordinary human beings are disregarded in a battle between financier and engineer on the one side and raw nature on the other. Financier and engineer, often the same man, probe the land for its secrets of gold, nickel, lead, zinc, copper, sulphur and, hopefully, they pray, some day oil. Nature resists with impossible terrain, muskeg-bogs, granitic rock, searing heat in summer (and swarms of black-flies, mosquitoes), and cryogenic cold in winter. The roads, such as they are, drive ruthlessly from mine to smelter to townsite and rail-head, with none of the careful urban planning which characterizes such modern Western developments as Thompson, Manitoba (Inco's newest mine complex) or the Rainbow and Zama Lakes oil drilling areas of northern Alberta.

Northern Ontario was developed long before those enlightened days, when a buck was a buck, and Roy Thomson, now Lord Thomson of Fleet, founding his fortune in Timmins, coined the immortal recipe for like-minded men, "a dollar down and chase me for the rest." Labor was cheap, plentiful and "Hunky" — the contemptuous term applied to all non-English-speaking European immigrants who labored in the mines and forests, and not just the Hungarians for whom it was devised.

But the curious thing about Northern Ontario is that while enlightenment has been forced on industry in so many places, things have changed little up in Timmins or Sudbury or Kapuskasing. Wages are high, certainly, and Inco can justly claim that its miners are among the highest paid in North America. But the quality of life, the aesthetics, have changed little.

In the towns, sidewalks are minimal or non-existent and the

great spruce hydro poles march down the street sides, marking the
edge of the pavement, dust swirling around them. But the worst
are the mines and smelters, surrounded by their scarred, man-
made wildernesses, billowing smoke that can pollute the air for
twenty miles around, waste that piles up into hideous slag heaps,
and effluent that turns clear trout streams and lakes into stinking
sewers. All in the name of profit, of course. It is little wonder that
the families who live and work in the ugly towns and villages of
Northern Ontario are angry about the callous spoilation which
characterizes so much of the development, a needless, mindless
process of blight.

They protest the only way they can without losing their jobs
or getting bounced by the establishment police — they vote for the
socialist option, the nirvana promised by the New Democratic
Party, or, to put it another way, they vote against the men who
permit it to continue, the men who control the parliaments of
Ontario and of Canada, the Progressive Conservatives and the
Liberals.

But the trouble with the NDP is that they are a protest party.
Frequently people vote NDP not so much for the party itself but
to spite one of the others. Douglas would declare bravely that the
party could become the official opposition — but in fact the best
it could hope for was a minority government which would allow
it to hold the balance of power once again.

With the arrival of Stanfield and Trudeau, and the apparent
seizure of power by the reform wings of both parties, the attraction of the NDP was diminished. Thinking people in Northern
Ontario, as elsewhere, were forced to realize that if they really
wanted a government that would change the social fabric of the
area, they would not get it by voting NDP.

Then there was the so-called ethnic factor. Northern Ontario is
much more French Canadian than most people realize: Timmins
is claimed to be 46% French-speaking whereas Kapuskasing is a
whopping 95% French — and whatever the good qualities of the
NDP leadership and candidates outside Quebec, the ability to
speak French fluently is not among them. Thus the French in
Northern Ontario must have felt doubly unrepresented by a party
that could neither obtain power nor speak their language.

The Liberals were counting on French Canadians voting for Trudeau because he was *un de nous-autres*, one of us. And, if their candidates had no other discernible qualities, they did speak French. Trudeaumania, they hoped, would do the rest. There's an old political adage in Quebec, borrowed from the loggers, which says "When the water's high, the good wood comes down with the bad." This year the water was high for the Liberals.

Douglas's trip through Northern Ontario that week took him in a high arc from Sudbury in the East, north-west to Timmins, further north to Kapuskasing and then around the top of Lake Superior to Prince Arthur and Fort William, on to Winnipeg and then home to Vancouver.

The campaign style was low-key and the approach almost leisurely. He traveled by commercial airline because the NDP could not afford a private plane. But far from making a virtue out of necessity, NDP strategists tried to tailor his campaign to the vagaries of an airline schedule and promised themselves that if the money came in they would rent Tommy a Lear-Jet for the final weeks of the campaign, just to get the sort of exposure such transport can give. Trudeau, by jet, they reckoned, could visit four places in a day. Douglas, by commercial airline or rented propellor aircraft, could reach about two, and the routes and distances were limited.

The Douglas style is deceptive. On the platform he looks and sounds like a doctrinaire little Scots socialist whose lifetime ambition is a chance to soak the rich. Off-stage, he is a different man who talks sadly of the rabid socialists of his own party who have not read Galbraith and do not realize that modern economics make monopolies a must rather than a monster, that much Canadian anti-trust legislation is not only out of date but downright damaging to a sound economy. What industry needs, he feels, is a watchdog and not a ball-and-chain.

The Douglas technique had changed subtly. There are no long prepared texts, but short "notes" of two or three pages which provide the nub of his message for reporters. Douglas filled out the rest with his gold medalwinner's oratory (he also won one for debating and dramatics at Chicago), telling his marvellous stories of political lore. One day he is going to write a book about humor in politics and one of his pastimes in Ottawa is going through British parliamentary debates of the 18th and 19th century, where he has discovered, with amusement, that many of Winston Churchill's celebrated sayings were borrowed from the era.

In Sudbury, he talked about pollution, tearing into Inco for the sulphur dioxide it belches out of its smelter, affecting 4,000 square miles of northern Ontario; into Canadian Industries Limited for the tons of sulphuric acid it had released into the rivers around Sudbury, accidentally of course. "Yet the fouling continues unabated, and the governments do virtually nothing," said Douglas.

At Timmins, he opened the new NDP service center, a joint project started six months earlier by the federal member, Murdo Martin, and his provincial NDP counterpart, to provide a central hospitality center and registry for constituents to bring their problems. Cases were coming in at a rate of 150 a month — immigrants with problems, workmen's compensation cases, pension rights of all sorts. "It's inevitable that as governments get more complex, it becomes almost impossible for many people to find their way around the bureaucracies — particularly the older people, the pensioners," says Douglas.

The bureaucratic runaround is becoming endemic, he says, and nothing cuts red tape faster than the threat of a question in the House. Douglas says Trudeau's "just society is just sloganeering. It's even more important to have a compassionate society."

He would hammer away at the government's economic policies. In a paid party telecast from Timmins' CFCL-TV, with Martin, Arnold Peters of Timiskaming (who was destined to be the lone northern NDPer to survive the Trudeau onslaught) and Ross Paterson, the candidate in Cochrane, Douglas used his favorite example of a young couple, buying an $18,000 house on a 9½% mortgage, who would wind up spending $44,000 for the house before it was paid off.

There was a typical NDP "bring your own" lunch at the Canadian Legion Hall, where 200 people paid 50 cents a head to hear Tommy talk. He talked about the need for Texas Gulf Sulphur to build a smelter in the area instead of sending all its raw material away to be processed in Quebec and Oklahoma.

His next stop was Timmins' six-month-old community college,

the Northern College of Applied Arts and Technology, built by the Liberal candidate's company, Roy Construction. It was graduation day and he told them Maeterlinck's famous story of the "Blue Bird of Happiness".

To get from Timmins to Kapuskasing, the Douglas party chartered two light planes, a five-passenger Aztec and an eight-seater Beechcraft. The journey is something over 90 miles.

At Kapuskasing he got a jam-packed welcome at the Civic Center where a four-piece band struck up with "Well, Hello Tommy! How are you Tommy!" A huge sign in aluminum foil read "Welcome Tommy". Douglas had tried to visit the Kap, as it's called, several times in past general elections but the weather had always been fickle. He told them about the government's failure to do anything to reduce the high cost of living, he told them about the $18,000 house. He talked about the need for a prices review board. "If labor has to justify an increase in wages, why shouldn't corporations justify an increase in prices?" He wound up with his famous story about Mouseland, where the mice elected cats to govern them until one day they realized "that you can't expect cats to pass good laws for mice. You can kill a man or a mouse," he added, "but you can't kill an idea."

The next day he talked for half an hour on an open-line radio show, but the questions were safe: housing shortage, corporate profits and how he stood on a national lottery (he didn't object).

Then it was on to Fort William, by road, because the weather had socked in again and the chartered plane couldn't fly under the conditions.

He set no fires but he did not dampen any enthusiasm either. He remained an immensely popular and respected figure, trying hard to shake a dated appearance in an age which seemed to demand excitement and novelty.

Meanwhile, Stanfield and Trudeau were winging their way across the country. Trudeau raced through Southern Ontario, speaking to huge crowds in shopping centers, kissing, shaking hands, gathering flowers in his open convertible and hammering away at the theme of national unity.

From London, Ontario he flew to Mont Joli, on the Gaspé peninsula, and to his first cool reception of the campaign. In

Matane, where his former executive assistant, Pierre De Bané was the Liberal candidate, he had a look at the new $8,000,000 deep water port and told a big crowd that he wanted De Bané with him in Ottawa.

De Bané had decided to run on the spur of the moment. He had been helping Trudeau get ready for the swearing-in ceremony at Government House on April 20, and the Prime Minister had asked him what he would like to do. "Well," said De Bané thoughtfully, as the Prime Minister pottered around in his undershorts, looking for his striped trousers, "if you can run for Prime Minister, Pierre Trudeau, I can run for parliament."

And so he did.

From Matane, Trudeau went to Rimouski to sign into action a $258-million rural development plan for the Gaspé region. The federal share was $212-million and the presence of Quebec Premier Daniel Johnson gave Trudeau a fine opportunity for a brief lesson in federalism. "It is precisely from the combination of the projects of each major region that will emerge a complete vision of Canada that will encompass and exceed the dreams of each province."

At Rivière du Loup, he visited the local *Cité des Jeunes* comprehensive high school and pickets outside carried placards reading, "From One Waterhole to Another" and "What About Our Lousy French?" and "$250-million for the plan, yes; Vote for Trudeau, no".

He opened a softball league in Three Rivers, Quebec, by smashing the ball deep into center field, to the cheers of the crowd; then he headed east for Halifax, and an uncharacteristic sulk in a Dartmouth, N.S. shopping center where he abruptly ended his speech saying: "If you don't want to listen, okay . . ." He had mistaken the noisy enthusiasm of Arnie's Army (teenage supporters of Liberal candidate Arnold Peterson) for heckling. He toured the Annapolis valley, abloom with apple blossom, but he was deep in Stanfield country and the crowds were muted, the weather miserable.

His jet took off from Greenwood forces base for St. John's, Newfoundland, but the Atlantic fog had rolled in and after approaching to within 200 feet of the runway with full flaps and wheels down, Captain Ralph Leek decided to abort the landing with a steep climb out of the crud which had newsmen quaking all the way to Gander.

Stanfield on the other hand, spent most of the week in Ontario. He told Tories in Sarnia that he was against Canada's entry into the OAS and two days later, in Wingham, said there were several things about the Criminal Code omnibus bill that he did not like.

As May turned to June, Trudeau went West again for a tour through the interior of British Columbia. In six small towns, crowds which totalled 15,000 turned out to meet him. The teeny-boppers were disappearing, too, put to useful work as "Trudeau Girls" in the orange and white shifts which became the rage of all Trudeau supporters after the convention (national headquarters sent color cards and patterns for the dresses and beanies to all Liberal ridings). The girls would act as crowd marshals, eliminating the need for police barriers, and getting guaranteed front-row positions for adoration.

In Kamloops, he told a crowd of 5,000 that the Tories were the ones who were making the constitution into an issue. "It is the Conservative Party who are speaking about two nations in one part of the country and trying to make the rest of the country forget about it." In Penticton, he had flap-jacks with a crowd that went well beyond the 2,000 anticipated, because the organizers quickly ran out of pancake mix. At Kelowna, he stood on an airport baggage cart to talk to the crowd and later they entertained him in turn by singing "Alouette" and "Frère Jacques". Each time he spoke French there was applause, warm, sincere applause that seemed to say 'We're with you, Pierre'. And it was "Pierre" everywhere. Never "Mr. Prime Minister", or "Sir", or "the Minister" as his supporters used to try to get people to call him during the leadership race. Even the Doukhobors were for Trudeau and in Castlegar they sang him some haunting old Russian songs of their own — plus one in French to make him welcome.

Few places on this earth are lovelier than the interior of British Columbia in early June when the broom, the lupins and Indian paintbrush are in flower and the orange blossom growing wild above Penticton gives the air its special fragrance.

But there was also sadness that week. In Edmonton, early in the morning of June 5, after another tumultuous rally, Trudeau heard the news of the shooting of Robert Kennedy in Los Angeles. He planned to fly back to Montreal that day for the funeral of his old friend, André Laurendeau, co-chairman of the Royal Commission on Bilingualism and Biculturalism, and the journey to Montreal was made more poignant by the hospital bulletins from Los Angeles, relayed to Trudeau's plane by Air Traffic controllers along the route.

Mike Berzoski, a 70-year-old pensioner, was pinned against the wall of the Macdonald Hotel in Edmonton as Trudeau left to catch his 5 a.m. flight. Berzoski, a quiet, gentle old man, had a box of stale bread rolls and old mashed potato that he wanted to show Trudeau so he would know what old age pensioners were forced to live on. But the police were afraid Berzoski might throw the box at Trudeau. They would take no risks from then until the campaign was over. Tough men with brush-cut hair and hard features would mingle with the crowds wherever Trudeau went, the bulges under their wind-breakers were guns and walky-talkies.

On Thursday, June 6, when Robert Kennedy died from his wounds, some teenage separatists at a rally in Rouyn, in northern Quebec, taunted Trudeau too far. He lashed out at them. "You," he shouted back, eyes narrowed with fury, "you little hate-pedlars! You are like the ones who killed Kennedy!" The separatists shouted back at him, *Vive le Québec Libre*, and he replied, *Vive le Canada Libre!*

Stanfield was in the Maritimes once more that week. A taping session in Toronto on his way to Prince Edward Island on Monday put the tour an hour behind — and there was no way of catching up. But P.E.I. is solid Tory country, and Stanfield had little to fear from Trudeaumania there. He visited the site of his grandfather's first woolen mill, at Tryon, on the south-west coast, and a local resident presented him with a long-forgotten photograph of the "Tryon Woolen Mills." The rest of the day he visited local school-houses where large numbers of children and small groups of adults listened gratefully to the platitudes.

The big event Monday evening was in Charlottetown's main arena, the Kennedy Coliseum, a building that could easily be mistaken for a cattle-barn with its red dirt floor, plank protected bleacher seats and green galvanized steel roof.

Colonel Grey's Legion Band warmed up the audience of 2,500 with oompah versions of "The Lonely Bull" and "Colonel Bogey", and, the Montague Teenaires choir sang a song about Prince Edward Island.

A giant blow-up of an idealized full-face portrait of Stanfield dominated the arena. "The more you think about it, Stanfield is the man," said the slogan underneath.

Stanfield was in a Grit-hitting mood on Monday night and the islanders loved it. "The Liberals issued their platform this week," he said, "It is profound — profound in its ignorance of the important problems facing Canadians." The crowd cheered. A few signs saying "Sock it to 'em, Bob", were wagged hard. And so it went. He was still hopeless at meeting people, which he had to do afterwards, offering a claw-like hand and croaked, plummy cordialities. But unlike Trudeau, he could read a speech. His austere, undemonstrative style fitted well with the need to glance down at the text, a need concealed by his sleepy eyelids and heavy eyebrows, while the very slowness of his ordinary speech makes reading aloud sound like flowing rhetoric.

He had also learned to wait for the laughter, even though he still appeared faintly bemused by it, like someone unaware that he has been funny. But it was better than the professorial deadpan which used to frost the audience in mid-guffaw.

When he got down to what the Conservatives would do, the partisan crowd began to sound like a revivalists.

He poured scorn on the "Marshall Plan for the Maritimes" Trudeau had promised the week before. "The people of these regions will not be taken for fools. The problems are much too real and much too serious to be dealt with by gimmicks and slogans such as a new department or a so-called Marshall Plan." He said the Tories would "beef up" the Atlantic Development Board by moving its headquarters to the Maritimes and bringing other programs such as ARDA and ADA under its control. They would raise old age pensions "rescuing the elderly from the subsistence level at which many of them are still trapped."

"That's right!" came the shouts.

He said the Liberals were "all old hangers-on of the Pearson administration."

"You tell 'em, Bob," yelled the crowd.

He said Liberal strategy was designed to "strike while the iron of publicity is still hot. Well now it's pretty cold and rusty," he said.

"Give 'em hell, Bob!"

The Lobster Carnival Queen turned out to welcome him to Shediac, New Brunswick, the following day, and a little Cessna towing an aerial sign, "Stanfield Is Here", announced Misajumax's arrival at Moncton Airport. He promised New Brunswick Acadians that a Tory government would favor a French language educational TV network and felt that CBC French broadcasting should be extended.

That night the Tories held a large meeting in Moncton High School and once again Stanfield put on a fighting display that pleased his supporters. "They must be the most inept government in the industrialized world," he declared, his scorn for the Liberals dripping from every word. "And yet they ask for a mandate on the 25th day of June. This is surely irresponsibility on a grand scale."

On Wednesday, the mood was somber. The news of Kennedy's assassination had filtered through the creaky corridors of Moncton's Brunswick Hotel soon after dawn. On the campaign plane, between Moncton and Saint John, people spoke about Kennedy or not at all. The heart seemed to go out of the campaign for the rest of the day. In Saint John people huddled in groups listening for news on transistor radios. At a press conference, Stanfield came out in favor of tighter firearms legislation.

That night, at the Paramount movie theater across the square from the Admiral Beatty Hotel, Stanfield made an unprecedented tribute to John Diefenbaker — a tribute that had observers guessing that things were not going well for the Tories on the Prairies. He talked about "the passionate zeal with which John Diefenbaker championed the oppressed and forgotten of the world" and said "his legacy of compassion and humanity will be honored and upheld".

On Thursday, Stanfield flew to Quebec. Kennedy died early that morning. Stanfield, pale and drawn from fatigue, spoke briefly about it to reporters in the lobby of the Admiral Beatty before leaving for the airport. The weather was glorious all the way and

by the time the DC-7 let down into Quebec City's Ancienne
Lorette airport, the depression had lifted. Stanfield's day in Quebec
was a strange one. He and his daughter Sarah and an aide, Bernard
Flynn, spent most of it visiting smaller communities in a chartered
DH-125 (the same one that Trudeau had used during his leadership campaign), rented from Montreal's Execaire at $600 per
hour. While the rest of the party took the DC-7 to Rivière du
Loup and Mont Joli. Stanfield caught up at Rivière du Loup for
a drive through town with the Tory candidate, lawyer Antonio
Dubé. The drive was a disaster. Not a soul came out to wave or
cheer and the cavalcade hastily saved face with a visit to St.
Patrice, where Sir John A. MacDonald's black and yellow clapboard summer house still stands, a Tory shrine of a sort.

Stanfield then jetted off to the town of Gaspé, on the other side
of the peninsula, while the DC-7 hopscotched to Mont-Joli, and
the rest of the party piled into buses for Matane, where Stanfield
would host a monster rally and "Habitant" bean supper later in
the evening.

But the only monsters at the rally turned out to be hungry little
boys and their older brothers and sisters, who were much more
interested in eating beans and dancing to the raucous yé-yé music
of Daniel and His Soul-Mates, Matane's answer to Lester Lanin.

Stanfield made the most of a bad scene with the help of a short
speech in French and a large plate of beans, topped with a frosted
bun. It was hard to say which he found more indigestible.

The next event was the "Great TV Debate" between the party
leaders which took place in Ottawa on Sunday, June 9, in a Gothic
set which suited Stanfield's physiognomy better than it did the
others. In fact he said he enjoyed it. "The two hours went very
quickly, I was not bored at all."

However the viewers seemed to agree with the Créditiste leader,
Réal Caouette, who called it "a waste of time", and Prime Minister
Trudeau, who said "I wouldn't want to impose another one on the
Canadian public."

In fact, the TV show was neither great nor a debate but a very
boring panel show in which each leader was asked questions by a
panel of newsmen. The Liberals had insisted that all the party
leaders take part, which eliminated the possibility of a confronta-

tion between the two important figures in the election, and ended
any chance of true debate. Imposing the newsmen was an even
worse idea. Trudeau quickly tired of the dreary progress of the
"debate", and his boredom was obvious.

Some critics said that Stanfield did best in the TV show, others
felt it suited Douglas better. While to Quebeckers, it was clearly
Caouette's practised TV personality (he has used television regularly since 1962) which gained the most from the exposure. Conventional wisdom said Trudeau flopped.

Yet, flop or not, it was Trudeau's campaign which caught fire in
the weeks that followed, not the others.

"Do you wear a hair-piece, Mr. Trudeau?" asked a cheeky
tike in Regina.

"No, it's all my own," replied the Prime Minister, tugging a
thinning forelock. The crowd roared with laughter. It was Monday
afternoon in Regina and the locals could not remember ever seeing a crowd like it in Wascana Park.

To be sure there had been a trace of post-debatum blues aboard
Flight 99 that morning, as it lifted off Upland's runway Three Left
and headed for Regina. Panelist Ron Collister was asked how he
felt his "Laugh-in" had gone — a sarcastic reference to the fact
that the debate pre-empted the popular Rowan and Martin show.
But, if Trudeau's image had slipped in debate, there was no mistaking the crisp focus he achieved in Saskatchewan. At Regina
airport, a Gay Nineties quartet belonging to the Buffalo Days
festival grabbed him on the ramp and ordered him to change there
and then into a maroon waistcoat, black ribbon tie, and a Stetson,
before he could shrug his way out of it. Once into costume, the
ham took over and, looking more like a Louisiana riverboat
gambler than a pillar of the West, he announced firmly: "I will
deal the cards."

He then smiled and murmured sweet appreciation to the inevitable group of teenagers dressed in regulation Trudeau orange
shifts. ("We changed the Liberal color from red to orange," claims
Merle Shain). The girls' leader told Trudeau proudly that they
had each made their own dress — though a glance would have told
him as much. "Did you *really*?" he said in his inimitable way, as
if he would never have guessed, if they hadn't told him. "They are

very nice, very pretty," murmured the old fraud, clearly at a loss for what to say next about a subject which was beginning to bore him stiff. But an organizer rescued him and he said a few words about national unity in the airport lobby before being swept away to a squadron of Cessnas for a tour of Prairie ridings. The crowd cheered and waved. "Trudeau is a Hunk", said one sign, while "P.E.T. is our Pet" enthused another. There were also bilingual signs in unilingual Regina. "Vive le Canada, Merci Pierre!"

The Trudeau campaign pattern was firmly established. A brief speech to an enthusiastic airport crowd of party stalwarts, a motorcade to a crowded shopping plaza or town square meeting, another brief speech, questions, then away again to the motorcade, passing through the crowd, squeezing hands, being touched by hands — though kissing was becoming rarer.

Of six pretty girls, who lined up with single roses for him at the entrance to the Regina Inn, only one long-stemmed blonde managed to hit her target. The others chickened out. The respect for the office finally seemed to be coming through, particularly in the West. Now, like some Caesar-cut Maharishi, it seemed to be sufficient to touch the man. Teenagers would drop back into the crowd after he passed, holding their hands and shrieking as if stung by a wasp. But then their admirers would cluster around and the hand-clutcher would shout happily, "I touched him! I touched him!"

The crowds were changing, too. They were not just teenagers, they were Everyman, from weather-beaten farmers who had driven wife and kids three hours in the pick-up truck to see "this here True-dough thet everybody's talkin' about," as one of them put it, to cool city lawyers, stopping off on their way home from the office. As Trudeau spoke in Wascana Park that evening, even the weather cooperated dramatically, and dark clouds that had hung low over the prairie all day started to peel away as he talked, letting the golden evening sun shine down.

He talked to them quietly, in conversational tones, and many people would say his speeches were more like lectures than political pitches, which was true. He showed great respect for the intelligence of his audience whether it was a group of red-necked farmers or school children.

Standing on the Provincial Youth Agency Showmobile in Wascana Park he made a speech that he had already made three, six, ten dozen times. But there was always some slight variation which made it a personal speech to them. He says he gets bored making the same speech twice.

He made a devastating rebuttal of the muddled Tory and NDP arguments for a special status for Quebec and gave his own, clear, cool logical argument for pluralism and for recognition of the languages that happen to be spoken by the country's two main linguistic groups. He said a few words in French, as he always did, and the crowd applauded hard, as it always did in English Canada. Only in French Canada were there boos when he said his piece in English — and the boos were quickly drowned in the cheers.

He went on to a provincial fund-raising banquet at Regina's Curlodrome and on his way met the province's oldest Trudeau fan, 91-year-old W. M. Martin, the oldest living premier of Saskatchewan. "Very good of you to show such an interest, Sir," said Trudeau. The old man was wearing a Trudeau button. "Someone pinned it on me when I arrived," explained Martin, with the guilelessness of the very old and very young.

At Brandon, Manitoba, it was the same thing. Crowds lined the streets for an hour in light drizzle just to watch him pass by. Once again, Trudeau took a light plane, a Piper Navajo, for quick visits to Neepawa, Dauphin and Portage La Prairie. In Neepawa, the Ukrainian community gave him a boxful of "real Ukrainian food"; in Dauphin, he talked about wheat and Canada's percentage of the world market. In Portage La Prairie, he talked about national unity in the parking lot in front of the Safeway supermarket. "I don't think it's through any historic right that English and French are the two main languages of Canada," he told the audience, largely descended from stock which was neither French nor English. But, he went on, the French and English languages are the main languages of Canada because the people who speak them make up the two major population blocs.

Then it was back to the DC-9, soaring high over thunderclouds at the Lakehead. The cumulo-nimbus anvil-heads stopped over northern Michigan, and as the jet flew clear of cloud, it seemed to float over the edge of a great cliff, 30,000 feet of clear air beneath the wings and a sun-dappled summer countryside. Then it was Windsor, huddled across the Detroit river from the proud, menacing skyscrapers of the city whose name is synonymous with superb automobiles and dreadful riots. The temperature was a stifling, near-tropical 87 degrees, a violent change from the cool 48 degree drizzle of Western Manitoba.

Trudeau spoke to the shirt-sleeved crowd down by the grey, ugly riverside, in a place named Dieppe Gardens in memory of one of Canada's greatest military sacrifices and blunders of the Second World War. Police were everywhere. On every roof and overpass, with rifles and field glasses, they watched and waited. The atmosphere was filled with forboding, a mood heightened by the dark towers across the river. Somehow in Windsor, within hailing distance of the United States, the problems were less parochial, the mood more nervous, the presence of a crueler, wider world much closer than the comfortable, cosy, sleepy Canada that lay to the extreme West and East.

Windsor is a strong NDP area, and Trudeau was in a fighting mood. The NDP obliged him with a persistent heckler who got much the worst of it, to shouts of "Attaboy, Pierre!" from the summery crowd and of course more "Sock it to hims" than Rowan and Martin could use in a dozen scripts.

"The NDP is talking about problems it can solve because it is not in power," said Trudeau. He pointed out that the NDP first broached a two-nations theory in 1961, but in eight years had got no further. "You are okay on housing. You are okay on giving more money to people, but on real problems, what have you done?" he asked the heckler. "We have heard the leader of the NDP in Quebec say that if the NDP were in power it would give us a new constitution in a year. What do you mean by two nations? What do you mean by special status for Quebec? You introduced an amendment in the House asking the government for special status for Quebec. Well, this might be something we would look at if you could tell us what you meant."

He turned back to the crowd, pointing a jabbing finger at the heckler.

"In seven years they have not been able to tell us what they want. A vote for the NDP is a vote for confusion and doubletalk."

The heckler said he didn't "give a damn about Quebec."

Trudeau was on him again in a flash.

"Here's a member of the NDP who doesn't care a damn about Quebec. And the other day we heard about the Quebec leader of the NDP who doesn't give a damn about the rest of Canada."

He said the NDP let Cliche say what he liked in Quebec while Douglas said what he liked outside. "In the Liberal party we want to say the same in all parts of the country. And that's why we don't want Quebec to have a special status."

He said Canada was not two nations sociologically, as two nations proponents claimed, because it was dozens of nations sociologically, with Eskimos and Indians getting prior claim.

He was interrupted by the NDP heckler — and invited him to go jump in the river, to the approval of the crowd.

"I am going on a bit, aren't I?" he said.

"You go on, Pierre Boy!" came the encouraging supporter again.

Then it was off again, in cars and buses — convertibles to the city limits for Trudeau and then a closed car to the next city. The police surveillance continued, RCMP, Ontario Provincial Police, city police — tall cops, squat cops, helicopter cops and motorcycle cops in golden helmets, plus dozens of plainclothesmen. The heat of the day had sent thunderclouds boiling up across the mid-West from Ohio, and as the motorcade raced along Highway 401 to Chatham, a brace of tornados were seen skipping along behind under the thunderheads.

At Chatham the thunderstorm broke, lashing the streets with floods and water, but the Trudeau juggernaut never faltered. An open-air park meeting had an alternative site in an armory, there was a brief talk about unity, bilingualism (cheers) and regional disparity. The rich provinces would help pay for the poorer provinces in Trudeau's Just Society. And the audience cheered that too.

Back in their air-conditioned highway cruiser bus, the press were feeling the pace of a 2,000-mile day in tropical heat. Liberal organizers had made sure the bus was equipped with toilet facilities and six cases of cool beer — all gratefully appreciated that night — and portable typewriters rapped out leads for late night and early morning editions as the big machine ate up the 80 miles to London, Ontario, in 80 minutes, for an on-schedule arrival at the "Treasure Island Shopping Center", in a Western suburb.

It was the eighth stop that day. The pace was killing. Trudeau looked washed out. But the magic thing called applause could still revive him. The arena was packed with the liveliest, prettiest, most enthusiastic crowd of the week. "It was like the Ottawa convention all over again," beamed one organizer, admiring the orange shifts, long-legged blondes and curvaceous brunettes, the balloons and the bunting, the banners and placards and all those excited, eager young faces.

The welcoming crowd cheered itself hoarse and Trudeau's nostrils flared like a thoroughbred. Suddenly, the fatigue was gone, the wan smile, too. And he was ready to perform again. "It's hard to believe that the country is going as badly as the others say, when you get a reception like this," he said. And he talked about the economy, how the GNP had doubled in a decade, how Canada was "one of the richest and most stable countries in the world."

He poured scorn on Stanfield's plan for a guaranteed annual income ("I would not buy a set of long underwear, if I didn't know how much it cost") because the Tories could put no price tab on it. He talked about unity, and his few words in French had them cheering again.

Exhilarated and exhausted, he was driven out to the airport for another tremendous farewell. Tie, jacket and shoes were off the moment he reached his seat and sat back. The jet took off home for Ottawa.

Wednesday morning was devoted to affairs of state and, in the afternoon, a taping session at City Hall, Toronto, for the "Public Eye". Hundreds of teenagers had staked out every possible exit at City Hall — but Trudeau escaped by way of the under-ground garage. At Malton the jet was waiting to take-off for Prince Edward Island. Trudeau spent that night in the bridal suite at the Garden of the Gulf Motel in Summerside, appearing reluctantly on the balcony to wave to some persistent fans who were clearly intending to stay outside shouting "We Want Trudeau" all night. To cries of "Speech!" he replied: "Since the events of last summer, I have decided never to make balcony speches. Good night." He waved. They laughed at the reference to de Gaulle. And everyone went home to bed.

Thursday was another triumph of Liberal organization, a helicopter tour across Prince Edward Island, a massive rally on the steps of the Confederation Memorial building in Charlottetown, and a motorcade through Summerside that brought out the staff of the general hospital, including what looked like the entire staff of the operating theater. "Did he live?" a newsman shouted as the bus went by. The nurses giggled.

From P.E.I., it was over to Cape Breton. Trudeau went by jet to Trenton and then by helicopter to Port Hawkesbury, where the Minister of Health, Allan J. MacEachen, was running in the new riding of Cape Breton-Highlands-Canso, and getting some tough competition from the Conservative, Hugh Gillis. (MacEachen won the seat by only 578 votes in the end).

The jet part of the trip was alright, and so was Captain Jos di Giacinto's helicopter flight plan until they ran into a bank of coastal fog and started bucking 65-mph head winds. They were an hour behind schedule when the helicopter fluttered down on Albert Malcolm's farm at Port Malcolm, 1½ miles off their target, the Stan Ellis farm at Port Richmond, where MacEachen was waiting.

Malcolm asked if the passenger was "that fella True-dough" and, on being assured it was, pointed the direction to the farm. The three-seater Bell took off again into the fog. Half an hour later Malcolm happened to peer out of his farmhouse window when that fella Trudeau whirly-birded down again, having failed to find Port Richmond for the second time.

This time Angus Cogswell, a friend of Malcolm's, offered to drive them over to the Ellis farm, where they duly arrived, unnoticed, while Ellis, MacEachen and a Mountie confidently peered upwards into the fog with binoculars assuring each other, "I can hear them, they're coming. . . ."

The light drizzle let-up for part of Trudeau's speech in the wet, puddled Port Hawkesbury shopping center. He talked about unity and regional disparity and the Cape Breton Development Corporation, and how by "designated means . . . the federal government helps bring resources to certain areas and certain provinces so that they will become self-sustaining — much like the Marshall Plan by which the United States permitted Europe to recover its economy — not for charity or even for humanitarian reasons, but because it was important to the peace of the world."

Then it was good-bye, "vote for Allan MacEachen", and a

65-mile drive back to Sydney by car through steady drizzle, hypnotized by the sweep of the windshield wipers and the swish of tires on wet roads and the twirling red flasher of the RCMP escort in front. The rain had stopped at Sydney and at the airport nearly 5,000 people, entire families, had come out to wave good-bye to Trudeau. Then Flight 99 spread her slats, her twin engines howled to life, and the big jet turned away down the taxi path to the runway, turned again, and raced down the rain-slicked tarmac and was gone, smoothly rotated and launched into the night, to battle stiff head-winds for two and a half hours, all the way to Toronto.

Friday dawned clear and sunny, but photographers waited in vain for him to come down for a morning dip at the Constellation Hotel pool. At Oakville's Holiday Inn they were luckier — campaign manager Bill Lee had thoughtfully arranged to have a pair of swimming trunks ready for Trudeau — and the world was treated to a diving display by the Prime Minister of All Canada that no other Canadian politician in memory could match. From the hotel pool's one-meter board, Trudeau's repertoire included front and back flips, a front layout with a half twist, and backwards somersaults and a one-and-a-half tuck. At someone's suggestion, he even showed how he thought Stanfield and Douglas might do in a similar situation. From beginning to end, it was a performance for the gallery, and a ham actor named Trudeau loved it. Sex reared its lovely head with a Prime Ministerial invitation to pretty U. of T. co-ed, Sharon Waterman, 19, to join him in the pool. She declined, saying she did not have a bathing suit. Trudeau suggested it was not necessary. "Marilyn Monroe did it," he said.

The rest of the day was a whirlwind tour of the Niagara peninsula, Burlington, St. Catharines, Hamilton — huge crowds in shopping centers, tremendous applause, little heckling. The Hamilton meeting took place in the Tiger Cats stadium where 18,000 people jammed into one section to hear him. The campaign was moving so fast now that places, events and people were beginning to blur. But there was no mistaking that Hamilton crowd. This was the start of a sweep. Mark it down, newsmen told themselves, the date was June 14. Then the jet was away again, to Chicoutimi, Quebec, the heart of the Kingdom of the Saguenay. A land of craggy hills and wide lakes, rushing rivers and deep gorges. It's a land Trudeau has known since childhood, hiking up through the forests from La Tuque to Roberval, canoeing down the Saguenay River or across that great inland sea, Lac St. Jean.

In Chicoutimi on Saturday morning, 60 members of the local "Asterix" motorcycle club donned scarlet jumpsuits and gunned their Yamahas and Triumphs in tribute to Trudeau, volunteering their services as traffic marshals for the man who has made leather jackets respectable. In St. Félicien, the local "Satanix" club took over. And all day, their supercharged motorcycles zipped up and down the motorcade like wheeled dragonflies.

He said the same things in the Quebec heartland as he had in English Canada, unity, participation, bilingualism. He praised Frère Untel, who was born in the little town of Alma, and he talked about regional disparities, "you don't build a great country by thinking only of your own little province or parish."

This was the day that Dr. Joyce Brothers entered the campaign with her assessment of Trudeau's appeal to women. Her conclusion was that Trudeau had machismo — a Spanish term for what she called a "sexy forcefulness and daring in a man."

The final week of the campaign confirmed the impression that a sweep was building up. Sunday and Monday, Trudeau was in British Columbia for huge rallies in Vancouver and Victoria; Tuesday, it was Calgary and Fort William; Wednesday a colossal rally in Toronto's City Hall plaza, Nathan Phillips Square, where 60,000 people turned out for a ticker-tape parade up Bay Street and for the rally; Thursday he streaked across the country to Edmundston, New Brunswick and a day in light planes around the Maritimes; Friday, it was Montreal, and another mammoth rally of about 45,000 in Place Ville Marie.

On Saturday, June 22, even Claude Ryan admitted the possibility of a Trudeau sweep. Trudeau himself spent the day in southeastern Ontario, visiting Brockville, Kingston and Oshawa to a series of big crowds, thunderous cheers and speeches about unity and participation. He wound up doing nip-ups in a Vic Tanny Spa.

As Trudeau's campaign soared, Stanfield's drooped. His wind-up rally in Toronto was a disaster, his Montreal visit was practically washed out by rain. When Trudeau appeared the clouds seemed to clear, the sun to shine; when Stanfield came by, the weather seemed to combine against him.

A Gallup poll the Saturday before the election showed the Liberals with 42% and the Conservatives with 26%, NDP 16% and others 5%. Political scientist, Peter Regenstreif would write the same day, "all the signs point to a victory for Prime Minister Pierre Elliott Trudeau. The big question is how much?"

Trudeau and Stanfield campaigned down to the last day. On Sunday Trudeau was in Winnipeg for the Red River Exhibition and parade.

Even the separatists helped publicize Trudeau. A story in the Montreal paper, Dimanche *Dernière-Heure* on Sunday, June 23, carried a separatist threat that an attempt would be made on his life if he attended the St. Jean Baptiste parade the following day.

That too, provided a triumph for Trudeau.

The election results seemed inevitable.

XVIII

The End of the Affair

A NUN CLASPED both of his hands in hers in motherly concern and exclaimed: "I am so glad you weren't killed last night!"

"But my goodness," replied Trudeau, "I was sitting beside the Archbishop!"

The school-room scene was repeated again and again after the *St. Jean Baptiste* parade riot. "You were so brave", "We prayed for you", "We admired your courage so much," they said, as he visited polling stations in Mount Royal on election morning, June 25, smiling, nodding, shaking hands and shyly disclaiming any credit. "I was just curious to see what was happening," he said. "I didn't want to miss anything."

Only one fan left him speechless, possibly for the first time in the campaign.

A pretty 14-year-old, who had already persuaded him to part with his *boutonnière* ("be kind to it" he said as he gave the rose away), and asked, but failed, to get a lift in his car downtown, finally tapped him on the shoulder, as he was about to leave. "Sir?"

"Yes, oh it's you again," said the Prime Minister.

"You know, you're a good shit, sir," said the girl.

"Well," said Trudeau. "Well, really." And trying hard to suppress a smile, he climbed into his car, and drove away.

"Well he is," said the girl, defensively, as a Mountie wagged a reproving finger at her.

Trudeau had a sandwich lunch in his committee rooms, dropped by a few more polling stations and then flew back to Ottawa in the DC-9.

There was nothing to be done except wait. He visited the Liberal Federation headquarters, in its quaint old Victorian house on Cooper Street, and then went home to change into fresh clothes to watch returns at the Chateau Laurier, in a private suite the party had rented for him and his guests. When he returned from Sussex Drive for the evening at the hotel, he was wearing a freshly pressed grey suit, the same one he had worn when he won the leadership convention, a tattersall check shirt, a maroon silk tie in a Macclesfield print, his favorite monk-strap loafers and a tiny rosebud in his button-hole.

He went straight upstairs to his fifth floor suite, Room 598, a lavish two-bedroom and drawing room layout, decorated in grey and white, with crystal chandeliers and French Provincial furniture. Many of his guests were already there — the Pearsons, Senator Nichol and his wife, members of the Trudeau family, party workers such as Porteous, Levasseur and Davey, friends and supporters like Marc Lalonde and television producer, Patrick Watson.

Newfoundland polls closed first, and the trend there was ominous. Seven Liberal seats were abruptly reduced to one, leaving Don Jamieson (Burin-Burgeo) as the only Grit left. "They jumped on the Tory bandwagon just as the wheels fell off," said Jamieson of his fellow Newfoundlanders.

Nova Scotia, which had lost one seat in redistribution, was predictably Tory and the province voted massively to support its former premier. Only one (out of two in 1965) Liberal survived, Allan MacEachen, who squeaked to victory in Cape Breton-Highlands.

Prince Edward Island, solidly Conservative federally in 1965, ignored the endorsement of Trudeau by its Liberal premier, Alex Campbell, and remained Tory in all four seats. P.E.I. was regarded as a trend area in any Liberal sweep. If the Liberals were going to win, they would do it there. They did not. The outlook was gloomy.

Even Liberal New Brunswick failed to deliver for Trudeau. The Liberals had six seats in the province in 1965, wound up with five in 1968.

Shortly after nine, the results began coming in from Quebec and Ontario. The mood in Room 598 improved, rapidly, and a bottle of the Chateau Laurier's best champagne, Dom Perignon (1961), at $29.35, was opened. Several more would follow, with good reason.

In Quebec, the Liberals were holding their own, and the Conservatives were being wiped out, their representation reduced from seven to three. Marcel Faribault was beaten in Montreal-Gamelin by Sauvé's nemesis, Arthur Portelance. In Quebec City, Jean Marchand won decisively in Langelier, while the National Union Conservative candidate, Rodrigue Pageau, came third, after the Créditiste. Heward Grafftey, Roger Régimbal and Russell Keays lost their supposedly solid Tory seats too. Trudeau's former executive assistant, Pierre De Bané, won in Matane; Eric Kierans beat the NDP Quebec leader Robert Cliche in Montreal-Duvernay; while the Prime Minister himself chalked up 94.6% of the vote in Mount Royal, the third highest majority in Canadian history. The Conservative runner-up got only 1,965 votes.

The Quebec returns did hold some shocks for the Liberals. Maurice Sauvé failed to unseat Théogène Ricard in St. Hyacinthe. In Bellechasse, the mercurial Auguste Choquette lost to a Créditiste, one of six Créditiste victories which would boost Réal Caouette's House membership from eight to 14. The resurgence of the Créditiste movement (all their gains were from Liberals) was a warning to the Trudeau administration that the concerns of rural Quebec are economic and not constitutional, since the Créditistes support the Liberals on their constitutional position but are sharply critical of the handling of the economy.

The Ontario results were just as dramatic. Dalton Camp, Ralph Cowan, Douglas Fisher, Wallace McCutcheon, all lost their contests with Liberals. Camp, in particular, was defeated by a political neophyte, 31-year-old Robert Kaplan. Cowan, running as an Independent Liberal after losing the nomination, got beaten by the party candidate. The NDP took a beating in Ontario with the defeat of Fisher, who was attempting a political come-back after three years as a newspaper columnist; with Murdo Martin's loss to Liberal Jean Roy in Timmins; and with the loss of Dr. William Howe in Hamilton-Mountain, a loss Howe himself blamed on drug-manufacturers backing his opponent. The accusation proved to be untrue, although Dr. Howe had led the NDP attack on drug manufacturers in Parliament and had demanded tougher price controls.

Though the results from Quebec and Ontario were encouraging, Liberals, they left them far short of the over-all majority they wanted.

As the polls started to close in the West, the Liberals seemed certain to equal their 1965 total (they had 131 in 1965 against

130 as the results passed from the Eastern to Central Standard time-zone), but whether they would get the magic 134 for a working majority would depend entirely on the West.

Manitoba had been a Tory stronghold in 1965 when the Liberals won just a single seat, St. Boniface, with ten others going Conservative and three NDP. In 1968, Manitoba lost a seat with redistribution, which theoretically reduced the Liberal chances still more.

Nevertheless, it was Manitoba that gave Trudeau the first indication that he would have a slim majority. Five ridings went Liberal. The Western trend had started.

Saskatchewan had not elected a single Liberal or NDP member in 1965. In 1968, redistribution reduced provincial seats from 17 to 13, and the NDP surged ahead, winning six of them, the Tories held five, and the Liberals won two.

Alberta's seat allocation was increased from 17 to 19 under redistribution, but the province remained heavily Conservative with 15 seats (same as 1965) to four for the Liberals. The 1968 election saw the disappearance of Social Credit as a federal party. Of their five members in 1965, one, Robert Thompson (Red Deer) turned Tory and the other four were defeated.

As British Columbia's results started to come in, the Liberals already had a clear majority of 141. British Columbia had returned seven Liberals in 1965, three Conservatives, nine NDP, and three Social Creditors. The Liberals could hope for seven or better — and they got 15 — taking the Liberal majority up to 156 for the best result since Louis St. Laurent's 170 in 1953.

The results from the West were as full of surprises as the East had been. In Vancouver's Burnaby-Seymour, the leader of the NDP, Tommy Douglas, lost a see-saw, suspense-filled contest to the former leader of the B.C. Liberal party, Ray Perrault, by 138 votes. In Kamloops, Davie Fulton lost to Len Marchand, a Liberal. In Regina, Alvin Hamilton lost his seat to the NDP. And in Winnipeg, Duff Roblin lost to Liberal E. B. Osler, a political first-timer.

In Prince Albert, John Diefenbaker saw his party fall from 96 seats to 72, and he termed it "a calamitous disaster."

The final party standings were Liberals 155; Conservatives 72; NDP 22; Créditiste, 14; independent one (the Speaker).

Pierre Elliott Trudeau had won his mandate, overwhelmingly.

Statistically, the results showed that 75% of all eligible voters had cast their ballots, and that the Liberals had won 45.3% of the popular vote, five per cent more than in 1965. The Conservatives had won 31.4% and the NDP 17.2%, dropping 1% since 1965. The Créditistes had increased their vote by 5%. In voting ages, the Liberals did better with the younger under-40 group than they did with those older, but they showed an increasing trend in all age groups, as did the NDP. The Conservatives showed a losing trend in all age groups.

The reshaped House of Commons would include the first Canadian Negro MP, Tory Lincoln Alexander, a 46-year-old lawyer from Hamilton West; and the youngest MP ever elected to the Canadian Parliament, 22-year-old Lorne Nystrom, of Saskatoon, the NDP member from Yorkton-Melville.

It took time for the full implications of the election to sink in. For the Liberals, there was the easy mental adjustment to majority rule, after five years as a minority government. For the Opposition parties, there was the unpleasant fact that they were now members of a simple minority. What use was the new Créditiste strength to Caouette when the Liberals did not need to be nice to him anymore? What use the results in Saskatchewan for the NDP, when their great hopes in the urban areas of Ontario and Quebec had vanished in the Liberal majority?

The man most cruelly used by the electorate was undoubtedly Robert Stanfield, who had worked so hard to make his party's constitutional policy understood — only to have representation reduced to a handful where it mattered most, in Quebec. Manitoba was a humiliation. Ontario was another disaster area, the party reduced to 16 rural seats and completely shut out of Toronto, once all Tory, where the new ideas and men of the reformed Progressive Conservative party proved devastatingly resistable.

The Tories came out exactly divided, 25 members in the Atlantic provinces and 25 in the West, plus 22 in central Canada. It was mathematically neat, but politically depressing, to say the least.

The Liberals dominated central Canada and British Columbia, but were thinly represented on the Prairies and down East.

The NDP were well represented out West but thin in Central Canada and still non-existent from Quebec to the Atlantic.

Some idea of what Prime Minister Trudeau planned to do with

his majority came on July 5, when he revealed his enormous new cabinet at an evening press conference. Of its 29 members, 22 were under-50. Notable freshmen in Parliament were Eric Kierans, who moved straight into the job of Postmaster-General and an imminent postal strike; James Richardson, 46, millionaire Winnipeg financier, head of the family-owned brokerage business, who became a minister without portfolio assigned to examine the financial structure of Air Canada; and Otto Lang, 36, former Dean of the Law School of the University of Saskatchewan, who became a minister without portfolio with special responsibilities in legal matters, trade and commerce.

Members of Parliament raised to cabinet rank were Newfoundland's only Liberal, Donald Jamieson, 47, Minister of Defense Production (soon to become the Ministry of Supply); Ronald Basford, 36, Minister of Consumer and Corporate Affairs; H. A. "Bud" Olson, 42, Minister of Agriculture; Robert Andras to minister without portfolio; Jean-Eudes Dubé, to Veterans Affairs.

Shifts among existing cabinet ministers saw George McIlraith, 59, go to Solicitor General; Arthur Laing, 63, to Public Works; Allan MacEachen, 47, to Manpower and Immigration; Charles M. Drury, 56, to Treasury Board; Joe Greene, 48, to Energy, Mines and Resources; Jean-Pierre Côté, 42, to National Revenue; Jean Chrétien, 34, to Indian Affairs and Northern Development; Bryce Mackasey, 46, to Labor; Donald Macdonald, 36, to the Privy Council and House Leadership; John Munro, 37, to Health and Welfare; Jack Davis, 51, to Fisheries.

In addition, there were the highly significant shifts of Jean-Luc Pépin, 43, to the senior cabinet post of Industry, Trade and Commerce, the first French Canadian ever to hold such a major economic position; of Jean Marchand, 49, into Forestry and Rural Development (soon to become the Ministry of Regional Development and key department for coping with regional disparities); of John Turner, 39, into the senior post of Minister of Justice, recognition of the powerful support he has within the party; and of old friend, Gérard Pelletier, 49, to Secretary of State, the cultural czardom of Canada.

Trudeau left five portfolios unchanged: Mitchell Sharp, 57, in External Affairs; Paul Hellyer, 44, in Transport; Edgar Benson,

45, in Finance; Leo Cadieux, 60, in Defense; and Paul Martin, 65, minister without portfolio and leader of the government in the Senate.

The cabinet showed that the new Trudeau government would not hesitate to use talent regardless of political experience (Richardson, Lang), conflicting views (Basford, Andras, Côté), previous opposition (Kierans, MacEachen, Greene, Turner), regional concentration (nine were from Quebec) or anything else.

But Trudeau made it clear that he would not tolerate cabinet indiscretions from that point onward. The cabinet oath of secrecy was to be strictly inforced.

In an appropriate footnote to cabinet indiscretion, as it were, on the day that Trudeau announced his new cabinet, and new rules to match, Gerda Munsinger became Frau Ernst Wagner in the registry office of the Swabing District of Munich. She wore a silk dirndl dress and carried a bridal wreath of myrtle. Wagner himself wore a collarless Bavarian suit and later was host to friends at a wedding breakfast of white Bavarian sausage at a nearby tavern.

Meanwhile, the political events of the last few weeks proved too much for Quebec's Premier, Daniel Johnson, who was taken to Laval's Institute of Cardiology on July 3 suffering from "a mild heart attack." His doctor said Johnson's heart was in an "intermediary or pre-thrombiotic state" which a rest in bed and slow convalescence could improve. Johnson gave up smoking three packs of cigarettes a day and by the end of July was fit enough to leave the hospital to go to Bermuda to recuperate.

In mid-July, the *Montreal Star* published the results of a poll on the election. The findings were optimistic for Trudeau watchers. The poll found that 57% of French Canadians approved Trudeau's decision to attend the St. Jean Baptiste Day parade; 50% thought they were most impressed with Trudeau as national leader (13% preferred Caouette, 1% wanted Douglas or Stanfield); and 54% felt that French Canadian influence was increasing in Ottawa.

With that good news to buoy him, Trudeau took off for a tour of the Arctic islands — Banks, Melville and Cornwallis — where no Canadian Prime Minister had ever been while in office. He travelled 9,780 miles in his Jetstar and by DC-3, Otter and helicopter, camping overnight at Grise Fjord, on Ellesmere Island,

1,200 miles from the North Pole, fishing for arctic char and shoot-ing at nothing in particular. He went to Frobisher Bay where he met some Eskimo Go-Go dancing girls and to Fort Chimo where he met Jennie Snowball, the person who invented Ookpik, the arctic owl. And, being a celebrity, he picked up quite a lot of goodies, ranging from a $300 sealskin parka at Tuktoyaktuk, to a walrus worry-ring at Frobisher Bay.

Early in August, the Prime Minister completed the reorganiza-tion of his personal staff and, not surprisingly, several faithful Tru-deau men wound up on top of the mushroom. Marc Lalonde, 39, was named *chef du cabinet* and special counsel to the Prime Minister. Former Pearson staffers, Roméo Leblanc, 40, and James Wightman, 43, continued as press secretary and assistant press secretary respectively. Vic Chapman, 36, the friendly giant of the campaign plane, joined them. Jim Davey, became program chief. Pierre Levasseur, became the regional councillor in charge of regional desks, with Gwen Clark, as one of his assistants. Ivan Head, 38, deputy chief of the task force on the constitution under Carl Goldenberg, gave up being a part-time academic to become legislative assistant to Trudeau. Tim Porteous, became a special assistant in charge of research and speeches. And Gordon Gibson continued as Trudeau's personal assistant in charge of appoint-ments and travel plans.

By mid-August, newsmen on Parliament Hill were complaining that Trudeau's rules of cabinet secrecy had locked things up so tight that it was hard to get the time of day without going outside to look at the Peace Tower. They were reduced to barbershop gossip, literally, with Canadian Press interviewing Robert Barton, architect of Trudeau's "sculptured look". Barton confided that Tru-deau was "losing his hair on top, so we try to fill in the spots."

But if leaks had dried up, Trudeaumania suffered no drought. When he went to Stratford to see "Tartuffe", in English, under the direction of his old friend, Jean Gascon, his followers were out in their hundreds. Two teenagers, Mary Pinkney and Anne Hayes, both 15, even jumped fully-clothed into the water when he went swimming at St. Mary's Quarry, a nearby water-hole.

On August 30, Trudeau said that the federal government would cancel its "winter works program", under which Ottawa had invested some $300 million over the last decade in subsidized municipal works projects. A chorus of doom and gloom arose immediately from just about every municipality in Canada, faced with raising their own taxes to pay for winter works programs which were increasingly exercises in municipal boondoggling. A monastery in Quebec, for instance, turned itself into a municipality to qualify for the federal subsidy.

The no-nonsense Trudeau approach was confirmed the following week with the appointment of a four-man board to study government information services with an eye to coordination and rationalization.

Donald Macdonald, the tough young government House Leader, ran into storms of protest from the Opposition on September 5 over a four-point plan to speed up the House of Commons that suggested:

1. A two-day limit on debate at second reading unless the House rules otherwise. 2. A limit of 15 days debate on departmental estimates and six motions of non-confidence in any one session. Canadian debates on departmental estimates have traditionally taken from 25 to 75 days. In Britain there is a limit of 29 days on departmental debates but no limit on confidence motions. 3. Changes in budget procedures. 4. Changes in question periods so that only certain ministers will be "on duty" on certain days; questions be limited to certain hours, etc. The Opposition called it Liberal arrogance and refused to discuss it further.

But if Trudeau was intent on changing parliamentary procedures, there were no signs that he intended to change certain other time-honored political practices, commonly known as looking after your friends.

On September 11, the day before the 28th Parliament opened, Bob Giguère, 56, was rewarded for long service to Quebec Liberalism with an appointment to the Senate, bringing Liberal membership to 66 out of 102.

In Manitoba, Roger Teillet, the Minister of Veterans Affairs who failed to get renominated, was nevertheless made a commissioner of the Canadian Pension Commission, while John Matheson, who lost the Ontario riding of Leeds on a recount to Desmond Code, a Conservative, was made a county court judge.

The Speech from the Throne, on September 12, was overshadowed by what became known as "the Rossillon affair", involving Philippe Rossillon, secretary general of the High Committee for the Defense of the French Language, and the five-day visit he made in August to St. Pierre, Manitoba, 30 miles south of Winnipeg, without informing the Canadian government.

Prime Minister Trudeau told a news conference that Rossillon was a senior civil servant reporting directly to the office of Premier Couve de Murville and had been responsible for arranging a visit of four New Brunswick Acadian French Canadians to Paris in the spring of 1968, also without the knowledge of the Canadian government. (Other sources in Montreal revealed also that Rossillon had been in frequent contact with separatist groups over the years.) He said a cultural agreement exists between Canada and France which allows the French government to promote cultural activities among French Canadians with prior notification to Ottawa.

"I am afraid that a good many Canadians who are not French-speaking will be very much annoyed at this intervention, and I rather think that if French Canadians are going to plot with more or less secret agents of France in Canada, this can harm the French-Canadian interests in Canada. It is rather distasteful that the French government should not act directly through the accord but should do so in this underhanded and surreptitious way. . . . I think that nothing could be more harmful to the acceptance of the bilingual character of Canada in the provinces where French-speaking Canadians are a minority than having free agents of a foreign state coming into the country and agitating, as it were, to get the citizens of that particular province to act in a given way."

The Prime Minister's revelations about Rossillon followed yet another press conference by President Charles de Gaulle (September 9), in which Canada was listed as one of a number of biracial trouble spots, in the same bracket as Nigeria, Rhodesia, Cyprus and Malaysia. Trudeau suggested France was still disturbed by recent troubles and had not yet recovered her "logic."

The Throne Speech had none of the excitement of the Rossillon press conference or its continuing reverberations. It was sober and businesslike and indicated that most of the first session of the new Trudeau Parliament would be spent clearing up left-over business from the Pearson Parliament. No less than 47 bills were mentioned and the highlights, such as they were, included reintroduction of the Criminal Code omnibus bill, speeding up government machinery, marketing freshwater fish, reconsidering the Canada Development Corporation, coping with pollution, correcting anomalies in the labor law, and so on.

By the following week, French foreign minister, Michel Debré, had replied that Trudeau was "very badly informed" about Rossillon's activities in Canada, but Jean Lesage, the Liberal Opposition leader in Quebec, had joined in to support Trudeau, adding that Quebec ministers would be better employed doing some work at home in Quebec and visiting France rather less often.

The Rossillon case sputtered out the following week as Jean-Noel Tremblay, Quebec's Minister of Culture, announced his 10-point program to make French the working language of Quebec. The St. Leonard Catholic School Commission in suburban Montreal had got a head start on Tremblay's plan by imposing French on primary grades that fall. Suddenly, just as the rest of Canada was getting around to the idea of bilingualism, it looked as if Quebec was going to become unilingual.

It was at this point that Premier Johnson returned from convalescence in Bermuda, reassured English Canadians that there was no danger to minority rights in Quebec and then, most tragically, died in his sleep the following night.

The death of Johnson — only two weeks before he was to go on a visit to France as the guest of President de Gaulle — came at a crucial moment in Canadian political history. In the short-term, the outlook was confusing.

If his successor, Jean-Jacques Bertrand, a federalist, can assert his complete authority over the National Union cabinet, the future for Quebec-Ottawa relations can only be encouraging. The ambivalence of Johnson, his indecision, his tendency to say one thing in French and another thing in English, served Quebec ill at a time when precision and decisiveness were badly needed.

And if Jean-Jacques Bertrand fails to control the party?

Then the National Union will collapse and the option will be passed to the reformed Quebec Liberal party, under Jean Lesage, with its cautious adoption of Trudeau's bilingual federalism, or to

René Lévesque and his separatist, Parti Québecois, which offers the other clear alternative.

With the National Union or without it, Quebec will be forced by events to make up its mind. The middle road, the status quo, the continuing crisis of uncertainty cannot last under Bertrand as it did under Johnson. But which way Quebec moves will depend as much on the other provinces as it will on Ottawa.

There is only so much that the federal government can do towards making bilingualism a reality in Canada. And unless bilingualism becomes a reality, French Canadians will not feel wanted by Canadian society as a whole and they will withdraw into Quebec, into nationalism, separatism and all the paranoid pettiness of a society that feels threatened. The Quebec birth rate has fallen steeply, immigration is virtually non-existent into the French community. The threat Quebeckers see is not imaginary.

So in the end it is not just up to Quebec, or up to Ottawa, or the ten provinces to decide whether Canada becomes bilingual, but up to each individual Canadian. What is Quebec without Canada? What is Canada without Quebec? Does it matter? Both Quebec and Canada would survive, of course they would, more or less, but what happens to the idea? What happens to that dream of a pluralist society which would be, in microcosm, what the world must become, one day, if man is to progress, to live in peace?

For if this is not the purpose of Canada, then what is it? A museum for archaic French and British customs, forcing everyone who wants to live here to fit into one of two boxes? United only in their anti-Americanism?

On June 25, 1968, 8,295,200 Canadians voted for federalism and for four main political parties which in their different ways favor the pluralist ideal. The man who described that ideal most compellingly was Pierre Elliott Trudeau, and the people gave him a mandate to realize his dream.

Index

Acknowledgements

THE FOLLOWING PEOPLE provided the author with original documentation and/or personal assistance that proved invaluable in the preparation of this book. Dalton K. Camp, Queen's University, Kingston; Brigadier Guy Gauvreau, Montreal; H. Carl Goldenberg, Q.C., Montreal; Senator L. de G. Giguère, Montreal; Jacques Hébert, Montreal; Senator Maurice Lamontagne, Ottawa; The Most Reverend Georges-Henri Lévesque, Rector, The National University of Rwanda; Professor Robert T. McKenzie, London; John de B. Payne, Montreal; Hon. Gérard Pelletier, Secretary of State; Gene Rhéaume, Ottawa; Roger Rolland, Montreal and Ottawa; and Hon. Maurice Sauvé, Montreal.

Acknowledgement is also made to the following individuals, publishers and corporations for material quoted in this book: Marsh Clark, Oliver Clausen, Dominique Clift, Richard Daignault, Jean Paul Desbiens, Paul Fox, Bill Lee, Frank Lowe, Peter Newman, Ed Ogle, Fraser Kelly, Roger Lemelin, Bob McKenzie, Claude Ryan, John Saywell, Herbert Steinhouse, Courtney Tower, Graham Watt and Tony Westell. The Canadian Broadcasting Corporation-Radio Canada; the CTV Network; CJOH Limited, Ottawa; Cité Libre and les éditions Cité Libre; le Devoir; Encounter Limited; Globe & Mail; Harvill Press; les éditions HMH Ltée; l'Observateur; la Presse; The Montreal Star; Penguin Books Limited; The Queen's Printer; Time Incorporated; The Toronto Daily Star; The Toronto Telegram; Weekend Magazine. Where source material was French, and no English version existed, the author has provided an unofficial translation which respects the original as much as possible but which is not definitive.